Language Anxiety

in memory of my brother
Michael J. Machan
1946–2007

Νῶϊ μὲν ὣς ἐπέεσσιν ἀμειβομένω στυγεροῖσιν
ἥμεθ', ἐγὼ μὲν ἄνευθεν ἐφ' αἵματι φάσγανον ἴσχων,
εἴδωλον δ' ἑτέρωθεν ἑταίρου πόλλ' ἀγόρευεν.

Homer, The Odyssey, 11.81–3

Language Anxiety

Conflict and Change in the History of English

TIM WILLIAM MACHAN

OXFORD

UNIVERSITY PRESS

OXFORD
UNIVERSITY PRESS

Great Clarendon Street, Oxford OX2 6DP

Oxford University Press is a department of the University of Oxford.
It furthers the University's objective of excellence in research, scholarship,
and education by publishing worldwide in

Oxford New York

Auckland Cape Town Dar es Salaam Hong Kong Karachi
Kuala Lumpur Madrid Melbourne Mexico City Nairobi
New Delhi Shanghai Taipei Toronto

With offices in

Argentina Austria Brazil Chile Czech Republic France Greece
Guatemala Hungary Italy Japan Poland Portugal Singapore
South Korea Switzerland Thailand Turkey Ukraine Vietnam

Oxford is a registered trade mark of Oxford University Press
in the UK and in certain other countries

Published in the United States
by Oxford University Press Inc., New York

© Tim William Machan 2009

First published by Oxford University Press 2009

British Library Cataloguing in Publication Data

Data available

Library of Congress Cataloging in Publication Data

Data available

Typeset by SPI Publisher Services, Pondicherry, India
Printed in Great Britain
on acid-free paper by
Biddles Ltd., King's Lynn, Norfolk

ISBN 978–0–19–923212–3

1 3 5 7 9 10 8 6 4 2

Contents

Acknowledgements

The chronological and geographical breadth of this book—conflict over change in the history of English, of all times and all places—has been both exhilarating and challenging. It has taken me, at least intellectually, to exotic locales and compelled me to work up material and disciplines with which I had had only passing familiarity. At the same time, it has introduced me to new kinds of complexity for the transmission of English and those who speak it, including the fact that certain kinds of concerns, institutions, and arguments evince a stubborn persistence across time. And this persistence has opened up not only new characteristics of English but also important, if also sometimes contested, shared experiences of those who speak it. If language since Babel has divided us, it can also provide the means to help us understand one another better.

For providing me with the opportunity to consider all these ideas and put them into a book, I am grateful to quite a few people. At OUP, John Davey has been friend as well as editor, seeing promise in the book's idea, offering encouragement and insight, and efficiently bringing it into production. I thank the press's anonymous reviewers for their valuable suggestions and comments, David Matthews for reading the typescript and improving its substance and style in many ways, and R. F. Yeager for his continued encouragement of my work. Shaun Hughes shared with me his knowledge of Maori and Maori English, and A. N. Doane offered several valuable opportunities to consider and critique the book's arguments with a learned audience. I thank Michael A. McKinney, former Dean of Arts and Sciences at Marquette University, for crafting an administrative schedule that allowed me to draft the book even as I was still Chair of English, and Krista Ratcliffe, for filling in as Chair and allowing that schedule to happen. The final version of the book was written with the generous aid of a full-year sabbatical from the Marquette Sabbatical Review Committee and a Summer Stipend from the National Endowment for the Humanities; any views, findings, conclusions, or recommendations expressed in this book do not necessarily reflect those of the Endowment. Closer to home, I thank Christine, Charlie, and Tim for indulging my passion for language and keeping me connected to those who speak it.

Throughout this book I make use of the International Phonetic Alphabet (IPA), a standardized system for representing sounds irrespective of the languages that use them. For readers who are unfamiliar with the IPA, I have tried to provide contextual information that will clarify what's being discussed, and I also include a brief note on phonetic transcription. Some passages of Middle English use two graphs no longer extant in English: ʒ (yogh) for *gh* and þ (thorn) for *th*. Citations of the *New York Times* are to the Chicago edition, and unless otherwise noted or taken from a published translation, translations of foreign-language materials are my own.

TWM

March, 2008

On the Use of Phonetic Symbols

Nearly any English word shows that sounds are very different things from letters or graphs. A word like *this*, for example, has four graphs: *t*, *h*, *i*, and *s*. The connection between these letters and the sound of the word they produce is in many ways conventional, since the graph *i* can sound quite differently in *right*, as can the graph *s* in *dogs*, where it is 'voiced' (articulated with vibrating vocal cords) and sounds more like a *z*. Conversely, the sound of the *i* in *this* can also be represented by *o* (*women*). And *th* of course uses two letters to represent one sound, which itself has two versions: a 'voiced' one in *this* and a breathy, 'voiceless' one in *thin*.

To talk about sounds as distinct from letters, linguists have developed their own abstract system known as the International Phonetic Alphabet. In some cases, as in *p* or *b*, the IPA symbol points to essentially the same sound as that predicted by English spelling conventions. In others, as in *i* or *e*, it can represent something entirely different. The following few correspondences should provide enough information for non-linguists to follow any of this book's phonological arguments.

IPA symbol	comparable sound
i	ee in beet
ɪ	i in bit
u	oo in boot
ʊ	u in put
ʌ	u in putt
e	ai in bait
ɛ	e in bet
o	oa in boat
ɔ	ou in bought
æ	a in bad
a	o in cod
ɑ	a in father
ə	a in about
θ	th in thin
ð	th in this
ŋ	ng in batting

One final important distinction in phonetic transcriptions is between phones and phonemes and, concomitantly, between phonetic and phonemic transcriptions. A phone is simply a sound in a language and is placed between square brackets, []. A phoneme is an abstraction—it is one of a group of the smallest distinct, meaningful sounds in a language and one that might actually be realized by several different phones. It is represented between slanted lines, //. So [e] refers simply to the vowel sound in *bait*, but /e/ signifies that that sound has phonemic status in English. In either case, a colon after the vowel indicates that its duration is sustained ('long'); [ma] is an old-fashioned diminutive for one's mother, but to [ma:] something, in a dialect that drops post-vocalic *r*, is to damage it.

1

Language, Change, and Response

Accents and attitudes

On 4 July 2000, I received a telephone call from a local radio station that had gotten my name from my American university's Experts Directory, where I was listed as a resource for the history and structure of the English language. Was it true, the woman inquired, that I was a specialist in English linguistics, and would I consent to a radio interview about the English used in the blockbuster movie *The Patriot*, starring Mel Gibson and then just-released? What about English in *The Patriot*, I asked, to which she replied: 'The Americans don't have British accents, and we want to know whether that's accurate or not.'

I was to be live on the air in fifteen minutes, and despite this, and despite the fact that I hadn't seen this film about the American War of Independence (though I since have) and had never really considered the issue, I quickly agreed to participate. What makes an accent an accent, I thought—a collection of features that a speaker uses or the perception of a listener? How determinative of a dialect is an accent? How and why do we make abstractions like a British accent from the demonstrable varieties of speech at any one time, thereby suggesting that all people from Britain (or America) speak alike? For that matter, to what extent would speakers on either side of the Atlantic at the time of the film's setting want to sound alike or unalike? How can we reconcile the various conflicting eighteenth-century comments on the consistent, regionally non-specific quality of American speech, on its inferiority to British speech, on its similarity to the language as spoken in the south and east of England, and on its status as the future of the language? There were simply too many intriguing issues to let this interview pass by, and specialists in English linguistics, after all, get precious few opportunities for radio exposure.

I did some quick fact checking and was ready when the interviewer called back to repeat her question on the air. I began with typical academic disavowals of the sort: dialect is a combination of various syntactic and lexical practices as well as phonological ones; speakers speak for all sorts of reasons of self-identification and social positioning as well as for the communication of ideas; the sound of earlier, pre-electronic forms of language is always a reconstruction; any language embraces social and regional variation, so that a British or American accent is an abstraction at a fairly high level; any individual may or may not approximate a regional norm; and so forth. Then I pointed out that to an American ear, two of the most prominent features of a loosely defined British accent were a low central vowel [ɑ] in words like *half* and *calf* and the absence of post-vocalic [r] in words like *fourth* and *floor*; in a loosely defined American accent the vowel would be realized as the front [æ] and the [r] generally articulated. These phonological differences, I noted, reflect changes that occurred in Britain but not America in roughly the late seventeenth and early eighteenth centuries, with the dropping of post-vocalic [r] characteristic of New England due to the later influence of British speech patterns on the American east coast.[1] If Mel Gibson's character in 1776 is presumed to have grown up in the American colonies, I went on, then he would have been born around 1730. And this means that, in all likelihood, he would not have had low vowels in *half* and *calf* and would not have dropped the [r] in *fourth* and *floor*, because these are features that developed in Britain but not the American colonies. The interviewer's response surprised me: 'You mean that the British are the ones who changed English and the Americans speak a more traditional, correct form?' Sensing that the points I had tried to make were losing their subtlety and precision, I said, 'Well, for these two features, at that time, much British but not American speech had changed, so that in these two features, at that time, yes, much American speech was more conservative'. 'So the British version of English is a development of the American version?' And my hunch that history, nuance, and theory were being utterly erased was confirmed when I hung up the phone and heard the interviewer and her co-host talk with satisfaction about how fascinating it was that Americans preserved a traditional accent and that the British were the ones who had changed the language.

In the end, this episode has become far more interesting to me than has the question of whether Mel Gibson should have spoken with some version of a British accent in *The Patriot*. Bringing together a number of popular and

---

[1] Roger Lass, 'Phonology and Morphology', in *The Cambridge History of the English Language*, iii, Lass (ed.), *1476–1776* (Cambridge: Cambridge University Press, 1999), 114–16, and John H. Fisher, 'British and American, Continuity and Divergence', in *The Cambridge History of the English Language*, vi, John Algeo (ed.), *English in North America* (Cambridge: Cambridge University Press, 2001), 75–7. Both changes took place over several centuries, with the dropping of post-vocalic [r] still a cause for comment in the early nineteenth century, and so by 'occurred' I mean that they became so extensive as to be decisive.

powerful notions of language, the question presupposed much about history, language, and identity. It is striking, for example, that on American Independence Day in the year 2000—a date of iconic if not historic significance for the United States—a popular radio talk show host should wonder at all about how the colonists sounded during the Revolutionary War. For the topic to be newsworthy, or at least chat-worthy, this long-ago accent must have been thought to have some consequence for Americans as they faced a new millennium, though it would never have occurred to me, even if I had seen the film, to raise the question on my own. Another striking presumption is that languages have a well-defined constancy and consistency, that a British accent has an absolute integrity and identifiablity tantamount to the qualities of a material object, regardless of who views it and when they do so. And this presumption is held, in part, by avoiding the messy complications of empirical data—involving, for example, the relation between two variable phonological features and an accent—and clinging instead to neat, simple truisms. Even more striking, by extension, is the implication that an accent serves as a marker of identity: we are how we speak. And perhaps most striking of all is the satisfaction inherent in the apparent recognition that Americans, somehow, speak an older, more original English. Not only is there a real English, then, but it resides in the United States and not England, where it was changed.

My radio interview was amiable enough (if also, alas, largely unnoticed), but this is not always the case when people talk about language variation and change and their relations to personal and social identity. In fact, for languages in general and so for English in particular—whether it's the English of the United Kingdom, the United States, New Zealand, or any other part of the Anglophone world—language change throughout the language's history has consistently figured as both tool and symbol in acrimonious conflicts over education, immigration, morality, and so forth. When English speakers have lamented the condition and goals of schools, they have cited the state of language usage as both cause and consequence of this condition. When they have worried over the integrity or diversity of society, they have argued for and against the persistence of non-English languages. And when they have identified signs of a literal or figurative apocalypse, they have pointed to language and how it, in turn, points to social and moral issues beyond itself. While English as such may never have caused a war, it has served as a cudgel to speakers of Celtic languages, Native Americans, and immigrants alike, whose own languages have been seen as communicatively inadequate, socially inhibiting, morally debilitating, and even unpatriotic. Bilingual education, dictionaries, and language planning—all of them responses to language variation and change—have been both burdensome and contentious. For those involved in their production and management, such activities have been lucrative as well, and the very fact that language change can provide economic opportunity itself reflects just how seriously Anglophones have historically taken the issue.

Language change produces, in a word, anxiety. And perhaps a better word than *produces* here is *focuses*, for part of the anxiety is in fact over the nature of the relationship between language change and transformation in the extra-linguistic worlds of politics, religion, and social interaction. Does language change portend changes in these worlds? Does it cause them? Is it the direct result of other kinds of change? Or does it merely accompany them? All this anxiety is already present in the earliest Western account of language change, that of the Tower of Babel, in which change and variation are figured as the divine punishment visited by God on humans for their arrogance and presumption. It is likewise already present in England in Alfred the Great's preface to his ninth-century translation of St Gregory's *Pastoral Care*, in which he cites the decline of Latin and English literacy as both sign and result of the general moral failure into which the Viking raids had plunged England. And this anxiety over change and variation has remained present through modern English's encounters with non-western languages and their speakers and through the recognition, driven home by standardized written English, that even among native Anglophones language continues to diversify.

Theories of change and variation

Underlying my discussion so far are two of the best-established and least disputable facts in social history. One is the fact of synchronic language variation—the existence of grammatical differences (in lexicon, syntax, phonology, and morphology) among contemporaneous varieties of a language, such as modern southern British English and modern southern United States English. Where the former has *lift*, the latter has *elevator*; where the former uses the plural *are* with mass nouns like *government*, the latter uses the singular *is*. The second fact is that of diachronic change, or change across time within the same language or dialect.[2] Thus, while medieval Londoners used *-eth* ([ɛθ] or [ɛð]) as the third person singular verbal inflection, modern ones use *-s* ([ɛs] or [ɛz]), making for a peace that *passes* rather than *passeth* understanding. And while the Anglo-Saxons used *déor* to mean 'four-footed

---

[2] Conventionally, *dialect* is used to refer to mutually intelligible social or regional forms of the same *language*. I will use these terms in this same way throughout this book, but most of the time I prefer *variety* as a neutral term that encompasses both *dialect* and *language* and thereby avoids the pragmatic and grammatical difficulties of distinguishing one from the other.

beast', contemporary Anglophones typically use *deer*, its modern reflex, to refer to specific kinds of quadrupeds—ruminants from a family (cervidæ) with deciduous antlers, such as *reindeer* and *whitetail deer*.

Scholars may argue about the origins of the universe or the demise of dinosaurs, politicians may dispute environmental causes and effects, and educators may contest the implications of standardized test scores. But these facts of change and variation, as I say, are indisputable, for nearly as early as the development of writing there is evidence both of them and also of speakers' awareness of them. It is variation among languages to which Homer nods in the *Odyssey*, when a disguised Odysseus, on his return to Ithaca, fabricates for his unwitting wife Penelope an account of his origins on Crete, an island that has 'many | peoples in it, innumerable; there are ninety cities. | Language with language mix there together'.[3] In the Book of Judges, variation among the dialects of Hebrew enables the men of Gilead to identify the fleeing Ephraimites, with catastrophic consequences:

The Gileadites captured the fords of the Jordan leading to Ephraim, and whenever a survivor of Ephraim said, 'Let me cross over', the men of Gilead asked him, 'Are you an Ephraimite?' If he replied, 'No', they said, 'All right, say "Shibboleth"'. If he said, 'Sibboleth', because he could not pronounce the word correctly, they seized him and killed him at the fords of the Jordan. Forty-two thousand Ephraimites were killed at that time.[4]

Looking back to the Antique over a millennium later in his *Troilus and Criseyde*, Geoffrey Chaucer imagines more beneficial consequences of these facts of language change and variation. In response to an audience that might express skepticism over how his lovers conducted themselves in word and deed, he observes with particular eloquence:

> Ye knowe ek that in forme of speche is chaunge
> Withinne a thousand yeer, and wordes tho
> That hadden pris, now wonder nyce and straunge
> Us thinketh hem, and yet thei spake hem so,
> And spedde as wel in love as men now do;
> Ek for to wynnen love in sondry ages,
> In sondry londes, sondry ben usages.[5]

---

[3] Homer, *The Odyssey*, trans. Richmond Lattimore (New York: HarperCollins, 1963), 19.173–5.

[4] *Judges* 12: 5–6.

[5] *Troilus and Criseyde*, 2.22–8, *The Riverside Chaucer*, ed. Larry D. Benson, 3rd edn. (Boston, MA: Houghton Mifflin, 1987).

As well established as the facts of language change and variation may be, the reasons behind them are a good deal more contested, even murky. All theories must account for the same aspects of variation and change, including: grammar (phonology, morphology, syntax, lexicon, and pragmatics), styles, strategies, and discursive conventions; alterations in an individual's or society's repertoire, such as the multilingualism of Homer's Crete; inconsistent regularity in the creation and transmission of forms and varieties; the relations between the speech of individuals and the aggregate language they use; and the impact of context, including language planning, on usage. Perhaps not surprisingly, this abundance of linguistic features in need of explanation has produced an abundance of explanations. According to Jean Aitchison, 'For centuries, people have speculated about the causes of language change. The problem is not one of thinking up possible causes, but of deciding which to take seriously.'[6] Whether it is the biblical account of the Tower of Babel, attributing diachronic change to divinely righteous indignation, or Dr Johnson's representation of synchronic variation, explaining neologisms as words that authors 'have introduced by their knowledge of foreign languages, or ignorance of their own, by vanity or wantonness, by compliance with fashion, or lust of innovation',[7] theories of linguistic change have indeed been as imaginative as they have been prolific. Very generally, contemporary approaches emphasize one of two ends of an explanatory spectrum, ascribing them primarily either to systemic pressures or to social ones.

Systemic explanations stress the structural characteristics of language, the ways in which various grammatical parts, by means of their contrastive distinctions with one another, mutually constitute a coherent and functional whole. What gives this whole meaning, and what allows speakers to make meaningful utterances with it, is the system of the language, and in such mechanistic theories speakers are not merely separate from but secondary to the language they speak. In Roger Lass's memorable phrase, linguistic change 'occurs over "geological" time, beyond the capacity of humans to act, since no actor can see the consequences of his actions. A speaker engaged in a change is not an agent, but a victim.'[8] As Lass's reference to 'geological time' suggests, systemic explanations situate a good deal of the explanation in metaphors

---

[6] Aitchison, *Language Change: Progress or Decay?*, 3rd edn. (Cambridge: Cambridge University Press, 2001), 133.

[7] Johnson, *A Dictionary of the English Language* (1755; rpt. New York: AMS, 1967), i, bi^r.

[8] Lass, *Historical Linguistics and Language Change* (Cambridge: Cambridge University Press, 1997), 367. Lass is synthesizing points initially made in Edward Sapir, *Language: An Introduction to the Study of Speech* (New York: Harcourt-Brace, 1921), 165–6.

from the hard sciences, if not in the hard sciences themselves. While most scholars would point to the anatomical developments of the head, mouth, and chest as prerequisites for the development of human speech, for example, mechanistic theories of change describe much closer, more intrinsic connections between language and biology. In this way, mechanistic theories reveal the mutually reinforcing connections between Darwinian evolution and comparative linguistics that have been present since the simultaneous nineteenth-century developments of both disciplines.[9] Derek Bickerton thus sees language change as intimately situated within evolutionary and social change. He posits a proto-language among early hominids that, with the development of syntax, sequentially enabled fully human language, meta-thinking (or double consciousness), social sophistication, and the increased record of artifacts in the period 100,000 to 50,000 BC.[10] One similar evolutionary theory of change imports the concept of punctuated equilibrium, by which long periods of structural stasis of organisms are interrupted by sudden periods of transformation, to describe the history of recorded (and unrecorded) languages.[11] Another, likening languages to species and individuals' grammars to the members of those species, conceives language change as the collective change of individual grammars; in this framework, it is language change that is gradual and grammatical change sudden.[12] Even more generally, Nikolaus Ritt, understanding systemic replication as a kind of linguistic survival imperative, suggests that languages don't so much change as evolve, using speakers as hosts and building new, coherent systems from the incompletely learned or transmitted earlier systems. For Ritt, 'the apparent similarities between languages and biological life forms are no coincidence... Instead, they reflect deeper and more general design principles, which may characterise the organisation of many systems within the universe.'[13]

Social explanations of language change, exemplified by the work of William Labov or Peter Trudgill, may grant that the process of a change—the way a

---

[9] David Lightfoot, *The Development of Language: Acquisition, Change and Evolution* (Malden, MA: Blackwell, 1999), 21–47.

[10] Bickerton, *Language and Human Behavior* (Seattle, WA: University of Washington Press, 1995). A comparable approach is that of Robbins Burling in *The Talking Ape: How Language Evolved* (Oxford: Oxford University Press, 2005). Rather than stress the development of human speech, however, Burling stresses the development of human understanding, for it is his argument that when the utterances of early humans were invested with meaning, this investment encouraged their further use and role in social development.

[11] R. M. W. Dixon, *The Rise and Fall of Languages* (Cambridge: Cambridge University Press, 1997).

[12] Lightfoot, *The Development of Language*.

[13] Ritt, *Selfish Sounds and Linguistic Evolution: A Darwinian Approach to Language Change* (Cambridge: Cambridge University Press, 2004), 110.

phonological alteration takes place, for example—is describable in mechanistic terms that reflect Ritt's 'general design principles'. The collective changes known as the Great Vowel Shift, thus, are often described as representing a push chain, whereby once the mid-high front and back long vowels /e/ and /o/ moved up in the mouth's phonological space, they pushed the falling and diphthongization of the highest front and back long vowels (/i/ and /u/) and dragged along the next lowest long vowels (/ɛ/ and /ɔ/) into the space they had left; these newly made mid-vowels, in turn, dragged the next lower long vowels into their own, previous space. In simpler terms, it's as if the vowel sound of *fate* rose in the mouth until it was the same as *feet*, which pushed the original *feet* to sound like *fight*. Since a push-chain mechanism like this has occurred in other languages at other times, it can at least be understood to reflect a general, systemic principle of organization for language. Where social explanations of change differ from systemic ones is that they go beyond such strictly mechanical principles to highlight the uniquely human features of speech, its use, and transmission. In the case of the Great Vowel Shift, Jeremy Smith and others have argued that the real explanation of why vowel raising and diphthongization occurred lies in increased immigration to London, particularly from East Anglia, in the late fourteenth and fifteenth centuries. This immigration, they say, brought differing phonologies into contact with one another, and with the matching of phonology to issues of solidarity and power—whether a speaker wants to be associated with a group or distinguished from it—the phonologies themselves came to have social valuations, thereby causing speakers to alter their pronunciations towards or away from particular speech patterns. In this way, it is the relative social prestige of speakers and their varieties that drives variation and change.[14]

More generally, sociolinguists have identified a number of social factors and contexts that demonstrate, to the extent that one can control the variables, intimate associations with various kinds of grammatical change. Like phonological mechanisms, these associations recur with sufficient frequency cross-linguistically as to merit consideration as sociolinguistic universals. The prestige of a given variety, as has been alleged in the Great Vowel Shift, can indeed figure significantly in change, as can the social desire to stigmatize or ameliorate a particular word. The noun *Miss*, for instance, has become marked in many varieties of modern English as a designation for an adult,

---

[14] See Jeremy J. Smith, *An Historical Study of English: Function, Form and Change* (London: Routledge, 1996), 79–111; and *Sound Change and the History of English* (Oxford: Oxford University Press, 2007), 127–53. More generally, see Lass, 'Phonology and Morphology', 72–85.

unmarried woman and has consequently been restricted to young girls, while *gay* has in most domains lost its earlier pejorative connotations in reference to homosexuals and become widespread as a neutral term. The history of *gay* provides a particularly rich illustration of how the connotations of words can shift in response to social pressure. The word began in the fourteenth century as an adjective describing light-heartedness, then by the seventeenth century designated a dissipated lifestyle (particularly that of prostitutes), and then, before its present usage as a noun, referred derisively to homosexuals.[15] Another social source of change, especially the introduction of new vocabulary, is contact with non-native speakers and the materials of their world; this was the case when English speakers encountered Native Americans and borrowed such words as *caribou, hickory,* and *moccasin.*

Change—or better, perhaps, resistance to change—can also arise from the explicit desire of members of a group to strengthen their solidarity by developing words and syntax that are intentionally obscure to outsiders. This is what M. A. K. Halliday calls 'the sociolinguistic play potential of one's own variety of the language'[16] and has been documented in Philadelphia, New York City, Belfast, and other urban environments, where the covert prestige of a non-standard variety may influence speakers to preserve it at the expense of an overtly prestigious standard and whatever social opportunities that standard might seem to provide. Conversely, when nineteenth-century speakers of Irish overwhelmingly switched to English as the language of both workplace and home, they revealed the extent to which economic opportunity (if not social prestige) and perceived connections between it and language can drive change. The relative social status of women and men has also been identified as a primary motivation for linguistic maintenance or change, with many studies suggesting that working-class women, perhaps better attuned to the possibility of social advancement, are more likely to speak a variety closer to a standard language than are working-class men. Still other studies have identified socially marginal groups, including adolescents, as the ones whose weak ties to a community bring them into contact with other speech communities and who risk no negative social consequences that would discourage them from transferring the words or practices of one community to another. For this reason, adolescents and other weakly tied speakers are sometimes identified as the instigators of change and variation. In short, any of the social characteristics and factors that one can imagine—age, sex, class, ethnicity,

---

[15] *OED,* s. v. *gay,* adj., adv., and n.
[16] Halliday, *Language as Social Semiotic: The Social Interpretation of Language and Meaning* (London: Edward Arnold, 1978), 160.

geographic origin, education, and so forth—might induce speakers to change their language in one way or another, and other speakers, in turn, to follow or resist them.[17]

In view of such diverse explanations for linguistic variation and change, the desire to throw up one's hands and explain language and its changes as neither mechanistic nor social, neither natural nor artificial, but as the proverbial third kind of thing altogether is not surprising.[18] In one way or another, all of the approaches I've outlined must presume an answer to the same fundamental question: What is language? Perhaps even more challenging than 'Why does language change?' this is ultimately a philosophical question, and unanswerable in absolute terms, too, for any response is inevitably a hypothesis. And for this reason, explanations of the ontology of language have been as diverse as have been those of language change. To philosophers from Descartes to Wittgenstein to Derrida, for example, language exists in a dynamic with extra-linguistic reality, which it variously processes or constructs, while for linguists it tends to be more of an abstract code that maps representations (sounds and words) onto objects and ideas.

Perhaps the most challenging ontological feature of language involves the relation between what an individual might say and what the collective of individuals speaking a given language might say. Is English what I speak, or what the majority of people in the United Kingdom speak, or an abstraction of what all the Anglophones in the world speak? And if the latter, how do we account for the diachronic and synchronic differences among all of us so as to be able to maintain that we all speak the same language? Similarly, how can English change for me as well as for hundreds of millions of other Anglophones whom I'll never meet and to whom I'll never speak? Oddly enough, an

---

[17] Some representative and particularly influential illustrations of the social approach to linguistic change are: John J. Gumperz and Dell Hymes (eds.), *Directions in Sociolinguistics: The Ethnography of Communication* (New York: Holt, Rinehart and Winston, Inc., 1972); Halliday, *Language as Social Semiotic*; Hymes' *Foundations in Sociolinguistics: An Ethnographic Approach* (Philadelphia, PA: University of Pennsylvania Press, 1974); William Labov, *Sociolinguistic Patterns* (Philadelphia, PA: University of Pennsylvania Press, 1972); Labov, *Principles of Linguistic Change*, i, *Internal Factors*, ii, *Social Factors* (Oxford: Blackwell, 1994, 2001); James Milroy, *Linguistic Variation and Change: On the Historical Sociolinguistics of English* (Oxford: Blackwell, 1992); Lesley Milroy, *Language and Social Networks*, 2nd edn. (Oxford: Blackwell, 1987); Salikoko S. Mufwene, *The Ecology of Language Evolution* (Cambridge: Cambridge University Press, 2001); Suzanne Romaine, *Socio-historical Linguistics: Its Status and Methodology* (Cambridge: Cambridge University Press, 1982); Peter Trudgill, *The Social Differentiation of English in Norwich* (Cambridge: Cambridge University Press, 1974); Trudgill, *Sociolinguistic Variation and Change* (Edinburgh: Edinburgh University Press, 2002).

[18] Rudi Keller, *On Language Change: The Invisible Hand in Language*, trans. Brigitte Nerlich (London: Routledge, 1994).

old textual-critical chestnut illuminates this ontological question with particular clarity. Addressing the ephemerality of a work of literature, the text of which may appear in multiple documents, F. W. Bateson once asked: 'If the *Mona Lisa* is in the Louvre, where are *Hamlet* and *Lycidas*?' Like Shakespeare's play or Milton's poem, which can be located in no one place but instead found in multiple books in the libraries of multiple readers, the English language is clearly limited to no one speaker or locale. But language is perhaps even more complex in this regard than are literary works. Unlike *Hamlet* or *Lycidas*, which are uniform in at least every copy of a particular edition, iterations of English differ from one time period to another, from one locale to another, from one speaker to another, and even, for that speaker, from one occasion to another.

Further, the facts that help to construct the ontologically problematic fact of English are themselves sometimes intractable, and this intractability accounts for a fundamental fissure in popular as well as professional definitions of language. On one side are those who see *the* language in the utterances that real people produce in real circumstances, replete with irregularities in pronunciation, word order, and phrasing, and verifiable in the spoken or printed record of English. On the other are those who conceive *the* language as an abstract system that is itself regular, even if it is irregularly realized by speakers; this abstraction would be Ferdinand de Saussure's *langue* or Noam Chomsky's ideal speaker-listener, and its data come from the knowledge and intuitions of its analysts. The nature of individual linguistic facts (such as in phonology) complicates even more this paradigmatic dichotomy and its relevance to the ontology of English. For example, a sound like [p], found in *sip*, is one kind of fact in English; this sound and the several variants of it are scientifically verifiable in the language through tools such as voice spectography, even if a speaker might be unaware of this verifiability or even the sound itself. The phoneme /p/ is an entirely different kind of fact. This exists only through an analysis that groups together a variety of sounds (such as the [p] of *sip* and the aspirated [pʰ] of *pull*) that are related in articulation (both are bilabial, voiceless stops) but cannot be used individually in a given language to differentiate one word from another, as the voicing of [p] as [b] can differentiate *bull* from *pull* in English. Without aspiration of /p/, *pull* might sound funny, but it would still be *pull*; with voicing, it would be another word. And yet a third kind of fact is something like the push-chain mechanism that I described above. As Lass has noted, in a case like the Great Vowel Shift, several linguistic facts (each already slippery) are understood to be part of a coherent process: 'The impact of the "establishment" of the GVS is this: once such an object as what we could now call a "covarying shift" is invented, a whole set of new questions becomes askable for the first time.'[19]

Philosophical speculation like this has relevance, I think, to the nature of language change and also, therefore, to responses to it, which are the concerns of this book. Given any distinction between English and the speakers of English, we need to account for how change can move among speakers at any one time—how English can change for both New Zealanders as well as South Africans, if in fact it does—since speakers develop their language primarily from individual contacts and their own native language capacity and not from consultation of books or some kind of a central linguistic clearing house. By extension, we need to determine how to draw distinctions between historical stages of a given language (Old English versus Middle English, for example) or between structurally similar languages (such as Danish and Faeroese). And precisely the same complex issues appear when we attempt to differentiate the variations peculiar to any individual (i.e., idiosyncratic forms) or to any group of individuals (i.e., dialect forms) from changes in the aggregate language. This might be done in several ways. We might, for example, distinguish dialect forms from forms in the early stages of diffusion through a language by the number of speakers using a form, by their social prestige, by their attitude, or by the duration of the form's usage. Each of these criteria would produce different, contestable results. In the contemporary United States, for instance, *dude* is widespread among younger speakers as (sometimes) a slightly ironic term of endearment. Measured solely by the percentage of speakers who use the form, given the overall youth of the American population, *dude* might well qualify as an ongoing lexical change for United States English, but this would not be the case if the prestige of these speakers, or the percentage they represent of all living Anglophones, were taken into account. The same is true for *guys*, which the same cohort (and this cohort alone) widely uses in reference to groups of men and women of all ages.

Given the character of linguistics as a discipline, philosophical resolutions of such linguistic problems are inevitable. First, there is not, nor ever can there be, an empirically demonstrable or even simply accepted quantity of structural features that by itself marks the differentiation of one language or dialect from another. There is no formula that dictates x number of unique phonological features, plus y number of syntactic features, plus z number of

---

[19] Lass, *Historical Linguistics and Language Change*, 36. More generally see his *On Explaining Language Change* (Cambridge: Cambridge University Press, 1980).

morphological ones create a language; or that a decrease of *x* can be offset by a specific increase of *y*; or that if *x*, *y*, and *z* are diminished by some value, the result is not a language but a dialect. This is so because in a very real sense outside the realm of structural linguistics, differentiation of dialects and languages draws on speakers' attitudes as well as their speech forms. Faeroese is thus a language and not a dialect of Danish in part because of the role it played in nineteenth- and twentieth-century nativizing movements in the Faeroes and in part because the Faeroese themselves regard it as a distinct language and have cultivated it accordingly.

The second factor that compels philosophical resolutions of some linguistic problems is that linguistics, unlike a hard science, cannot isolate its subjects in a laboratory, control for all variables but one, and replicate situations in order to verify results. In the twenty-first century it cannot take a medieval population from London, introduce a late-medieval population from East Anglia, and watch to see whether social differentiations and something like the Great Vowel Shift develop. This means that all of its explanations lack the predictive power of those from biology, chemistry, and physics. And this leaves the linguist needing to find English even more desperately than the literary critic needs to find *Hamlet*.

From another fundamentally philosophical perspective, whether one understands the English language as an abstract system or as the conflicting and inconsistent usages of its speakers, any kind of change seems counter-intuitive. Optimal communication, an often-cited motivation for change, makes this very point. When the Old English long vowels /e:/ and /e:o/ merged in the tenth and eleventh centuries as /e:/, for instance, homophony would have arisen between the personal pronoun used for males (*hé*) and the one used for females (*héo*). On the presumption that such homophony would create communicative confusion, scholars have cited a drive for optimal communication—for the need to maintain crucial semantic distinctions—as the factor that led to the new form *she*, presumably through palatalization of the initial [h] in *héo*. Theoretically and practically, this makes a good deal of sense. But while optimal communication might have strong explanatory power in the very narrow context of vowel mergers, its general explanatory power is limited. If even a subconscious desire for optimal communication is pre-eminent, then once this communication has been reached, additional change would seem to be both superfluous and counter-productive. And since by most theories humans have been speaking for at least 100,000 years, there would seem to have been plenty of time to achieve optimality.

Yet variation and change continue, and the results of change occasionally render its persistence even more counter-intuitive. While biological evolution is the process by which random variation produces contextually successful features, which are then 'selected' in the sense that they are the ones that survive, linguistic change sometimes has strikingly unsuccessful results. Indeed, as Labov has noted, language actually points to conclusions that oppose natural selection: 'the major agent of linguistic change—sound change—is actually maladaptive, in that it leads to the loss of the information that the original forms were designed to carry'.[20] More generally, change and variation are responsible for a great many socially debilitating situations. They produce mutually unintelligible languages and their attendant barriers to communication, the communicative obstacles that even regional variation can present, and the sociolinguistic drive to instruct generation after generation of students in the details of spelling, punctuation, and usage, which are never internalized and transmitted to subsequent generations in some Lamarckian fashion. In view of the tumult of history and the blame placed on inadequate communication, I would venture that if there truly is a general drive to optimal communication, it has failed miserably.

Linguists sometimes neutralize the counter-intuition of change and variation by drawing a distinction between teleology and direction. They say that when one sound becomes another, the transformation may be directional—[e] may move in the direction of [i], for example—but it is not teleological, because it does not go towards any specific end for any specific purpose. As with a found fact like a push-chain shift, however, whatever issues such a distinction resolves, it also enables new questions about why change occurs, where, and when. And in so doing, it also leaves unanswered questions that emerge from other found facts, such as how or why such a non-directional change could be irreversible, a quality commonly attributed to all linguistic change. If change just happens, that is, it would seem just as likely as not that a sound would happen to become once again what it once was. Nor does this distinction between teleology and direction answer questions that challenge its own validity as a fact. In the most common push-chain explanation of the Great Vowel Shift, to which I've already alluded, the restoration of balance in phonological space—the distribution of vowels by height and frontness—would very much seem to be a goal for the changes (once begun) and not simply their direction. And this quality, like all linguistic versions of Ritt's 'general design principles', would seem once more to reflect at least a kind of teleology.

From a pragmatic as well as a philosophical view, indeed, perhaps the most challenging ontological issue is that linguistic change and variation don't

---

[20] Labov, *Principles of Linguistic Change*, ii, *Social Factors*, 10.

simply persist. They thrive. It's worth recalling here that while animal life has been on earth for well over 100 million years, humans have spoken for perhaps only 100,000 of these years. Broadly speaking, then, if the language faculty is at least partially biological, as (again) most linguists would argue, the extent of the structural differences among the roughly 6,000 to 6,500 languages that are current today would seem to exceed natural differentiation of a shared feature, particularly (but not only) if they all developed from the speech of a common population.[21] It could even be argued that change and variation have exceeded any rational explanation of what causes them or, consequently, how they might be curtailed. More narrowly, what the *Oxford English Dictionary* shows diachronically, a journey across any sizeable Anglophonic region shows synchronically: however counter-intuitively, change and variation have continually outweighed any systemic and social advantages of linguistic uniformity. Such change is in fact so extensive and intrinsic to languages that for Lass and his mechanistic approach to change, English or French or Latin are not so much stable communicative codes as loosely affiliated sets of changes: 'A language is a population of variants moving through time, and subject to selection.'[22] In this same vein, the recent school of 'emergent linguistics' emphasizes that whatever syntactic and phonological rules govern human speech do not precede language but emerge variably in the act of speech.[23] And inherent variation and change are the implications, significantly, not only of evolutionary models that see languages as replicating systems subject to the same kinds of mutation of all such systems, but also of the static Chomskyan model. One of the original insights of generative grammar, thus, is that any theory of language must account for the fact that speakers have the recursive ability to reuse syntactic structures and thereby to produce grammatically correct sentences that nonetheless have never been uttered before. As rule-governed as transformations may be, their primary explanatory focus is variation.

Nearly a century ago, Robert Bridges, then England's Poet Laureate, argued that the advent of the wireless radio would control the evolution of speech and be conducive to the standardization of English. It didn't happen, of

---

21 See Daniel Nettle, *Linguistic Diversity* (Oxford: Oxford University Press, 1999), 2–3.

22 Lass, *Historical Linguistics and Language Change*, 377.

23 See Brian MacWhinney, 'Emergent Approaches to Language', in Joan Bybee and Paul Hopper (eds.), *Frequency and the Emergence of Linguistic Structure* (Amsterdam: John Benjamins, 2001), 449–70. See also Charles-James N. Bailey's argument for 'developmentalism', or the notion that change and variation are not simply fundamental to language but rather are language (*Essays on Time-Based Linguistic Analysis* [Oxford: Clarendon Press, 1996]). I return briefly to this issue in the second chapter.

course. Indeed, as Labov noted towards the end of the twentieth century, 'change is continuing at a rapid rate in every city of North America that has been studied with any care. This result clashes sharply with the common-sense expectation that constant exposure to the network standard on radio and television would lead to convergence and the gradual elimination of dialects.'[24] Whatever their origins, powerful diversifying mechanisms must indeed be at work.

From sentence structure to social upheaval

'Tongues, like governments, have a natural tendency to degeneration,' Dr Johnson once observed; 'we have long preserved our constitution, let us make some struggles for our language'.[25] This linking of language, government, and degeneration demonstrates Johnson's characteristic wit, but it also highlights the anxiety that can be produced by language change. In Johnson's formulation, governments are like the lost boys in William Golding's *Lord of the Flies*: if left to their own devices, they will evidently by nature regress to their unprincipled, undisciplined condition. And in view of this inherent drift towards decline, the struggle against regression is arduous and constant, requiring the unvarying attention of the governing and governed alike. In comparing language to government, Johnson implies that the two share a constructed nature, that they are designed and produced by human beings for the benefit of other human beings. For language to be like government, further, it must share not only government's natural qualities but also its natural tendency to degeneration, which needs to be resisted as much as governmental decline is resisted. Tantamount to one another, language and government (for Johnson) are members of the same natural category.

To be sure, not every scholar or popular commentator shares Johnson's anxiety. During the nineteenth-century development of comparative linguistics, linguists like Max Müller, the first Professor of Comparative Philology at Oxford, saw the reduction of inflectional morphology among Indo-European languages, English in particular, as unambiguous improvement. Otto Jespersen, one of the last of these critics, once tied this improvement to improved interpersonal communication in particular: 'In the evolution of languages the

---

[24] Labov, *Principles of Linguistic Change*, ii, *Social Factors*, 3; Bridges, 'The Society's Work', Society for Pure English, Tract XXI, excerpted in W. F. Bolton and David Crystal (eds.), *The English Language*, ii, *Essays by Linguists and Men of Letters, 1858–1964* (Cambridge: Cambridge University Press, 1969), 93–4.

[25] Johnson, *A Dictionary of the English Language*, i, cii[v].

discarding of old flexions goes hand in hand with the development of simpler and more regular expedients that are rather less liable than the old ones to produce misunderstanding.'[26] And some recent critics have enthusiastically embraced both the modern development of world English*es* and the apparent resurgence of non-English languages (or non-standard varieties of English) in largely Anglophone populations.[27] Without going so far as to connect change to improvement, Lass and still other linguists maintain that at least in the abstract, change is neither positive nor negative: 'Languages are imperfectly replicating systems and therefore throw up variants during replication; the fact of variation itself is neutral.'[28] Nevertheless, the anxiety expressed by Johnson and the suspicion implied by my radio interviewer have insistently animated responses to changes in English, whether the changes involve the structure of the language or its relations with other languages.

One of the improbable best sellers of 2004, for instance, was Lynne Truss's *Eats, Shoots & Leaves*, a diatribe, somehow both witty and irascible, that linked together an eclectic group of putative changes—specifically declines—in punctuation, education, communication, and standards in general. Rife with emotive images like a 'zero tolerance for bad punctuation', a 'dismally illiterate world', and a 'swamp from which [English] so bravely crawled less than two thousand years ago', Truss's book captured popular imagination (and hysteria) by reviving Johnson's view of language change—in this case, alleged changes in punctuation practices—as a degeneration homologous with the degeneration of the world at large: 'The reason it's worth standing up for punctuation is not that it's an arbitrary system of notation known only to an over-sensitive elite who have attacks of the vapors when they see it misapplied. The reason to stand up for punctuation is that without it there is no reliable way of communicating meaning.'[29] More ambitious in scope and execution, another widely read response to language change and variation (John Honey's) concentrates on the values to be gained from fostering linguistic uniformity. He sees a reduction of dialects as an ethically good thing, since 'accent differences are one of the greatest obstacles to genuine social equality' in England and 'causing children to learn Standard English is an act of empowerment which will give them access to a whole

[26] Jespersen, *Language: Its Nature, Development and Origin* (London: G. Allen & Unwin, 1922), 263. Also see Lass, *Historical Linguistics and Language Change*, 292.

[27] On the cultivation of the plural Englishes as an academic discipline, see Tom McArthur, *The English Languages* (Cambridge: Cambridge University Press, 1998), 56–77.

[28] Lass, *Historical Linguistics and Language Change*, 354.

[29] Truss, *Eats, Shoots & Leaves: The Zero Tolerance Approach to Punctuation* (New York: Gotham, 2004), 20.

world of knowledge and to an assurance of greater authority in their dealings with the world outside their own homes, in a way which is genuinely liberating'. The 'function of prescription', then, 'is not the prevention of change but rather the *management* of change—a process of control which allows change to be seen as an orderly process'.[30]

Truss and Honey further a popular tradition of linguistic anxiety that Deborah Cameron has aptly labeled 'verbal hygiene' and to which I'll return in Chapter 5.[31] This tradition of popular anxiety over language change remains as healthy today as it did when Cameron coined the term; for that matter, since Johnson was not an academic but a popular critic, the tradition was healthy as far back as the eighteenth century. Every year, perhaps improbably, Lake Superior State University in Sault Ste. Marie, Michigan, issues its 'List of Words Banished from the Queen's English for Mis-Use, Over-Use and General Uselessness'.[32] While the list is compiled in fun—and fun it most certainly is—its appeal for over thirty years now rests on readers' suspicion of new words, like *blog* and *carbs*, much as my radio interviewer's response drew on a suspicion of new pronunciations and dialect variation. Similarly, when in a 1999 *Washington Post* column Bob Hirschfield whimsically announced the existence of a new computer virus—the Strunkenwhite virus, which would prevent the transmission of any emails containing grammatical errors—his satire had effect and humor precisely because computer users could be presumed to be aware of the divergence between traditional written Standard English (as advocated in Strunk and White's landmark *Elements of Style*) and the casual variety that has developed for Internet communication.

Such suspicion cannot be dismissed as merely a popular fad, for it is shared by linguists, too. What Müller saw as morphological improvement, Franz Bopp, his rough contemporary and like him one of the founders of comparative linguistics, saw as decay. More recently, John McWhorter, in his own best-selling book whose subtitle contains the phrase 'The Degradation of Language', has described modern America as having changed its attitudes towards language in such a way that it has lost the ability to produce, understand, and enjoy any rhetoric but the colloquial. By tracing what he sees as the poverty of political discourse to this rhetorical change, McWhorter agrees with Truss and Johnson about the linking of language and government: 'Modern America,

---

[30] Honey, *Does Accent Matter? The Pygmalion Factor* (London: Faber and Faber, 1989), 174, and *Language is Power: The Story of Standard English and its Enemies* (London: Faber and Faber, 1997), 42, 147.

[31] Cameron, *Verbal Hygiene* (London: Routledge, 1995).

[32] http://www.lssu.edu/banished/.

then, is a country where rigorously polished language, of a sort only possible when channeled through the deliberate activity of writing, is considered insincere. And this is not a Yankee keystone, but a trait only a few decades old. And it leaves us culturally and even intellectually deprived.'[33] David Crystal invests the same degree of significance in change and variation, though from a diametrically opposed perspective. Writing specifically in response to Truss and other verbal hygienists, he champions the diversity they attempt to control. His book, Crystal says, tells 'the story of the fight for English usage— the story of a group of people who tried to shape the language in their own image but, generation after generation, failed. They looked at language around them, and didn't like what they saw. "Fight" is not my metaphor, but theirs.'[34]

Linguists' anxiety about language change, however, characteristically focuses on issues of social and even global upheaval rather than on grammar and usage. The spread of English as a world language has been a particular concern for analysts who see the issue as not simply linguistic but cultural and economic. Provocatively titled books like *Language in Danger: The Loss of Linguistic Diversity and the Threat to Our Future* and *Language Death*—the cover of which displays the heartbeat line from an EKG, presumably on the point of cessation—offer statistics on the worldwide decrease of languages since the expansion of English and American interests in the past several centuries. By one estimate 75–90% of the languages spoken today will disappear by the next century; according to another, by 2070 'fewer than one-tenth of the languages spoken [in North America] before European contact will still survive'; and according to still another, of the 250 Aboriginal languages spoken when Britain annexed Australia in the late eighteenth century, 90 remain in use, and of these 70 are near extinction.[35]

---

[33] McWhorter, *Doing Our Own Things: The Degradation of Language and Music and Why We Should, Like, Care* (New York: Gotham, 2003), 67. McWhorter's work, like Deborah Tannen's studies of language and gender, reflects how anxiety about language change bridges the academic/popular divide; the appearance of *Doing Our Own Things* from a popular press was accompanied by Emily Eakin's lengthy article entitled 'Going at the Changes in, Ya Know, English' in the *New York Times* (15 November 2003, A15, 17). A similar bridge appears in Tony Crowley's critique of John Honey's views of standards and dialects; while taking a distinctively academic position opposite Honey's on nearly every issue, Crowley shares his popular inflammatory style and tone. See 'Curiouser and Curiouser: Falling Standards in the Standard English Debate', in Tony Bex and Richard J. Watts (eds.), *Standard English: The Widening Debate* (London: Routledge, 1999), 271–82.

[34] Crystal, *The Fight for English: How Language Pundits Ate, Shot, and Left* (Oxford: Oxford University Press, 2006), ix.

[35] Dixon, *The Rise and Fall of Languages*, 116–17; Andrew Dalby, *Language in Danger: The Loss of Linguistic Diversity and the Threat to Our Future* (New York: Columbia University Press, 2003), 148; and Stephen May, *Language and Minority Rights: Ethnicity, Nationalism and the Politics of Language* (New York: Longman, 2001), 145.

The reasons such change occasions interest and concern vary from the intellectual to the cultural to the economic. Robert Dixon, thus, describes as urgent the 'task to document ... before they disappear' languages whose speakers are shifting to another language, while Crystal sees language death as rapidly increasing and the changes involved in language shift as qualitatively different from those involved in other kinds of linguistic change. He speaks of the need to develop 'in people a sense of the value of a language, and of what is lost when a language dies ... there is an urgent need for memorable ways of talking, to capture what is involved: we need to develop ear-catching metaphors—language as a "national treasure", perhaps, or as a "cause for celebration", or a "natural resource" '.[36] More subtly, Daniel Nettle and Suzanne Romaine have connected the retraction of languages not simply to the emergence of political units but to the economic history of human society. First agriculture and then the industrial revolution, they suggest, produced social reorganizations that favored shared language as opposed to the multilingualism fostered among isolated, undeveloped communities.[37] Language shift and death may thus stand as the inevitable byproducts of social sophistication.

Since language instruction, much less use, is not value-free, the global expansion of English at the expense of indigenous languages has alarmed other critics not simply because it will facilitate the demise of these languages, but because it necessarily brings with the language Anglo-American cultural, economic, and political values. Merely to speak English, in this analysis, is to further imperialism (to 'inhabit' its discourse), and the subtitle of one relevant critical essay is the catchy 'The Threat from Killer Languages'.[38] The

---

[36] Dixon, *The Rise and Fall of Languages*, 117; and Crystal, *Language Death* (Cambridge: Cambridge University Press, 2000), 98. For similarly emotive arguments, see Peter Mühlhäusler, *Linguistic Ecology: Language Change and Linguistic Imperialism in the Pacific Region* (London: Routledge, 1996), 269–81; and Michael E. Krauss, 'Keynote—Mass Language Extinction and Documentation: The Race Against Time', in Osahito Miyaoka *et al.* (eds.), *The Vanishing Languages of the Pacific Rim* (Oxford: Oxford University Press, 2007), 3–24.

[37] Nettle and Romaine, *Vanishing Voices: The Extinction of the World's Languages* (Oxford: Oxford University Press, 2000). An effective extension of this argument is K. David Harrison's *When Languages Die: The Extinction of the World's Languages and the Erosion of Human Knowledge* (Oxford: Oxford University Press, 2007). Demonstrating how issues like animal taxonomy, calendars, and conceptions of time manifest language-specific ways of organizing experience, Harrison argues that as language diversity atrophies, so, too, does that of world views.

[38] See, for example, Robert Phillipson, *Linguistic Imperialism* (Oxford: Oxford University Press, 1992); Tove Skutnabb-Kangas and Phillipson (eds.), *Linguistic Human Rights: Overcoming Linguistic Discrimination* (Berlin: Mouton de Gruyter, 1994); Alastair Pennycook, *The Cultural Politics of English as an International Language* (London: Longman, 1994); and Skutnabb-Kangas, 'Linguistic Diversity and Biodiversity: The Threat from Killer Languages', in Christian Mair (ed.), *The Politics of English as a World Language: New Horizons in Postcolonial Cultural Studies* (Amsterdam: Rodopi, 2003), 31–52.

fact that non-Anglophones shift to English thereby raises as much alarm—even hysteria—as the fact of the internal changes that Truss and Honey describe. And in each case, enormous significance and power are understood to reside in change and variation, the very phenomena that Lass presents as neutral.

Changes in the status of English have also raised concerns for English itself, beginning with the fact that speakers of English as a second language vastly outnumber native speakers. Indeed, of the one billion speakers currently estimated to have some command of English—and some estimates are twice that—perhaps only 400 million use English as their primary, mother tongue. Native speakers have thereby been transformed into minority stake-holders in a language that has become increasingly pre-eminent in international business and communication. Even if other languages are unable to challenge the status of English as a global language, an increase in the numbers of their speakers, coupled with the changing character of the population of Anglophones and the varieties of language they speak, could have adverse economic as well as social consequences for the United Kingdom, the United States, and other traditional Anglophone powers. 'We may find the hegemony of English replaced by an oligarchy of languages,' notes David Graddol, 'including Spanish and Chinese. To put it in economic terms, the size of the global market for the English language may increase in absolute terms, but its market share will probably fall.' Here, it is English that is threatened by the changes of other languages, and the metaphor from economics would not seem to be coincidental: the future of English, so this argument goes, needs to be monitored as a way of monitoring the future of English markets.[39]

To an extent, anxiety about language change could be understood as a manifestation of a more general kind of nostalgia for golden ages and halcyon days. While the proliferation of grammatically casual electronic communication on the Internet may have catalyzed this kind of non-historical memory, then, it certainly did not create what may partly be a feature of the human condition.[40] Like Dylan Thomas looking back on his childhood Christmases

---

[39] Graddol, *The Future of English?: A Guide to Forecasting the Popularity of the English Language in the 21st Century* (London: British Council, 1997), 3. As a publication of the British Council, which describes itself as 'the United Kingdom's international organisation for educational opportunities and cultural relations', this volume, replete with tables, charts, and statistics, lays claim to a peculiar kind of hybrid authority, part linguistic, part social, and part economic.

[40] Cf. Aitchison, *Language Change*, 13.

in Wales, or middle-aged individuals remembering the fashion, music, and culture of their youth, speakers of all ages can imagine language as once having attained a standard never reached again. This kind of anxiety is always powerful, precisely because it rests on memory, which can be measured in neither quantity nor quality and therefore provides no internal check on the concerns it might foster.

But the fact that nostalgic complaints are generally unmeasurable and therefore unverifiable goes only part way towards understanding why changes in grammar, vocabulary, or usage should occasion the concerns I have sketched so far. Is the language of *Beowulf* truly a swamp, back to which our 'dismally illiterate world' is slouching? Does the appearance of a word like *blog* truly diminish language and thought? Is modern America truly 'culturally and even intellectually deprived' because the general adult population, now nearly entirely literate, does not cultivate the stylized rhetoric of an age that restricted literacy by sex, race, and class? And is the shift of language any more unusual—and therefore any more alarming—than the transformation of Old English into Middle, or Middle into Modern? When even the persistence of multilingualism causes concern—not because it resists the economic power of a majority language group or works against national unity, but because languages mediate power and multilingualism therefore simply has the potential to be coopted in various kinds of power relations[41]—one begins to suspect that anxiety about language change and variation is really about something else. That something is the subject of this book.

The scope of this book

Language Anxiety explores how anxiety over language change and variation has transhistorically motivated and underwritten sociopolitical behavior, ideological formation, and mythological construction—how it has been largely a constant in the Anglophone world. It suggests that as a constant, further, this anxiety has served to displace and channel other kinds of social concerns, whether of economics, race, ethnicity, sex, or class. Put much more directly, my thesis is that anxiety over language change has euphemistically displaced anxiety about other issues and that so long as the anxiety remains centered on language, the other issues can never be fully addressed.

---

[41] Louis-Jean Calvet, *Language Wars and Linguistic Politics*, trans. Michel Petheram (Oxford: Oxford University Press, 1998).

In order to depict and understand this anxiety, my approach to language change is quite broad. As my preliminary examples have already suggested, I approach change at a level encompassing the grammatical (such as phonological variation or lexical addition), the pragmatic (such as discourse conventions and standardization), and the social (such as language contact and bilingualism). And I do this because a word like *hopefully* as a sentential adverb, pronunciations like *wanna* ([wɑnə]) for *want to* [wɑnt tu], and the mere presence of non-native speakers can in fact all elicit moral outrage, calls for educational reform, and even, in some instances, legislative ministrations. Much of what I examine has parallels among at least other Western European languages, in which the myth of Babel has been as foundational as it has been for English. While a more broadly focused book is thus certainly possible, and while I will offer comparative evidence from other language traditions, practical and theoretical considerations limit my concerns to English: it is the tradition I know best and the one I want most to understand.[42] In my linking of change with language and the speakers who use it, I also hope both to conceptualize a range of change and variation within one critical category and to suggest the mutual effects speakers and their language have upon each other.

And though I speak of an English tradition, neither my outlook nor my method is chronological. In discussing specific illustrative examples (whether government policies, literary expressions, or published volumes), I will indeed concentrate on the historical context that gives a particular example its particular force. Alfred's anxiety about England's change from multilingualism, for example, is rooted in both the immediate Viking raids and also, more generally, in discursive traditions about conquest as a visitation by God that go back, in England, to Gildas's sixth-century *De excidio Britanniae liber querulus*. And in some cases, as in the eighteenth-century codification of English, particular arguments and publications are predicated on and developed from earlier published positions, all of which therefore can be connected to one another in ways useful to the understanding of sociolinguistic thinking. But in the main, this book's orientation is not chronological but topical, not exhaustive but thematic. The reason for this orientation is simply put: although it may take various forms at particular moments in history and

---

[42] The difficulty of a comparative approach is that it almost inevitably produces generalities so broad as to work against focused, detailed conclusions. For an example of just such an approach, see Peter Burke, *Languages and Communities in Early Modern Europe* (Cambridge: Cambridge University Press, 2004).

although it may be particularly insistent in the current moment, the kind of anxiety I address does seem to be a historical and social constant, it does seem to have run through a lot of English sociolinguistic activity irrespective of historical specifics. Language change and variation are by no means the only social phenomena to mediate such extra-linguistic anxieties, nor is such mediation the only social work that variation and change accomplish. It remains the case, however, that connections between change and anxiety have been particularly prominent in the history of the English language. In fact, this anxiety has demonstrated greater durability across time and space than have many grammatical features; it has been a constant for English, even as words, inflections, and syntactic structures have come and gone. In this sense, I would argue that anxiety about change might even be regarded as one of the language's distinctive characteristics, as one of the features that justify the single label English for fifteen hundred years and thousands of miles of linguistic variation.

The next chapter expands on the theoretical propositions of this one by surveying the kinds and contexts of synchronic variation and diachronic change that have affected English, including grammatical changes and changes in linguistic repertoire through contact with other languages. There I want to flesh out two simple but enormously consequential claims: that English always changes—typically in regular fashions—and that the social meanings assigned to changes are distinct from the changes themselves. Together, the first and second chapters provide the theoretical and practical premises for the following three chapters, each of which identifies a different nexus of social institutions, principles, and actions and surveys the ways in which these invest sociolinguistic meanings in variation and change. The third chapter considers how language change has been represented in myth, beginning with the Tower of Babel and the myths and miracles associated with language shift. From there I proceed to the ideological and cultural impact of languages like Esperanto and Volapük, which have been invented to counter-act language change, and then to representations of language change and variation in literary works, where dialect writing and related rhetorical devices have conceived such linguistic transformation as the object of humor and social critique and also as a reflection of social and individual deviation. Chapter 4 examines how Anglophone governments have responded to linguistic change by using language planning to manage contact between English and other languages. As was the case when English came into contact with Welsh, American Indian languages, and Maori, such contact has sometimes arisen through expansion by Anglophones, but it has also resulted from

immigration by non-Anglophones into predominantly Anglophone countries, as has been the case with the spread of Asian languages in both Australia
and the United States today. In these circumstances, whether through laws,
military action, or court decisions, Anglophone governments have often used
English to further the construction of national identity. In the fifth chapter,
I shift my focus to the linguistic reasoning that has underwritten efforts to
retard or eliminate language change. Here I consider how approaches to both
language and the instruments of its codification (such as dictionaries) have
themselves produced and channeled extra-linguistic concerns. As a conclusion I draw together the evidence of the book to argue for the importance of
distinguishing the fact of language change from the social meanings assigned
to it. Redirection of anxiety about language change and variation to the social
concerns it mediates, I maintain, is the most effective way to approach (not to
mention resolve) the latter.

All this sounds dispassionate and academic, and these are precisely the
notes I hope to sound in what follows: to dissociate the personal as well as the
political from the processes of language change and variation. At the same
time, as I will emphasize on a number of occasions, I take the recognition that
English is not simply a structured code but a lived experience to be foundational to understanding all these matters. I may here strive to be an objective
analyst, but I am also an academic and a native Anglophone from the
Midwestern region of the United States. Whatever I say about language,
including whatever social meanings I see invested in it, will necessarily be
shaped in some way by my own linguistic background.

As an English teacher, I've had plenty of opportunity to witness and
experience the channeling of social issues into language. I've heard students
attribute poor grades in science classes to the alleged English deficiencies of
their Asian American, but native Anglophone, teaching assistants, and I've
had a non-American acquaintance summon me to a conversation at a conference wine hour in order to have me demonstrate how Midwesterners
talked. I've been told that the appearance of Spanish signs in local department
stores is an indication of just what's wrong with the United States today and,
at a dinner party, that I was an 'idealist'—and this was meant as an insult—if
I didn't think that the active suppression of non-standard English was in the
best interests of everyone, especially minorities.

What puzzles, offends, amuses, or outrages me may not always affect other
speakers in the same way. And this is to be expected, for it testifies yet again
to the variability inherent in natural language and speakers' responses to it.
More importantly, the variable judgements of Anglophones about the social

meanings of any particular linguistic form or act underscore the experiential quality of language. And perhaps most importantly, such variability manifests the fact that what we agree or disagree about is often not linguistic but social and that if our conversations on such matters are to progress, they sometimes need to leave language behind.

2

A Moveable Speech

Where sounds go when they go away

Sometimes, the oddest questions, the ones that would seem to be the most easily dismissed, end up requiring unexpectedly complex answers. Here's one: since the globe spins, could one travel around the earth by floating over the ground in a helicopter and waiting for the world to turn? Here's another: if lime and orange are colors as well as fruit, why isn't grapefruit? An intuitive response to both questions may well be that they're simply naive and not worth answering. But the truth of the matter is that effective answers end up being anything but simple. Responses to the first question must draw on issues like the physics of time, friction, gravity, and relative motion, while cogent responses to the second depend on semantics, lexical history, and usage. Without recourse to these admittedly sophisticated heuristics, replies can take on the peremptory, even mystical quality of an answer like 'because that's the way it is'. And that quality only serves to make the questions appear even more complex.

Another of these unexpectedly complex questions is, where does pain go when it goes away? There's a strong philosophical streak in it, since it presumes something about the ontology of pain. A physician might say that pain isn't so much a 'thing' as a response to something, specifically to stimulation of the nerves or muscles or bones, but to anyone suffering it, particularly children, pain seems real enough. If anything, its reality seems confirmed by its disappearance. If a thorn in one's hand causes pain, and when the thorn is removed from one's hand, the pain disappears, too, the pain would seem to have been extracted along with the thorn. And if pain can be removed like a thorn, which can be discarded in the trash, what happens to the pain afterwards? What does one do with it?

The answer to this odd question requires the same kind of sophistication that I directed at my earlier questions. A physician would simply insist that one doesn't really do anything with pain, because as a biochemical response of the nervous system, pain ceases when what's causing it ceases. If I've cut my finger, once the cut closes and heals over, the factors eliciting a painful response from my nervous system cease, too. What does not cease, however, at least so long as I am alive, is *some* biochemical response from my nervous system. I will continue to feel with some of the same nerves that once registered pain, but with my cut healed what I feel will be, variously, something rough, soft, wet, or—in the case of minimal tactile stimulation—effectively nothing at all. Medically, when pain goes away, much of it in effect becomes a new response, no longer painful but perhaps indifferent rather than pleasurable.

The implicit comparison I am drawing, of course, is with language change and variation. When a sound, word, or syntactic structure changes, what happens to the original linguistic form? More generally, when change involves an aggregate of features from a language—when Old English becomes Middle English, say—what becomes of the original form of the language? Do sounds and varieties ever truly go away, and if so, where do they go? Or, like painful nervous stimulation that becomes non-painful, do they effectively become other sounds and other varieties? In looking at the dominant language of a particular region like modern Ireland, how does one decide whether that language is the same as what was spoken three centuries before, or an altered version of that language that is still somehow the same language, or a different language entirely? What sociolinguistic consequences follow from the various possible answers to such questions? Presuming we can differentiate an original form or variety from its developments, does the former take any conceptual, social, or linguistic precedence over the latter? On what grounds?

What I mean to suggest is that questions about what happens to forms and varieties that change have the uncomfortable impact of an odd question about pain. On one hand, they might seem simplistic, predicated on misconceptions about natural language as a category. Granting that Irish and English are distinct languages that have been used by real people, we can't (or perhaps shouldn't) ask whether one simply became the other or treat the languages as if they existed independently of their speakers. The English spoken in most of Ireland today is clearly not the same language as the Irish that predominated in the eighteenth century: even leaving aside the genealogy of the languages, their structural differences are so great that no mutual communication between their speakers would be possible. On the other, like a question about pain, these kinds of questions are rooted in experience, specifically speakers' experiences with language. In that regard, they are predicated on a view of language as a social phenomenon, and it is after all in a social context—whether of speakers addressing one another or confronting historical documents—that linguistic change and its consequences are particularly salient. Indeed, it is in this kind of context that anxiety about change and variation arises and has its greatest significance, for (I contend) speakers ultimately worry not about forms or languages as such but about the presumed social implications of those forms and languages. When language changes, its forms—phonology, morphology, lexicon, and syntax—reconfigure the language as a system, but it is the meaning speakers assign to these forms, their changes, and the reconfigured system that define speakers' interest and response. Just as the structural boundaries between dialects and languages can be malleable, depending partly on speakers' attitudes towards their environment, culture, and fellow speakers, so the outcome of change—in effect, its teleology—can rest on speakers' perceptions of how language mediates their social world.

In asking where sounds and languages go when they go away, I am really asking something about speakers' views of themselves and their language. Change itself, Lass has maintained, is neutral. It is also inevitable, multiform, and structured for both grammatical alteration and language shift, which is a community's (or speaker's) replacement of its own language with another. While not absolutely predictable, such change for any one language proceeds in patterned fashions that replicate similar, non-random patterns in other languages and other time periods. The social consequences of variation and change are likewise not random but structured, deriving their meanings from the way they challenge or support ideas, practices, and institutions. But if structured change is neutral, the significance speakers attach to it always reflects individual and collective preference and partiality. Even though linguistic changes and their meaning share the qualities of regularity and inevitability, they thus diverge in this crucial way.

This is the issue I want to explore in this chapter, then: this sometimes shifting distinction between social evaluations of change and change itself. Changes to the structure of a language, I will argue along with Lass, are simply neutral linguistic facts: a vowel disappears or acquires a new quality, a syntactic structure gains complexity, vocabulary expands, and so forth. Whatever social impulses might contribute to change and whatever institutions or ideas might assign them significance are entirely different matters, for the social meanings that facilitate and accrue to change and variation reflect the partiality of speakers and speech communities. If change is inevitable and constant, these meanings necessarily vary. They do so, moreover, in ways that both respond to and further extra-linguistic considerations. I will also argue that the same kinds of inevitability and regularity that describe structural change apply to social and regional variation as well as to language contact. Perhaps the most important concomitant point here is that empirical judgements about change and the social recognition of them do not necessarily coincide with one another. At a structural level, for example, it may be possible to demonstrate that prevailing vowel articulations reflect alterations in a word's pronunciation or, more broadly, phonemic change, but such demonstration has not prevented speakers from judging the new pronunciations as 'good', 'bad', or 'wrong'.

It is the disjunction between the fact of linguistic change and the social meanings that accrue to it that produces much of the anxiety with which I am concerned in this book. Further and perhaps most importantly, if in theory a clear distinction exists between change and its social significance, in practice—in the historical development of English in various speech communities—this distinction has been both situational and strategic. Specifically, immediate social concerns have led to the judgement of some linguistic phenomena as natural—and therefore neutral—change and other phenomena as socially meaningful in their manifestation or violation of sociolinguistic norms. Clear, empirical distinctions between synchronic variation, diachronic change, shift, faulty grammar, and discursive impropriety cannot always be easily drawn.

The regularities of grammar

In the opening chapter I described change and variation as indisputable facts of social history. To their inevitability I here add their regularity and, in view of this regularity, the qualification that in a fundamental way language *is* change. Whether at the level of sound, word, syntax, or linguistic repertoire, change and variation are not random processes or the simple byproducts of laziness and ineptitude but rather develop in structured ways that allow for empirical analysis and explanation and that figure in various languages of various epochs. They are, in fact, linguistic universals. If this simple claim might seem unremarkable to most linguists, the anxiety associated with linguistic change and variation suggests that it is not more generally understood or accepted.

The regularity of which I speak operates at several levels of linguistic structure. Nouns, for example, are everywhere the most heavily borrowed category, and function words, like determiners and prepositions, the least borrowed. When languages come into contact with one another, similarly, the survival of any particular language generally depends more on the kinds of domains in which it is used than on merely the number of its speakers. And phonological variation is so consistent and inevitable as to play an essential role in the differentiation of meaning. So-called strong verbs like *sing* and *drink*, for instance, form their preterites by altering the root vowel to produce *sang* and *drank*. And they do so because in many Indo-European languages, including the Germanic family, the universal process of context-conditioned vowel gradation (*Ablaut*) came to carry the functional load of verb tense. In these verbs, thus, the distinction between present and preterite—a distinction that probably all Anglophones would accept as not only normal but crucial to the production of meaning—rests, ultimately, on the fact that early speakers were inconsistent in their articulations of the same vowel.

The collection of changes affecting tense vowels in English and collectively designated the Great Vowel Shift offers an elaborate example of just this point: how in its non-random regularity, change serves as a vital defining feature of English (and, for that matter, all natural languages). Occurring at various times in various locales—and echoed by parallel changes in German and the Scandinavian languages—these changes generally originated in the early fifteenth century and were completed within two centuries. As a reconfiguration of English phonology, the Great Vowel Shift represents a transformation of the language's grammar—of what it means to speak English. What had been /a/ became /e/, for example, and what had been /i/ diphthongized (eventually) as /ai/, so that in an oral recitation of Chaucer's 'Wife of Bath's Tale' the Knight would address his *lady* and his *wife* as [ladi] and [wif], while in one of John Dryden's translation she'd be his [ledi] and his [waif].[1] As I noted in Chapter 1, it's as if the first syllable of *fodder* were to be pronounced like *fate*, whose vowel in turn came to be like the one in *feet*, whose own vowel became like the one in *fight*. Far from being haphazard, changes like the Great Vowel Shift manifest such regularity, with the same sound under the same circumstances tending to alter in the same way, that the nineteenth-century neogrammarians regarded sound change as admitting no exceptions, though recognition of synchronic variation and the messiness of the historical record would relax this claim for most linguists since then. 'All grammars leak', observed Edward Sapir,[2] and the Great Vowel Shift had at least one leak: in northern England and Scotland, the high back vowel /o/ seems to have moved forward as well as up to (eventually) /ü/ rather than directly up to /u/, with the result that in those regions the original /u/ was not pushed to diphthongize as /au/, as it did in other early modern dialects of English. Modern English

---

[1] For the sake of clarity, my transcriptions here are intentionally broad. Dryden, for example, could well have realized the stressed vowel of *lady* as [ɛ:] or even as a diphthong like [ei], while its final vowel would likely have had an off-glide for Chaucer if not Dryden. Since the Great Vowel Shift affected only stressed long vowels, it would have had no impact on the final syllable of *lady*, thus leaving it the same for Chaucer, Dryden, and, indeed, most modern speakers.

[2] Sapir, *Language: An Introduction to the Study of Speech* (New York: Harcourt, Brace, 1921), 3.

house, pronounced [hus] (rhymes with *loose*) in Old and Middle English, thus became [haus] via the Great Vowel Shift but retained the former pronunciation in most Scots varieties. This northern leak was in fact so steady that Jeremy Smith has argued it represents a distinct co-varying shift.³ This may well be the case, but for my purposes, the same conclusion emerges: both shifts (and any leaks) were so consistent as to support a claim for the regularity of sound change.

Further support emerges from the strikingly parallel set of Primitive Germanic phonological phenomena collectively known as the First Consonant Shift. Like the Great Vowel Shift, the First Consonant Shift describes a series of changes (these involving voiced and voiceless stops) that occurred over several centuries and that, in the way they relate to one another, constitute evidence for the found fact of a co-varying shift. To offer just one example, the voiced Indo-European aspirant /bʰ/ (a breathier version of the *b* in *bull*) became the continuant /ß/ and eventually the unaspirated stop /b/ (the *b* of *stab*); the original voiced stops, in turn, devoiced, so that what had been /b/ became /p/; and an original voiceless stop like /p/ became a fricative like /f/. Also like the Great Vowel Shift, the First Consonant Shift leaked a bit. The new voiceless fricatives became voiced in certain circumstances, for example, while in much of what is now Germany this co-varying shift was extended in a series of changes known as the Second Consonant Shift. One measure of their regularity is the fact that the shifts I have described are among the most established and crucial in conceptualizing the Germanic languages as a group. It is the First Consonant Shift, ultimately, that accounts for some of the most pervasive etymological doublets in English: *dentists* who work on *teeth*, *podiatrists* who work on *feet*, *brothers* of a *fraternal* order, *paternalistic fathers*, *wheeling cycles*, and all *kinds* of *gender*. The leaking of the voiceless fricatives explains why the singular preterite of the verb *be* is *was* but the plural *were*, and the leaking of the extended co-varying shift explains why Germans drink *Wasser* in place of the *water* drunk by Anglophones.⁴ But the Shift also significantly helped define the methods and objectives of comparative linguistics in general. It was the early nineteenth-century linguist and folklorist Jacob Grimm, indeed, whose 'law' provided the earliest comprehensive account of these changes and served as a model for subsequent attempts to define putative co-varying shifts.

---

³ Smith, *Sound Change and the History of English* (Oxford: Oxford University Press, 2007), 127–53.

⁴ Accounts of the First Consonant Shift and the leaks described by Verner's Law (*was*) and the Second Consonant Shift (*water*) can be found in most comparative or historical Germanic grammars.

In calling the Great Vowel Shift and the First Consonant Shift regular, I do not mean to suggest that such change is necessarily, or perhaps even characteristically, rational. For one thing, as the school of 'emergent linguistics' has increasingly suggested, such changes depend not simply on pre-existing grammatical structures but on the individual articulations of speakers. Indeed, the basic idea of emergent structure, according to two of its adherents, is that 'what may appear to be a coherent structure created according to some underlying design may in fact be the result of multiple applications or interactions of simple mechanisms that operate according to local principles and create a seemingly well-planned structure as a consequence'.[5] And another factor that works against strict rationality for linguistic change is that in both examples of co-varying shift, however the changes began and proceeded, they eventually produced a phonology strikingly similar to the one they had replaced. Although two new diphthongs emerged in the process of the Great Vowel Shift, excepting lengthened /ɛ:/ English began and ended the changes with essentially the same inventory of long tense vowels: /i/, /e/, /a/, /ɔ/, /o/, and /u/.[6] And as for the First Consonant Shift, Primitive Germanic had the same inventory of voiced and voiceless stops as had Indo-European; where it did differ from Indo-European was in having phonemic voiceless fricatives (/f/, /θ/, /x/) rather than phonemic voiced aspirated stops (/bʰ/, /dʰ/, /gʰ/), but even in this case, there was phonetic overlap in aspiration, articulation, and, in words described by Verner's Law (e.g., *was* / *were*), voicing.[7] In very casual terms it's as if in each case, after centuries of phonological reconfiguration extensively affecting the language's lexicon, sounds mostly traded places, both going away and remaining at the same time—which would not seem to reflect any preconceived, rational structure.

---

[5] Joan Bybee and Paul Hopper, 'Introduction', in Bybee and Hopper (eds.), *Frequency and the Emergence of Linguistic Structure* (Amsterdam: John Benjamins, 2001), 10. See also Bybee's *Phonology and Language Use* (Cambridge: Cambridge University Press, 2001); and *Frequency of Use and the Organization of Language* (Oxford: Oxford University Press, 2007).

[6] For the sake of argument, I simplify here by omitting the varying glides described by many phonologists for the realization of the vowels in many varieties of Modern English.

[7] Phonological balance is sometimes claimed as the motivation of and improvement provided by the First Consonant Shift. That is, after the changes Germanic, unlike Indo-European, had pairings of not only voiced and voiceless stops but also voiced and voiceless fricatives. As a mechanistic explanation, however, phonological balance is limited in the same way as functional optimality, which I discussed in Chapter 1. Beyond that, even granting this explanation this fundamental fact remains: after the Shift, Germanic had virtually all of the sounds it had before it. A perhaps more striking example of this kind of non-rational change involves the vowel in modern English *that*. In Primitive Germanic, this vowel was /a/; in Old English it became, variously, /æ/ or /ɛ/; in Middle English it became /a/ or /ɛ/; and in Early Modern English it generally became /æ/ once more; then, in certain phonological environments in varieties of British English, it returned yet again to [a] or [ɑ].

For the Great Vowel Shift, accordingly, an answer to an apparently simple question like 'Where did /i/ go?' is anything but simple. Did it, ontologically, become /ai/, so that this very same vowel now somehow appears with a different sound in words like *wife*? Is a vowel, in other words, much like individuals who might be understood to retain the same identity, even when they put on new hats and coats? Or did the sound remain the same, irrespective of the words in which it occurred, so that it in effect became what had been /e/ in words like *feet*, previously pronounced [fet] but now pronounced [fit]? In this case, is a vowel like a furnished room that stays unchanged, whoever occupies it? Or did it in some fundamental way simply disappear, replaced by an entirely new /i/ and generating the new diphthong /ai/?

These are not idle questions. Judgements that Middle English /i/ becomes /ai/ in words like *wife* accept the fact that language is a system incorporating change and transcending its speakers and forms at any one time. In this system, change and variation, at least in certain phonological circumstances, occur as natural processes that do not disturb the essential character of a language. By such analyses, English is still English, even if its vowels trade places and we now designate it Early Modern rather than Middle. And this kind of analysis identifies certain kinds of change as systematic not only in the way they unfold but also in the fact that their occurrence is as grammatical as specific rules of syntax or morphology. It is a syntactic rule, for example, that articles placed before their nouns do not violate but rather adhere to the grammar of English, just as it is an apparent systematic rule that certain kinds of change and variation, as in co-varying shifts like the Great Vowel Shift, can occur without violating the integrity of the language.

The interesting thing about rules like these is that while their positive forms parallel one another, their negations do not. A violation of an English syntactic rule would take the form of a structure like *dragon the*, in which the article postposes its noun. Such violations are empirically verifiable, practically infinite (there are many kinds of incorrect structures, like *the dragon the*, *the the dragon*, and so forth), in many cases relatively stable over time (*dragon the* has always been ungrammatical in English), and recognizable as unacceptable by all speakers. I know of neither a grammar handbook nor a variety of English that would recognize *dragon the* as well formed.[8] Violations of rules about change and variation are not so simply illustrated, however, because these kinds of violations reflect not empirical facts but

---

[8] Within the Germanic language group, however, Old Norse did allow for enclitic articles on nouns not preceded by an adjective: *drekinn*, literally 'dragon the', but *inn grænn dreki*, 'the green dragon'. Modern Scandinavian languages show reflexes of this structure.

judgement calls over which linguistic phenomena exceed *permissible* change and variation for a language and thus transgress the language's integrity. It is by this kind of situational evaluation that the pronunciation of *lady* can change from [ladi] to [ledi] and still qualify as grammatical English, while *want to* becoming realized not as [want tu] but [wanə] (*wanna*) can illustrate non-standard or incorrect speech.

One might well ask on what grounds a distinction like this has been drawn. And one way to approach this important and complex issue is through the common distinction between prescriptive and descriptive grammar, which underwrites all manner of government and educational as well as purely linguistic activity. Prescriptive grammar, generally, refers to what the word *grammar* invokes in the minds of most educated people: rote drills about *i* before *e* in spelling or never ending a sentence with a preposition that often seem to run contrary to what people naturally wish to do with English and that were learned partially and sometimes painfully in schoolrooms and through exercises. Locatable in dictionaries as well as grammar books, this kind of grammar has standards of absolute right and wrong that provide, in the form of explicit rules, a way to measure grammatical competence.

While prescriptive grammar might be thought akin to the driving rules of the road, whose violation results in accidents and citations, descriptive grammar is like the rules that fashion a car from metal, rubber, plastic, and so forth; driving a car the wrong way down a street, while proscribed as illegal, is nonetheless physically possible, but an object is not a car if it lacks wheels. Descriptive grammar, then, provides an account of how well-formed—i.e., natural and acceptable—utterances are made in a language. Its grammatical rules describe what it means to speak English: what sounds are used, how words are made, and the ways in which words combine in sentences. In this sense, learning descriptive rules means learning the language, whether passively as an infant or actively in an adult second-language course. And rather than something like 'don't split an infinitive', a descriptive rule would be of the sort I noted above: 'adjectives are positioned between determiners and nouns', so that *the great green dragon* is a well-formed English noun phrase, but *great green the dragon* is not. Given the variability of how people speak, of course, descriptive grammar allows a good deal of latitude in identifying what's well formed and resists passing evaluative judgements on the variation it identifies. Where prescriptive grammar would enjoin speakers not to use 'double negatives', descriptive grammar would note that in some modern varieties, such as African American Vernacular English, multiple negation has the same intensifying effect that it did for Chaucer and Shakespeare.

Or so it goes in theory, at least. As several critics have noted, as crucial as the categories of prescriptive and descriptive grammar may be, an impermeable distinction between the two is not easy to maintain.[9] The latter, which characteristically draws its data from the critics' experiences, ultimately makes many of the same kinds of value judgements about acceptable and unacceptable language as the former. Descriptive grammar may label correct structures well formed instead of right, and it may refrain from attaching any moral or intellectual significance to them, but like prescriptive grammar it remains in the business of distinguishing English from non-English. In the case of something like the voiceless bilabial stop [p] as opposed to a click from a language like Xhosa, it is essentially accurate to say that a simple description of English would include the one but not the other. But many grammatical rules are less clear. There doesn't seem to be a strict rule that precludes the phrase *the green great dragon*, for instance, but to my ear, there's nonetheless something odd about its ordering of adjectives. And if the reason it sounds odd is that in English we prefer adjectives of size to precede those of color, this remains a feature of style and not one of the structure of the language: the phrase's ordering of determiner, adjectives, and noun is well formed.[10] Even a descriptive rule as apparently innocuous as 'in most cases form English preterites by adding the suffix *-ed*' (variously articulated as [d], [t], [ɪd], or [ɪt]) works against an easy distinction between descriptive and prescriptive rules. Above all, it fails to account both for varieties that include the deletion of final stops and for ones regarded as creoles or pidgins, in which preterite formation typically follows an entirely different, periphrastic paradigm by forming verbs with the root and *done* or *been* (e.g., *he done walk* rather than *he walked*).

What grammatical descriptions can easily overlook is that simply by virtue of the identification of a base form from which other forms develop—or against which they are measured—the description of certain rules necessarily becomes the prescription of a particular variety of English. Many analyses of preterite verbs, for example, describe the deletion of final stops as a rule that sequentially follows the one adding the suffix *-ed*, and this kind of rule has the effect of rendering varieties that employ deletion as secondary and derivative. It's certainly true that grammatical precedence might well be based on history and thereby in this example justify a claim for the voiced stop preterites as being the base form from which other preterites develop. Yet this same claim

---

[9] e.g., Roy Harris, *The Language Machine* (Ithaca, NY: Cornell University Press, 1987).

[10] If there is a stylistic 'rule' here, it's not easy to state. *Green happy dragon*, with an adjective of color preceding one of disposition, seems unexceptionable to me; and even *green small dragon* doesn't sound as odd to me as *green great dragon*.

simplifies the diversity of the historical record, for competition between these two preterite forms dates at least to the eighteenth century and is therefore scarcely ephemeral. More generally, similar kinds of competition characterize the history of English; throughout the fourteenth and fifteenth centuries, for example, alternate forms of the singular third person indicative verbal inflection ([ɛθ] and [ɛs], spelled *eth* and *es*) were in use, and in certain isolated rural districts that competition continued until fairly recently. The most important point for my purposes, however, may be the fact that arguments that draw on historical precedence tacitly bypass the role social evaluations play in identifying variation as acceptable or erroneous. The existence of both dental preterites and periphrastic ones is a simple linguistic fact. The decisions to derive the second from the first and then associate it with a particular group of speakers and even pronounce it incorrect—these are all, to varying degrees, value judgements.

While fictional, Mark Twain's *Adventures of Huckleberry Finn* makes these points about both the malleability but also the social implications of grammar with particular effect. Even before the book begins Twain voices the descriptive dispassion of a linguist in claiming that he has utilized seven dialects in the book. He further dispassionately maintains that he has done so not haphazardly but 'pains-takingly, and with the trustworthy guidance and support of personal familiarity with these several forms of speech'.[11] He thereby grants these kinds of variation status as markers of legitimate social and regional varieties of English; his characters are not, as he observes, all trying to speak the same way, for the simple reason that not all Anglophones speak the same way. Yet the novel's moral and rhetorical force relies precisely on the disjunction between Huck's ignorance of prescriptive grammar, due to his lack of formal education, and the rectitude of his conscience. His language marks him as an ignorant social outcast, while his heart declares his conscience, and language and heart together thereby undermine neat truisms about prescriptive grammar, class, and virtue.

As tenuous as this distinction between descriptive and prescriptive grammar may sometimes be, it does more for English than simply underwrite many educational and government actions—though this is significant in and of itself. The distinction also supports a broader categorical distinction between change and variation that are judged internal to a language, and change and variation that violate its essential character and to which social meanings can accrue. Here, too, the distinction can seem permeable, even

---

[11] Twain, *Adventures of Huckleberry Finn*, ed. Henry Nash Smith (Boston, MA: Houghton Mifflin, 1958), 2.

impressionistic. Trivial phonological variation such as the pronunciations of [ɪn] as the termination of words ending in -*ing* (often represented as *in'*) can elicit indignation as corruptions of English, even as extensive phonological changes such as the First Consonant Shift have been readily accommodated as internal changes that leave the integrity of the language and its speakers intact. By way of an explanation for the Shift, for example, Grimm himself dispassionately regarded the consonant changes, somehow, as reflections of Germanic pride and impetuosity: the same life force that gave rise to Germanic culture gave rise to the Germanic languages. In a similar collapse of language and culture, Grimm's contemporary Heinrich Meyer-Benfey thought that the changes may have arisen from the effects of mountain air on Germanic speakers. In each case, it's as if Germanic predates the co-varying shift that defines it, for change was presumed to be inherent in the language as the expression of circumstances and social identity; beyond speakers' control, it was therefore also beyond the purview of value judgements. Recently, Smith has offered a far more empirically sophisticated explanation for the Shift by tracing it to social and linguistic contact between early Germanic speakers and the Raeti to their south.[12] While this account transcends Grimm's and Meyer-Benfey's in every way, it shares with them the sense that some changes, even ones that affect many of a language's consonantal phonemes, can occur without undermining the integrity of that language. All three analyses seem fundamentally essentialist: German is still German, whatever changes it undergoes, so long as those who speak German speak it.

Comments on the Great Vowel Shift reflect the impressionism of much linguistic categorization with just as great a force, precisely because, unlike any modern discussions of the First Consonant Shift, they sometimes do involve not only Grimm's dispassionate acceptance of change as part of a language's grammar but also the indignant response to unnatural change that Honey, McWhorter, and other modern critics express. On one hand, for example, Lass describes the essence of the Great Vowel Shift as a systemic change much like that of the First Consonant Shift: 'each non-high long vowel raises one height, and the high vowels diphthongise, dropping their first element by one height'.[13] John Hart, who witnessed (or perhaps heard) the Shift as it occurred and who in his *Orthographie* provided one of the richest sources for phonological discussion, can share Lass's dispassion. On occasion he, too, makes simple and scientific observations about, for instance, the fact

[12] Eduard Prokosch, *A Comparative Germanic Grammar* (Philadelphia, PA: Linguistics Society of America, 1939), 55; Smith, *Sound Change and the History of English*, 84–7.

[13] Lass, 'Phonology and Morphology', in Lass (ed.), *The Cambridge History of the English Language*, iii, *1476–1776* (Cambridge: Cambridge University Press, 1999), 73.

that the English and the Scots 'doe at any time sounde i, in the foresayde sounde of ei'. Yet on the other hand, Hart also evokes a present-day value judgement on the changes when he sees them as detrimental to communication. While he resists connecting the changes to specific social groups or assigning them specific social valuations, he does consider them illustrative of the kinds of deviations (from putatively correct pronunciations of graphs) that characterize what he sees as the period's general abuse of language.[14]

As impressionistic as distinctions between natural, grammatical change and its converse may be, they nonetheless figure significantly in the kinds of meanings that can accrue to a particular change. When changes are judged natural, discussion typically focuses on their mechanics—on how they change the grammar of a language—so that their meanings are purely linguistic and not social. For Western European languages, for instance, the First Consonant Shift figures not as a corruption of Indo-European but as a catalyst in the creation of the Germanic languages, which themselves then represent a separate group of languages with its own linguistic integrity. And, Hart notwithstanding, the Great Vowel Shift likewise typically represents not deterioration of medieval English pronunciation but an aspect of a categorical grammatical transformation that produced Modern from Middle English; despite the extensiveness of the change, we use the same noun, 'English', to refer to the language spoken before and after its occurrence.

More narrowly, incidental grammatical change can be accepted without comment, when categorized as an ordinary internal development, or as a linguistic and social mistake, when otherwise categorized. Thus, a Primitive Germanic form like *horso remained *hors* in Old English but through the process of metathesis became *hross* in Old Norse and *hros* in Old High German and Old Saxon; Old English *brid* became Modern English *bird* in the same way. In all cases metathesis occurred without popular or scholarly disapproval.[15] Yet in the realization of *professor* as *perfessor* ([pərfɛsər]), a common form in popular representations of colloquial speech, r-metathesis very clearly correlates with ignorance. It is by this same phonetic process that Modern English *ask* is sometimes realized as [æks], with the two final sounds reversed, and here again the metathesis has frequently been identified as a problem—and served as the subject of jokes—even though, as has often been noted, the metathesized pronunciation has a long history. Though the Old English form of the verb was in fact *ascian* ([ɑskiɑn]), the spelling *ks* occurs

---

14 Hart, *An Orthographie* (1569; rpt. Menston: Scolar Press, 1969), 32.

15 A similar example may be Old English *yrnan* and Modern English *run*, though the derivation of the former is complicated; see *OED*, s. v., *run*, v. The asterisk in front of *horso* means that the form is unattested—necessarily so, since Primitive Germanic was not a written language.

already in the Anglo-Saxon period and persists afterwards in the United States as well as in Britain. In his 1789 *Dissertation on the English Language*, Noah Webster in fact remarks not only that 'the word *ax* for *ask* was used in England' but also that '*ax* is still frequent in New England'.[16] The significant point here is that it is not simply a phonetic change or a sound that is inherently marked for Anglophones. As Labov comments, indeed:

> The force of social evaluation, positive or negative, is generally brought to bear only on superficial aspects of language: lexicon and phonetics. However, social affect is not in fact assigned to the very surface level: it is not the sounds of language which receive stigma or prestige, but rather the use of a particular allophone for a given phoneme. Thus the sound [iːə] is not stigmatized in general, since it is the prestige norm in *idea*, but it is stigmatized as an allophone of /æ/ in *man*.[17]

A process like metathesis or a diphthong like [iːə] becomes stigmatized as external corruption rather than internal change only when speakers, for whatever non-linguistic reasons, assign negative value to these linguistic phenomena in certain circumstances.

One way that changes accepted as internal and natural differ from those that are not is that descriptions of the former often take the form of plain tables of cognates like this:

> *name*: *Name* (G), *nomen* (L), ὄνομα (Gr), *ainm* (OIr), *nafn* (ON)
> *two*: *zwei* (G), *duo* (L), δύο (Gr), *tveir* (ON), *dwa* (Pol)

What is characteristically absent in discussion of changes perceived as grammatical and represented in this fashion is any consideration of the demonstrable and necessary social processes like migration and colonization that would have produced, in this case, the cognates or their consequences. It is as if, as Lass observes of linguistic facts like co-varying shifts, the establishment of a category of natural grammatical change enables certain kinds of questions but precludes others, in this case ones about how cognates come into existence and what they imply sociolinguistically. Perhaps the most significant of these questions is about the legitimacy of a variety as a language.

A table of cognates simply accepts as given the fact that social processes like immigration and colonialization have resulted in new languages. No one, to the best of my knowledge, has lamented—has attached any social meaning to—the shifting of stops and fricatives that helped define the Germanic language group, or the creation of new diphthongs by means of the Great

---

[16] Webster, *Dissertations on the English Language* (1789; rpt. Menston: Scolar Press, 1967), 386. See further *OED*, s. v. *ask*, v., and *DARE*, s. v. *ask*, v.

[17] Labov, *Principles of Linguistic Change*, ii, *Social Factors* (Oxford: Blackwell, 2001), 28.

Vowel Shift. By comparison, when immigration and colonization have figured in the development of creoles or the diffusion of global English, discussion has indeed focused on issues like the competence of speakers or whether particular varieties can even be labeled English. And so even though similar processes of sociopolitical expansion and regular grammatical change underwrote both the emergence of the Germanic languages via the First Consonant Shift and the development of new, transplanted varieties of English in previously non-Anglophone countries, the former has been categorized as natural change while the latter, lacking this categorization, has produced anxiety and even outrage. Lass's scheme of 'each non-high long vowel' raising one height, similarly, depicts the Great Vowel Shift as a purely internal linguistic phenomenon and as such one that precludes value judgements of the sort modern critics can make of the variant pronunciations they hear. Absent from Lass's scheme and from the category of natural grammatical change more generally is any sense that Middle English phonology is a swamp from which Modern English phonology climbed. Conversely, neither does his scheme imply that Middle English phonology was the dry land from which modern pronunciation retreated—that vowel raising was a diminishment of language and thought or diphthongization a source of the modern world's intellectual and cultural deprivation.

The primary distinction I have been drawing so far is between structural change and social meaning. While the former is regular, constant, and, perhaps, irrational, the latter is often impressionistic and even opportunistic, depending a good deal less on the nature of the linguistic phenomena and a good deal more on the context of the evaluation. The entire tense vowel system of English might change—has changed—without violating the integrity of the language, while the deletion of final stops or the realization of final [ŋ] as [n] (*ing* becoming *in*') contributes to utterances that are judged no longer English. Or, as significantly, such utterances might be classified as bad English in one sense or another and thereby justify an evaluation of an individual's worth and ability. As Henry Higgins says of Liza Doolittle's pronunciation in Shaw's *Pygmalion*, 'A woman who utters such depressing and disgusting sounds has no right to be anywhere—no right to live. Remember that you are a human being with a soul and the divine gift of articulate speech: that your native language is the language of Shakespear and Milton and The Bible; and don't sit there crooning like a bilious pigeon.' What gives Higgins's observation its linguistic force is its recognition that Liza's phonology varies so considerably from his own. What gives it its social force, of course, is not simply the categorization of this variation as outside the kinds of variation permitted within English grammar but also the attribution of social meaning to it within a nexus of socially described varieties of English: 'You see this creature with her kerbstone English: the English that will keep her in the gutter to the end of her days. Well, sir, in three months I could pass that girl off as a duchess at an ambassador's garden party. I could even get her a place as lady's maid or shop assistant, which requires better English.'[18]

Prescriptive and descriptive grammar, I have suggested, overlap in their reliance on categories of acceptable and unacceptable forms. I have joined to that claim an even more far-reaching one. Built on this shifting and permeable foundation, judgements of a change as natural and inevitable or aberrant and regrettable can themselves largely be functions of extra-linguistic attitudes. In effect, both sets of distinctions are situational and adaptive, with the same linguistic phenomena potentially pointing to different categorizations, interpretations, and responses in ways and for reasons that have nothing to do specifically or necessarily with language. Truss's advocacy of zero tolerance for errors in punctuation, for example, rests on a sense of punctuation as intrinsic to the grammatical expression of meaning—as something constitutive of the descriptive grammar of English. But she also represents punctuation as subject to socially constructed standards of absolute correctness. Her stylized outrage evokes the conflict and controversy of putatively unnatural grammatical dissolution, even though its instigation simply illustrates the variation and change that have historically characterized English. Punctuation is in fact a particularly fraught topic in grammar. In English, it is sporadic in the Old and Middle English periods, typically directed towards oral recitation and rarely transmitted in the copying of a work. And yet as medieval manuscripts amply illustrate, the absence of punctuation was in no way a hindrance to the production of meaning. While punctuation practices expanded with the introduction of print, into the nineteenth century they remained primarily rhetorical (rather than syntactic) and largely the results of publishing houses' styles. It is only in the modern period that writers like Hemingway began consistently to exercise authorial concern over punctuation in ways that justify Truss's sense of its centrality to a work's meaning, a sense that other modern writers, like Thomas Wolfe, who relied on the extensive editorial ministrations of the editor Maxwell Perkins, completely undermine.

This kind of interpretation has an opportunistic quality, though the opportunities are all the interpreters' and not the language's. Depending on contextual factors, various critics may variously judge punctuation to be largely an irrelevancy, a quality of descriptive grammar, or a prescriptive

---

[18] Shaw, *Complete Plays with Prefaces* (New York: Dodd, Mead, 1962), i, 206.

feature that can be left to others as a means to clarify, but not create, meaning. I don't see anything nefarious in such variable categorization. It is an example, rather, of how change and variation acquire social meaning. But for this very reason, I also don't see the impact of grammatical classification, however shifting it may be, to be of any less significance. And for this reason, beyond any social consequences that accrue to variations judged violations of a language's prescriptive grammar, the decision of whether or not to treat particular linguistic phenomena as internal variation and change goes a long way towards defining the contours of a language along with the groups of individuals who do—and do not—speak it.

The history of gender in English grammar illustrates this point especially well. As an Indo-European and Germanic language, Old English inherited a system of anaphoric pronoun usage and inflectional concord that correlated words for *he* (*hé*), *she* (*héo*), and *it* (*hit*) with particular declensions of nouns and, by extension, particular declensions of adjectives as well. In the strictest terms, the presence of such grammatical gender means that a noun's morphology rather than its semantic content determines which pronouns and adjectival forms concur with it. An Old English *bóc* (*book*), thus, is a *héo*, a *stán* (*stone*) is a *hé*, and a *lið* ('fleet') is a *hit*. While initially distinctions like these were largely the matter of systemic grammar—specifically morphology—already in the Anglo-Saxon period modifications took place that suggest speakers' intentional interventions and reclassifications of gender as a grammatical feature. This was so, evidently, because for certain animate nouns, grammatical and natural gender conflicted:

Word	Sense	Grammatical gender
wíf	adult female; married female	neuter
wífmann	adult female	masculine
mægden	young unmarried female	neuter

For words like these, the pronoun *héo*, matching natural rather than grammatical gender, became typical, although in non-animate nouns grammatical gender continued to predominate into the twelfth century. Patterns of usage complicate grammatical analysis in still other ways suggestive of Anglo-Saxon speakers' influence not simply on pronoun usage but on grammatical classification and the language itself. As the distance in an Old English sentence between a pronoun and its antecedent noun increases, for example, so, too, does the likelihood that the pronoun will follow natural and not grammatical gender. Grammatical categorization, in other words, was determined by the social impulses of discursive conventions. The general shift to natural gender is likewise social in the geography of its history, for like later Middle English changes in the third person plural pronouns and inflection of third person singular indicative verbs, it seems to have begun in the north and east of England and gradually spread southwards and westwards.

All these changes commenced in a period of extensive contact with Old Norse, which, in Anne Curzan's view, may not have instigated the shift but did help it along: 'Whether or not confusion over inflectional endings or gender between Old English and Old Norse speakers was a cause of the grammatical change in English is a matter of speculation; but the evidence supports theories that language contact can and will speed changes incipient in one language.'[19] In these ways, speakers' attitudes, conversational strategies, and social interactions—all of them strategies for prescribing usage—influenced and even reshaped English's descriptive grammar. This influence appears in yet another way. When the decisive shift away from grammatical gender took place (roughly 1150 to 1250), it initially affected masculine nouns more than feminine ones, with the result that feminine pronouns co-occurred with inanimate nouns longer into the history of English than did masculine ones.[20] To this day a version of grammatical gender persists with *she*, in references to the moon, days, cars, or ships, even if such usage strikes many modern Anglophones (including me) as odd or obsolete.

The historical variation of grammatical gender in Old English suggests, then, not absolute, impermeable categories of grammar and usage but fluid ones subject to redefinition by (in this case) Anglo-Saxon speakers. For largely social reasons, inherited grammatical gender remained strong with inanimate nouns, but among animate ones referring to humans, natural gender came to have an established and increasing significance. And it did so apparently with neither social conflict nor confusion, despite the extensive and non-trivial reconfiguration of English grammar that it involved: its concomitant was a complete reconfiguration of the morpho-syntax of the English noun phrase. And it did so, too, despite the fact that it was implicated in, if not driven by, social processes, which have in many cases focused all manner of anxiety on change. 'The diffusion of natural gender', Curzan observes, 'seems to follow

---

[19] Curzan, *Gender Shifts in the History of English* (Cambridge: Cambridge University Press, 2003), 123. It is worth noting that sign language has been susceptible to the same kinds of management that other natural languages have experienced. There have been increasingly successful attempts, for example, to modify signs that might have racist or sexist overtones, as for *Chinese* or *homosexual*. Such management has not been without controversy, raising the same charges of 'political correctness' that Curzan addresses. See Jennifer Senior, 'Sign Language Reflects Changing Sensibilities', *New York Times*, 3 January 1994, A1, 8.

[20] Curzan, *Gender Shifts in the History of English*, 110. On the statistical probabilities of grammatical gender with animate Old English noun, see 62 ff.; and on the influence of a pronoun's distance from an antecedent nouns, see 99.

patterns of historical syntactic change such as reanalysis and extension without a cataclysmic disruption in this diffusion.'[21]

And yet by the sixteenth and seventeenth centuries, grammatical and natural gender had again been reanalyzed in ways that pointed to just such cataclysms. Handbooks like Thomas Wilson's 1553 *Arte of Rhetorique* had then begun to see pronominal usage as not only a grammatical issue involving what was and wasn't correct or even real English but also a reflection of a larger natural social order: 'Some will set the carte before the horse, as thus. My mother and my father are both at home, euen as thoughe the good man of the house ware no breaches, or that the graye Mare were the better Horse. And what thoughe it often so happeneth (God wotte the more pitye) yet in speakinge at the leaste, let vs kepe a natural order, and set the man before the woman for maners sake.'[22] Reiterated in the eighteenth-century proliferation of grammar books and strengthened by laws that described wives as legally subsumed by their husbands, such pronominal prescriptions straddle a line between the prescriptive and descriptive, proscribing particular usages as both socially unacceptable and wrong but also claiming to situate such proscriptions within the describable grammar of English. As with Truss's complaints about punctuation some four and one-half centuries later, Wilson effectively elides distinctions between grammar and usage in ways that enhance the claims of the latter by putatively situating them not in stylistic choice but in the objective, descriptive facts of English.

Such elision likewise has underwritten consideration of the noun *man*, whether alone or in compounds like *chairman*, when it was argued to retain a sense of 'human being' over that of 'male human being' on the grounds that this would have been an original, etymological meaning. And it underwrites advocacy for generic *he* (rather than *they*) as necessary for references to singular non-gendered antecedent nouns like *author* or *president*, on the grounds that concord in number transcends other grammatical issues and that the masculine pronoun subsumes the feminine. Both kinds of arguments defy history as well as logic in order to make putatively grammatical claims about what are ultimately social discourses and practices. The etymological fallacy (as Curzan labels it) may account for some of Milton's verbal excess in *Paradise Lost*, but it explains little else about how the meanings of words evolve. While the use of generic *they* with singular antecedents has been

---

[21] Curzan, *Gender Shifts in the History of English*, 123.

[22] Wilson, *The Arte of Rhetorique* (1553; rpt. Gainesville, FL: Scholars' Facsimiles and Reprints, 1962), f. 89ʳ. See also Ann Bodine, 'Androcentrism in Prescriptive Grammar: Singular "They", Sex-indefinite "He", and "He or She"', in Deborah Cameron (ed.), *The Feminist Critique of Language: A Reader* (London: Routledge, 1990), 166–86.

recorded since the Middle Ages, early modern advocacy of generic *he* rather than *she* presumed and appealed to the typicality (if not naturalness) of men in certain professions, such as the law and medicine, and thereby blurred still further any distinction between internal grammar and external usage. And this kind of reasoning *to* language *from* social expectations, in turn, helps sustain other gendered patterns in English language usage: the fact that insults specifically directed at females tend to be more sexually charged than those directed at males, and the fact that in pairs of semantically parallel words (such as *bachelor* and *spinster*, or *stud* and *bitch*), the female word has been the more likely to take on a negative connotation.

Changes involving the gender of English pronouns have been as consistent and structured as phonological change, and their significance has been just as situational. Indeed, usage continues to evolve in response to social pressures, with the quasi-natural generic *he*, itself the replacement of grammatical gender, still sometimes advocated in formal discussions of the pronominal system alongside (more typically) *they, he or she, he/she*, or *s/he*. All these pronominal changes have likewise not been absolutely rational, since there is no morphological or semantic analysis by which it would be true to claim that a language with grammatical gender is somehow clearer or superior to one with natural gender; today, many languages have one, many languages the other. And though the movement from primarily grammatical to primarily natural gender may have been structured and may have proceeded along clear chronological and geographic axes, there is no evidence in its earliest stages for the kind of social motivations (of class, age, or provenance) that have been identified in modern changes and claimed for the Great Vowel Shift, nor is there any evidence of conflict or anxiety occasioned by the movement. Anxiety did arise, of course, when the pronominal system became implicated in social attitudes and institutions. Just as the history of gender and pronouns in English thus complicates any easy distinction between descriptive and prescriptive grammar, so it undermines an interpretation of changes sub-sumed by the former as more natural and internal than those subsumed by the latter. An initial movement towards natural gender was less a monolithic grammatical transformation and more a shift in emphasis among competing Old English systems, just as a shift in analytical emphasis reconceived patterns of usage as not simply grammatical but connected to social verities. Gram-matical gender in effect became natural gender, gaining significance and controversy in the process. The classification of linguistic change, it seems, can be as opportunistic as the change itself, and as this classification changes, so, too, does the language.

Phenomena like the Great Vowel Shift, the First Consonant Shift, and the history of gender in English illustrate several crucial features of change and the social meaning that sometimes accrues to it. The immediate question of where sounds and grammatical forms go when they go away turns out to require an answer that responds to several levels of language and its use. From a purely structural perspective, it could be said that wherever grammatical forms go, they characteristically go away in fashions that are structured, multiform, and, if not strictly speaking rational, then comprehensible. Once begun, push-chain mechanisms like that which describes the Great Vowel Shift organize disparate data into coherent and stable patterns that imbue phonological change with a kind of simplicity and inevitability. And the incipience of natural gender among Old English nouns that referred to human males likewise fosters the understandable and structured impact of discursive practices on the development of language. Where sounds and forms go, from this perspective, depends on certain empirical tendencies and limitations for languages and their changes. Methodologically, that is, historical linguistics relies on the same premise that underwrites historical inquiry in general. This is the Uniformitarian Principle, by which, as Lass describes it, 'Nothing (no event, sequence of events, constellation of proper-ties, general law) that cannot for some good reason be the case in the present was ever true in the past'.[23] What is impossible in modern theories of linguistic structure, change, and even novelty thereby becomes impossible for historical periods of a language: stops may add or lose voicing, but they cannot become vowels; vowels and consonants may change in quantity and quality, but for a given language they cannot all disappear at once, leaving the language with only glides; inflectional morphology may atrophy and alter, but syntax cannot be completely random. And novelties may appear among both individual forms and general linguistic principles, but they can do so only in ways allowed by the principles or in ways that require reconfiguration of the principles.

From another perspective, where sounds and forms go is significantly con-nected to speakers' attitudes. Most immediately, speakers may consciously modify the direction of a change by (say) accelerating the leveling of inflectional

---

[23] Lass, *On Explaining Language Change* (Cambridge: Cambridge University Press, 1980), 55. The whole of Lass's discussion on 45–63 is valuable, as is his further consideration of these issues in *Historical Linguistics and Language Change* (Cambridge: Cambridge University Press, 1997), 24–32. See also Suzanne Romaine, *Socio-historical Linguistics: Its Status and Methodology* (Cambridge: Cambridge University Press, 1982), 122–3; William Labov, *Principles of Linguistic Change*, i, *Internal Factors* (Oxford: Blackwell, 1994), 10–27, and 'On the Use of the Present to Explain the Past', in Philip Baldi and Ronald N. Werth (eds.), *Readings in Historical Phonology: Chapters in the Theory of Sound Change* (University Park, PA: Pennsylvania State University Press, 1978), 275–312.

morphology or by avoiding socially stigmatized vocabulary. Or, whether consciously or unconsciously, they may collectively use one vowel realization more than another and thereby produce change. But speakers also effect change in a more conceptual fashion. They may, that is, interpret some linguistic phenomena as internal and natural (and therefore permissible) and other phenomena as external and artificial (and therefore to be resisted and rejected from a language's grammar). Or they may conflate these categories, regarding a stylistic choice such as 'father and mother' as grammatical in a way that 'mother and father' is not, and in this way utilize grammatical claims to sustain a particular social view of the relationships between males and females. Here is where the ontology of language becomes a factor, for it seems to take its identity from speakers' perceptions as well as from empirical data. From a purely structural point of view, for instance, Smith's definition of language change makes good sense by tying change to speakers' usage: 'a sound change has taken place when a variant form, mechanically produced, is imitated by a second person and that process of imitation causes the system of the imitating individual to change'.[24] Yet as for many linguistic topics, the simple criterion of the number of domains or users does not allow for a precise classification built on the principle of majority-rule. Otherwise, the widespread pronunciation of *ask* as [æks] or the use of double negatives would occasion no comment. These limitations of use-based definitions also appear in the evaluation of varieties of English as well as of specific forms. Received Pronunciation thus continues to be cited as the most prestigious and socially advantageous accent in the United Kingdom, the accent from which all other accents necessarily deviate, even though estimates routinely claim no more than 3% of the population speak what is itself a variable accent.[25]

From this vantage, then, where grammatical forms go depends on what speakers understand them to be and where they want them to go. To describe linguistic phenomena as change is to categorize them as modifications of English's descriptive grammar and to claim, implicitly, that one form has become another, retaining its former self only as a historical trace and without violating the language's integrity. Middle English /i/ thus became Modern English /ai/ and no longer exists except in its transformed state; the /i/ in words like *feet* represents a new /i/, arising from a different but related change. To regard linguistic phenomena as violations of either descriptive or prescriptive grammar, however, is to represent them not as change but as error; pronunciation of a word with a historic Middle English /i/, like *five*, as if

---

[24] Smith, *Sound Change and the History of English*, 70.
[25] e.g., David Crystal, *The Cambridge Encyclopedia of the English Language* (Cambridge: Cambridge University Press, 1995), 365.

the vowel were /o/ rather than /ai/ would thus generally be considered simply wrong, however many speakers actually used the pronunciation and whether the error is due to circumstance or imperfect acquisition. And in this case, particularly with respect to prescriptive grammar, the categorization of error can carry with it moral valuations dependent on whatever social meanings have been invested in the forms. Here, one form remains as the standard against which other forms can be identified as imperfect or corrupted.

Judgements like these thus derive not simply from empirical data and a fixed taxonomy of linguistic phenomena. One of the fundamental achievements of Labov's pioneering sociolinguistics work, indeed, was the demonstration, in both New York City and Martha's Vineyard, that the origins of phonological diachronic change can lie in synchronic variants, their distribution, and valuation.[26] Yet only retrospection allows such a demonstration, since not all synchronic variation will result in diachronic change, and at any given moment speakers have little way truly to predict which variation, whether of structure or repertoire, will result in change. Classifications of variation, error, and change, then, also depend on speakers' choices: over which phenomena have social meanings, over what the consequences of those meanings may be, and over how much variation is tolerable for both linguistic form and social meaning. In effect, the conceptual category of change *validates* linguistic transformation—it constitutes affirmation that one form has become another while still preserving the essential characteristics of the language and that as such the form and its change preclude additional value judgements. And yet as categorical and consequential as this affirmation may be, it is also fundamentally *situational*. What speakers choose to classify as change, variation, or error, indeed, bespeaks their larger senses of their language, their society, and the relations of the two. Speakers' concomitant judgements about a particular change—whether it's good, bad, or indifferent—ultimately testify more for their views of themselves and their language than for the change itself. Variation and change in the gender of pronouns began to matter, then, when they were invested with sociolinguistic meaning.

Among linguists it has become axiomatic that many linguistic phenomena have situational and not transcendent meanings. Discourse analysis has shown that features like intonation or silence, depending on who is using them, when and how, can sometimes supplement meaning in one way and sometimes in another. Sometimes silence can signal power, other times submission. In this vein, I do not believe there is anything conceptually revolutionary in the claims I have made about change and variation. This

---

[26] Labov, *Sociolinguistic Patterns* (Philadelphia, PA: University of Pennsylvania Press, 1972), 1–69.

same situational force that discourse analysis recognizes, I am arguing, underwrites interpretations and categorizations of varying grammatical forms and, ultimately, of what is and is not English. Whether particular linguistic features are judged synchronic variants, diachronic developments, errors, or inconsequentialities depends a good deal on who is doing the judging and when.

Sociolects, dialects, history

Turning from the details of grammar to the larger structures they make up, I want now to consider how the inevitability, regularity, and susceptibility to social valuation that I have traced in the change of grammatical forms figure in the change and variation that produce linguistic varieties. Inevitability appears in the fact that, irrespective of the internal mechanisms that drive grammatical change, social and regional variation arises from geography, history, economics, and politics. To some extent, as I noted earlier, this kind of variation can be passive. Faced with social and cultural phenomena for which their language has no expression, speakers may quite unconsciously borrow words and structures that strike them as better suited to describe the world around them. This is why Anglophone visitors to North America borrowed words like *raccoon* and *toboggan* from Algonquian.

Such variation can also be active, however, in the sense that speakers can use varieties as well as forms for social definition. Like music, clothing, or hair style, forms and varieties of a language are in part social display, and as such they have meaning against a variety of sociolinguistic institutions and attitudes, such as sixteenth-century prescriptions on the syntactic ordering of *father* and *mother*, which reflect social gender more than linguistic structure. Beyond whatever cognitive content they convey, that is, particular forms (e.g., pronunciations) and regional and social varieties can sometimes (but not always) have pragmatic significance with potential implications for social status. In this way, whether speakers realize as much or not, linguistic forms serve self-identifying purposes for speaker and listener alike. For the former, they are ways to declare one's solidarity with or separation from others by willy-nilly evoking a particular variety and its sociolinguistic associations; for the latter, drawing on the same heuristic framework, linguistic forms and varieties serve as means to assess a speaker's ethnicity, provenance, education, reliability, and so forth. And in this way, so long as speakers move about, meet one another, and engage in social interaction with one another—which is as much to say, so long as they and their language are alive—change and variation must take place. The presence of regional and social variation, indeed, might well be regarded as illustrative of the Uniformitarian Principle; if a monolithic language without any variation is impossible now—and it is—so must it have been impossible at any moment in the past. The histories of transplanted English in post-colonial regions in fact make just this point. By consistently enacting the same basic processes in changing from an imposed language to one with its own indigenous norms, structurally as well as sociolinguistically, the English of regions like India and Nigeria seems to bespeak a uniformly shared pattern for adapting and nativizing language.[27]

Together, internal linguistic variation, speakers' needs to respond to new experiences, and the uses of language for self-identification have produced—and continue to produce—a proliferation both of national versions of English and of regional and social varieties of those same national versions. As a national version, Australian English paradigmatically illustrates this conflux of regular internal linguistic and external contextual pressures. The influence of the former appears in the fronting of the vowels /ʌ/ (*up*) and /ɑ/ (*father*), which seems to be common to both Australia and eighteenth-century London and thus attests to the linguistic substratum of the language of southeast England spoken by many of the original immigrants. It is sociolinguistic context, however, that accounts for historical regionalisms like *frisk* for *pick* and *cly* for *pocket*, both of which point to the storied role of prisoner transportation in the country's history. Similarly, contact with Aboriginal languages, other non-English languages, and the region's landscape is evident in *bettong*, *cooliman*, and *billabong*—distinctively Australian English words for distinctively Australian phenomena: a kangaroo rat, a wooden water vessel, and a branch of a river.[28] In Robert Burchfield's overview of how national and regional varieties of English developed in general, 'the introduction of English in different physical and cultural environments has everywhere produced a similar set of results: markedly distinguishable speech patterns in each of the regions, considerable diversity of local vocabulary (the need

[27] Welsh offers an interesting qualification about the persistence of regional varieties, for with the language's revival centered on schools and not at home, a standardized variety has spread at the expense of previous regional ones. If the language were to be fully revived, however, one would expect the re-emergence of regional varieties and sociolects. See Mari C. Jones, *Language Obsolescence and Revitalization: Linguistic Change in Two Contrasting Welsh Communities* (New York: Oxford University Press, 1998). On the development of transplanted English, see Edgar W. Schneider, *Postcolonial English: Varieties around the World* (Cambridge: Cambridge University Press, 2007).

[28] See John Gunn, 'Social Contexts in the History of Australian English', in Tim William Machan and Charles T. Scott (eds.), *English in Its Social Contexts: Essays in Historical Sociolinguistics* (New York: Oxford University Press, 1992), 204–29; and George W. Turner, 'English in Australia', in *The Cambridge History of the English Language*, v, Robert Burchfield (ed.), *English in Britain and Overseas: Origins and Development* (Cambridge: Cambridge University Press, 1994), 277–327.

elements being chiefly drawn from the languages of the indigenous inhabitants) and the essential sameness (with only limited exceptions) of the acci-
dence and syntax'.[29] Put another way, social and regional varieties of English
have been inevitable and inevitably reflective of the circumstances of language
change and variation.

Regularity as well as inevitability appears most simply in the consistency of
divergences between corresponding grammatical forms among varieties.
These forms diverge not necessarily because speakers of one variety are trying
and failing to achieve the grammar of another but because their own variety
represents a nativization of that or another grammar. Among speakers of
South Asian English, for instance, Standard British English [t] and [d] are
characteristically realized with the tip of the tongue curled back ('retroflex'),
in accordance with indigenous phonologies. Similarly, African American
Vernacular English speakers who delete final stops regularly articulate present
(e.g., *walk*) and dental preterite (*walked*) forms in the same manner ([wɔk])
and thereby reflect the influence of a substratum of creoles and West African
languages. Earlier I noted that the interpretive maneuver of deriving one form
from another—perhaps retroflex [t] from alveolar [t]—can misleadingly use
the objectivity of descriptive grammar to present what is ultimately a presumptive judgement about which form is normative. Such representation can
represent South Asian English in general, that is, as not only derivative but
wrong. An additional important point here is that just as rules like 'use
retroflex [t]' and 'delete final stops' are themselves not absolutely regular
but variable, speakers of Standard British or American English, whether they
recognize it or not, realize converse rules like 'use alveolar [t]' and 'add [d] or
[t] to form preterites' with similar variability. And thus the crucial point is
that the same kind of regularity underwrites both prominent and historical
national varieties of English and regional or social varieties of comparatively
recent development. To paraphrase Mark Twain, not only are we not all trying
to talk the same way, but we couldn't do so even if we did try.

Both regularity and inevitability also appear in the persistence of social and
regional variation across time. The named varieties of English may have
changed, as have some of the features that are used to define them, but the
fact of identifiable types of English characterized by unique combinations of
shared linguistic features and attitudes has remained constant. Presumably,
when Bede's Angles, Saxons, and Jutes arrived in England, mostly in the fifth
and sixth centuries, they did so speaking not a uniquely monolithic language

---

[29] Burchfield, 'Introduction', in Burchfield (ed.), *English in Britain and Overseas: Origins and Development*, 13.

but varieties of West Germanic that reflected their origins and culture as much as Australian English reflects its own. Some variations in the extant Old English record, indeed, such as that between the 'retracted' Anglian form *haldan* and West Saxon *healdan*, may well owe to pre-migration, continental linguistic diversity, and the continental proximity of the Angles to speakers of North Germanic varieties (Old Danish and Old Swedish in particular) may account for other dialect differences in Anglo-Saxon England.[30]

The earliest English writs and charters survive from the seventh and eighth centuries, and already by this time the written record certainly reflects structured regional variation. This early record means, then, that there has *never* been a time in the recoverable history of English when the language did not embody variation and change. The Venerable Bede himself, though indirectly, provides a vivid illustration of this point. On his death bed in 735, reflecting on this life and ordering his soul for the next, Bede (according to tradition) looked back from his Latin literacy to Anglo-Saxon oral traditions of his youth and uttered a hymn about the unpredictability of inevitable death:

> Fore them neidfaerae   naenig uuiurthit
> thoncsnotturra   than him tharf sie,
> to ymbhycggannae,   aet his hiniongae,
> huaet his gastae,   godaes aeththa yflaes,
> aefter deothdaege   doemid uueorthae.[31]

Or that, at least, is how the hymn appears in Bede's native Northumbrian dialect in a version written down one century after his death. Several centuries later still, a slightly different version of the song circulated, this one showing some forms that characterize West Saxon, the variety of Old English that became a kind of tenth-century koine and that remains the form most commonly taught and read today:

> For ðam neodfeore   nænig weorðeð
> ðances snotora   ðonne him ðearf sy,
> to gehycgenne,   ær his heonengange,
> hwæt his gaste,   godes oððe yfeles,
> æfter deaðe heonen   demed weorðe.

---

[30] The reason why I suggest 'retraction' may be pre-migration is that it is virtually complete in even the earliest Anglian texts. See Alistair Campbell, *Old English Grammar* (Oxford: Clarendon Press, 1959), 55–6. On the possible linguistic consequences of the Angles' continental proximity to speakers of North Germanic, see Smith, *Sound Change and the History of English*, 88–106.

[31] A. H. Smith (ed.), *Three Northumbrian Poems* (London: Methuen, 1933), 42–3. In S. A. J. Bradley's translation, the poem reads: 'Before the inevitable journey no man shall grow more discerning of thought than his need is, by contemplating before his going hence what, good or evil, will be adjudged to his soul after his death-day' (*Anglo-Saxon Poetry* [London: Dent, 1982], 6).

Even for a reader not conversant with Old English, the structured variation among these versions recalls the regularity of the phonological changes I described above. Leaving aside differences in wording (e.g., *gehycgenne* for *ymbhycggannae* and *deaðe heonen* for *deothdaege*), which may owe to the vagaries of transmission in a predominantly oral culture, we see consistent variation in orthography (*ð* for *th* and *w* for *uu*) and inflectional morphology (*e* for *ae*, *eð* for *it*). At least some of the variation, additionally, would seem to have phonological significance, reflecting differences in Old English accents; *neodfeore* for *neidfaerae* suggests as much, as does *oððe yfeles* for *aeththa yflaes*. While much written Modern English may erase or conceal such variation, it has continued and, in doing so, has proliferated national varieties of English, much as it did in the continental Germanic homeland as well as in Anglo-Saxon England. And this same inevitability and regularity that created national varieties like Canadian or Nigerian English produces regional varieties of particular national ones. When completed, the five-volume *Dictionary of American Regional English* will document the history, usage, and vicissitudes of millions of words in American English alone.[32]

Again as with judgements of grammatical forms like pronunciations, the cultural valuation of such sociolects and regional dialects has a situational quality that casts 'English' as an abstraction into sharp relief. Above all, as Jonathan Marshall has argued, the spread and identity of such varieties is not simply a structural matter: 'mental attitude, solidarity, or orientation is the driving force behind choices made about levels of social network integration and language use. This can account for a high degree of correlation between network indices and language uses, as well as for low degrees of correlation.' In this way, a kind of 'mental urbanization' may conduce rural speakers to model their language not on nearby varieties but on a desirable one found in far away cities.[33] In a related situational vein that likewise reflects the 'mental attitude' involved in the valuation of varieties, pidgin forms of English that are stigmatized in Africa may have no social meanings at all in other Anglophone communities, while overtly non-prestigious sociolects like Geordie (spoken in Newcastle) often have a good deal of covert prestige among their speakers. The mere fact that such valuation has a history—that there is a beginning and development in the social valuation of regional varieties of English—also points to this same situational quality, and it is to this history that I now turn.

---

[32] Frederic G. Cassidy, chief editor, *Dictionary of American Regional English* (Cambridge, MA: Belknap Press of Harvard University Press, 1985–), 4 vols., with one in progress.

[33] Marshall, *Language Change and Sociolinguistics: Rethinking Social Networks* (New York: Palgrave Macmillan, 2004), 228–9.

To begin with Bede, whose own death song records regional variation, the *Ecclesiastical History* identifies social variation in its account of Imma, one of Elfwin's thanes. Captured by King Ethelred, Imma feigns to be only a poor peasant, but 'his appearance, clothing, and speech' allow others to recognize his noble background.[34] The important point in this early recognition of dialect varieties is that while Bede acknowledges Imma's sociolect, he offers no value judgement on it, nor does he assign social meanings of any kind to the varieties being used. Similar recognition of regional variation in Anglo-Saxon England appears in certain eighth-century manuscript evidence that reveals speakers altering the forms of their native dialects in approximation of forms from Mercia, whose political ascendancy at that time could be thought to render its variety of English prominent, if not prestigious.[35] Like the tenth- and eleventh-century propagation of West Saxon forms through the scriptorium at Winchester, this kind of linguistic activity embodies an ambivalence about regional variation comparable to Bede's. On one hand, it certainly indicates awareness of regional and social variation; on the other, it reflects a lack of recognition of or interest in the relative sociolinguistic merits of varieties or the pragmatic utility of any one variety in particular. The implication of these shared sentiments is that the influence of both Wessex and Mercia lay in their political power, not in their varieties of Old English. And all this is to say that in the Anglo-Saxon period, however obvious the variations of English may have been, a clear distinction existed between them and their social valuations, since speakers do not in fact seem to have assigned the latter at all.

By the Middle English period, especially the fifteenth century, there are indications that speakers had begun to conceptualize varieties of the language within a linguistic repertoire of not only English dialects but also non-English languages. The survival of works in multiple copies, for example, increasingly reveals dialect translation, by which a text written in one regional variety was rendered in another one, presumably for reasons of intelligibility and marketability. A colophon in a copy of Richard Rolle's fourteenth-century *Form of Living* even records that the text has been 'translat out of Northarn tunge into Sutherne that it shulde be the bettir vnderstondyn of men that be of the selve countre'.[36] Likewise, scribes sometimes drew attention to variation in English

---

[34] See Bede, *A History of the English Church and People*, trans. Leo Sherley-Price (Harmondsworth: Penguin, 1955), 244.

[35] See Thomas E. Toon, 'The Social and Political Contexts of Language Change in Anglo-Saxon England', in Machan and Scott (eds.), *English in Its Social Contexts*, 28–46.

[36] M. B. Parkes and Richard Beadle (eds.), *The Poetical Works of Geoffrey Chaucer: A Facsimile of Cambridge University Library MS Gg.4.27*, 3 vols. (Norman, OK: Pilgrim Books, 1979–80), iii, 55. See also *Cursor Mundi*, ed. Richard Morris, EETS os 57, 59, 62, 66, 68, 99, 101 (London: Trübner, 1874–93),

by specifying the regional form they used, as did Dan Michel in his 1340 *Ayenbite of Inwyt*, for which he used the 'engliss of kent'.[37] Perhaps the most famous (if still general) comments of this sort are William Caxton's remarks in his preface to the *Eneydos*, where he observes that 'our langage now vsed varyeth ferre from that. whiche was vsed and spoken whan I was borne' and then recounts the confusion confronting a merchant who, while in Kent, uttered the northern form *eggs* rather than the regional *eyren*.[38]

Although sporadic comments like these do not imply a clear hierarchy or social valuation of dialects, Middle English itself did help to sustain institutionalized conceptions of England's three most prolific languages: English, French, and Latin. In his 1387 *Testament of Love* Thomas Usk described with particular clarity the distinct roles for each of these languages: 'Let than clerkes endyten in Latin, for they have the propretee of science, and the knowynge in that facultee; and let Frenchmen in their Frenche also endyten their queynt termes, for it is kyndley to their mouthes; and let us shewe our fantasyes in such wordes as we lerneden of our dames tonge.'[39] And the preface to the *Cursor Mundi* distinguishes its primary, ignorant ('lewed') readership from knowledgeable readers conversant with Latin and French:

> And on Inglysch has it schewed
> Not for þe lerid bot for þe lewed:
> For þo þat in þis land wone
> Þat þe Latyn no Frankys cone.[40]

It is not until the early modern period, with the concomitant spread of printing, literacy, regularized orthography, and standardized language, that widely shared social valuations of English dialects emerge, however. Even as it lauds the emergence of English as a national language, for example, George Puttenham's 1589 *The Arte of English Poesie* offers a sociolinguistic

---

ll. 20,061–4. On Middle English dialects more generally, including dialect translation, see Margaret Laing (ed.), *Middle English Dialectology: Essays on Some Principles and Problems* (Aberdeen: Aberdeen University Press, 1988); James Milroy, 'Middle English Dialectology', in *The Cambridge History of the English Language*, ii, N. F. Blake (ed.), *1066–1476* (Cambridge: Cambridge University Press, 1992), 156–206; and Felicity Riddy (ed.), *Regionalism in Late Medieval Manuscripts and Texts: Essays Celebrating the Publication of 'A Linguistic Atlas of Late Medieval England'* (Woodbridge: D. S. Brewer, 1991).

[37] Dan Michel, *Ayenbite of Inwyt*, ed. Richard Morris, EETS os 23 (London: Trübner, 1866), 262.

[38] Caxton, *The Prologues and Epilogues of William Caxton*, ed. W. J. B. Crotch, EETS os 176 (1928; rpt. New York: Burt Franklin, 1971), 108.

[39] Usk, *Testament of Love*, in *Chaucerian and Other Pieces*, vii, *Complete Works of Geoffrey Chaucer*, ed. W. W. Skeat (Oxford: Oxford University Press, 1897), 2.

[40] *Cursor Mundi*, ll. 5–8. Also see ll. 21–6 and 237–40. For more discussion of the conceptualization of dialects in the Middle English period, see Machan, *English in the Middle Ages* (Oxford: Oxford University Press, 2003), 86–96.

conceptualization of English varieties that bespeaks attitudes far advanced from those of Dan Michel or Caxton. The language of the court and town, he observes, is much superior to that of 'marches and frontiers' or even universities,

> where Schollers vse much peeuish affectation of words out of the primatiue languages, or finally, in any vplandish village or corner of a Realme, where is no resort but of poore rusticall or vnciuill people; neither shall he [the aspiring poet] follow the speach of a craftes man or carter, or other of the inferiour sort, though he be inhabitant or bred in the best towne and Citie in this Realme, for such persons doe abuse good speaches by strange accents or ill shapen soundes, and false ortographie. But he shall follow generally the better brought vp sort, such as the Greekes call [*charientes*] men ciuill and graciously behauoured and bred.[41]

In effect, Puttenham conflates social and regional variation by linking proscribed varieties, 'vplandish' locales, and 'vnciuill' speakers, and, as Chapter 5 will consider in detail, this kind of linking develops and spreads in the seventeenth and eighteenth centuries in ways that firmly attach valuations to synchronic variation in general and certain varieties in particular. For the first time in a systematic and institutional fashion, then, the facts of linguistic change and variation were thereby broadly implicated in social significance and institutional propagation; and if codification proliferated grammatical prescription, schools came to embed it in business, politics, and the processes of social advancement. By the nineteenth century, as the next chapter will discuss, a hierarchy of English varieties and their sociolinguistic implications was well enough established that writers like Dickens and Twain could use it for literary effects.

Today, as Denis Preston's studies of what he calls perceptual dialectology demonstrate, such a hierarchy has become a naturalized part of speakers' sociolinguistic horizons. Indeed, Preston's work shows just how far the social valuation of English varieties—as distinct from empirical recognition of their existence—has developed since the Anglo-Saxon period. Over several years he has surveyed speakers on what they judge to be the spectrum of best to worst varieties of American English and also on where on this spectrum they would place their own variety. What he's found is that speakers' perceptions of the spatial limits of American regional dialects are not empirically based but rather reflect their own geographic biases, while their evaluation of their own variety often reflects more broadly shared views, even when those might involve the devaluation of their own variety. Testifying still more forcefully to the internalization of value judgements on variation is the widespread

---

[41] Puttenham, *The Arte of English Poesie* (1589; rpt. Menston: Scolar Press, 1968), 120.

acceptance of the very notion of language as a mediation of social status within a fixed interpretive framework. 'By placing language itself outside both social environment and cognitive embedding,' observes Preston, 'folk linguists in the USA are able to posit an easily accessed exterior standard, one which good people will access with little effort and place themselves where they belong—in the mainstream of US society.'[42] The influence of this standard can be apparent whether it is endorsed or resisted. In the case of a predominant working-class variety of English in New York City—variously labeled Brooklynese or New Yawkese—characteristic speech patterns that reflect the city's immigrant history now compete with both the social stigmatization of the variety (as in forms like [ɔɪ] for [ɚ], roughly *oi* for *er*, in *thirty-third*) and the influx of new forms reflecting new patterns of immigration. To some speakers, such competition inspires greater dialect loyalty to a stigmatized yet historical and unique variety; to others, it suggests progressive, sociolinguistic assimilation. To all such speakers, the fact that this kind of competition has meaning reflects naturalized social responses to what is in the end, to return to Lass, neutral linguistic variation.[43]

The absence of standard language in the middle ages may make medieval dialect diversity the most apparent in the written record of English,[44] but *every* period in the language's history has been dialectal. Whatever impression the regularity of modern written English may give, this regularity has done nothing to decrease the persistence and proliferation of regional and social varieties. In fact, given the factors that produce social and regional variation, and given the one billion people now commonly estimated to speak English, the modern period would seem likely to be quantitatively *more* dialectal than the Middle English one. This claim can be pushed even further. Identifying, counting, and comparing varieties from one epoch of English with those of another is a fraught enterprise, complicated in the early periods by the relative paucity of written records, in later periods by the absence of electronic media for preservation, and in the contemporary period by the leveling of spoken variation in written representations. Yet with perhaps two-thirds of the world's Anglophones residing outside of the United Kingdom and the United States combined, current sociolinguistic conditions would seem to offer more

[42] Preston, 'The Story of Good and Bad English in the United States', in Richard Watts and Peter Trudgill (eds.), *Alternative Histories of English* (London: Routledge, 2002), 148. Also see Preston, *Perceptual Dialectology: Nonlinguists' Views of Areal Linguistics* (Dordrecht: Foris Publicatons, 1989).

[43] Deborah Sontag, 'Oy Gevalt! New Yawkese An Endangered Dialect?', *New York Times*, 14 February 1993, A1, 18.

[44] e.g., David Crystal, *The Stories of English* (Woodstock, NY: Overlook Press, 2004), 194; and Seth Lerer, *Inventing English: A Portable History of the Language* (New York: Columbia University Press, 2007), 99.

opportunities for dialect diversity than at *any* moment in English's history. Even if, for the sake of the argument, one accepts Chomsky's ideal speaker-listener and its implications about the foundational grammatical regularity and sameness of English, there remains an abundance of grammatical and discursive diversity among the linguistic varieties subsumed by this label. For this reason, as the designation of a coherent and stable variety, Modern English—even just South African or Australian English—represents an abstraction of a high order. And just plain English, with its almost cavalier disregard of synchronic variation and diachronic change, is an abstraction of a still higher order.[45]

Discussions of the history of English often contain illustrations that show historical change as documented in a repeatedly reissued work such as the Bible. Here, then, is Genesis 3: 1 in four versions stretching from the Anglo-Saxon period, through Middle and Early Modern English, to Modern English:

Old English Heptateuch: Eac swylce seo næddre wæs geapre ðonne ealle ða oðre nytenu ðe God geworhte ofer eorðan. And seo næddre cwæð to ðam wife: 'Hwi forbead God eow ðæt ge ne æton of ælcon treowe binnan Paradisum?'

Second Wycliffite Version: But and the serpent was feller than alle lyuynge beestis of erthe, whiche the Lord God hadde maad. Which serpent seide to the womman, 'Why comaundide God to ʒou that ʒe schulden not ete of ech tre of paradis?'

King James Version: Now the serpent was more subtil than any beast of the field which the Lord God had made. And he said unto the woman, Yea hath God said, Ye shall not eat of every tree of the garden?

New International Version: Now the serpent was more crafty than any of the wild animals the Lord God had made. He said to the woman, 'Did God really say, "You must not eat from any tree in the garden"?'

Comparisons like this usefully highlight significant features of diachronic change in English, including: orthography (*treowe* > *tre* > *tree*); morphology (*seo næddre* > *the serpent*); lexicon (*geapre* > *feller* > *more subtil* > *more crafty*); and syntax (*God geworhte* > *God hadde maad* > *God had made*). They attest to continuity as well as development in the expressive potential of English and its grammatical structure. Like matter-of-fact listings of Indo-European cognates, what such comparisons do not do is acknowledge

---

[45] For a variety of reasons, such as the difficulty in empirically identifying levels of linguistic competence and the well-known tendency of speakers to misreport their own competence in one way or another, hard and fast figures on the numbers of Anglophones today are impossible to produce. See the data—and qualifications—in David Crystal, *English as a Global Language*, 2nd edn. (Cambridge: Cambridge University Press, 2003), 59–71.

their tacit distinctions between change and variation or engage the theoretical and social investment in such distinctions.

Bopp and Müller may have passed value judgements over alterations in inflectional morphology, but, as I argued in the previous section, for the most part long-term, expansive transformations of the sort that distinguish Middle from Old English (or Germanic consonants from Indo-European ones) have been categorized as change and therefore less subject to the charge of being errors than are those linguistic phenomena that are considered synchronic variations. Here again, however, the neutrality of change can be deceptive. I would venture that of these four versions the structural differences between all but the King James and New International texts of Genesis would seem to exceed the difference between any two modern varieties, such as Australian and contemporary British English. And I would also venture that there would similarly seem to be greater structural difference among these four biblical versions than there is between any two varieties of either Old English or Middle English, or between any two current United States varieties. And yet despite such differences, all these varieties are labeled 'English' on the conviction—and with the implication—that they arise through diachronic change that is accepted as internal and natural for the language.

There is, of course, something profoundly circular in such reasoning: diachronic change is that which maintains a language's integrity over time, while a language like English remains English over time, so long as its alterations reflect diachronic change. And it is this fundamentally impressionistic value judgement, I suggest, that works to preclude controversies comparable to those associated with social and regional varieties of English from the end of the seventeenth century. By extension, such a judgement fashions language and its history as simple, objective facts. Whether or not a change is accepted as historical, however, has social significance for both it and the language. While *seo næddre* 'became' *the serpent* without violating the integrity of English—at least according to histories of English—some of the most trivial synchronic differences can take on the greatest significance, as when the popular commentator John Simon described the construction 'between you and I', a construction that dates to the early modern period, as 'an *unsurpassable* grossness' that must be eradicated before it produces 'every kind of deleterious misunderstanding'.[46]

At the outset of this section I noted that judgements about linguistic forms and varieties conditionally and contextually reflect the speakers who make them. This same point can now be made more pointedly as a question: when

---

[46] Simon, *Paradigms Lost* (New York: Potter, 1980), 18, 21. The emphasis is in the original.

is language, its change, or its variation a significant part of social or cultural identity and therefore subject to social valuation? The evidence of English varieties, their histories, and their evaluations suggests that the answer is: when someone to whom the issue matters and who has the authority to influence others, whether or not that person is part of the relevant speech community, says it does. It is in this way that the categorization and social meaning of particular linguistic forms or varieties are assigned; they are not transcendent or based on empirical, structural categories. However strong some sentiments about language can be, clear distinctions between change and variation are in fact often difficult to maintain. To put the matter concisely: the history of English is itself a value judgement about which forms and varieties constitute the language and which do not. In the next section of this chapter I extend this argument by considering how English, through contact with other languages, not only underwent variation and change but also affected the contact languages, frequently including the shift of their speakers to English.

When languages collide

In 1599, barely a decade after the defeat of the Spanish Armada and England's emergence as a world power, Samuel Daniel published a small volume of poetry entitled *Poeticall Essayes*, which included the poem *Musophilus, Containing a General Defense of All Learning*. Despite England's stature and growing prominence, some of the country's most consequential global achievements still lay in the future: the founding of the British East India Company in 1600; the settlement of Jamestown, Virginia, in 1607; and the arrival in New Zealand of Captain James Cook in 1769. Nonetheless, in a display of optimism and foresight, Daniel waxed rhapsodic about the spread of not only English power but also the English language:

> And who, in time, knowes whither we may vent
> The treasure of our tongue, to what strange shores
> This gaine of our best glory shall be sent,
> T'inrich vnknowing Nature with our stores?
> What worlds in th'yet vnformed Occident
> May come refin'd with th'accents that are ours.[47]

In the first flush of English expansion, language and all the ideas and institutions it enabled would be England's gift to a less fortunate world.

---

[47] Daniel, *Musophilus: Containing a General Defense of Learning*, ed. Raymond Himelick (West Lafayette, IN: Purdue University Studies, 1965), ll. 957–62.

Expressing widely shared views, Daniel saw English as inherently a treasure and glory and therefore, like English government, religion, and technology, a means for improving the unknown, primitive world. Slightly over three centuries later, Mahatma Gandhi took a rather dimmer view of this gift: 'To give millions a knowledge of English is to enslave them. The foundation that Macaulay laid of education has enslaved us. I do not suggest that he had any such intention, but that has been the result.'[48]

Such differing views partly depend on the individual speakers, of course, but also on these speakers' differing epochs and the varying outcomes of English's contact with other languages in Daniel's and Gandhi's lifetimes. Whether individual or institutional, this kind of contact has always characterized all natural languages, occurring whenever speakers travel for business, pleasure, war, or adventure. And language contact and its effects upon the languages involved displays the same kind of inevitability and regularity that I have traced in structural and dialectal variation and change. Since monolinguals predominate in many Anglophone populations, including those of England and the United States, to many speakers the normativeness of language contact and multilingualism may seem less apparent. Yet they are institutionalized in the multiple official languages of Belgium, Switzerland, and South Africa, evident in the hundreds of languages that co-exist in India and Indonesia, and personalized in the fact that nearly the entire adult population of Israel is at least bilingual.[49] Even in predominantly Anglophone societies, however, multilingualism is the norm. According to one study, as many as 307 different languages are used by London school children in their homes, while the 1996 Australian census records 240 languages and the fact that over a quarter of the population of both Melbourne and Sydney speak a language other than English at home.[50] The 2000 United States census indicates that nearly 18% of the population over the age of five speak a language other than English at home, with over half this group (10% of the total population) speaking Spanish; about 3.8% speak another Indo-European language and roughly an additional 2.5% speak an Asian or Pacific Island language. All totaled, perhaps four hundred languages besides English are spoken in the United States.[51] In Canada, the 2001 census offers similar

---

[48] Quoted in Richard W. Bailey, *Images of English: A Cultural History of the Language* (Ann Arbor: University of Michigan Press, 1991), 144.

[49] On Israel, see Eliezer Ben-Rafael, *Language, Identity, and Social Division: The Case of Israel* (Oxford: Clarendon Press, 1994).

[50] Kingsley Bolton, *Chinese Englishes: A Sociolinguistic History* (Cambridge: Cambridge University Press, 2003), 111; and Michael Clyne, *Dynamics of Language Contact: English and Immigrant Languages* (Cambridge: Cambridge University Press, 2003), 23.

[51] US Census, Table 5 (http://www.census.gov/).

numbers: approximately 82% of the population know only one or both of the official languages—English and French—and the remaining individuals, though they may speak one of these languages, also speak another.[52]

A claim for the ubiquity of multilingualism is supported by the past of English as well as its present. In the twelfth century, for example, Great Britain's majority language was certainly English, and many of its approximately three million residents were monoglots. But Latin was still spoken in monasteries and schools and remained the dominant written language in theology, science, philosophy, law, and other such ecclesiastical and civil activities. In the southeast in particular, descendants of the Norman and Angevin aristocracy spoke French, which was also increasingly used in legal and ecclesiastical domains. Cornish was spoken in the southwest, Welsh in most of modern Wales (with much of the population being monoglots), Gaelic in most of Scotland, and Irish in most of Ireland. Beyond this, Flemish would have been heard in Wales and Norse in the Shetland and Orkney islands and also, possibly, in Yorkshire and the London area, where Hebrew was spoken, too.[53]

But if England's political expansion in the early modern period continued rather than initiated English's interactions with other languages, it also accelerated such contact. And this acceleration significantly involved not only new contact languages (such as Maori, Zulu, and Navajo) but also new contact situations, in which English served as the colonial language of tradition, government, education, and technology. At the same time, the contact languages served as the mediums of indigenous cultures and the varying desires of individuals to maintain their culture or assimilate with the Anglophones. Such dynamics of language contact have been well documented as the impetus that frequently turns the potential for change, which is always present, into its reality.[54] It was continental contact with North Germanic,

---

[52] Language Composition of Canada: Highlight Tables, 2001 Census (http://www12.statcan.ca/english/census01/home/index.cfm).

[53] R. I. Page, 'How Long Did the Scandinavian Language Survive in England? The Epigraphical Evidence', in Peter Clemoes and Kathleen Hughes (ed.), *England Before the Conquest: Studies in Primary Sources Presented to Dorothy Whitelock* (Cambridge: Cambridge University Press, 1971), 165–81; M. L. Samuels, 'The Great Scandinavian Belt', in Laing (ed.), *Middle English Dialectology*, 106–22; Austin Lane Poole, *From Domesday Book to Magna Carta 1087–1216*, 2nd edn. (Oxford: Clarendon Press, 1955), 88 and 290; M. T. Clanchy, *From Memory to Written Record: England, 1066–1307*, 2nd edn. (Oxford: Blackwell, 1993), 201–2.

[54] Classic statements are Uriel Weinreich, William Labov, and Marvin I. Herzog, 'Empirical Foundations for a Theory of Language Change', in W. P. Lehmann and Yakov Malkiel (eds.), *Directions for Historical Linguistics: A Symposium* (Austin, TX: University of Texas Press), 95–188; and M. L. Samuels, *Linguistic Evolution, with Special Reference to English* (Cambridge: Cambridge University Press, 1972).

Smith argues, that produced some Old English phonological variation, and contact with Norse in England, for Curzan, that may have accelerated changes in the status of grammatical gender. From these dynamics, accordingly, arose linguistic as well as social transformations that once more reveal not only the regularity and inevitability of change but also the easily elided distinction between language change and the social meanings that accrue to it.

When English has come into contact with other languages, that contact has often taken on the quality of a collision in which the non-English language (or languages) experienced similar sociolinguistic dynamics, leading to essentially the same curtailment and even eradication of domains and speakers. Anglophones involved in the expansion of English have perhaps invariably been the politically and technologically dominant group, for example, although they have not also been (at least initially) numerically superior. In fact, given their numerical disadvantages and inexperience in many colonial areas, such as North America, the Caribbean, Africa, India, and the antipodes, Anglophones often found themselves dependent on indigenes for information on local geography, climate, and foodstuffs. Beyond this, in order to maintain a colonial state, Anglophones depended on indigenous populations for service, whether forced or at least nominally voluntary. In this way Anglophones typically not only cultivated a degree of English competence among some locals, even as they resisted acquiring for themselves full competence in indigenous languages, but also, as in India, thereby restructured a region's prevailing linguistic repertoire.

Because of shared characteristics like these, the spread of English has often been likened to that of Latin in the late Antique and Middle Ages. Through the expansion of the Roman empire, that is, Latin experienced extensive contact with a range of languages, including Greek, Oscan, Venetic, Etruscan, Punic, Gaulish, Germanic, Hispanic, Aramaic, and Thracian. And yet of all these, with few exceptions Greek was the only second language widely acquired by speakers of Latin, and this was not because of any interest in Greek ethnicity but because of that language's cultural and political associations.[55] For English, the list of contact languages is even longer—perhaps five hundred indigenous languages in North America alone at the time of European settlement—and the resistance and even xenophobia towards them sometimes as strong. Just as through contact with English most of these five hundred languages are now moribund or extinct, so, too, did the introduction of English to Australia, Canada, and New Zealand in particular lead

[55] J. N. Adams, *Bilingualism and the Latin Language* (Cambridge: Cambridge University Press, 2003), 293.

to significant reduction of indigenous languages in these areas. Even in England, of course, contact between English and non-English languages has had adverse effects on the latter. As in other regions, economics and technology influenced the shift to English, but so, too, did Anglophones' explicit judgements about the languages they encountered. In his famous essay in praise of Celtic literature, for example, Matthew Arnold nonetheless echoed comments also made about Maori and Hawaiian by observing, 'The sooner the Welsh language disappears as an instrument of the practical, political, social life of Wales, the better; the better for England, the better for Wales itself'.[56]

Arnold's seventh-century countryman Oswald, king of Northumbria, took a rather more sympathetic attitude towards the Celtic languages. After his victory over the Welsh king Cadwallon and the reassertion of his own power, Oswald invited the monk and bishop Aidan to come from the Irish monastery at Iona and direct the conversion of Northumbria in 635. According to the Venerable Bede's account, Oswald served as Aidan's translator, thereby embodying the sociolinguistic transactions between English and Irish culture: 'And while the bishop, who was not fluent in the English language, preached the Gospel, it was most delightful to see the king himself interpreting the word of God to his ealdorman and thegns; for he himself had obtained perfect command of the Irish tongue in his long exile'.[57] In situations involving such extreme differences in power and numbers—one influential king or official in the company of many indigenous people—the compulsion to learn another language can weigh heavily on both Anglophones and non-Anglophones. Indeed, this same situation arose among early European missionaries and colonists in North America, though for significantly different reasons. Colonists taken captive of course had no choice but to learn the indigenous languages. Yet missionaries, vastly outnumbered by the American Indians they hoped to convert, had little more flexibility: like Europeans taken captive, they needed to learn the indigenous language in order to survive.[58] But while specific missionaries may initially have learned non-English contact languages in these cases, the ultimate result of such contact has been virtually the same in every colonial situation: the expansion of English at the expense of other languages.

---

[56] Arnold, *On the Study of Celtic Literature and On Translating Homer* (New York: Macmillan, 1904), 10.

[57] Bede, *A History of the English Church and People*, 147.

[58] Karttunen, 'Interpreters Snatched from the Shore: The Successful and the Others', in Edward G. Gray and Norman Fiering (eds.), *The Language Encounter in the Americas, 1492–1800: A Collection of Essays* (New York: Berghahn Books, 2000), 221.

In such contact situations, change and variation as inevitable linguistic phenomena contrast with the variable social meanings that speakers assign to them. To the extent that Oswald's knowledge of Irish suggests his magnanimity—and Bede certainly seems to interpret it that way—it might be treated as evidence of his power and his ability to reach out with his learning both to those around him in exile and to his subjects. Yet this same presumptive magnanimity was a non-issue among early Anglophones on the North American continent, for it was trade with indigenous peoples that essentially compelled many to learn the language of the very people they sought to dominate. Even among European missionaries, who would have shared at least some of Bede's sentiments, the social significance of indigenous languages varied in ways that reveal its contingent nature. While Protestants sought to learn American Indian languages and to translate Scripture into them as an extension of the Reformation's project for individuals to know God's word in their own languages, Catholics pursued these same activities in order to provide a bridge to Latin and the institutional hierarchy it supported.[59] Contact between English and Celtic languages provides yet another illustration of the contingency of social evaluations. It is commonly asserted that eighteenth- and nineteenth-century Irish, Gaelic, and (to a lesser extent) Welsh speakers shifted to English in part from socioeconomic desperation—from a sense that the inability to speak English was socially and financially deleterious—and this explanation certainly has much to commend it. Yet in the face of similarly enormous odds and despite similarly negative economic consequences, some indigenous people, such as the North American Navajoes, have maintained their language so well as to suggest on their part a kind of indifference to or defiance of emerging linguistic and economic norms. The learning of a second language, whether by a speaker of a socially dominant or subordinate language, clearly can be a submissive as well as an empowering gesture—the latter for reasons of economics or cultural identity. In the same vein, refusal to learn another language can reflect the dominance of some speakers (e.g., Anglophones) and the subjection or defiance of others (e.g., Navajoes).

When colonial Anglophones have compelled the acquisition of English by non-Anglophones, they have done so in ways that emerge from and sustain this same conditional and contextual categorization of language change and its meaning, irrespective of the change itself. Lord Macaulay's educational minute of 2 February 1835 is a case in point. Building on a century of

---

[59] Edward G. Gray, *New World Babel: Languages and Nations in Early America* (Princeton, NJ: Princeton University Press), 1999.

sentiment, this minute established government policy on the status of English in subcontinental Indian education by directing funds for the instruction of the native population in English language and literature. Its professed, non-altruistic objective was the creation of a new Anglophone group of indigenes who could act as intermediaries between the English and their colonial subjects: 'We must at present do our best to form a class who may be interpreters between us and the millions whom we govern—a class of persons Indian in blood and colour, but English in taste, in opinion, in morals and in intellect.'[60] In one interpretation, the minute was highly successful, leading to the use of English in 60% of India's primary schools by 1882; in another, by transforming English from a foreign language to a dominant, institutionalized one within an already multilingual society, the minute fostered the linguistic slavery of which Gandhi spoke. And in either interpretation, the purpose of inculcating or learning English differs markedly from the economic motives prominent in Celtic communities or the religious ones among Native Americans.

The changing views of English held by the prolific and influential Nigerian novelist Chinua Achebe offer another vantage on how the meaning and the fact of language contact can diverge from one another. In his influential 1964 essay 'The African Writer and the English Language', published just four years after Nigeria's independence, Achebe viewed English (like French) as one of the factors by which colonial governments forged African countries from disparate ethnic groups. To use a nativized English was to be part of that nationalizing process: 'I feel that the English language will be able to carry the weight of my experience. But it will have to be a new English, still in full communion with its ancestral home but altered to suit its new African surroundings.'[61] By the early 1970s and after the Nigerian civil war had perhaps dispelled any illusions about post-colonial life, Achebe had begun to speak more forcefully about the cultivation of indigenous African beliefs and practices and the rejection of those sustained by English. In 1982 he even helped establish the bilingual journal *Uwa Ndi Igbo: a Journal of Igbo Life and Culture*. Achebe's experience is far from unique, however, for such shifts in sentiment and the interpretation of linguistic phenomena have become widespread in former British colonies in Africa. In his 1986 *Decolonising the Mind*, in which he eloquently details how language shift served larger colonial goals

---

[60] Quoted in Henry Sharp (ed.), *Selections from Education Records*, i, *1781–1839* (Calcutta: Superintendent Government Printing, 1920), 116. See also Kachru, 'English in South Asia', in Burchfield (ed.), *English in Britain and Overseas: Origins and Development*, 500–8.

[61] Quoted in Ezenwa Ohaeto, *Chinua Achebe: A Biography* (Bloomington, IN: Indiana University Press, 1997), 101. Also see Bailey, *Images of English*, 170.

of economic and social dominance in Africa, the Kenyan writer Ngũgĩ wa Thiong'o thus expressed a rejection of English similar to Achebe's. This book, he says, 'is my farewell to English as a vehicle for any of my writings. From now on it is Gĩkũyũ and Kiswahili all the way.'[62] Today, this kind of anxiety over the spread of English as a global language and its disruption of local linguistic repertoires is not restricted to post-colonial areas. It has become increasingly strident, indeed, in continental Europe, where a recognition of the utility of English for business and computer communication accompanies a sense that such utility comes at the expense of cultural autonomy.[63]

For English itself, the effects of its global contact have been equally fraught. Beginning with predominant Anglophone populations of what Braj Kachru has called the Inner Circle—the United States, the United Kingdom, Canada, Australia, and New Zealand—English has spread increasingly as both a transplanted language (as in India, Nigeria, and South Africa) and a supplementary means of communication (as in South America or eastern Europe).[64] Since the early modern period, whether through choice, coercion, or incentive, non-Anglophones have acquired or even shifted to English at spectacular rates and in the process reconfigured prevailing cultural relations among education, finance, and ethnicity so as to include English alongside indigenous languages.[65] English has spread so much, in fact, that while estimates vary, today, as I noted above, perhaps one-sixth of the world's 6.5 billion people know English as a primary or secondary language, and of this group, only about 350 million reside in the United Kingdom or the United States.

Given its own structured differences of social and regional varieties, the English that has contacted other languages in these many circumstances was not necessarily or even likely the standard language of dictionaries and grammar books but rather had its own peculiarities of lexicon and syntax, just as surely as did the languages it contacted. One structured, variable language, in other words, contacted other structured, variable languages in ways that have been themselves structured and variable, and so in some cases of what is blithely described as contact between English and another language,

[62] Wa Thiongo, *Decolonising the Mind: The Politics of Language in African Literature* (London: James Currey, 1986), xiv.

[63] Suzanne Daley, 'In Europe Some Fear National Languages are Endangered', *New York Times*, 16 April 2001, A1, 10; and John Tagliabue, 'In Europe, Going Global Means, Alas, English', *New York Times*, 19 May 2002, A15.

[64] Kachru, 'The Second Diaspora of English', in Machan and Scott (eds.), *English in Its Social Contexts*, 230–52.

[65] For a useful overview of the spread of English and its variable roles in multilingual societies, see Viv Edwards, *Multilingualism in the English-Speaking World: Pedigree of Nations* (Malden, MA: Blackwell, 2004).

several regional and social variations of English and its contact languages may have been involved. In New Zealand, for example, the label Maori subsumes a number of distinct dialects, and in the United States patterns of immigration affected some areas more significantly than others. To say that Yiddish influenced American English would certainly be true, but at least initially so only in urban areas like New York City, where there were significant numbers of Yiddish speakers in the nineteenth century; the impact of Yiddish on the English of the plains states would be negligible until print and electronic media began to disperse words like *schlock* and *schmuck*.[66] The stylized maps in the *Dictionary of American Regional English*, which depict the concentration of words like *cooter* ('freshwater turtle') in the southeast United States, make a similar point with visual clarity, for as former slave-holding territory this is just the part of the country where one would expect to find a word related to Bambara and Malinké *kuta*. Unlike *schmuck*, however, *cooter* has not entered general American speech. For all languages in a contact situation, such fluctuations in speech communities extend the normal, structured process of grammatical transformation and variation by group. And these fluctuations raise the same issue that appeared in my consideration of sociolects and dialects: the regular processes of borrowing and grammatical innovation developing alongside the distinct conditional and contextual categorization of language change and its meaning.

The status of American English among early British critics provides an apt example. Although English was firmly established in North America early in the seventeenth century, it is not until the eighteenth century, as England's relations with its colonies deteriorated, that speakers came to comment on the issue of whether American English was the same as British English, a dialect of it, or its corruption. Perhaps motivated by the same sociolinguistic impulses as my radio interviewer but reaching the exactly opposite conclusion, many early commentators stressed the barbarity of American English, emphasizing how much the language had already changed from that used in England. This early modern and modern divergence of conclusions rooted in the same motivations points to just how opportunistic judgements about change and its meaning can be, and the same is true of comments by colonists like Benjamin Silliman, who visited England late in the eighteenth century. Of British Anglophones he observed, 'they imagine it [United States English] is a colonial dialect, with a corrupt and barbarous pronunciation, and a vocabulary, interspersed with strange and unknown terms of transatlantic manufacture'.[67] Yet for all this putative barbarity and distinctiveness, Silliman was astounded (and perhaps secretly relieved) that he himself was not recognized as an American but rather judged English on the basis of his pronunciation. Drawing on presumably the same evidence, other critics distanced American speech from British still more—if with less vituperation—by regarding United States English as essentially a different language instead of a corruption of the one used in England. According to an anonymous 1807 piece in the *Edinburgh Review*, the root of Joel Barlow's language in his epic poem *Columbiad* 'may be English, as that of the Italian is Latin; but the variations amount already to more than a change of dialect; and really make a glossary necessary for untravelled readers'.[68] Just as opportunistically, while both American and British analysts could also argue that the language of the United States was a regionally or socially undifferentiated variety that diverged only in its general characteristics from the English of England, the former might interpret this putative uniformity as a mark of a national character, the latter as confirmation of the predominant depravity of American speech.[69] In 1832, for instance, Jonathon Boucher prefaced his *Glossary* by stating, 'With little or no dialect, they [i.e., Americans] are peculiarly addicted to innovation: but such as need not excite our envy, whether we regard their elegance, or their propriety'.[70] And still other, more dispassionate critics, including David Hume, saw the prosperity and population of North America as the means for the worldwide spread of English and the increase in the number of its speakers.

The global dispersion of English in the past two centuries has produced new linguistic varieties that highlight in still other ways the disjunction between regular, inevitable change and the value judgements that can be assigned to it. As with language in the early modern period, contact with both indigenous languages and the languages of other European explorers and colonists—such as French, Dutch, Swedish, Spanish, and German—did not alter natural processes of variation and change, but it did provide input fundamentally different from that which affects an isolated Anglophone community. And it sometimes did so in socially charged situations involving

---

[67] Quoted in Bailey, *Images of English*, 129. On the barbarism of colonial English, see Allen Walker Read, 'Milestones in the Branching of British and American English', in *Milestones in the History of English in America*, ed. Richard W. Bailey (Durham, NC: Duke University Press, 2002), 3–21; see also Read's 'British Recognition of American Speech in the Eighteenth Century' in the same volume, 37–54.

[68] Quoted in Read, 'Amphi-Atlantic English', in *Milestones in the History of English in America*, ed. Bailey, 60–1.

[69] See Bailey, *Images of English*, 130–57.

[70] Quoted in Read, 'British Recognition', 42.

differences in race, ethnicity, level of education, and economic class. Jamaica, for example, has a particularly rich and diverse linguistic history, involving indigenous languages as well as those transplanted from Europe and Africa, from all of which have developed both distinctive varieties of English and also creole varieties. As a British colony and then post-colonial society, Jamaica has equally experienced shifting social dynamics in which language has served as a means of identifying cultural stability and also various threats to it. One such perceived threat, in Jamaica and elsewhere in the Anglophone world, has been racial difference. Already in 1858 Major Alan Chambre focused on variation in English as an indication not only of intrinsically debased speakers but also of the pernicious influence such variation can have on British speech and, perhaps more importantly, society: 'There is scarcely a black in a hundred who speaks pure English, and the white people take no pains to correct them. Sometimes they even adopt the barbarous idiom of the negro, thinking to make themselves understood. The consequence is, their pronunciation is abominable, and the rising generation, not withstanding [sic] the pains taken to educate them, retain the villainous patois of their parents.'[71] In Charles Leland's 1876 *Pidgin English Sing-Song*, such blending of racial judgement and linguistic variation acquires a strange, academic kind of respectability: even though Leland himself was a well-known comic writer who wrote (among other works) burlesque legends in a mixed German-English language, his book became the best-known nineteenth-century handbook on Chinese English. Focusing less on race and more on the social class of colonial Anglophones, an 1829 Australian commentator noted that the language of new immigrants would do much to sustain the region's debased variety of English: 'bearing in mind that our lowest class brought with it a peculiar language, and is constantly supplied with fresh corruption, you will understand why pure English is not, and is not likely to become, the language of the colony'.[72]

It is perhaps easy to identify how comments like these filter non-linguistic concerns through change and variation, but the same filtering has sometimes occurred more recently in the championing of the plural concept of 'Englishes'. Pointing to a variety of structural and contextual features, some critics of the past quarter century have described the transplanted varieties that disturbed someone like Chambre not as ineffective attempts to replicate a standard British or United States variety but rather as fully developed versions

---

[71] Quoted in Barbara Lalla and Jean D'Costa, *Language in Exile: Three Hundred Years of Jamaican Creole* (Tuscaloosa, AL: University of Alabama Press, 1990), 97.
[72] Quoted in Gunn, 'Social Contexts in the History of Australian English', 211.

of English that respond to the social needs and contexts of those who speak them. Chicano English, Singapore English, Asian English, Philippine English, and Chinese English have thus all been identified as distinctive varieties because they all have distinctive phonologies, lexicons, and syntax, because they all have their own histories, and, in the case of Chicano English, because it can be spoken as the birth language of individuals who are not bilinguals of Spanish and English. If Chambre and other early critics filtered prejudices about race and class through their assessments of English change and variation, these kinds of analyses can filter a kind of identity politics. By responding directly to the discussions of earlier generations and championing the non-linguistic rights and integrity of particular speakers, that is, they, too, separate language from its sociolinguistic status and become driven by racial, ethnic, and social concerns. In his valuable study of Chinese English, Kingsley Bolton has thus noted that for nineteenth-century colonialists, 'the notion of "pidgin English" was being actively promoted in Britain and the United States in the conscious attempt to create a racially derogative stereotype of the Chinese in the minds of the western public'.[73] It is of course this stereotype that the promotion of contemporary Chinese English—or Chicano English or Singaporean English—just as actively seeks to erase, replacing it with a different view of the variety and its speakers.

Similar kinds of anxious, social meanings, whether derogatory or vindicating, have been assigned to various kinds of interlanguages that have been produced through contact between English and non-English languages. Whether judged as code-switching, pidgins, or simply dialects with extensive borrowing, Franglais, Denglish, Japlish, and Spanglish (for French-English, German-English, Japanese-English, and Spanish-English) share certain grammatical principles (e.g., English nouns are the most heavily borrowed word class) and pragmatic effects: those who speak them often regard the varieties as creative and contemporary, while traditionalists see them as linguistic corruptions of both languages and diminishments of cultural identity, perhaps every bit as threatening as those that indigenous American Indian languages experienced in their own contact with English. Even as some critics celebrate varieties like Spanglish as cultural phenomena with their own history and socially defining force that is neither entirely English nor entirely Spanish, for Roberto González Echevarría, 'Spanglish, the composite language of Spanish and English that has crossed over from the street to Hispanic talk shows and advertising campaigns, poses a grave danger to Hispanic culture and to the advancement of Hispanics in mainstream America.

---

[73] Bolton, *Chinese Englishes: A Sociolinguistic History*, 186.

Those who condone and even promote it as a harmless commingling do not realize that this is hardly a relationship based on equality. Spanglish is an invasion of Spanish by English.'[74]

The assignment of social meaning to change and variation (at least in the modern world) thus appears as consistent and even inevitable as the change and variation themselves. As intensely as anxieties of one kind or another may be channeled through what are value-free (to reprise Lass) linguistic phenomena, the anxieties over change are not identical to the change, and in many cases they betray an innocence about the structure and history of natural languages like English. From a purely historical perspective, for example, concerns over interlanguages present several difficulties. First, the interlanguage switching in Spanglish or Denglish is not random but structured, following grammatical principles as regularly as did the First Consonant Shift or the development of natural gender in English; and its pragmatic motivations are as clear and consequential as those underlying the formation of regional and social varieties of English around the globe. Second, intermixing of languages has accounted significantly for the growth and vitality of English and other living languages. It is, in fact, perhaps the pre-eminent impetus behind the lexical diffusion that many popular commentators identify as English's most distinctive and valuable trait.[75] For English, the third person singular indicative verbal inflection -*s* as well as the third person plural pronouns *they, them,* and *their* are not native Anglo-Saxon forms but derive directly from Old Norse, the language spoken by the descendants of Viking raiders and colonizers in the Midlands and northern parts of England; a kind of Norslish gave rise to them, as surely as Franglais has produced *qu'est-ce que tu veux pour lunch.* Through mixing such as this, which keeps a language vital and personally meaningful for its speakers, a language like Afrikaans can remain alive in South Africa, despite its comparatively small number of

[74] Echevarría, 'Is "Spanglish" a Language?', *New York Times*, 28 March 1997, A19. For arguments in support of Spanglish as a mediation of cultural hybridity, see Ed Morales, 'Introduction: What I'm Talking about When I Speak in Spanglish, or the Spanglish Manifesto', in Morales (ed.), *Living in Spanglish: The Search for Latino Identity in America* (New York: St Martin's Press, 2002), 1–29; and Ilan Stavans, *Spanglish: The Making of a New American Language* (New York: Rayo, 2003). More generally, see Lizette Alvarez, 'It's the Talk of Nueva York: The Hybrid Called Spanglish', *New York Times*, 25 March 1997, A1, 14; and Richard Bernstein, 'A Snappy Slogan? In German? Don't Smile. Try English', *New York Times*, 21 December 2004, A4.

[75] e.g., Bill Bryson, *The Mother Tongue: English & How It Got That Way* (New York: W. Morrow, 1990); Howard Richler, *A Bawdy Language: How a Second-Rate Language Slept Its Way to the Top* (Toronto: Stoddart, 1999); Kate Burridge, *Blooming English: Observations on the Roots, Cultivation and Hybrids of the English Language* (Cambridge: Cambridge University Press, 2004); and Guy Deutscher, *The Unfolding of Language: An Evolutionary Tour of Mankind's Greatest Invention* (New York: Henry Holt, 2005).

speakers, its role as only one of eleven official languages, and its historical associations with apartheid.[76]

A third difficulty with many contemporary concerns over interlanguages is that the historical record suggests that such varieties are inevitable and valuable features of human communication. In the colonial era of North America, the principles of grammatical and pragmatic regularity motivated the production of pidgins that were used not only between Europeans and Native Americans but among the Europeans themselves.[77] In the Middle Ages England's linguistic repertoire similarly came to include entire linguistic codes structured like Spanglish or Denglish in the forms of a Latin-English macaronic variety utilized in sermons and a French-English-Latin interlanguage employed in late-medieval business, alongside of which Latin, French, and English each continued to exist.[78] At that time, code-switching among Latin, French, and English could also achieve significant rhetorical effects, much like the style-shifting effected by modern novelists. This is the case in William Langland's fourteenth-century poem *Piers Plowman*, where switches from English to Latin both help foreground moments of thematic importance and portend, perhaps overly optimistically, the eventual emergence of English as England's dominant language in all domains of business, education, and government. Langland emblemizes the spiritual and intellectual faculties that define humans in the character of Anima, for instance, who is also one of the most linguistically gifted figures in the poem. She easily lapses into extended Latin passages and quotations, such as the following:

> Prelates of cristene prouinces sholde preue if þei myȝte
> Lere hem litlum and litlum *et in Iesum Christum filium,*
> Til þei kouþe speke and spelle *et in Spiritum sanctum,*
> Recorden it and rendren it wiþ *remissionem peccatorum*
> *Carnis resurreccionem et vitam eternam amen.*[79]

---

[76] Kimberly J. McLarin, 'To Preserve Afrikaners' Language, Mixed-Race South Africans Join Fray', *New York Times*, 28 June 1995, A4.

[77] See Ives Goddard, 'The Use of Pidgins and Jargons on the East Coast of North America', in Gray and Fiering (eds.), *The Language Encounter in the Americas*, 61–78.

[78] See Siegfried Wenzel, *Macaronic Sermons: Bilingualism and Preaching in Late-Medieval England* (Ann Arbor, MI: University of Michigan Press, 1994); and Laura Wright, 'Macaronic Writing in a London Archive, 1380–1480', in Matti Rissanen *et al.* (eds.), *History of Englishes: New Methods and Interpretations in Historical Linguistics* (Berlin: Mouton de Gruyter, 1992), 762–70, and *Sources of London English: Medieval Thames Vocabulary* (Oxford: Clarendon, 1996).

[79] Langland, *Piers Plowman: The B Version*, rev. edn., ed. George Kane and E. Talbot Donaldson (Berkeley and Los Angeles, CA: University of California Press, 1988), XV.609–13. See further Machan, 'Language Contact in *Piers Plowman*', *Speculum*, 69 (1994), 359–85.

Syntactically, this is a difficult sentence to describe, combining as it does quotation, code-switching, and relic English ('litlum') in a rhyming, alliterative, and thematic tour de force. As the conclusion to passus XV, these lines are also in part an introduction to passus XVI and the Tree of Charity, the most powerful mnemonic and theological icon in *Piers Plowman* and an image that recapitulates not only Anima's teachings but also those of *Piers Plowman* in its entirety. It is thus with the ingenuity of an interlanguage— of Latlish—that Langland pragmatically foregrounds this section as one of the poem's climaxes.

Change, shift, death

In order to account for the persistence of variation and change among European languages, Leonard Bloomfield, in his ground-breaking 1933 book *Language*, formulated a 'principle of density':

The reason for this intense local differentiation is evidently to be sought in the principle of density. Every speaker is constantly adapting his speech-habits to those of his interlocutors; he gives up forms he has been using, adopts new ones, and perhaps oftenest of all, changes the frequency of speech-forms without entirely abandoning any old ones or accepting any that are really new to him. The inhabitants of a settlement, village, or town, however, talk much more to each other than to persons who live elsewhere. When any innovation in the way of speaking spreads over a district, the limit of this spread is sure to be along some lines of weakness in the network of oral communication, and these lines of weakness, in so far as they are topographical lines, are the boundaries between towns, villages, and settlements.[80]

Implicit in Bloomfield's principle is the fact that people talk for all sorts of reasons: to convey information, to ask questions, to deceive, to seduce, to entice, and, simply, to get along. More generally, as I noted earlier, they speak to identify themselves socially, in their linguistic forms as well as their topics, and they use these same criteria to pass judgement about their interlocutors' age, politics, education, credibility, familiarity, congeniality, honesty, and ancestry. What Bloomfield points out are the linguistic consequences of motivations like these. Whether they want to display solidarity with one

---

[80] Bloomfield, *Language* (New York: Holt, 1933), 476. Bloomfield here lays the groundwork for the theory of social networks, which has become a powerful and valuable way for understanding how speakers interact with language and how it changes through these interactions, depending on how closely tied particular speakers are to particular groups. See further Lesley Milroy, *Language and Social Networks*, 2nd edn. (Oxford: Blackwell, 1987); James Milroy, *Linguistic Variation and Change: On the Historical Sociolinguistics of English* (Oxford: Blackwell, 1992); and J. K. Chambers, *Sociolinguistic Theory: Linguistic Variation and Its Social Significance* (Oxford: Blackwell, 1995), 34–101.

another or to claim dominance or distinction, speakers who live in close proximity necessarily use language to accomplish social as well as communicative objectives, and this means that they use it in ways that affect their language's grammar and pragmatics. Language, in turn, necessarily continues to vary and change in regular if often unpredictable ways.

From this perspective, the processes conventionally understood as language variation, change, and shift have much in common. All are responses to the impact of time and geography; all proceed in regular, structured fashions; all correlate language with group and individual identity; all are temporal phenomena that confirm and define the temporality of language; all have diversified and enriched English in general and in the idiolects of individual speakers and literary artists; and all occur with a frequency that projects inevitability. For reasons like these, in fact, it has become increasingly common for critics to approach a language not as a discrete system (or set of systems) but as a continuum; like a creole, then, the varieties of a language gradually shift, by speaker and form, from one to another, even including the creole varieties that have developed from it.[81]

Perhaps not surprisingly, the consequences of such phenomena can preclude easy distinctions among change, variation, and shift and even challenge the categories themselves. Whatever their diachronic differences, for example, shift and historical change can produce strikingly similar results. From the viewpoint of structural complexity and arrangement, creole languages, whether they arose instantaneously or developed gradually from pidgins, share the characteristics of all natural languages, and so without any historical background and with only the grammar and corpus of a language, distinctions between interlanguage creoles and historically developed monogenetic languages are likewise not easily drawn.[82] Synchronic variation blends into diachronic change when contact with an immigrant language leads to the grammatical restructuring of a dialect, producing features that eventually spread throughout the language; this was the case with the third person plural pronouns *they*, *them*, and *their*. And, to return to the biblical examples that I cited above, even the discreteness of an individual language across time can sometimes be difficult to maintain. We may identity the *New International Version* of Genesis as the linguistic descendant of the version in the *Old English Heptateuch*, but I would venture that for a modern reader the latter

---

[81] For a careful case study that illustrates this very point, see John R. Rickford, *Dimensions of a Creole Continuum: History, Texts & Linguistic Analysis of Guyanese Creole* (Stanford, CA: Stanford University Press, 1987).

[82] Salikoko S. Mufwene, *The Ecology of Language Evolution* (Cambridge: Cambridge University Press, 2001).

is only marginally more intelligible—or even recognizable as English—than would be (say) the first Welsh version, initially published in 1588 and beginning 'Yn y dechreuad y creawdd Duw y nefoedd a'r ddaiar'.[83] To that reader, in fact, Modern English might nearly as easily have developed from Middle Welsh as from Old English.

What does strongly distinguish language variation and change from shift, death, and even simple error or inadequate linguistic achievement are the responses of both the speakers themselves and the succeeding generations. When viewed and described as natural or internal (i.e., structured grammatical development), linguistic transition across time tends to be regarded as change that does not raise controversy. Except in very arch ways, speakers don't lament—and linguists don't regret—vowel mergers, morphological leveling, or syntactic elaboration. Linguistic transition within time, judged variation, can raise controversy, but it doesn't do so necessarily. Regional variation may evoke some social stereotypes but often passes without comment. When it seems to morph into external, diachronic change, however, as in the cases of Nigerian or Indian English, variation can enfold racial and cultural issues in such a way that it does become quite controversial, even though precisely the same process brought in the third person pronouns without comment. And controversy can likewise surround synchronic sociolects, such as African American Vernacular English or Black South African English.

M. L. Samuels has explained change as follows:

Every change is, at least in its beginnings, present in the variants of the spoken language; it is the process of continuous selection that ensures its imitation, spread, and ultimate acceptance into one or more systems. The selection takes place both at the level of idiolect (and interlocutor) and at the level of system proper; and it may consist of a preference for a commoner variant rather than a rare one, or vice versa.[84]

This is as concise and clear an account of the mechanics of change and its implication in variation as I know. Yet I also think that as a definition Samuels's account is limited by its own restrictions to the mechanics of linguistic change. If language truly were a value-free system, unconnected to the desires, whims, and foibles of its speakers, the definition would be exhaustive. But language—English—isn't this kind of system. It's a system whose speakers do not simply articulate its elements but also assign meaning (and controversy) to them in their daily lives. In many ways, indeed, it is in

---

[83] *Y Bibl Cyssegr-lan: Sef yr Hen Destament a'r Newydd* (London: Robert Barker, 1630), sig. al[r].

[84] Samuels, *Linguistic Evolution*, 138.

speakers' lived sociolinguistic experience that the clarity of technical distinctions among variation, change, corruption, and shift becomes most obscure. The mere ability of phenomena as structured and recurring as variation and change to generate controversy points to the significance of this experience. So, too, does the fact that just as the teaching of language and the categorization of its change and variation are not value-free, neither, it seems, is identification of its history.

Structural rearrangement has been so consequential as to render Old and much Middle English unintelligible to most modern Anglophones, whatever variety they speak. And yet as histories of English are conventionally written, some varieties—and only some varieties, such as Standard British or United States English as opposed to South Asian English—can claim a kind of linguistic lineage from these historical versions. Such a claim both endorses their primacy above other varieties and obscures how much they, too, have changed over time. In effect, history becomes a positive value judgement in a way that shift is not, since the former implies continuity and integrity, while the latter evokes all at once cultural rupture and loss from the speakers who have shifted and (sometimes) only a kind of liberal guilt from those to whose language the shift has occurred. Diachronic change simply has sociolinguistic advantages that are lacking to shift and, to a large extent, variation. Indeed, the classification of new varieties as corruptions or even interlanguages (and thus entirely new languages) is an interpretive gesture that recalls some nineteenth-century British responses to American English. Linguistic shift thereby comes to describe a non-Anglophonic population's loss of its indigenous language but also to quarantine its newly acquired language from the Anglophone mainstream. And in this way speakers of Chicano English, for example, may be judged to speak neither Spanish, nor, unless one is willing to allow the identification of a variety through structure, history, and so forth, a coherent, recognized variety of English.

There is something particularly insidious about where analyses like these, however well intentioned, leave the concerned speakers. While speakers of Maori, Welsh, and Native American languages—and in the United States, to a much lesser extent, Spanish—have generally adopted English in place of their historical languages, they have often sought to remain ethnically and culturally identified with their indigenous history and traditions. If linguistic shift has occurred, this identification necessarily must come through the medium of another language—English—much as Anglophones can continue to identify with the Anglo-Saxon and medieval past by reading (or perhaps only knowing that they can read) *Beowulf* and the *Canterbury Tales* through the medium of Modern English translations. The important difference is that

Anglophone populations in Britain, the United States, and elsewhere at least in Kachru's Inner Circle can assert a historical connection with Old English, even if it is no more intelligible to them than would be Maori or Welsh. And it is just such a connection that can be denied not only to Maori speakers but also to speakers of varieties like Jamaican English, which may be no structurally farther from Old English than is Standard United States English but which, unlike Standard United States English, can be marked as a non-standard interlanguage.

To the extent that since the Romantic period Anglo-American criticism has fostered the notion that language and culture are immanent in one another, there's an additional difficulty here. If language is an essential determinant of culture, then when language is lost, as through shift, so might culture be. By extension, just as a shifted variety might be linguistically excluded from English as an interlanguage or an inadequate level of achievement, so would the shifted speakers be excluded from the cultural traditions of their original language. If speakers of varieties recognized as English—such as Standard British English—can claim the patrimony of historical style, language, and literature, speakers of creole varieties or other interlanguages cannot. And if such speakers are denied the patrimony of English, Romantic notions of nation and language can equally deny them the patrimony of their own indigenous languages. The implication would seem to be that there can be no Irish culture independent of Irish, no Maori culture independent of Maori. It might thus be argued that beyond the forcible ways in which Anglophones have sometimes imposed their speech and culture around the world stands another kind of violence and rupture: this set of interpretive sociolinguistic strategies that variously advocate protection of indigenous people but also serve to erase them in the onrush of Anglophone culture. In this way, where languages go when they go away is into oblivion, and their speakers with them.

The larger, crucial issue here is how sociolinguistic meanings and values like these are assigned to the phenomena associated with language change and variation. Whatever structural and historical criteria may be used to differentiate among change, variation, shift, and corruption, I am maintaining, the classifications themselves are to an extent value judgements—gestures of sociolinguistic approval, disapproval, or disregard. It is not simply an empirical decision but an exercise of judgement that certain forms of English qualify as legitimate natural variation, other forms as linguistic corruptions, and still others as evidence of a new interlanguage. In order to define what the English language is, this judgement rests on a selection of some of the hundreds of millions of structural forms uttered in the course of a millennium and a half. And this definition, in turn, has profound consequences for the social standing of various speakers, for the cultural significance of the varieties they speak, for their ethnic and national identities, and for their ability to appropriate English literary and linguistic history as their own. As distinct as linguistic phenomena may be from their interpretation, the latter has a great deal to do with how the former not only are perceived but also function in society. At the outset of this chapter I asked where linguistic forms and languages go when they go away. The answer I would give now is where they go—into new varieties, languages, or corruptions—and whether they go away at all or simply are treated as the same forms and languages in new guise depend a great deal on the partiality of judgements about language, its variation, and its change. It turns out that linguistic change, as distinct from shift or error, can sometimes be even less empirically identifiable than pain.

In asking how sociolinguistic meanings and values are assigned, I am of course partly asking who assigns them and why they are accepted. Who judges which linguistic phenomena represent change, which variation, which shift, and which errors, and how do they do so? Why do some kinds of structured, irrational variation engender hostility, while other kinds do not? Why do some languages or forms become other languages or forms, some continue, and some disappear? Why are some varieties accepted as versions of English whereas others are not? These questions point to fundamental issues for understanding how language change and variation have occasioned so much anxiety, which is itself as contingent as the phenomena it accompanies. When a variation is judged a corruption, as with putting the cart of *mother* before the horse of *father*, the anxiety can be the result of the assigned values. But the anxiety can also produce such values, as in the case of British educational policy in colonial India or American policy with indigenous peoples, where anxiety over language contact and its effects ironically led to additional variation in the form of English acquired by indigenes and thus additional anxiety. In this kind of contingent balance, it is often the case that the responsibility for a particular sociolinguistic meaning lies less with one person or group and more with a complex nexus of institutions, principles, and actions. In the three chapters that follow, I look at three such nexuses and the way they have shaped linguistic anxiety.

3

Narratives of Change

Stories, confusion, and the Tower of Babel

In his discussion of the formal content and moralizing impulses of historical narrative, Hayden White observes that the events of daily life, whether intimate social interaction or epic international struggle, do not transpire in the well-motivated, balanced, and thematized plot of a story. These kinds of coherence are imposed by the historian, who selects events, arranges them in a linear order, and necessarily provides cause-and-effect explanations. As the matter of narrative, such coherence is also the product of imagination. For White, in fact, it is historical narration that renders the phenomena of the world real and desirable by positing in these phenomena the form and coherence characteristic of imaginative acts: 'These events are real not because they occurred but because, first, they were remembered and, second, they are capable of finding a place in a chronologically ordered sequence.'[1] As an act of imagination, historical narration must also posit its own closure, and the need for such closure—for comprehensible completion, purpose, and meaning in historical events—is ultimately moralizing: 'The demand for closure in the historical story is a demand, I suggest, for moral meaning, a demand that sequences of real events be assessed as to their significance as elements of a moral drama.'[2] But the moralizing and authenticating powers of the historian can be evoked only when the imaginative narrative form assigned to human experience is contested, only when the reality to be made desirable is contested. 'In order to qualify as historical,' White contends, 'an event must be susceptible to at least two narrations of its occurrence. Unless at least two versions of the same set of events can be imagined, there is no reason for the historian to take upon himself the authority of giving the true account of what really happened. The authority of the historical narrative is the authority

[1] Hayden White, *The Content of the Form: Narrative Discourse and Historical Representation* (Baltimore, MD: The Johns Hopkins University Press, 1987), 20.
[2] White, *The Content of the Form*, 21.

of reality itself; the historical account endows this reality with form and thereby makes it desirable by the imposition upon its processes of the formal coherency that only stories possess.'[3]

While White's concerns are with historical narratives, their applicability to myths and stories leads me to use them as a point of departure in this chapter, where I am concerned with the kinds of stories and myths individuals and epochs have told to explain language change and variation, specifically as it relates to the history of English. These narratives might have language as either their subject or their ideological background, and the explanations might be either direct or implicit, in the sense that the use of change and variation for stylistic effect presumes a particular interpretation of them. In any case, such narratives of language change and variation are powerful ways to organize and interpret sociolinguistic experience. They make real not simply the inescapable facts of language use but, like historical narratives, also the extra-linguistic social meanings that accrue to them. Beyond simply acknowledging that change and variation take place, such narratives position these phenomena in relation to historical events, cultural beliefs, and political expectations. They state chronological connections between language and social process, and in this way the stories provide the form and coherence that give change and variation substance, implicitly classifying them (as change, variation, shift, or error) and providing them with causes, conse-quences, and moral meanings. What these stories contest, to stay with White's analysis, are other accounts of change and variation, which themselves, neces-sarily, offer other sociolinguistic meanings and other versions of reality. The ultimate effect of many of these stories for English, I will argue, is to use language change and variation as means to advance particular social positions, neutralize challenges to these positions, and displace discussion from social issues to linguistic ones.

In the most general terms, myths can perform many extra-linguistic tasks. Whether images, ideas, or fully developed stories, they can narrate history, explain social practice, justify beliefs and prejudices, define aspirations, and give shape to fear. If the Norse myth of the Ragnarok expresses hope for a new, less violent world in its account of the final, cosmic battle among the gods and giants, the Judeo-Christian myth of Adam and Eve assures us of divine love and explains why the world can sometimes be a painful and hostile place. Myths may achieve their prototypical and pre-eminent shape in a particular literary work—such as the Norse *Völuspá* or the Book of Genesis—but they attain their force not through the influence of one work nor through any

---

[3] White, *The Content of the Form*, 20.

verisimilitude to historical events but through the way they respond to cultural needs and circulate in a variety of formats. The Ragnarok and other Norse cosmological myths, for example, echo a pervading medieval Norse anxiety over the passage of time and daily life in the relentlessly harsh northern world. And while the Norse cosmology is echoed in this anxiety, it also helps to explain it. Formed from the body of a giant in a primeval struggle, that is, the world necessarily has an agonistic quality that will be realized on one last occasion in a climactic battle at the end of time. This explanatory power is the quality that gives a story or picture mythic status: not simple recitation of or allusion to the myth, but the fact that the myth can be applied as an organizing principle to cultural experience, as a paradigm that makes a variety of experiences real.

For language change and variation, no myth has been more powerful—has explained more or has had more echoes not simply for the history of English but for the history of other European languages as well—than the account of the Tower of Babel, as told in Genesis 11: 1–9. According to this account, some time after the Great Flood, 'the whole earth was of one language, and of one speech'. Concerned that they would 'be scattered abroad upon the face of the whole earth' and thus their memory and achievement obliterated in their dispersion, the people build a city with a tower 'whose top may reach unto heaven'. For His part, the Lord seems motivated by concerns about what a united people might accomplish, whether in and of itself or as a challenge to His own authority: 'And the Lord said, Behold, the people is one, and they have all one language, and this they begin to do: and now nothing will be restrained from them, which they have imagined to do.' In order to thwart the construction of the Tower and thus the people's ambitions, the Lord resolves to 'confound their language, that they may not understand one another's speech', and as a result the people leave off building the Tower and disperse around the world. 'Therefore', concludes the account, 'is the name of it called Babel; because the Lord did there confound the language of all the earth: and from thence did the Lord scatter them abroad upon the face of all the earth.' As bleak a future as this story seems to foretell, however, it offers some hope to the people: this same chapter concludes with the introduction of Abram, later Abraham, the patriarch of Israel. If the people's pride leads to their dispersion, their dispersion in turn leads to the building of a nation.

Perhaps Babylonian in origin, this story represents the earliest, recorded explanation for what the Middle Ages called the *confusio linguarum*, the confusion of tongues, although analogues exist in other traditions. Through folk etymology of the Hebrew roots, the account interprets Babel to mean 'dispersion' rather than the actual 'gate of God' (or 'gates of the gods') and connects the story with Babylon, the city founded by Nimrod according to Genesis 10: 10. In this way, what might have begun as simply a story of a tower, perhaps even a tower of piety, was overtaken by a story of language change.[4] While Genesis never addresses the matter, later traditions presumed that from the one language spoken at the Tower arose the seventy-two languages that exegesis understood to have been scattered with the people across the earth—seventy-two, both because it matched the number underlying the Septuagint and because it represented the total number of Noah's grandsons from Shem, Ham, and Japheth.[5]

It is not always recognized that the narrative of the Tower of Babel is in fact the second mythic explanation for language change and variation in Genesis. The previous chapter, Genesis 10, relates the multiplication of Noah's descendants (including Nimrod) in a Table of Nations, and in so doing refers with parallel phrasing to the peoples and languages associated with each of his sons. At the end of the chapter, for example, Genesis 10: 31 reads, 'These are the sons of Shem, after their families, after their tongues, in their lands, after their nations' (also 10: 5 and 10: 20). It is possible to reconcile the two explanations in the way St Augustine does, by regarding the references in chapter 10 as proleptic of the general sociolinguistic groupings that would develop as a result of the events at the Tower.[6] There was one language, in other words, but when change and variation began, they did so along the patterns foreshadowed in Genesis 10, with the descendants of Shem tending to scatter in one direction and speak one kind of language, those of Ham in another, and those of Japheth in a third. It's also possible that the two explanations are just that—two different accounts of change and variation, much as the four Gospels offer sometimes inconsistent views of Jesus's life.

More significant than the divergence in narrative lines between Genesis 10 and 11 is the divergence in the stories' implications for language, for this divergence produces a dialogue that dominates subsequent narratives and representations of language. It is this kind of dialogue, following White's analysis, that constructs the form, coherence, and reality of change and variation. According to the account in Genesis 10, change and variation exist as ordinary features of ordinary human experience. They help define

---

[4] Arno Borst, *Der Turmbau von Babel: Geschichte der Meinungen über Ursprung und Vielfalt der Sprachen und Völker*, 4 vols in 6 (Stuttgart: Anton Hiersemann, 1957–63), i, 116–17. Also see *OED*, s. v. *Babel*. For accounts of Greek, Kenyan, and Aboriginal analogues, see Richard Bailey, *Images of English: A Cultural History of the Language* (Ann Arbor, MI: University of Michigan Press, 1991), 93–4.

[5] Borst, *Der Turmbau von Babel*, ii, 480.

[6] St Augustine, *The City of God against the Pagans*, ed. and trans. R. W. Dyson (Cambridge: Cambridge University Press, 1998), 702.

who we are as human beings, both by reflecting our history and culture and by taking place as naturally as does the succession of generations; children are born, and languages change. In Genesis 11, conversely, change occurs as divine punishment. For St Augustine, the Tower, which he allows may be a metaphorical representation of an entire city, was built as 'an affront to God' and symbolizes Nimrod's 'ungodly pride'. 'Because the power of a ruler lies in his tongue,' Augustine continues, 'it was there that Nimrod's pride was condemned, so that he who refused to understand and obey God's bidding was himself not understood when he gave his bidding to men.' Having scattered human language, God leaves the Tower standing, and in this way He reconfigures its symbolic significance. Observes Augustine, 'The safe and true way to heaven is built by humility, which lifts the heart up to the Lord, not against the Lord'.[7] A personal tower of modesty and submission thus replaces Nimrod's literal tower of pride. Elsewhere, Augustine amplifies the moral import of the story by claiming that 'certain proud' men built the Tower, ostensibly so that they might not be destroyed by another flood: 'For they had heard and recalled that all iniquity had been destroyed by the Flood.'[8] What they had not heard, evidently, was God's pledge not to destroy the world by flood a second time, and so their hubris in resistance to God is compounded by their ignorance of His Testament and the folly of their belief that were God to send another flood, they could build a tower high enough to rise above the water.

If the injunction against pride provides the moral axis of the Tower story, however, its emotional axis is the all-too-human anxiety over being left alone in the world, particularly in the pre-modern world with its limited networks of social support. Indeed, this threat of being scattered would seem to appeal to an almost primeval fear: the action the people specifically dread and build the Tower to forestall is the very action with which the Lord punishes them. As powerful as it is, such fear might well better account for the persistence and emotional power of the story over time than does its explanation of language change.[9] Already in this etiological myth of language change, then, anxiety over language thus stands in for other, greater anxieties: over the forced abandonment of a homeland that is known and familiar for one that is not, and over forced separation from an individual's family and friends.

---

[7] St Augustine, *The City of God against the Pagans*, 703.

[8] St Augustine, *Tractates on the Gospel of John 1–10*, trans. John W. Rettig, i of *The Fathers of the Church: A New Translation* (Washington, DC: The Catholic University of America Press, 1988), 138–9.

[9] Cf. Bailey's comment: 'This terror of being "scattered" is a key to understanding this central myth of Western linguistic culture' (*Images of English*, 93).

Within this interpretive framework, whenever language changes, it reminds us all at once of our pride, isolation, and punishment, just as surely as the sweat of toil and the pains of childbirth remind us of Adam and Eve's fall in the Garden of Eden and our own mortality. By extension, if before the fall humans were without sin or death, before Babel they spoke one language, which allowed such complete and perfect communication as to enable them to build a tower that captured divine attention. For St Augustine, additionally, such complete communication is possible again only through Christ and His Church: 'If pride created differences of tongues, Christ's humility has joined the differences of tongues together. Now what that tower had dispersed, the Church binds together. From one tongue came many; do not be amazed, pride did this. From many tongues comes one; do not be amazed, love did this.'[10] Total, invariable communication is thus mythologized at once as an original attribute of humans and a quality that elevates us above human limitations to the point where, to echo Tennyson, we might strive with God. And hence the significance of God's choice to scatter language and humanity rather than simply destroy the Tower: another Tower might be built, but not, evidently, without a shared language.

Peter Bruegel the Elder's famous depiction of the Tower of Babel strikingly accommodates both of these narratives. Painted with oil on oak in 1563 and approximately 45 inches by 61 inches, the picture shows an aristocratic Nimrod surrounded by his councillors and facing several prostrate workers.[11] Other craftsmen shape and lever stone blocks. In the distance to the left appears a village with houses too numerous too count, while up the right side of the painting a river extends into the distance; alongside the Tower are docked several large ships, from which, presumably, supplies and workers have been unloaded. The Tower dominates the central space of the painting, stretching from Nimrod, who through foreshortening stands at the Tower's base, through the clouds in the picture's upper margin. A ziggurat partly inspired by the Colosseum, which Bruegel had seen in Rome, this Tower climbs upward by levels graduated so slightly that, if the enormous proportions were ever completed, it might indeed reach unto Heaven. Each level develops in the same way: tall archways with two windows above them that are grouped in pairs by buttresses and three additional windows spanning the top of the buttressed space.

---

[10] St Augustine, *Tractates on the Gospel of John 1–10*, 139.

[11] In or around 1563 Bruegel painted another representation of the Tower of Babel, one less developed and considerably smaller (approximately 24 inches by 30 inches) than the better-known version I discuss here.

What is striking about Bruegel's picture from a sociolinguistic perspective is its ambivalence about the origins of language change and variation. On one hand, in its scale and complexity, Bruegel's Tower exudes the hubris to which Genesis 11 alludes. In comparison to the simplicity of the depicted construction procedures, it additionally testifies to what can be accomplished through human cooperation (and perhaps coercion) of a sort that the medium of a shared language allows. On the other hand, Bruegel's Tower allows for the realization of variation and change that Genesis 10 describes and Genesis 11 initiates. With the innumerable houses stretching into the distance behind it, the Tower's many rooms would seem superfluous, prepared for a population that either is already housed or does not yet exist. More provocatively, the repeated design of individual chambers, each with exterior access, images the separation and isolation of a world already linguistically divided.

The account of change and variation expressed by the Tower of Babel is the better known of the two versions in Genesis. It certainly better lends itself to visual depiction, so much so that Bruegel's painting is perhaps best seen as part of a tradition of early modern representations. Between about 1550 and the beginning of the seventeenth century, in fact, 140 depictions of the Tower were published.[12] Yet the other version has had explanatory power as well. As the expansion of the known world made it more and more difficult to adhere to the seventy-two languages predicated on Genesis, and as developments in linguistics made change and variation more empirically comprehensible, so it became more difficult to posit one parent language for all the world. Colonization of North America alone presented Anglophones with evidence of hundreds of languages structurally dissimilar not only to European languages but also to one another. In the early modern period, indeed, recognition of the diversity of human speech proceeds at an almost logarithmic rate: by 1660 Andreas Müller had identified ninety languages, by 1787 Lorenzo Hervás y Panduro over three hundred, and by 1806 Adelung and Vater five hundred.[13]

While this early modern identification of so many languages provided empirical arguments against Genesis 11, Enlightenment thought strengthened these arguments with a theoretical underpinning that had much the same effect. The arbitrary connection between words and things that was advocated by John Locke and other early modern thinkers, for instance, rendered language artificial and therefore a polygenetic rather than monogenetic phenomenon.[14] Even if early modern Anglophones regarded indigenous peoples

---

[12] Vivien Law, *The History of Linguistics in Europe from Plato to 1600* (Cambridge: Cambridge University Press, 2003), 262.

[13] Law, *The History of Linguistics in Europe from Plato to 1600*, 218.

[14] Umberto Eco, *The Search for the Perfect Language* (Oxford: Blackwell, 1995), 73–116. Also see Chapter 5.

in North America and other sites of Anglophone colonization as savages, moreover, they increasingly came to grant that all languages primarily reflected their speakers' shared cultural experience.[15] And this, too, is as much as to accept both the inevitability of variation and the absence of descent from a single linguistic fountainhead.

The greatest influence of the Table of Nations, however, may be indirect—as the competing version that motivates echoes of the Tower of Babel and that makes its account, and the sociolinguistic anxieties it projects, real. Behind every insistence on the decline of language, punctuation, and pronunciation uneasily lurks the anxiety that such transformations may be natural and inevitable. Behind every claim that language and variation are unnatural lies the recognition that this might not be true. Between them, the narrations of Genesis 10 and 11 thus dialogically compete over the causes of variation and change, the mechanics of their development, the consequences of their existence, and their moral implications for life on earth.

Earlier I noted that mythic power depends not simply on the historical accuracy of stories. It may partly arise in this fashion, although since myths can also be outright fabrications, equally important are discursive traditions that include explicit reference to a story as part of an argument. Yet the greatest power of a myth lies in its responsiveness to lived experience, in the way it can be used to organize and explain unfolding events that would seem to have no chronological or causative connection to it. In the case of the Tower of Babel and the alternative account of Genesis, the history of English and other European vernaculars affords multiple examples of all kinds of such mythic affirmation. Since the earliest Christian era, specific allusions to the stories and their presumed historical accuracy have occurred in a variety of contexts, as have sociolinguistic developments implicitly underwritten by the myth's account of the origins of variation and change. What many of these narratives share, accordingly, is the implication that language change and variation are wrong—even unnatural and immoral—and can thereby serve as justifications for all the sociolinguistic practices that proceed from this judgement.

The predominant approach of early Christian exegetes takes a very literal reading of the story. Late in his fourteenth-century *Confessio Amantis*, for example, John Gower follows Augustine in identifying sin as the cause of Nimrod's pride and linguistic division of humankind as its consequence:

---

[15] For a discussion of how the North American experience affected traditional thinking about languages and language development, see Edward G. Gray, *New World Babel: Languages and Nations in Early America* (Princeton, NJ: Princeton University Press, 1999).

And over that thurgh Senne it com
That Nembrot such emprise nom,
Whan he the Tour Babel on heihte
Let make, as he that wolde feihte
Ayein the hihe goddes myht,
Wherof divided anon ryht
Was the langage in such entente,
Ther wiste no what other mente,
So that thei myhten noght procede.[16]

By this common medieval reading, Nimrod's pride is archetypal, since it is sin that produces division of all kinds:

For Senne of his condicioun
Is moder of divisioun
And tokne whan the world schal faile.[17]

Three centuries later, in *Paradise Lost*, John Milton shared and developed the medieval moralizing impulses in the story, if not Gower's religious sentiments more generally. To Milton, Nimrod is driven by 'ambition', and the very material he uses to build the Tower—'a black bituminous gurge' that boils up from 'the mouth of Hell'—morally orients his ambition as well as the Tower itself. Here, however, Nimrod appears less as someone who might challenge God and more as the object of scorn, and in this way the Tower emerges as truly the act of folly St Augustine understood it to be. It is in 'derision' that God divides human language into a 'hideous gabble' and 'hubbub strange', and once language has been divided, 'Great laughter was in Heaven'. The Tower itself is, very simply, 'Ridiculous'.[18]

Consideration of just what 'the langage' was that preceded the Tower's destruction exercised many medieval and early modern commentators, and it, too, had a distinctly moral cast. According to St Augustine, in the pre-lapsarian world of the Garden of Eden, humans and God managed both external, vocal speech and also a kind of silent, inner communication. 'He speaks', says Augustine of God, 'in His own ineffable way. His speech is explained to us in our fashion; but God's speech is indeed more sublime than ours. It precedes His action as the immutable reasons of the action itself, and it has no audible and transient sound, but it has a power which endures

---

[16] *The English Works of John Gower*, ed. G. C. Macaulay, EETS es 81 (London: Oxford University Press, 1900), Prologue, ll. 1017–25.

[17] Prologue, ll. 1029–31.

[18] Milton, *Paradise Lost*, 12.38–62, in *The Poems of John Milton*, ed. Roy Flannagan (Boston, MA: Houghton Mifflin, 1998).

for eternity and operates in time.'[19] In Eden and before the Tower, communication was direct and unmediated, uncorrupted by any intermediate signs or lapses in interpretation. Some of this quality of complete and perfect communication was lost with the fall, when humans, in a sense, fell from direct knowledge of God and into flawed and indirect communicative channels, including writing. To some exegetes, indeed, writing could therefore be regarded as the earliest indication of the hazards of change and variation. By these accounts, well before Nimrod built his tower, had Adam not sinned, we would not have needed writing, the Bible, or exegesis to understand one another or God with complete comprehension.[20]

While some commentators regarded the original Adamic language as lost either in the Garden of Eden or at the Tower of Babel, prior to the seventeenth and eighteenth centuries identification with Hebrew was so typical as to be commonplace. As Isidore of Seville simply put the matter in his influential *Etymologies*, 'the Hebrew language is the mother of all languages and literatures'.[21] This connection may have strained linguistic explanation, inasmuch as Hebrew is neither the parent nor even genetic relative of any indigenous European language—not to mention South African, Asian, South American, North American, and Pacific Rim languages. But a genealogy that postulated an intrinsic, genetic connection between Hebrew and the European languages did respond to historical and theological imperatives: the medieval need to connect Europe to the culture and language of the Old Testament.

Such a connection served ideological purposes as well, implicating the development of languages and all that entailed culturally within the development of Christianity. To the twelfth-century English exegete John of Salisbury, for example, pre-Babel Hebrew wasn't simply originary; this original language was also 'more natural than the others, having been, so to speak, taught by nature herself'.[22] By this reasoning, a fall from Hebrew in particular was simultaneously a fall from God and nature. In *De Vulgari Eloquentia* Dante similarly invested Hebrew, the putative original language, with an innately moral quality, noting that only it was worthy enough for Christ to utter. 'In this form of speech Adam spoke,' Dante observes, 'in this form of speech all his descendants spoke until the building of the Tower of Babel...and this

---

[19] St Augustine, *The City of God against the Pagans*, 705.

[20] Eric Jager, *The Tempter's Voice: Language and the Fall in Medieval Literature* (Ithaca, NY: Cornell University Press, 1993), 52–97.

[21] Isidore of Seville, *Etymologiarum sive Originum Libri XX*, ed. W. M. Lindsay, 2nd edn. (Oxford: Clarendon Press, 1962), i, 3.4.

[22] Quoted in Jesse M. Gellrich, *The Idea of the Book in the Middle Ages: Language Theory, Mythology, and Fiction* (Ithaca, NY: Cornell University Press, 1985), 99.

form of speech was inherited by the sons of Heber, who after him were called Hebrews.' Dante goes on to imagine the *confusio linguarum* as a *felix culpa*, however, for if it shattered pre-Tower linguistic uniformity, it also allowed the history of faith to become written in the history of languages. 'With them alone', he observes of the Hebrews and their continued use of the original language, 'did it remain after the confusion, in order that our Redeemer (who was, as to his humanity, to spring from them) might use, not the language of confusion, but of grace'.[23] That apparently simple formulations about the origins of language have an ideological edge likewise appears in St Augustine's discussion of translation in *De Doctrina Christiana*. There, stressing that a knowledge of languages is a necessary pre-requisite to any scriptural analysis, he explains how dangerous mistranslation can be, not simply to the reading of the Bible but, in light of its role as the foundational text for Christianity, to the book's larger implications. As he had said in his *Confessions*, while divine speech is eternal and immaterial, human speech is temporal, the result and source of further errors.[24] To read Scripture and thereby participate in the understanding and even governance of the medieval world is to resist the errors in communication that have characterized human experience since the fall and that now include errors in written transmission: 'for the attention of those who wish to know the divine scripture must first focus on the task of correcting the manuscripts, so that uncorrected ones give place to corrected ones, assuming that they belong to the same class of translation'.[25] For St Augustine, then, sin led to Babel, which led to the confusion of tongues, which led to failed communication in general, which led to failed transmission and understanding of the Bible in particular, which leads to the forces that challenge medieval Christian society. Through this influential analysis, resistance to variation and change becomes resistance to social dissolution and, simultaneously, conservation of the ecclesiastical and political institutions that counter it.

A similar ideological edge informs the fourteenth-century comments of Nicholas Oresme, who proceeds from recognition that a diversity of languages works against civilian and political conversation to the affirmation that a people should never accept a king from another nation who does not speak their language.[26] And the Babel story serves such political purposes even more

---

[23] Dante, *De Vulgari Eloquentia*, in Alex Preminger *et al.*, ed. and trans., *Classical and Medieval Literary Criticism: Translations and Interpretations* (New York: Frederick Ungar, 1974), 417.

[24] *Confessions*, trans. R. S. Pine-Coffin (Harmondsworth: Penguin, 1961), 256–60.

[25] St Augustine, *De Doctrina Christiana*, ed. and trans. R. P. H. Green (Oxford: Clarendon Press, 1995), 81.

[26] See Serge Lusignan, *Parler Vulgairement: les intellectuels et la langue française aux xiiie et xive siècles*, 2nd edn. (Paris: J. Vrin, 1987), 109.

so in the sometimes unconventional arguments of the early modern French scholar and thinker Guillaume Postel (1510–81). His 1538 *De Originibus seu de Hebraicae Linguae et Gentis Antiquitate* maintains not only that Hebrew was the original language, spoken by Noah and his sons, but that Arabic, Chaldean, Hindi, and even Greek developed from it. In his *Linguarum Duodecim Characteribus Differentium Alphabetum Introductio*, published in the same year, Postel further argues that in fact all languages share a common origin, and from there, Umberto Eco notes, 'he went on to advance the project of a return to Hebrew as the instrument for the peaceable fusion of the peoples of differing races'.[27] Within the mythological tradition of Babel, a unity of language would correspond to the unity of the world and God, would foster the unity of humanity, and would thereby demonstrate the transcendent truth of Christianity to believers as well as non-believers. The histories of language, the Church, and politics once more become homologous.

In these ways, then, Christian exegesis mythologizes language change and variation as unnatural and sinful conditions; they may persist, in fact must do so, but they persist both as confirmations of a world that fell in Eden, at Babel, and ever afterwards and as catalysts of the confusion towards which humans seem drawn by their fallen nature. In a telling comparison that suggests just how far down the chain of being linguistic dispersion has cast humans, St Augustine claims that 'if two men, each ignorant of the other's language, meet, and are compelled by some necessity not to pass on but to remain with one another, it is easier for dumb animals, even of different kinds, to associate together than these men, even though both are human beings'.[28]

While the story of Pentecost offers what is in some ways a competing biblical account of change and variation, it shares with the Babel myth this notion that such linguistic phenomena are unnatural. At Pentecost, when the apostles were gathered together, 'there appeared unto them cloven tongues like as of fire, and it sat upon each of them. And they were all filled with the Holy Ghost, and began to speak with other tongues, as the Spirit gave them utterance'. When they go out to speak, they encounter people 'of every nation under heaven', who 'were confounded, because that every man heard them speak in his own language. And they were all amazed and marvelled, saying one to another, Behold, are not all these which speak Galilaeans? And how hear we every man in our own tongue, wherein we were born?'[29] Here, change and variation in the miraculous form of glossolalia may represent

---

[27] Eco, *The Search for the Perfect Language*, 76. See 73–116 in general for discussion of the putative status of Hebrew as the original language.

[28] St Augustine, *The City of God against the Pagans*, 928.

[29] *Acts*, 2: 1–12.

divine gifts for faith rather than punishments for pride, but like the confusion of tongues at Babel they originate outside of ordinary human experience, they transform this experience, and they hold out the possibility of perfect, unmediated communication. For St Augustine's teleological historiography, as a gesture of Church unification Pentecost stands simply as Babel's fulfilment: 'The apostles were sent to the nations: if to the nations, to all tongues. The Holy Spirit, parted in tongues, united in the dove, signified this. On this side tongues are parted; on that the dove joins them together.'[30] Three centuries later, the Venerable Bede invested even more spiritual potential in a putative return to divine, unmediated communication. For him, not only does Pentecost restore what Babel cast apart, but also it is this restoration that enables humans to begin to recover the nearly God-like wisdom they were to have had at creation: 'The humility of the Church brings together again the unity of languages that the pride of Babylon had scattered; spiritually, however, the diversity of languages signifies the gifts of holy favors. Indeed, the Holy Spirit is not improperly therefore understood to have given the first gift of languages to men, for whom human wisdom is learned and taught from without, in that it can be shown how easily men can be made wise through the wisdom of God, which is within them.'[31]

Although the story of Babel offers an overt reference point for discussions of language in the Middle Ages and later, it is perhaps even more significant that its conceptualization of change and variation can underwrite and organize historical experience so as to demonstrate the very thing that gives the story its mythic power. First ancient Greece and then Rome, though decidedly not Christian, effectively strove towards a pre-Babel condition in their imperial aspirations and their linguistic practices. To the Greeks, anyone who didn't speak Greek was βάρβαρος—foreign, with speech sounding like ba-ba-ba and behavior that was crude and uncultivated. Many of these same connotations appeared in the Latin borrowing *barbarus*, epitomizing Rome's own indifference and condescension to those outside the empire who shared neither their language nor their customs. The world may necessarily have been multilingual, but conceptually, Greece and Rome were not.

Lacking imperial ambitions of its own, the early Christian church concomitantly demonstrated little interested in the unity or diversity of speech, but by the eleventh and twelfth centuries it, too, had begun overtly to conduct itself in ways consistent with a Babel model of change and variation.[32]

30 St Augustine, *Tractates on the Gospel of John 1–10*, 138.

31 Bede, *Expositio Actuum Apostolorum et Retractatio*, ed. M. W. Laistner (Cambridge, MA: Medieval Academy of America, 1939), 16.

32 Borst, *Der Turmbau von Babel*, ii, 366.

This shift in outlook owes to several developments, in each of which linguistic attitudes supported political concerns. First, by that time Christianity had in fact begun to exercise pan-European expectations, seeking to establish hierarchical institutions that were networked to carry out its administration and to cultivate shared practices and beliefs as a way of defining, maintaining, and expanding the faith. Second, such an exercise necessarily required the assistance of writing. This period witnessed, indeed, the proliferation of Bibles, commentaries, and other heuristic works, all of them written in Latin and all of them helping to define a limited class of *literati* who alone were able to participate fully in political and ecclesiastical administration. And third, it is around this same time, not coincidentally, that various vernacular traditions underwent significant and diverse expansion: critical grammatical works like the Icelandic *First Grammatical Treatise* and Sir Raimon Vidal's Provençal *Razos de trobar* date to the period, and to the following centuries stylistic ones like the Icelandic *Prose Edda* or the Welsh *Bardic Grammar* and literary traditions like Provençal lyrics and the Icelandic sagas. In such a context, the efflorescence of painted representations of the Tower, particularly after the eleventh century,[33] affirms concern over the reality and development of multilingualism and belief in the importance of a mythic common language for the functioning of the Christian world. Outside of iconography and myth, this same anxiety manifested itself in an insistence on Latin as the language of government, the church, and political power, on the conduct of all kinds of business through writing, and on the effective exclusions of some groups (such as women) from both kinds of sociolinguistic activity. In effect, such procedures fashioned a world that, while perhaps more efficient than the one it replaced, ultimately endeavored to resist variation and change and instead to reproduce the imagined communicative achievement of the time before Babel.

For an emblem of this world, I return to a passage I've already cited (*Paradise Lost*, 12.56–61) in which Milton uses *hubbub* to describe the 'hideous gabble' of post-Babel speech:

> Forthwith a hideous gabble rises loud
> Among the Builders; each to other calls
> Not understood, till hoarse, and all in rage,
> As mockt they storm; great laughter was in Heav'n
> And looking down, to see the hubbub strange
> And hear the din.

---

[33] Eco, *The Search for the Perfect Language*, 17.

Only a century old at the time *Paradise Lost* was written, *hubbub* is an onomatopoeic word that described, initially, a 'confused noise of a multitude shouting or yelling; esp. the confused shouting of a battle-cry or "hue and cry" by wild or savage races'. Its first recorded use, according to the *OED*, illustrates a twofold linguistic anxiety, comparing as it does the 'confused noise' of African languages to that of Irish: the Ichthiophagi of Africa, William Watreman observes in his 1555 translation of Boemus's *Fardle of facions conteining the aunciente maners of Affrike and Asia*, 'flocke together to go drincke…shouting as they go with an yrishe whobub'.[34] Beyond this striking contemporary anxiety, which is characteristic of the early modern global expansion of English, Milton's word choice joins the moral and institutional imperatives of Christianity to the xenophobia of Greece and Rome. The wicked, in other words, are at once damned *and βαρβάροι*. That a simple word like *hubbub* can encapsulate such capacious traditions says much about the acceptance and naturalization of the Babel account of change and variation.

International language and perfect communication

Later, in a letter to Catherine the Great dated 26 May 1767, Voltaire claimed to have heard a woman at Versailles observe, 'What a great shame that the bother at the tower of Babel should have got language all mixed up; but for that, everyone would always have spoken French'.[35] As stereotypical as such a comment from the age of the ancien régime might seem, there is more than hubris or xenophobia here. As I noted above, global European expansion in the early modern period made it increasingly difficult to adhere to the biblical tradition of a monogenetic language fragmented into seventy-two other languages at the Tower of Babel; it became obvious that there were (and are) many more languages than seventy-two, and also that many of the ones newly encountered in North America, Africa, and Asia could have had little direct connection to European languages, not to mention Hebrew. At the same time, Enlightenment belief in the power of reason and the intrinsic merit of human beings rendered an unnatural, punitive origin for language change and variation more difficult to accept intellectually. Even in these circumstances, however, the Tower model for change and variation has remained both adaptable and persistent. That the events of Babel could

---

[34] *OED*, s. v., *hubbub*. Cf. Seth Lerer's discussion of *hubbub* in *Inventing English: A Portable History of the Language* (New York: Columbia University Press, 2007), 149–50.

[35] Quoted in David Crystal, *Language Death* (Cambridge: Cambridge University Press, 2000), 28.

have fashioned this kind of general template for organizing linguistic experience, long after spiritual much less literal belief in them has ceased to be commonplace, suggests again that their appeal is not simply linguistic but rather to some profoundly felt anxiety about separation.

Already in the *Paradiso* Dante had come to question Hebrew's originary status by having Adam observe,

> The tongue I spoke had vanished utterly,
> long before Nimrod's people turned their hands
> To the work beyond their capability.

God's linguistic gift as Dante here conceives it, then, is not a specific language but the ability to speak—something like universal grammar—and in this way Dante redeems the status of all European vernaculars and implicitly invokes Genesis 10 as the competing narrative that dialogically has helped fashion the form and coherence of language change:

> That man should speak is Nature's own behest;
> but that you speak in this way or that
> nature lets you decide as you think best.[36]

The French aristocrat's substitution of her own national language for the Hebrew of tradition offers still another use of the Babel story, not by following Dante's substitution of critical faculties for a natural language but by appropriating the story for her own nativist purposes. Her claim reflects a compromise between biblical tradition and Enlightenment thinking with which many other early modern thinkers were comfortable.

Over a century earlier the Englishman Richard Verstegan had noted that Goropius Becanus had claimed it was in fact Teutonic that was 'the moste ancient language of the world; yea the same that Adam spake in *Paradise*'.[37] Still others traced to Eden, or identified as the original language, Spanish, German, Swedish, Hungarian, and Celtic.[38] More modest proposals (which were also more reminiscent of Dante's views) were advanced by critics like the anonymous author of the 1689 etymological dictionary *Gazophylacium Anglicanum*, who merely traced their own language to the linguistic big bang of Babel. Before Babel, the author observes, 'all the then World speke one and the same Dialect, supposed to be Hebrew', but Babel gave rise to many languages, 'of which, the primitive language of the Nation was one, and, had it not been corrupted, perhaps as good and intelligible as the best; but being so alter'd by

---

[36] Dante, *The Paradiso*, trans. John Ciardi (New York: Mentor, 1970), XXVI.124–6, 130–2.
[37] Verstegan, *A Restitution of Decayed Intelligence* (1605; rpt. Ilkley: Scolar Press, 1976), 190.
[38] Eco, *The Search for the Perfect Language*, 95–103.

the aforesaid Accidents, it has quite lost its primitive Glory, as well as that of the French, and other Nations'.[39] For his part, Verstegan was skeptical of such arguments, though he allows that if Teutonic is not the first post-Babel language, 'it cannot bee denied to bee one of the moste ancientest of the world'.[40] In this way, the myth of Babel came to accommodate the competing narrative of Genesis 10 and, along with it, language variation and change, English nationalism, and the early modern insistence on distancing the present, positively or negatively, from what had come before.

Perfect languages offer another example of the way in which sentiments reflected in the Babel story have framed and made real variation and change. Rooted in kabbalistic traditions as well as in Christian exegesis on the Garden of Eden and the Tower, perfect languages are artificial constructions that attempt to transcend the vagaries of communication produced by time and space. Whether numerical, symbolic, or lexical, they seek to offer a medium of communication that is transparent, unmediated, and reflective of constant universal truths, and in this way they foster community and intellectual achievement. They seek, in short, to reproduce the unchanging language from before Babel. Flourishing in the sixteenth and seventeenth centuries in particular, the perfect languages developed by scholars like George Dalgarno and John Wilkins have all the esoteric characteristics of a cultic secret code, known only to a few and never acquiring many users, much less enough to restore the presumptively lost linguistic world. Having at length identified the natural categories from which all concepts in general derive, for example, Wilkins proceeds to devise a symbolic 'philosophic language' that both manifests the conceptual reality of the universe and in so doing provides for perfect communication: 'The first thing to be enquired after, is to find out fitting Marks for the common Genus's or Heads in the former tables of Integrals, which are there reduced to the number of forty.'[41] There follow seventy pages demonstrating this 'philosophic language', which is written in a kind of geometric script in which characters receive additional lines in a fixed pattern reflecting the 'tables of Integrals'.

By the late eighteenth century, there emerged still another heuristic for change and variation that sustained the Babel model and its narrative of perfect communication: the discipline of linguistics. Beginning with Sir William Jones's 1786 hypothesis of the common origins of Sanskrit, Greek, Latin, Gothic, and Celtic, comparative linguistics in particular focused

---

[39] *Gazophylacium Anglicanum* (1689; rpt. Menston: Scolar Press, 1969), a4^r.

[40] Verstegan, *A Restitution of Decayed Intelligence*, 192–3.

[41] Wilkins, *An Essay towards a Real Character, and a Philosophical Language* (1668; rpt. Menston: Scolar Press, 1968), 386. On Wilkins see further Eco, *The Search for the Perfect Language*, 238–59.

increasingly on the definition of principles of historical reconstruction and on the classification of languages that such reconstruction allows. Jones, to be sure, built on the work of previous scholars, but it was his own 'Third Discourse' to the Asiatick Society that he helped found in Calcutta that specifically served as both a catalyst to nineteenth-century philologists like Bopp and Müller and, for several schools of modern linguistic thought, a critical affirmation of the importance of what lies beyond variation and change. Bopp and Müller, for example, devoted themselves to the reconstruction of Indo-European, the parent language from which nearly every European language, as well as several subcontinental Indian ones, evolved. Moving back through regular sound changes like the Great Vowel Shift and the First Consonant Shift, philologists traced modern language forms to medieval ones, medieval ones to antique ones, antique ones to hypothetical ones, and hypothetical ones to a Babel-like time, perhaps in the fifth millennium BC and perhaps in the area between the Black and Caspian Seas, when Indo-European speakers began to migrate and their putatively single language began to diversify.

While I don't mean to suggest either that comparative philologists believed in a literal Tower of Babel or that their specific goal was the reconstruction of a perfect language, I do mean to underscore that the descent of language as they traced it harmonized well with the Babel model of Genesis 11. Similarly, and from wholly different critical perspectives, although neither structural nor transformational linguistics share much methodologically with Indo-European studies, much less biblical exegesis, they, too, concentrate on the recovery of a moment beyond variation and change—the timeless synchrony of Saussure's *langue* or Chomsky's ideal speaker-listener. In bracketing off the mistakes and misstatements of ordinary speech, both approaches imagine the possibility of language uncomplicated by the realities of daily communication.

The Babel model embraces still other schools of linguistics. It may seem just as counter-intuitive to link Benjamin Lee Whorf with Bopp and Müller and then with Saussure and Chomsky, since the primary concerns of Whorf's research and reputation were the individual and sometimes mutually exclusive ways in which languages represent empirical phenomena. The Sapir-Whorf hypothesis, to which he lends his name, embraces Genesis 10 in its insistence that language is infinitely variable and significantly determinative of speakers' perceptions of their experience, so that speakers of different languages might be judged to live, effectively, in different worlds. And yet it was Whorf who wondered about the viability of 'restoring a possible common language of the human race or perfecting an ideal natural tongue constructed of the original psychological significance of sounds, perhaps a future common speech, into which all our varied languages may be assimilated, or, putting it differently, to whose terms they may be reduced'.[42]

Most recently, this same aspiration for a common language and unmediated communication informed the controversial linguistics of Joseph Greenberg, who sought to construct super-families of languages, encompassing, for example, enormous numbers of American Indian languages, and from these languages to reconstruct in turn a proto-world language.[43] Like St Augustine, Verstegan, Bopp, Chomsky, and even Truss—in imagining, as she does, perfect punctuation for a perfect language—Greenberg begins with the presumption that there is or can be or once was a unified language, providing stable and unmediated communication to all speakers. In all these approaches, change and variation and the way they reflect the realities of human social experience, travel, and history are, in a word, wrong. They and the historical specifics they articulate are to be resisted and undone. And if variation and change attest to these specifics, then an unchanging language of perfect communication would in several senses transcend them.

In this chapter so far, in tracing out ways in which the Tower of Babel has offered an epitome of thinking about change and variation and the anxiety they generate, I have touched on the mythic, the exegetical, the fanciful, and the scientific. I want to conclude this portion of my discussion by looking at another kind of narrative, one that seems to embody all these qualities: Esperanto. While there have been other artificial and artificially modified languages before and since its creation—including Volapük, Latino Sine Flexione, and Tutonish—none has had the success of Esperanto in terms of numbers of speakers, institutional support, or public recognition.[44] Like most of these languages, Esperanto is meant to be auxiliary, supplementing but not replacing indigenous languages. Also like most of these languages, Esperanto points towards a world in which communication is immediate and straightforward and language is transparent and constant. As with the Tower of Babel and perfect languages, therein lie several provocative contradictions.

While Esperanto may claim to be a world language dissociated from any particular nationality, region, or group, for instance, it is very much the creation of a single individual—Dr Lazar (or Ludwik) Zamenhof—and the

---

[42] Whorf, *Language, Thought, and Reality: Selected Writings*, ed. John B. Carroll (Cambridge, MA: Technology Press of Massachusetts Institute of Technology, 1956), 12.

[43] See Greenberg, *Indo-European and Its Closest Relatives: The Eurasiatic Language Family* (Stanford, CA: Stanford University Press, 2000). A great many linguists have called into question the reliability of Greenberg's conclusions and methods, which claim genetic connections among sounds or words on the basis of morphological similarities that seem to be no more than chance.

[44] The Conlang Directory of International Communication lists well over 150 invented languages. See http://www.langmaker.com/db/condir_internationalcommunication.htm.

circumstances of his life. Born into Tsarist Russia in 1859, Zamenhof grew up in a polyglot society at a time of active suppression of ethnic groups. As a Haskalah Jew, he was raised in both strongly intellectual and religious traditions, and while a medical student in Warsaw he became actively engaged with Jewish groups involved in emigration to Palestine and the United States.[45] Zamenhof's interest in the integrative qualities of language, religion, and society emerged from the experiences of this specific time and place, and already at the age of ten he wrote a five-act tragedy based on the Tower of Babel and staged in Bialystok. By nineteen he had begun developing and teaching early versions of Esperanto (meaning 'one who hopes'), although the earliest grammar did not appear until the 1887 Russian-language *The International Language: Preface and Complete Manual (for Russians)*.[46] Described very briefly, Esperanto is an absolutely regular language, with no grammatical exceptions, minimal inflectional morphology, and a derivational morphology that, like Wilkins's 'philosophical language', allows for the easy and consistent conversion of one part of speech into another. Semantically, while it is not an avowed perfect language, it does seek to represent experiential categories that transcend situation, time, and geography.[47] In the eastern European political climate of Esperanto's formative period, dominated by contentious and repressed ethnic and national identification, the popularity of this regularized language grew quickly, leading to two landmark events in 1905: first, Zamenhof published the *Fundamento de Esperanto*, an extensive grammar that has served as the reference point for all discussions of Esperanto and its growth, and, second, the First International Congress of Esperantists took place in Boulogne.

From these beginnings, two issues have remained prominent in Esperanto studies that have particular relevance to the anxiety associated with language change and variation. The first is grammatical, involving the nature of Esperanto and the distinction between correct and incorrect forms. As a living if artificial language, Esperanto very early became subject to the same forces that change completely natural languages, moving away from what Zamenhof had designed and raising the question of whether the language should be left to the use of its speakers or monitored in some way to preserve a particular, presumptively essential, character. Put another way, the question

---

[45] Peter G. Foster, *The Esperanto Movement* (The Hague: Mouton, 1982), 51–2; Marjorie Boulton, *Zamenhof: Creator of Esperanto* (London: Routledge, 1960), 23–7; Eco, *The Search for the Perfect Language*, 324–6.

[46] Foster, *The Esperanto Movement*, 50.

[47] See further George Alan Conner *et al.*, *Esperanto: The World Interlanguage* (London: A. S. Barnes, 1948).

early Esperantists faced was to what extent should the language, created almost instantaneously in its own Edenic moment, be allowed to advance towards its own Tower of Babel? The *Fundamento* provided an answer if not the resolution to this question by not only establishing the language's basic grammar but also articulating the essential paradox of a language meant to be of the people that can be maintained only through authoritarian management of what those people say. While it lays out all the grammatical rules, 'in which nobody has the right to make change', it also claims that the language can be adapted to accommodate new expressions, 'as is done in any other language'. Indeed, according to the *Fundamento*, 'The material master of this language is the whole world and anyone who wishes can publish in or about this language all works that he wishes, and can make use of the language for every possible kind of action'. The *Fundamento* complicated the issue of change and variation even further by going on to embed Esperanto, the pre-eminently neutral language, in government policy. Once Esperanto is 'accepted by the governments of the most important nations and such nations by a special law guarantee to Esperanto certain life and use', the *Fundamento* claims, then 'an authoritative committee' can be established to change 'the foundation of the language', if necessary. Until that time, Esperanto 'must strictly remain absolutely unchanged'.[48] In this division of responsibility, governments would have the authority to approve neologisms but not alterations of the language's grammar. All by itself Esperanto thus came to express the historical dialogue between narratives of change as natural and those of change as divisive.

By the Fourth International Congress, held in Dresden in 1908, Zamenhof, while guarding his privilege as the inventor of Esperanto, was attempting to disqualify himself as its pre-eminent grammatical arbiter. The language sub-committee of the Congress there elected an Academy from its own membership, charged with the task of conserving the basic principles of Esperanto and also, on a two-thirds vote of its members, mandating change. In fact, no radical changes were ever implemented, and throughout Zamenhof's life (he died in 1917) tension remained between anti-reformists, who considered the *Fundamento* absolutely unchangeable, and those who sought to allow Esperanto to transform like any living language.[49] In the process, in 1907, yet another language developed from Esperanto: Ido, which attempted to respond to the most frequent criticisms about concord, the accusative case, and morphological derivation in Esperanto. Rooted in a more fundamental tension over the nature of linguistic change and variation, the tension

---

[48] Quoted in Foster, *The Esperanto Movement*, 90, 111.
[49] See Foster, *The Esperanto Movement*, 154–66.

between reformists and anti-reformists of Esperanto could never be finally resolved, because it rested on a paradox reminiscent of perfect languages and the Tower of Babel: the maintenance of a putatively natural language by decidedly unnatural means.

The second issue involving Esperanto that has significance for the study of change and variation is the claim, made early and insistently, that the language is ethnically and politically disinterested, a claim that often took on a millenarian quality. The 'Declaration of Boulogne' issued at the 1905 Congress, for example, pronounced Esperanto a 'neutrally human language' that 'would give men of different nations the possibility of understanding between one another' and could be a 'peace-keeping language' in countries where there was linguistic contention. All this recalls Postel's aspiration for the revival of Hebrew. Indeed, in his own speech to the Congress Zamenhof, invoking the Tower of Babel and Pentecost and ending with a prayer for God to reunite humanity, spoke about a golden age when all people would understand one another and there would be no more linguistic confusion leading to war.[50] Yet the notion of a politically neutral, living language, echoed at the 1906 Second International Congress in Vienna and afterwards,[51] was as unreachable as centralized management of change and variation in a living language. As there was tension between reformists and anti-reformists, so there was tension between local, national Esperanto organizations and the international movement centered on Zamenhof. The paradox of a politically neutral, living language is perhaps emblemized by the League of Nations' response to Esperanto. An avowedly neutral organization, the League nonetheless consistently supported the language. In 1920 (at its first meeting) the League debated a proposal to make Esperanto a second language for all and thus a de facto world language; in 1921 it legislated a study of the status and viability of Esperanto; and in 1924 it passed a resolution that recommended the use of Esperanto in telegrams.

More pointedly political, as Tsarist Russia had suppressed Esperanto as a threat to its authoritarian rule, so the Soviet Union initially supported it as a means to disseminate socialism around the world. In 1921 the Soviet Union even formed the Soviet Esperanto Union for this very purpose. This same international applicability led France to resist League of Nations resolutions in favor of Esperanto and the Soviet Union itself, eventually, to reject it and imprison Esperantists in the Gulag.[52] Nazism, the other face of

---

[50] Foster, *The Esperanto Movement*, 81–9.
[51] Boulton, *Zamenhof: Creator of Esperanto*, 106.
[52] Foster, *The Esperanto Movement*, 172–203.

twentieth-century totalitarianism, invested Esperanto with equal political force. In *Mein Kampf*, Adolf Hitler, coming from much the same sociolinguistic background as Zamenhof, had said: 'As long as the Jew has not become the master of the other peoples, he must speak their languages whether he likes it or not, but as soon as they become his slaves, they would all have to learn a universal language (Esperanto, for instance!) so that by this additional means the Jews could more easily dominate them.'[53] With its avowed political neutrality attracting increasing political attention, in 1935 the German Esperanto Association excluded all Jews from its ranks and affirmed its desire to advance Nazi objectives; the Association even offered to translate Hitler's works into Esperanto. Seen as the medium of communist and international thinking antithetical to the goals of the Third Reich, however, Esperanto was outlawed in Germany in July of 1936.

In short, Esperanto could not escape politics, not of France, Germany, or Russia. Even the claim of political neutrality, as the efforts of the League of Nations indicate, itself proved political. The language has served as a cipher to be invested with successive cultural meanings: initially, for Zamenhof, a means to international peace; to the Tsarists, a weapon of ethnic revolution; to early Soviets, a vehicle to disseminate socialism; to later Soviets, a manifestation of bourgeois internationalism; and to the Nazis, an instrument of Jewish and communist separatism. For his part, Zamenhof increasingly devoted himself to his millenarian concerns, moving his focus from Judaism to Hillelism to what he called Homaranismo, a quasi-religious concept expressing belief in the brotherhood of all human beings, rejection of racism and ethnic prejudice, and acceptance of equal rights for all. In 1913, in fact, he renounced control of Esperanto in order to devote his time and effort to Homaranismo.[54]

Esperanto is often regarded as the work of a crank, utilized only by cranks for cranky purposes. It is for this very reason that I have dwelt at some length on it. Grammatically, it does indeed have a rigidity that poorly reproduces the expressive flexibility of natural languages; and if its semantic suppositions about universally shared truths and language's ability to express them may have seemed merely odd in the late nineteenth century, they are completely untenable in a post-modern world. The very notion of an individual building a language evokes the quirky charm of an eccentric intellectual and the monomania of a messianic complex. Belief that such a language might ever

---

[53] Quoted in Foster, *The Esperanto Movement*, 221; see also 218–19. On Nazi suppression of Esperanto, see Boulton, *Zamenhof: Creator of Esperanto*, 208–18.

[54] Boulton, *Zamenhof: Creator of Esperanto*, 178.

be widely used seems naive or disingenuous or both, and the entire enterprise invests language academies with far more direction over usage than has ever proved possible. For all these reasons, competency in the language— not to mention fluency—raises questions of priorities and time management, questions that if anything become more insistent as the world, a century after Zamenhof's death, seems closer to the dissolution that his millenarian linguistic vision sought to hold at bay.

And yet, Esperanto shares a good deal with the biblical, exegetical, and scientific traditions I have already considered. Like them, the language conceptualizes change and variation as problems in themselves, which lead to additional communication problems among speakers and thence to additional social problems, like conflict and war. Even leaving aside Zamenhof's belief in a global religion, which the leading Esperantists rejected anyway, Esperanto conceives of a world in which perfect, unmediated communication is possible, and, once possible, remains. Far from Leibniz's best of all possible worlds, our own world is a damaged and deteriorating one, with language as both sign and cause of the current situation, yet it is also a world that has the potential for improvement. It is not coincidental that Zamenhof should have invoked Babel, for like St Augustine, early grammarians, and later philologists, Zamenhof presupposed a fundamentally conservative, even reactionary, view of the world. Esperanto may be a language, but ultimately what it resists, as its origin and history suggest, is the extra-linguistic sphere of politics and ethnicity. In this vein, the very idea of a neutral language, central to Zamenhof's thinking, is preposterous, for it is the absence of neutrality— partiality of one kind or another—that gives speakers a reason to talk, something to say, someone to say it to, and the means to say it. In constructing his auxiliary language, Zamenhof, again like St Augustine, worked at cross-purposes with the nature of change and variation in natural languages.

In many ways, then, Esperanto enacts a Babel-model of communication and thereby epitomizes many of the issues I consider in this book. The paradox that confronted early Esperantists—that of maintaining a natural language through unnatural control—is the very paradox that animates the dialogue of Babel. That being the case, it is striking that speakers of Esperanto should be judged cranks, when those who champion global English and rail against variant pronunciations, the influx of non-Anglophones into predominantly Anglophonic countries, bilingualism, the development of new varieties through second language acquisition, and changes in usage— all of which share Babel's presuppositions about perfect communication and its anxieties about change—are not. Indeed, if Zamenhof worked at cross-purposes with change and variation, the same might be said of attempts to engineer pronoun usage, vocabulary, and contact between English and other languages. It is also striking that the narrative of Babel model should provide such explanatory power for responses to change and variation, since the ultimate moral of Nimrod's efforts is that perfect communication is not simply impossible; it is lethal. Like Icarus or Prometheus, Nimrod aspired to be god-like and was destroyed for his efforts. Perfect communication would seem to be even more lethal than wings or fire, since Icarus and Prometheus failed as individuals but Nimrod's downfall was the world's as well. Encouraged by narratives of change and variation, we may resist the linguistic realities of this world—the grammatical, pragmatic, and demographic fluctuations across time—in pursuit of a golden era wherein meaning was transparent, language constant, and communication flawless. But in so doing we relive Nimrod's pride and resist the extra-linguistic world in an attempt to transform it in our own image. As the history of Esperanto suggests, this world, ultimately, may be as irresistible as the linguistic one.

Diglossia, Early Modern English, and dialect-writing

While the Tower of Babel supplies a theoretical model for change and variation in the English language—the linguistic equivalent of a unified theory—narratives of fiction supply that model's details. They can and do make change real in two ways. First, following White's analysis of narrative, fictional stories offer competing ways of remembering and representing linguistic phenomena. In the case of the origins of change and variation, the dialogue between Genesis 10 and Genesis 11 emblemizes the competition between representing these origins in ordinary human experience (i.e., language is shown or presumed to change as naturally as Noah's descendants moved about) or in extraordinary divine punishment of human pride. The competition represented in English fiction over the centuries is more complex than that in the biblical account, however, reflecting as it does the intimate connections between language, art, and daily experience. As the sociolinguistic variables of class, ethnicity, nationality, and age have historically continued to produce variation, so fiction, increasingly, has served as a forum for more involved, persistent conflict and argument.

The second way by which fiction makes change and variation real involves its mimetic qualities. To the extent that fiction seeks to evoke a world recognizable by its readers, that is, it portrays human experience with at least some degree of familiarity: characters need to act, think, and, most importantly for the current discussion, speak in fashions that resemble those known (if not used) by readers. If a writer is to make any particular point about a speech act like a church sermon, such as that the congregation is ironically indifferent to the message it hears, the portrayal of the scene must have enough of the qualities of a real-life sermon for the reader to see the parallel. And the same is obviously true of speakers' discursive strategies, conversational structures, and other aspects of how language mediates human behavior. As I will suggest below, this must be the case even in works of science fiction or fantasy, which portray worlds that may be profoundly different from the ones their readers experience but which require some similarities for the reader to make an invested identification with them. By the same token, so long as a threshold of familiarity is met, fiction may represent parts of the world—including the role of language—as writers might fear or wish them to be, even if these representations would seem clearly to differ from readers' lived experience. In view of fiction's power to make change real, then, and in order to suggest the range of both representations of linguistic variation and the anxieties these representations can evoke, I want to survey a range of works from throughout the chronology of English literature. My intention is not to suggest an evolutionary development in fictional treatments of change and variation, though certain devices are historically specific. Nor is it to argue that one particular treatment has been inevitable or even predominant; there certainly are exceptions to what I talk about here. Rather, I want to sketch out some of the conflicting narratives of change, variation, and the social issues they reflect in order to lay open how fictional narratives have served as one means for speakers to organize their thoughts on language and channel real-world responses to it.

I have already alluded to the biblical account of Pentecost, which shares with the Tower of Babel the connection of change and variation to other-worldly causes and consequences: both stories depend on God's intervention in human affairs, elicited by the weaknesses of humans and directed, ultimately, at their improvement. This same notion that change and variation are non-normative and even supernatural informs several written traditions, both English and non-English. One particularly well-developed tradition shaped English historiography of the eleventh, twelfth, and thirteenth centuries, a time following the Norman Conquest and the imposition of a Francophone nobility. Like any other sizeable region, the British Isles had always been multilingual, with English, Latin, Cornish, Welsh, and Gaelic co-existing in various regions. The Norman Conquest introduced not simply a new language to this repertoire—French—but also a more rigid structural differentiation among languages known as diglossia, in which the use of a specific language helps to define specific domains and speech acts. Conventionally, Latin was the language of ecclesiastical and many legal domains, French of the court and law, and English, the only language of most of

England's inhabitants, a largely oral language, heard in many places (including the court and legal proceedings) but restricted in writing, at least in the early Middle Ages, to ephemeral traditions of lyrics, romances, and chronicles. To be sure, this situation changed as the centuries advanced, with more English writing appearing in more domains and with some multilingual individuals exploiting for stylistic effect the lexical, syntactic, and rhetorical resources of Latin, French, and English. For example, John Gower wrote a long narrative poem in each of these languages. His was a situationally strategic approach to multilingualism and diglossia, leading him to offer an interpretation of the unnatural outcome of Babel (which I quoted above) that matched neither his own multilingual background nor the well-established distribution of languages in universities and business enterprises but that did fit his lament about the decline of English society in the days of King Richard II. While fluent in Latin and French as well as English, and while well versed in the status of each within England's linguistic repertoire, Gower could situate what was in effect the origin of his own multilingualism in Nimrod's sinful pride, simply because of the narrative demands of the *Confessio*.[55]

Although I do not want to minimize the nuances in the multilingualism of someone like Gower, I do want to assert that the infrastructure of diglossia continued to inform England's linguistic repertoire until the waning of the Middle Ages, offering a theoretical model that assigned particular roles for particular languages and therefore conservatively working against changes in any language's grammar and discursive functions. Diglossia also provided a framework for sociolinguistic behavior and, in turn, for the mediation of non-linguistic concerns through language in ways that could facilitate the divergence of linguistic reality and discursive representation from one another. For post-Conquest English historiography—written mostly in Latin but also in French and English—the reality of diglossia did in fact contrast with narrative accounts that represented England as predominantly monolingual by passing silently over events in which English, French, and Latin would have co-occurred. While chroniclers like Orderic Vitalis and Richard Devizes noted, respectively, that William I failed in his attempts to learn English and that the equally Francophone Queen Eleanor (the wife of William's great-grandson Henry II) lacked the ability to speak English,[56] and while other writers

---

[55] See further Machan, 'Medieval Multilingualism and Gower's Literary Practice', *Studies in Philology*, 103 (2006), 1–25.

[56] Orderic Vitalis, *The Ecclesiastical History of Orderic Vitalis*, ed. and trans. Marjorie Chibnall, 6 vols. (Oxford: Clarendon, 1969–80), ii, 257; Richard of Devizes, *The Chronicle of Richard of Devizes of the Time of King Richard the First*, ed. and trans. John T. Appleby (London: Thomas Nelson and Sons, 1963), 59.

implicated diglossia in England's social and geographic landscapes, most episodes in which language contact would have occurred pass without comment.
This is the case not only with daily business or religious encounters in England
but also in battles between the English and their Saracen foes on the Crusades
and even in battles that do not involve the English.

Such silence expresses the resistance to change and variation that Babel
mythologizes, but an even stronger expression comes from the depiction of
multilingualism as the byproduct of preternatural experiences like Pentecost.
If early historiographers bypass English–French contact, that is, they also do
much to define variation in general as outside the norm of ordinary human
experience and often occurring with dangerous as well as other-worldly
consequences. It is Orderic Vitalis who again provides an apt illustration in
his account of the French and English affirmation of William I as England's
proper king. 'But at the prompting of the devil, who hates everything good,'
Orderic observes, 'a sudden disaster and portent of future catastrophes
occurred. For when Archbishop Ealdred asked the English, and Geoffrey
bishop of Coutances asked the Normans, if they would accept William as
their king, all of them gladly shouted out with one voice if not in one language
that they would. The armed guard outside, hearing the tumult of the joyful
crowd in the church and the harsh accents of a foreign tongue, imagined that
some treachery was afoot, and rashly set fire to some of the buildings'.[57] The
joyous affirmation of William may suggest the harmony and righteousness
of his reign, but the devil's appearance brings together language variation,
social upheaval, and the supernatural, rendering all three as latent, literally
inflammatory threats to the prosperity of post-Conquest England. Other
chroniclers, such as Walter Map, Ralph Coggeshall, William of Newburgh,
and Gerald of Wales, correlate multilingualism with enchanted knights, evil
spirits, spectral children, and pygmies, while in attributing glossolalia to
St Bernard and others Gerald also evokes Pentecost and attaches hagiographic
and spiritual qualities to language variation:

There is the story of St. Bernard, who spoke to the Germans in the French language,
which they were wholly ignorant of, and filled them with such devotion and com-
punction that he called forth floods of tears from their eyes. With the greatest of ease
he softened the hardness of their hearts so that they did and believed all he told them.
Yet when an interpreter faithfully set forth to them, in their own tongue, everything
Bernard had said, they were not moved at all. It is clear from this incident that what
was accomplished was more the result of holiness than of words.[58]

---

[57] Orderic Vitalis, *The Ecclesiastical History*, ii, 185.
[58] Gerald of Wales, *The Jewel of the Church*, ed. and trans. John J. Hagen. (Leiden: E. J. Brill, 1979),
117. Hagen notes that this incident is also recorded in the *Vita et Res Gestae Sancti Bernardi Libris*

St Bernard's accomplishment may well have resulted more from holiness than from words, but Gerald's words testify as much for the displacement of social anxiety to language as for Bernard's sanctity. A Norman claim on the English throne rested, in the first instance, on a tenuous story (much amplified by Norman historians after 1066) that Edward the Confessor had committed the kingdom to William of Normandy, an arrangement that had been accepted and then treacherously ignored by Harold Godwinsson, Edward's nephew and immediate successor. More than this, the Norman claim rested on the success of the Conquest and subsequent reorganization of the Anglo-Saxon church, courts, and political system, which included positioning of Normans in the most influential positions. The Normans may have felt the justice of their claim, and they certainly highlighted Anglo-Saxon foibles in order to present themselves as God's scourge, but the historiographic presentation of variation and change betrays an anxiety about their presence in England. Through discursive practices that did not simply erase English–French contact but also displaced all multilingualism to the realm of the dangerous and supernatural, Norman historiographers did much to exclude variation and change from the orbit of ordinary human experience. In the process they also did much to justify Norman political activities. By muting the sociolinguistic consequences of the Conquest—the inescapable fact of multilingualism and French–English contact in England— they also muted much post-Conquest regnal upheaval, including the twelfth-century anarchy during the reign of King Stephen, as well as the daily evidence that the Normans had appeared in the country as invaders. Because of the breach in writing, history, and tradition that they themselves produced, the Normans would have benefitted from the suppression of all such breaches, and the representation of change and variation in post-Conquest chronicles, whatever the chroniclers' individual motivations, served this very purpose.

By the early modern period, England's diglossia had weakened considerably. The Reformation produced English prayer books and Bible translations and mandated the use of English, rather than Latin, in religious services, giving impetus to the use of English in other domains. English had already begun to pervade business activities, and by 1600 it had largely replaced French in courts of law; throughout the seventeenth and eighteenth centuries, it became the dominant language in grammar schools and at Oxford and Cambridge. And yet even in this period diglossia and the resistance to change and variation that it modeled continued to animate rhetorical representations

Septem Comprehensae, by William of St Thierry. See further Machan, 'Language and Society in Twelfth-Century England', in Irma Taavitsainen *et al.* (eds.), *Placing Middle English in Context: Selected Papers from the Second Middle English Conference* (Berlin: Mouton de Gruyter, 2000), 43–66.

of language. For instance, even as the status of English continued to change, with expansion of its domains and codification efforts that I will consider in Chapter 5, the value of Latin was reiterated in various ways. Sir Thomas Elyot, in his widely read and reprinted 1531 *Book of the Governour*, encouraged the use of Latin 'as a familiar langage' for a noble's son, with him 'hauynge none other persons to serue him or kepyng hym company / but suche as can speake latine elegantly'.[59] Much as would be the case with Standard English in the centuries to come, Latin's value was understood to be the stature, durability, and constancy that accrued to it as a classical language and that granted permanence and intelligibility to works written in it, as opposed to those written in English. In his 'Of English Verse' the seventeenth-century poet Edmund Waller thus opined,

> But who can hope his lines should long
> Last in a daily changing tongue?
> While they are new, envy prevails;
> And as that dies, our language fails.
>
> When architects have done their part,
> The matter may betray their art;
> Time, if we use ill-chosen stone,
> Soon brings a well-built palace down.
>
> Poets that lasting marble seek,
> Must carve in Latin, or in Greek;
> We write in sand, our language grows,
> And, like the tide, our work o'erflows.[60]

Waller goes on to instance Chaucer, whom late-medieval poets like Thomas Hoccleve and John Lydgate had lauded for his 'illumination' of the English language, as someone whose verse the passage of time and the change of language have diminished and obscured. For Waller, change and variation in English cause us to forget who we are and the world, in turn, to forget us.

Inasmuch as paeans to Chaucer's accomplishments continued through the early modern period and into the nineteenth century—to Spenser, he was famously a 'well of English undefiled'—there is of course a contradiction between the putative originary status of Chaucer's language and its obscurity, between English as an established tradition and English as a flawed medium subject to time and changing in ways that impede communication. This

---

[59] Elyot, *The Boke Named the Gouernour* (1531; rpt. Menston: Scolar Press, 1970), 30.
[60] Waller, *The Poems of Edmund Waller*, ed. G. Thorn Drury (London: Lawrence and Bullen, 1893), 197–8.

contradiction appears with particular prominence in Sir Francis Kynaston's *Amorum Troili et Creseidae Libri Duo Priores Anglico-Latini*, issued in 1635 and containing, in facing-page format, the first two books of *Troilus and Criseyde* in English (printed in the already old-fashioned black letter font) and in a Latin translation (printed in roman italic). A sequence of prefatory poems by Kynaston and his acquaintances emphasizes that it is Chaucer's poetic and rhetorical achievement that justifies the volume. Kynaston himself begins his preface by referring (in Latin) to Chaucer as a 'venerable and ancient poet', who is 'the ornament of this island and distinguished glory of poetry'. Yet Dudley Digges (likewise in Latin) notes that by writing in English Chaucer, unlike Homer or Virgil, has restricted his own worthy reputation: 'The fame of such a name ought | to lie before the world, not just an island.' If Chaucer's reputation motivates the continued reading of his poetry, then, the impermanence of language effectively victimizes the *Troilus* and impedes communication between poet and reader. Chaucer, Kynaston notes, is 'not only growing old, diminishing in value beneath the obsolete and already scorned clothing of the ancient English idiom, but—how sad!—wholly wasting away and nearly dead'. Later, in his dedication to Book One, he avers, 'I desired the preservation from ruin and oblivion of his gem of poems, which was nearly lost and scarcely understood by us (at least as the favorite of none) because of ignorance of the obsolete words in it which have fallen into disuse'. In response, Kynaston's objective is to resist such obsolescence by securing Chaucer 'with the lasting support of Roman eloquence' and rendering him 'again stable and immobile through all ages (however many we have left)'.[61] Ironically, then, even as in the *Troilus* Chaucer earnestly entreats his audience to accept the fact that in language as well as in love, there is 'chaunge' in the course of a millennium, Kynaston (and others) advanced the poet's claim to greatness by citing this same 'chaunge' as both a sign of the world's transience and a justification for their own literary ministrations.

While the *Amorum Troili et Creseidae Libri* is not a unique early modern production—in 1690 William Hogg published a volume containing Latin translations of Milton's *Paradise Lost*, *Paradise Regained*, and *Samson Agonistes*—it is certainly unusual in the individual and collective effort it embodies. To this end, Kynaston and his coterie may well have been motivated largely by novelty, by a desire to see whether an exercise as peculiar as

---

61 Kynaston, ed. and trans., *Amorum Troili et Creseidae Libri Duo Priores Anglico-Latini* (London: John Lichfield, 1635), sigs. 1ʳ, †1ʳ, *ʳ, †1ᵛ, and A3ᵛ. See further Richard Beadle, 'The Virtuoso's *Troilus*', in Ruth Morse and Barry Windeatt (eds.), *Chaucer Traditions: Studies in Literature in Honour of Derek Brewer* (Cambridge: Cambridge University Press, 1990), 213–33; and Machan, 'Kynaston's *Troilus*, Textual Criticism, and the Renaissance Reading of Chaucer', *Exemplaria* 5 (1993), 161–83.

translating an English poem in accentual rhyme-royal stanzas into syllabic Latin verse could be carried off; and truth be told, they do just this rather well. At the same time, set against a background of shifting social classes, the incipient cultivation of nationalism, economic instability, and religious and political upheaval—set in a century that began with the uncertainty surrounding Elizabeth's succession, passed through the interregnum and Civil War, to the Restoration and Glorious Revolution—Kynaston's concerns with the dangerous mutability of language echo the concerns of others. Robert Crowley, the first editor of *Piers Plowman*, had observed already in 1550 that English had changed in so many ways since the poem's fourteenth-century composition as to leave Langland's language difficult and obscure: 'The Englishe is according to the tyme it was written in, and the sence somewhat darcke, but not so harde, but that it maye be vnderstande of such as wyll not sticke to breake the shell of the nutte for the kernelles sake'.[62] Even earlier, in the preface to his 1532 edition of Gower's *Confessio Amantis*, Thomas Berthelette tried (albeit halfheartedly) to put something of a positive spin on language change, asserting that it was deficiencies in English vocabulary that had led early writers to borrow words from 'latyne / frenche, and other langages'. But such borrowing ultimately only obscured communication for readers who were unable to read these languages, while the creation of new vocabulary does not set 'a president to vs / to heape [new words] in / where as nedeth not / and where as we haue all redy wordes approued and receyued of the same effecte and strength'.[63] Language change elicited similar (if similarly overstated) anxiety in discussions of English literature well after Kynaston's translation, as in 1700, when in the preface to his *Fables* John Dryden described Chaucer as 'the Father of English poetry... a perpetual Fountain of good Sense; learn'd in all Sciences', but went on to note that in the time since his death, Chaucer's language has become 'so obsolete, that his Sense is scarce to be understood'. 'Chaucer', Dryden confesses, 'is a rough Diamond, and must first be polish'd, e're he shines.'[64]

So, contemporary discursive traditions as well as novelty may indeed partly underlie the *Amorum Troili et Creseidae Libri*. At the same time, within the framework of the Babel model and early modern social upheaval, the volume evokes other anxieties associated with language change and variation. Kynaston himself, obviously, was an aristocrat. Born in 1587 he took degrees

---

[62] Crowley (ed.), *Piers Plowman* (London: Crowley, 1550), ii^{r-v}.

[63] Berthelette (ed.), *Jo. Gower de Confessione Amantis* (London: Berthelette, 1532), aaii^v. See further Machan, 'Thomas Berthelette and Gower's *Confessio*', *Studies in the Age of Chaucer* 18 (1996), 143–66.

[64] Dryden, *The Works of John Dryden*, ed. Edward Niles Hooker and H. T. Swedenberg, Jr. (Berkeley, CA: University of California Press, 1956–), vii, 39–40.

from both Oxford and Cambridge, was knighted in 1618 by James I, and in 1625 was made an esquire of the body to the new King Charles I. In 1635, with funding from the king, he founded the Museum Minervae, an institute devoted to the education of the sons of the nobility, and continued to write sonnets and romances until his death in 1642. Kynaston was thus wealthy, well connected, and professionally invested in the crown and high culture of England. If like his contemporaries he exaggerates the obscurity of Middle English in view of the continual change and variation in English, he also benefits in several ways from the exaggeration. For one thing, the ravages of time require the ministrations of men like Kynaston, specially educated and qualified to maintain continuity with the past and bring that past to the present. For another, men like Kynaston, uniquely qualified as they are, hold a prerogative on assertions about how language relates to history and society and about which issues are linguistic and which extra-linguistic. They represent a social group whose membership is closed but empowered to make sociolinguistic pronouncements for all speakers—in effect, to define the history of the language. And for a third, linguistic conservatism in the face of the disruptions of variation and change can serve as a model for a more general conservatism of political structure and social values. Because of his education and position, Kynaston would profit as surely from stability in English society as he would from the kind of stability he advocates in language—for however many (as he ominously observes) ages as we have left.

Not coincidentally, I think, the period in which Kynaston produced his translation is also the one that witnessed the increased emergence of the use of regional and social dialects for literary effect. I say 'for literary effect' because so long as English lacked a standard variety—codified in grammar books and dictionaries, inculcated in schools and universities, and constitutive of powerful domains of business, law, and government—all English writing was necessarily dialectal. As I noted in the previous chapter, prior to the modern period written variations among regional dialects could be copious and consistent enough to enable a poem written in one dialect, such as Bede's 'Death Song', to be translated into another. This kind of dialect translation persisted throughout the Middle English period, but the use of dialect differences for literary effect dates only to the fourteenth century and is sporadic for some time thereafter. In the *Second Shepherds' Play* of the fifteenth-century Towneley Cycle of mystery plays, for example, the sheep-stealing Mak, who is a farcical character and the victim of others' jokes and machinations, speaks in an erratic southern variety, setting him off from his fellow characters, whose English is northern. One of the Shepherds asks of him,

> Bot, Mak, is that sothe?
> Now take outt that Sothren tothe,
> And sett in a torde![65]

Caxton's preface to his 1490 edition of the *Eneydos* offers a similar example, when he tells the story of a merchant who said the northern *eggs* instead of the southern *eyren* and was accused of speaking French.[66] Even if true, this story has a local stylistic effect similar to that of Mak's 'Sothren tothe': it enhances a self-conscious passage on the importance of Caxton's new edition and provides emphasis in the way metaphors or other tropes might. Also like Mak's southern tooth, I would add, Caxton's vignette shows variation and change as disruptive and dangerous: Mak, after all, is a sheep stealer, and the merchant is angered by his exchange, which epitomizes the delay and business costs of having to remain in the Thames estuary until the wind shifts and he can sail to Zealand. Change and variation make even Caxton melancholic. His nostalgic summarizing comment, again, is that 'our langage now vsed varyeth ferre from that. whiche was vsed and spoken whan I was borne'.

Chaucer's 'The Reeve's Tale' offers a more sustained engagement with the expressive capabilities of language variation, describing as it does a bawdy and tempestuous encounter between a southern miller and his family and a pair of northern Cambridge clerks. The contrast between the characters and their speech patterns appears in the morphology, vocabulary, and lexicon of their first exchange:

> Aleyn spak first: 'al hayl, Symon, y-faith!
> Hou fares thy fair doghter and thy wyf?'
> 'Aleyn, welcome', quod Symkyn, 'by my lyf!
> And John also, how now, what do ye here?'
> 'Symond', quod John, 'by God, nede has na peer.
> Hym boes serve hymself that has na swayn,
> Or elles he is a fool, as clerkes sayn'.[67]

While speech differences among the characters are not topics in 'The Reeve's Tale', they do pervade it and necessarily seem to invite consideration of language variation as integral to the themes of the story, which revolve around pride, malice, violent sexuality, and overweening ambition. In this regard,

---

[65] A. C. Cawley (ed.), *The Wakefield Pageants in the Towneley Cycle* (Manchester: Manchester University Press, 1958), 48.

[66] William Caxton, *The Prologues and Epilogues of William Caxton*, ed. W. J. B. Crotch, EETS os 176 (1928; rpt. New York: Burt Franklin, 1971), 108.

[67] *The Riverside Chaucer*, ed. Larry D. Benson, 3rd edn. (Boston, MA: Houghton Mifflin, 1987), *Canterbury Tales*, 1.4023–8.

Chaucer's aberrant use of language—his mixing of regional varieties—offers the linguistic equivalent of the social upheaval that the tale describes. In language as well as theme, that is, 'The Reeve's Tale' depicts a frighteningly imbalanced world, maintained neither by the strictures of proscribed sexuality or social rank nor by the linguistic stability manifested in diglossia. Change and variation thereby become as alarming, even apocalyptic, as they are for Kynaston or the twelfth-century chroniclers.[68]

When I say that the early modern period witnessed an increase in the use of social and regional variation for literary effect, then, I might better say that it witnesses its creation. The efforts of Chaucer, Caxton, and the *Second Shepherds' Play* do not offer a consistent presentation of linguistic variation's rhetorical potential, even if they do, in various ways, suggest it produces the same kind of anxiety that I have discussed elsewhere in this chapter. By comparison, just as the early modern period featured the proliferation of grammars, dictionaries, and rhetorical manuals, all further helping to define a fixed written standard, so its writings displayed increasingly nuanced use of variation and change. As I will argue in Chapter 5, this connection is not fortuitous, since the identification of non-standard language, not to mention the rhetorical exploitation of it, requires the presence and acceptance of a standard language. It is at this point that, in the terminology of William Labov, variation and change cease to be indicators, becoming instead markers. Labov has in fact identified a three-stage development for the rhetorical significance of regional and non-standard forms, and these can be traced in English literature.[69] The initial stage is when a form is an indicator, evoking the speech patterns of some social group, whether social or regional, and connecting a speaker to that group. In the above passage from 'The Reeve's Tale', thus, Chaucer restricts to the Cambridge clerks the verbal inflection -s (rather than -eth) and the graph *a*, suggesting a pronunciation [a] or [ɑ], in words where some Middle English varieties had *o*, presumably for [o] (e.g., the final vowel in John's *na* as opposed to Symkyn's *also*). He thereby evokes speech associated with the north of England both through works and manuscripts produced there and through dialect translation of such features in non-northern works.

---

[68] For further discussion, including consideration of why the regional variety of 'The Reeve's Tale' lacks the humor in and of itself that is sometimes attributed to it, see Machan, *English in the Middle Ages*, 112–38.

[69] Labov, 'On the Mechanism of Linguistic Change', in John J. Gumperz and Dell Hymes (eds.), *Directions in Sociolinguistics: The Ethnography of Communication* (New York: Holt, Rinehart, and Winston, Inc., 1972), 512–38.

But as the desultory and disparate quality of such representations suggests, this kind of variation achieves only local rhetorical effects rather than evokes broadly shared conceptualizations of a variety within what might be called the ecology of languages, varieties, and domains in a speech community. It begins to do so in Labov's next stage, that of marker. Here, not simply are forms and varieties associated with a particular group but that association and the group themselves have recognizable sociolinguistic meanings—involving social rank or credibility, for example—which representations of the language can manipulate. Shakespeare's depiction of the northern language of the Scottish captain Jamy in *Henry V* offers a case in point: 'It sall be vary gud, gud feith, gud captens bath, and I sall quit you with gud leve, as I may pick occasion. That sall I, mary.' While this language shares certain graphic features with 'The Reeve's Tale' (as in *bath* for *both*), it goes beyond it through its contributions to a comic subplot involving the Irish captain Macmorris and the Welsh captain Fluellen, whose language is similarly spelled so as to evoke their own regional accents. More generally, such linguistic variation draws on traditions of comical Celtic stereotypes on the stage and contributes to the play's nationalizing themes centered on an England surrounded, in several senses, by a Celtic fringe. Similar nationalizing (even anti-foreign) traditions underwrite the presentation of the French princess Katherine, who, in a memorable passage, confuses English *foot* and *count* for homophonic French obscenities: 'De foot et de count! O Seigneur Dieu! ils'ont les mots de son mauvis, corruptible, gros, et impudique, et non pour les dames d'honneur d'user.'[70] While muted and turned to comic effect, variation in such early modern representations still conjures images of aberration and deviance from linguistic and social stability. One of the central concerns of *Henry V*, it should be noted, is the early modern fashioning of an English nation from disparate social groups, and this can take place once Jamy, Macmorris, Fluellen, and even Katherine speak the same English.

It is thus not coincidental, to offer one final example, that alongside *Henry V* some of the earliest uses of linguistic variation for rhetorical effect are sixteenth- and seventeenth-century dictionaries of cant and slang. When an increase in vagrancy attendant on decreases in subsistence farming and other social instabilities led to concomitant increases in crime, these works appeared as, in effect, defensive weapons, identifying a thieves' sociolect and helping magistrates and honest citizens by keeping them informed of secret methods of communication directed against them. If for Shakespeare

---

[70] *Henry V*, III.ii.94–6 and III.iv.48–50. Quoted from *The Complete Works*, ed. Alfred Harbage (London: Penguin, 1969).

variation in language projected a kingdom in need of unification, handbooks of cant suggest that deviance in language accompanied deviance in behavior.[71]

Modern fiction and language change

The third stage of Labov's model occurs when, framed by the norm of a standard written language and discursive traditions that shape the use of non-standard language, forms and varieties become stigmatized. They are then stereotypes with instantly recognizable social implications. If such implications provide opportunities for rhetorical exploitation, figuring in characterization and so forth, they also reinforce the stigmatization of the variation. In response to the way stereotypes foster the continued subordination of a particular variety or those who use it, moreover, speakers may in fact decrease their usage of subordinated forms, but the power of stereotypes is such that they can continue to define a speech community even after any empirical basis for them has disappeared.

Throughout his novels, for example, Dickens uses spellings like *wot* for *what* to represent pronunciations that voice the initial glide, i.e., [wat], rather than preserve the historically voiceless [ʌat] or even [hwat], suggested by the Old English form *hwæt*. And he uses this spelling and its implied pronunciation only for low-class speakers, such as cockneys, with whom the pronunciation had become negatively identified in the eighteenth century. Yet by the middle of the nineteenth century, when Dickens was writing, nearly all British varieties and speakers voiced an initial [w] (creating homophones of *witch* and *which*), and this pronunciation remains widespread, even typical, today. While most speakers of his era—including, presumably, Dickens himself—would have said [wat] and not [ʌat] or [hwat], the voicing evoked by *wot* remained conceptually a novelty and distinction of only lower-class speech.[72] As Lynda Mugglestone observes, the success of techniques like this—and not only this but also final *-in* for *-ing* and the presence or absence

---

[71] See further Julie Coleman, *A History of Cant and Slang Dictionaries*, i, *1567–1784* (Oxford: Oxford University Press, 2004). For additional examples and discussion of the use of regionalisms for literary effects in this period, see Manfred Görlach, *Aspects of the History of English* (Heidelberg: Carl Winter, 1999), 94–161.

[72] See E. J. Dobson, *English Pronunciation 1500–1700*, 2nd edn. (Oxford: Clarendon Press, 1968), ii, 974; Michael K. C. MacMahon, 'Phonology', in *The Cambridge History of the English Language*, iv, Suzanne Romaine (ed.), *1776–1997* (Cambridge: Cambridge University Press, 1998), 466–7; Joan C. Beal, *English Pronunciation in the Eighteenth Century: Thomas Spence's 'Grand Repository of the English Language'* (Oxford: Clarendon Press, 1999), 176–80; and Roger Lass, 'Phonology and Morphology', in Lass (ed.), *The Cambridge History of the English Language*, iii, *1476–1776* (Cambridge: Cambridge University Press, 1999), 124.

of initial *h* and post-vocalic *r*—'depends not on the fidelity which may or may not exist between the written and spoken forms selected but instead on the clear perception of notions of form and deviation which are offered to the reader'.[73] And they depend, too, on readers' recognition of the stylistic device, which is a kind of recognition that developed over the course of the eighteenth and nineteenth centuries and on which Dickens could depend implicitly.

This is the stage at which writing in dialect has become dialect writing: a fully developed system that isn't necessarily or even usually accurate (as Dickens's *wot* suggests) but that maps recognizable social valuations onto an artificial arrangement of spelling, italicization, capitalization, hyphenation, and punctuation. And it is a stage so thoroughly ingrained in modern fictional narratives that its history and development can be taken for granted. Easy generalizations about literature written from the eighteenth through the twenty-first centuries certainly fail, since non-standard spellings throughout this period suggest regional and social variation in many ways, directed at different literary effects. One could not detail a line of continuity and development from, say, Mrs Malaprop in Sheridan's *The Rivals*, through Sir Walter Scott's *Heart of Midlothian* and Mark Twain's *Adventures of Huckleberry Finn*, to William Faulkner's *The Sound and the Fury*, and finally to Toni Morrison's *Beloved* and Irvine Welsh's *Trainspotting*. What many such works do share is the general association of non-standard spellings with particular pronunciations and, by extension, speakers and groups, as well as a link between this association and particular social attitudes, qualities, or beliefs. And unlike in 'The Reeve's Tale' or even *Henry V*, these connections are not novelties that might require foregrounding or overt explanation. Rather, they constitute a kind of horizon of literary and social expectations on which writers can draw, knowing full well that their stylistic methods and thematic implications will be instantly recognizable. In a sense, modern dialect writing is less a way to think about change and variation than a reflection of how it has been thought about. This will be so even if—perhaps especially if—writers work against type, as did Thomas Hardy in his representations of a Wessex dialect. A correspondent of Sir James Murray, the general editor of the *OED*, Hardy took particular interest in language, regarding regional dialects as 'intrinsically as genuine, grammatical, and worthy of the royal title [of English] as is the all-prevailing competitor which bears it'.[74] Hardy's non-standard,

---

[73] Mugglestone, *'Talking Proper': The Rise of Accent as Social Symbol*, 2nd edn. (Oxford: Oxford University Press, 2003), 119. See the whole of her discussion on 95–134.

[74] Quoted from Hardy's personal writings in Dennis Taylor, *Hardy's Literary Language and Victorian Philology* (Oxford: Clarendon Press, 1993), 160.

Wessex-speaking characters, then, achieve their moral force precisely because they can be seen to undermine Victorian England's received expectations about class, integrity, and language.

Works in which dialect is a Labovian stereotype often share another quality, and that is the displacement of non-linguistic social anxieties to variations in language that I have described throughout this chapter. As keen as Hardy was about language, for example, novels like *Jude the Obscure* ultimately rage against social institutions and the limitations of a class system that they support, not merely individuals' speech patterns. Regionalisms may be 'genuine', but neither they nor their speakers are socially normative, and if their variance from normative language channels the intrinsic virtue of their speakers, it equally channels the tensions of social class. Such is the case, too, with Dickens, whose novels prominently employ stereotypes (in Labov's sense) that, whether they overtly sustain or challenge social hierarchies, associate language variation with broader kinds of disruption. *Great Expectations*, for instance, opens with scenes of intimacy between the youth Pip and the illiterate blacksmith Joe Gargery, which take on additional emotional force from the contrasting violent scenes with the escaped convict Magwitch or Mrs Joe, stifling ones with Mr Pumblechook, and eerie ones with Miss Havisham. Pip shares with Joe resiliency, honesty, and a compassionate spirit born of brutal backgrounds, all of which are expressed in the scenes describing Pip's efforts to learn to read and in the non-standard representations of Joe's speech: ' "Well!" Joe pursued, "somebody must keep the pot a biling, Pip, or the pot won't bile, don't you know?" ' As the story progresses and Pip realizes a change in character along with his great expectations, the simple integrity focused on Joe and emblemized in his non-standard speech contrasts sharply with the affectations of wealth and power in London. 'I'm wrong in these clothes', he tells Pip on a visit to London, 'I'm wrong out of the forge, the kitchen, or off th'meshes'.[75] It may be an ironic twist of the dialect stereotype that it is Pip's variation from regional to standard speech that accompanies his self-destructive change in values, but the association of linguistic variation with social disruption still follows the pattern that I have been tracing.

Dickens's *Nicholas Nickleby* reveals the range of expressive possibilities for dialect-writing as well as the ways in which it can direct comments on language change and variation to social ends. For Mr Mantalini, a minor character who provides comic relief in his tumultuous marriage and philandering ambitions, the pronunciation of a single word (*damn*) serves as a kind

---

[75] Dickens, *Great Expectations*, ed. Angus Calder (London: Penguin, 1965), 77, 246.

of signature. In the course of one brief conversation he remarks, 'Oh dem! ...Demnition discount...Demd scarce....demd trifling...Oh demmit!' In contrast is the language of Lord Frederick Verisopht, who first appears as a shallow rake but who eventually rejects his malicious mentor Sir Mulberry Hawk and is in fact killed by him in a duel. Irrespective of particular words, he displays a habit of clipped speech and lengthened vowels. 'What–the–deyvle?' he exclaims at one point, continuing during the same dinner with 'it's not a wa-a-x work', 'How de do', 'deyvlish pitty', 'the most knowing card in the pa-ack', 'how can you a-ask me', 'Gad, so he has', 'deyvle take me','it wouldn't be a good pla-an', 'it's too ba-ad of you', and 'ma-ake one effort'. While Mantalini's *dem* comes across as a kind of verbal tic or prop, the spoken equivalent to a comedian's cigar, the more nuanced portrayal of variation in Lord Verisopht's language mimics the snobbish affectation of the monocle that he moves from eye to eye as he talks. And in that nuance linguistic variation, which for Mr Mantalini evokes only laughter, projects a disingenuous and even manipulative quality.

The language of John Browdie, a Yorkshire grain merchant, varies in still more lexical and phonological detail from Standard English. Upon giving a destitute Nicholas money to keep him on the road, John exclaims, 'Dean't be afeard, mun...tak' eneaf to carry thee whoam. Thee'lt pay me yan day, a' warrant.'[76] John shares with Joe Gargery a genuine and decent spirit; he is delighted to aid Nicholas's escape from the miserly schoolmaster Squeers, whom Nicholas has just beaten, and later in the novel he will enable the escape of the feeble-minded and mistreated Smike, confront Squeers himself, and aid the flight of the abused boys of Squeers's Dotheboys Hall. In this regard, his non-standard speech, like Joe's, suggests the absence of affectation and deceit. At the same time, however, the variation in their language marks both characters as uneducated, financially limited, and socially circumscribed. They may be decent men, but their language indicates that, unlike Pip or Nicholas, they will never succeed in London's normative world. Put more directly, decency appears as socially marked as regionalisms.

While in many ways Hardy, Dickens, and other nineteenth-century novelists affirmed prevailing notions about the social instability associated with change and variation, dialect-writing itself came into criticism as a rhetorical device that undermined the stability of written standards and what they imply

[76] Dickens, *Nicholas Nickleby*, ed. Mark Ford (London: Penguin, 1999), 407–8, 230–5, 161. For some examples of mid-nineteenth-century American dialect writing put to rhetorical (including comedic) effect, see F. G. Cassidy, 'Geographical Variation of English in the United States', in Richard Bailey and Manfred Görlach (ed.), *English as a World Language* (Ann Arbor, MI: University of Michigan Press, 1982), 189–95.

about social stability. In the United States, whose population increased dramatically through immigration at this time, the language of regional writers and immigrants concentrated a number of political issues, including nationalism, education, ethnic and racial identity, geographic difference, and financial opportunity. Writers like Mark Twain, Theodore Dreiser, Willa Cather, and Upton Sinclair found themselves in the double-edged position of all writers who employ non-standard language for stylistic effect: dialect-writing could be a way to challenge accepted sociolinguistic views and thereby affirm that the non-standard language was worthy of representation, but to do so inevitably involved drawing on comedic and disparaging traditions that, just as inevitably, it perpetuated. If dialect-writing has celebrated ethnicity and challenged social stereotypes, it thereby has also affirmed the implication of social disruption in linguistic variation.

A particularly voluble authority on this subject was *The Dial,* a literary journal published in Chicago from 1880 to 1929. One of the leading proponents of international modernism in its later years, *The Dial* devoted many early editorials to regional and non-traditional writing, a topic that resonated particularly in Chicago, which was the focal point and catalyst of much nineteenth-century non-traditional writing in the United States. Despite its advocacy of modernism, *The Dial* was a largely conservative review, anchored by a conviction in the prestige and importance of a shared Anglo-American culture. Accordingly, *The Dial* echoed Waller and Kynaston on the pre-eminence of immutable language by arguing against non-standard writing on the grounds that it failed to achieve the transcendency characteristic of great literature. One editorial asked, 'Does the speech of Tommy Atkins and Marse Chan, the dialect of Drumtochty and Donegal, the locution of the Hoosier farmer and the Bowery tough, have anything of the antiseptic quality that preserves a story or a poem and enables it to delight successive generations of readers?' Another lamented the state of reading and writing in American universities, warning of the dire consequences attendant upon the liberties taken with English 'morphology, phonetics, syntax, and meaning, for no more adequate reason than the supposition that such linguistic butchery is humorous'.

An anxious link between linguistic and non-linguistic concerns appears as well in *The Dial.* Citing Athens and Transcendentalist Boston as models of what a homogenous population can accomplish, one writer wondered: 'Can a really great literature grow up in the midst of a heterogenous population, and how far are we Americans a heterogeneous people?' More pointedly, another editorial in effect glossed the xenophobic, even racist, connotations of 'heterogenous population':

There are few features of the recent literary situation as noteworthy as the large production and wide vogue of writings which exploit some special form of idiom and rely for their main interest upon the appeal of curiosity thus made. The idiom of the sailor and the soldier, the rustic and the mechanic, have elbowed their way into literature, and demand their share of the attention hitherto accorded chiefly to educated speech. The normal type of English expression has to jostle for recognition with the local and abnormal types of the Scotchman and the Irishman, the negro and the baboo, and, in our own country particularly, with such uncouth mixtures as those of the German-American and Scandinavian-American.[77]

While the emphasis on the relation between an individual's democratic expression and the collective character of a nation may have cast this argument on literary voice in a distinctively American way, the anxiety about change and variation is familiar from other writers and periods. By the logic of these kinds of argument, linguistic instability and imprecision result from the affectations of particular marginal groups (such as university students) and, more significantly, from immigrants and ethnic communities; this kind of social instability undermines national identity as well as the clarity of speech and writing; various national goods would be served by curtailing change and variation; an efficient way to curtail these linguistic phenomena would be to curtail the process that putatively gives rise to them—immigration in particular, as well as, perhaps, access to higher education. It is this same access, of course, that loosened the conceptual hold of men like Kynaston and Arnold on the history of English and contributed to the variation that critics like Honey, Truss, and McWhorter find so disturbing.

As the literary use of non-standard and regional writing has proliferated since the early twentieth century, the double-edged effect of perpetuating stereotypes in order to resist, exploit, or expose them has persisted. Novels like *Trainspotting* or James Kelman's *How Late It Was, How Late* use regional variants as effectively their normative language, requiring of readers both linguistic agility and the empathy to apply it. A fairly typical narrative passage in the latter reads: 'And there were shoppers roundabout; women and weans, a couple of prams with wee yins, all big-eye staring at him; then a sodjer was here and trying not to but it looked like it was too much of an effort and he couldnay stop himself, he stuck the boot right in, into Sammy's belly, then another.'[78] In a passage such as this, non-standard spellings evoke regional pronunciations, word choice regional dialect more generally, and syntax the

---

[77] All passages quoted from Lisa Woolley, *American Voices of the Chicago Renaissance* (Dekalb, IL: Northern Illinois University Press, 2000), 24, 25, 23. It should be noted that this *Dial* is not the one founded in 1840 in Boston by Ralph Waldo Emerson, Margaret Fuller, and others.

[78] Kelman, *How Late It Was, How Late* (London: Secker and Warburg, 1994), 6.

style of conversation. Unlike in *Nicholas Nickleby*, however, in *How Late It Was, How Late* regionalisms mark not one or more characters within the work but the work itself. Linguistic and social variation still correlate with one another, but here it is the entire world of the novel, which includes sociolinguistic stratification among its non-standard speakers, that deviates from sociolinguistic norms.

A work like Chinua Achebe's *Anthills of the Savannah* deploys non-standard language more sparingly—using allusions and lexicon to summon the exoticism of culture and context without provocatively, even belligerently, challenging the comprehension of many readers: 'Agwu does not call a meeting to choose his seers and diviners and artists: Agwu, the god of healers; Agwu, brother to Madness! But though born from the same womb he and Madness were not created by the same *chi*.'[79] Similarly, Patricia Grace, who is widely praised for the distinctive Maori voice of her fiction, writes stories that are imbued with Maori myths, culture and social practices, but creates her distinctive voice through fairly restrained use of proper names and allusions: 'Now they've come to this. It fits, you see. We have a twenty percent Maori here. We've tried to put programmes in place, kapa haka, etcetera, but it's not enough. No *depth*. We're keen to have a whanau class, whether it be total immersion or bilingual. With the children coming from Kohanga we'll have numbers enough, enough kids for an extra teacher.'[80] More whimsically, in Malcolm Pryce's fictional renderings of Aberystwyth, language variation serves as one more marker of a post-modern world everywhere filled with drollery and surrealism: 'She switched to Welsh. "*Beth ydych chi eisiau? Dydw I ddim yn siarad Saesneg....*" I could speak in tongues, too. "*Edrychwch Hombré, agorwch y drws! por favor*".'[81] Writers like Grace may well seek to undo social stereotypes with dignity, as some critics have argued, using variation to effect opposition to continued colonization or to enact cultural hybridity.[82] And Pryce may attempt much the same through humor. But the linguistic stereotypes they use achieve much of their force through their associations with the demeaning implications of earlier dialect-writing. And like Dickens or Hardy, they cannot challenge these implications without affirming them. In all cases, social disruption still accompanies linguistic variation.

---

[79] Achebe, *Anthills of the Savannah* (New York: Anchor, 1987), 114–15.

[80] Grace, *Baby No-Eyes* (Honolulu, HI: University of Hawaii Press, 1998), 146.

[81] Pryce, *Last Tango in Aberystwyth* (London: Bloomsbury, 2003), 5.

[82] e.g., Chadwick Allen, *Blood Narrative: Indigenous Identity in American Indian and Maori Literary and Activist Texts* (Durham, NC: Duke University Press, 2002); and Evelyn Nien-Ming Ch'ien, *Weird English* (Cambridge, MA: Harvard University Press, 2004).

The key point about such contemporary dialect-writing is this: while each of these cases, to varying degrees, may aggressively challenge dominant culture and its views on language, evoke the multilingual character of the Anglophonic world, or celebrate diversity, they can do so only through explicit and self-conscious recognition of change and variation. And such recognition again fails to be politically neutral, for modern fiction in non-standard language ultimately seeks political transformation as actively as did Zamenhof or St Augustine. While Zamenhof advocated language as a means to foster community, for example, Achebe and Grace see it as an expression of individual, resistant culture. Further, the same dialogue about variation that animates Christian exegesis obtains here. If Dickens and *The Dial*, in their own very different ways, articulate sociolinguistic yearnings for the world of Genesis 11, wherein communication was direct and complete, Kelman, Achebe, and Grace affirm variation with the competing narrative of Genesis 10.

Futuristic novels offer their own versions of these competing narratives. While language and its variations may be even more prominent in these kinds of narrative than in those I have already considered, the utopian or dystopian world of such books necessarily focuses on social concerns, thereby providing a now familiar link between linguistic and disruptive extra-linguistic change. Here, too, language variation and change can thus serve as symptoms or concomitants of extra-linguistic ideas, practices, and institutions. An early version of the use of change for this purpose occurs in Evelyn Waugh's short story 'Out of Depth', originally published in 1933. In it, a wealthy American, through the magic of a doctor with the transparent surname of Kakophilos, finds himself transported to London five centuries hence. In the area of present-day Piccadilly Circus, by then reduced to a marsh with mud huts and naked children, he asks whether he is still in London: 'The men looked at each other in surprise, and one very old white bear giggled slightly. After a painful delay the leader nodded and said, "Lunnon".' As the men squat to discuss what to do with their captive, the narrator observes: 'Occasional phrases came to him, "white", "black boss", "trade", but for the most part the jargon was without meaning.' Adding to the extra-linguistic import of Waugh's story is the fact that in this futuristic world, the grunting, primitive men are white, while the uniformed group who take the captive in trade, the group who have won some sort of racial war, are black.[83] In this vision of the future, the collapse of culture, language, and racial hierarchies has been simultaneous and complete.

---

[83] Waugh, *The Complete Stories of Evelyn Waugh* (Boston: Little, Brown, and Co., 1998), 136.

The Nadsat of Anthony Burgess's *A Clockwork Orange* offers perhaps the best-known version of a sociolinguistically disintegrating world, in which the slang of rebellious youths has combined with the Russian of England's Cold War enemy to produce a version of English, in structure and style, severed from its cultural and historical roots and articulating violence, disillusion, and boredom: 'It was nadsats milking and coking and fillying around (nadsats were what we used to call the teens), but there were a few of the more starry ones, vecks and cheenas alike (but not of the bourgeois, never them) laughing and govoreeting at the bar.'[84] A generation later, in describing a world reduced by nuclear holocaust to primitive, warring bands, Russell Hoban's *Riddley Walker* similarly utilizes linguistic change to underscore individual and institutional devastation: 'Peopl talk about the Cambry Pul theywl say any part of Inland you myt be in youwl feal that pul to Cambry in the senter. May be its jus in the air or may be where the Power Ring ben theres stil Power in the groun.'[85] In both works, as if in fulfillment of what twelfth-century Norman chroniclers and Chaucer's 'Reeve's Tale' prophesy, language change is at once sign, cause, and consequence of apocalyptic social upheaval.

From a utopian perspective in his 1933 *The Shape of Things to Come*, H. G. Wells imagines a future in which a world-state will be created in 2059, foreshadowed by the League of Nations and ending what he calls the Age of Frustration. Among the concerns of the new world order is the elimination of national and racial prejudice: 'Next, a lingua-franca had to be made universal and one or other of the great literature-bearing languages rendered accessible to everyone.' While writing of the future, Wells is necessarily a product of his present, and to identify this lingua franca he turns to the then-popular efforts of C. K. Ogden to develop a simplified version of English—one with only 850 words, just 18 of which were verbs—that might facilitate the acquisition of English as a second language and thus its spread around the globe. 'One of the unanticipated achievements of the twenty-first century', Wells thus later observes, 'was the diffusion of Basic English as the lingua franca of the world and the even more rapid modification, expansion and spread of English in its wake.' As with contemporary arguments for the spread of Basic English as a global language, English of the future, to Wells, achieved its status not through any language planning but simply by virtue of the fact that, compared to other European languages, it 'was simpler, subtler, more flexible and already more widely spoken'. A language academy in the form of the Dictionary Bureau solves the dilemma of Esperanto by monitoring further change,

---

[84] Burgess, *A Clockwork Orange* (London: Penguin, 1972), 24.
[85] Hoban, *Riddley Walker: A Novel* (New York: Summit Books, 1980), 106.

with the result that English of the twenty-first century has far greater 'delicacy and precision of expression' than did English of the eighteenth and nineteenth centuries—though it's still not perfect—and all speakers can now 'understand one another and they are all in one undivided cultural field'.[86] Writing between the world wars, Wells (like Zamenhof) imagined that language would change to reflect the eradication of the nationalistic threats then present in Europe. For Wells, Babel stands as a desirable and perhaps reachable future, while for Waugh, Burgess, and Hoban it seems to have receded, regrettably, far into the past, leaving a future as bleak, scattered, and isolated as the moment after the *confusio linguarum*. What all four writers share is the desire for a world of total communication and, more importantly, a sense that the structure of languages serves as a measure of how close or far away a world of social and political stability may be.

Back to Babel

And so, metaphorically and conceptually, I come back to Babel. As an explanation of language change and variation, the story of Nimrod's Tower has offered, throughout the history of English, a powerful theoretical framework for organizing conceptions of language and for understanding both the past and the present. Indeed, perhaps the greatest testament to the explanatory power of this model is through its explicit extension into Christian exegesis and the Enlightenment, as well as through the unacknowledged justification it provides for the stylistic choices of individual writers. The competing treatments of these writers and, more generally, the competing models offered by Genesis 10 and 11 have made change and variation real in White's sense: they have made linguistic topics matter at more than simply an intellectual level. As the Babel model has informed literary representations of language across time, in fact, it has figured in extra-linguistic concerns as disparate as medieval hagiography, early modern economics, nineteenth-century immigration, and the rise of totalitarianism in the twentieth century. From another, explanatory perspective that I have been sketching out so far, the specter of Babel allows for the displacement of such concerns to language. In this way, language change and variation serve as pre-emptive

---

[86] Wells, *The Shape of Things to Come* (New York: Macmillan, 1933), 381, 415–18. A polymath, Wells seems to have been particularly intrigued by language and its social implications. For discussion of the variety of ways in which science fiction writers have responded to the issues of language change and variation, whether in time-travel narratives or in narratives set in the future, see Walter E. Meyers, *Aliens and Linguists: Language Study and Science Fiction* (Athens, GA: The University of Georgia Press, 1980), 12–37. Also see Bailey, *Images of English*, 215–35.

issues, represented as more general and therefore more consequential; and by substituting for issues of economics, race, nationalism, and so forth, they in effect preclude those issues. As the twenty-first century looks to the future, this dialogical fashion in which the narratives of Genesis 10 and 11 have shaped the reality of change and variation and defined the history of English continues to prevail in the world of social practices as well as in literature.

Language revivals exhibit the recognition, even celebration, of change and variation as ordinary features of human language that Genesis 10 describes. For certain languages, such as Cornish, Manx, and some American Indian languages, the revival truly is just that—an attempt to make a living language out of one that had reached a moment when no living native speakers remained. In the case of Cornish, whose last native speaker is generally thought to have died late in the eighteenth century, revival attempts began almost immediately thereafter, drawing on the childhood memories of older monoglot Anglophones, written records, and the comparative evidence of genealogically affiliated languages like Breton. Less drastic situations have involved languages that are still spoken but whose numbers of speakers and domains have been severely reduced. Bosnian, Provençal, and Aramaic have all been cultivated and revivified in the face of a culturally dominant language, and in the ambit of English contact languages alone the list of revitalizations (some still quite tenuous) includes Welsh, Irish, Yiddish, Maori, and various Aboriginal languages. Whether a revival is complete or partial, all these cases share something with each other besides the enabling notion that language variation is a good, normal, and useful thing. And this is that the revival, like the literary examples I considered above and like most acts of language planning, responds to the effects of largely extra-linguistic motivations in politics, culture, ethnicity, and so forth. It was the eighteenth-century English clearance of Highland farms, for example, that both displaced Gaelic speakers and infused Anglophones to such an extent as to leave Gaelic today with a small population of ageing speakers, just as it was English farming and whaling in New Zealand that led to the reduction of Maori speakers by approximately 75% during the nineteenth century.

By the same token, since revivals are predicated on the notion that language is a vital and intrinsic part of culture, their ultimate goal is the emergence and affirmation of a culture and not simply a language associated with it. Revitalization of economically depressed Gaelic and Maori speech communities, for instance, would redress a history of social oppression and reassert their financial and social viability. In this same vein, commenting on the cultivation of Bosnian as a distinct language beside Serbian and Croatian, the director of education for the Bosnian National Council observed, 'Language defines the identity of a people. Having the Bosnian language brings recognition to a people who have lived in Serbia and Montenegro for centuries.'[87] It is this very reasoning that produced formal recognition of variation and change—ratification of Genesis 10, as it were—in the 1992 European Charter for Regional or Minority Languages and the 1996 Universal Declaration of Linguistic Rights, endorsed by PEN, UNESCO, and other linguistic organizations. The former considers minority languages to be cultural wealth and therefore as worthy of protection as are those who speak them, while the latter begins with similar affirmations of how the contexts of politics, geography, and ideology contribute to a language's identity. The Declaration goes on to assert, among other things, the basic human right of individuals to retain their language, the equality of all languages, regardless of their political status in any one region, and the role of language in expressing individual cultural views.[88] As with the literary efforts of Kelman and Welsh, such political strategies and policies invest language change and variation with terrific social impact that, while self-affirming to those who use a particular variety, is necessarily meant as a challenge, even a threat, to those who do not.

The competing narrative of Genesis 11 underwrites its own competing versions in narratives of the linguistic and social future. In some accounts, a return to a single language of unmediated communication is every bit the achievement that rendered Nimrod's ambitions divine. English, more than any other language, often bears the sobriquet 'global language' today, and having already played this role in diplomacy, the language is increasingly expanding into areas without large indigenous Anglophone populations. While earlier generations in Mongolia cultivated Russian or Chinese as second languages, for instance, English is today taking their place. 'We see English not only as a way of communicating', observes Tsakhia Elbegdor, the prime minister of Mongolia, 'but as a way of opening windows on the wider world.'[89] This same empowering quality informs the embrace of English as the dominant language of world telecommunication, now including the Internet.[90] Contesting narratives invoke not a putative communicative idyll before Babel but rather the presumed oppression by which Nimrod made it possible. As I indicated in the first chapter, for many speakers worldwide,

---

[87] Quoted in Nicholas Wood, 'In the Old Dialect, a Balkan Region Regaining Identity', *New York Times*, 24 February 2005, A4.

[88] See the 'Universal Declaration of Linguistic Rights' at http://www.linguistic-declaration.org/index-gb.htm.

[89] Quoted in James Brooke, 'For Mongolians, E is for English, F is for Future', *New York Times*, 15 February 2005, A1.

[90] See David Crystal, *Language and the Internet* (Cambridge: Cambridge University Press, 2001).

particularly in Europe, the role of English in rebuilding Nimrod's Tower is a sinister one indeed. France, Germany, Russia, and Brazil have all taken steps to curtail the reduction of linguistic variation through the spread of English, whether these be formal, legislative efforts to limit the influx of English vocabulary or informal ones to discourage its presence on shirts and in advertising.

As with linguistic revivals, these various uses of the Babel model ultimately serve non-linguistic ends. In advocating the diffusion of English as a second language, thus, the president of Chile observed, 'As a country, we want to be a bridge and a platform for flows of international trade and in the Asia-Pacific region', while the rector of one of the country's largest universities, in explaining the introduction of a requirement for all students to study English, noted, 'Our mission is to train professionals for an internationalized world, and this is the only way for this country to develop the way it wants'.[91] From the very different perspective of a native Anglophone, Arthur Schlesinger, Jr., protests what he calls the 'cult of ethnicity' in modern America but likewise uses the Babel model for non-linguistic purposes. Mixing literary and biblical allusions with emotive metaphors, he bluntly warns of what will happen if variation is allowed to proceed unchecked: 'Will the center hold? Or will the melting pot give way to the Tower of Babel?'[92]

In the end, narratives of change and variation function much like the found facts of co-varying phonological shifts. Bringing together institutional and conceptual impulses into meaningful patterns, the explanations they provide become templates for organizing and interpreting linguistic phenomena. Out of their competition—out of the disjunction between narratives that grant the human origins of linguistic diversity and those that affirm its unearthly status—they make these phenomena real. They have also made them, in the case of English, the conduit for anxieties over the speakers of particular varieties, the economic and ethnic consequences of their presence in a community, the character of a national population, and the direction of a country's future. When we tell stories about change and variation, we talk about something far more consequential than language alone: we talk about ourselves.

---

[91] Quoted in Larry Rohter, 'Learn English, Says Chile, Thinking Upwardly Global', *New York Times*, 29 December 2004, A4.

[92] Schlesinger, *The Disuniting of America: Reflections on a Multicultural Society*, rev. edn. (New York: W. W. Norton, 1998), 22.

4

Policy and Politics

Victimized by sound change

In the first chapter, when discussing theories of language change, I quoted Roger Lass's characteristically witty and insightful observation that linguistic change 'occurs over "geological" time, beyond the capacity of humans to act, since no actor can see the consequences of his actions. A speaker engaged in a change is not an agent, but a victim.'[1] Lass's perspective is that of a historical linguist interested in structural changes like consonant shifts and syntactic elaboration, and from this perspective 'geological time' is indeed an apt metaphor. Including the exceptions accounted for in Verner's Law, for example, the consonantal changes designated as the First Consonant Shift probably required at least half a millennium for completion, while the expansion of English periphrastic verb phrases, whereby modals like *should* came to create progressive structures like *should have been going*, took place over several centuries. Any one speaker at any one moment in either change might well be aware of the existence of variation, with certain eighteenth-century speakers already saying something like *the house is being built*, even as others retained the historical *the house is building* or *the house is on building*. Speakers might associate variants with particular social groups, or know that they are socially stigmatized, or suspect, like H. G. Wells and many of the verbal hygienists described by Deborah Cameron, that they can extrapolate the linguistic future, whether utopian or dystopian, from what they hear around them. And after the fact, speakers certainly can look back, identify the one variant that would prevail, and reconstruct its development as inevitable.

But in Lass's critique, such linguistic foresight is illusory. All linguistic history is written retrospectively, and it all therefore benefits from the possibility of identifying patterns and developments among phenomena that

---

[1] Lass, *Historical Linguistics and Language Change* (Cambridge: Cambridge University Press, 1997), 367.

transpired in a non-teleological fashion. Typically, I have maintained, language change merely happens, since a specific use of language is only rarely directed to produce an identified result, even if that result can later be connected to it. And given competing linguistic forces (such as phonetic assimilation and dissimilation) and the vagaries of population movement, individuals living during a 'geological' sound change have no way of knowing its outcome. In fact, it might well be difficult for them even to recognize a change as change, both because not all synchronic variation produces diachronic change and because, as sociolinguistic interviews often show, speakers can be poor, even unaware, witnesses of the language they use. Indeed, the Northern Cities Vowel Shift in the United States illustrates how the 'geological' progress of change can sometimes render a change elusive to the very speakers who propagate it. In this change, which has been documented for several decades, lax vowels are participating in a small co-varying shift whereby [ɔ], for instance, has moved down to [a] and [æ] up to [ɛ], so that *caught* is pronounced *cot* ([kat]) and *cat* has the same vowel as *kept* ([kɛt]).[2] As long-standing and widespread as the change is, it seems to pass unnoticed by the majority of northern United States speakers, including my students, who regularly deny that the Northern Cities Vowel Shift exists, even as they demonstrate it in their denials. And to the extent that speakers are unaware of a change in progress, they obviously cannot intentionally further it. For such speakers, the existence and progress of the Shift can be identified only retrospectively.

Such after-the-fact identification of a change's direction is readily apparent in structural issues, as when critics identify the origins of periphrastic verbs in the gradual restriction of the verb *will* from a word meaning 'to wish' to a grammatical marker of futurity and in the extrapolation from this restriction to similar uses of modal verbs (e.g., *shall* and *must*). But the retrospective definition of coherence and teleology can occur with sociolinguistic issues as well. Recent discussions of Middle English, for instance, have used post-medieval sociolinguistic developments in literature, nationalism, and technology in order to project into the Middle Ages notions of Standard English and a resistant vernacular culture, which have then been understood to constitute the pre-eminent and inevitable trend in the late-medieval English linguistic repertoire. At the very moment Chaucer is sometimes credited with creating and fostering a modern notion of English literature and language, however, Latin still dominated ecclesiastical domains, and French legal and

---

[2] See William Labov, *Principles of Linguistic Change*, i, *Internal Factors* (Oxford: Blackwell, 1994), 177–201.

aristocratic ones. Even within the repertoire of English alone, varieties besides the southeast one Chaucer used (such as the northwest variety that figures in many late-medieval alliterative poems, like *Sir Gawain and the Green Knight*) furthered their own literary traditions and left it uncertain, at least prior to the late-fifteenth-century emergence of print, from which region a standard might develop—if, in fact, any would.[3]

Noah Webster's 1789 *Dissertations on the English Language* provides a more recent example of how linguistic history can be appropriated—maybe even created—to serve the sociolinguistic present. As I will argue later in this chapter, Webster certainly had a well-formed sense of a strong central government reflected in a centralized and stable linguistic tradition, and in the *Dissertations* he thus observes that a '*national language* is a band of *national union*'. But while he gave voice to a forceful and developing argument in early America, his was only one, competing view at the time. Other critics, such as Benjamin Franklin, put a priority on restricting the number of German speakers in the colonies, while still others, like John Adams, championed the creation of an American language academy. Webster could not have imagined two hundred years of American sociolinguistic history and how events would advance his views over those of Franklin and Adams: the extensive European emigration of a century later, the nationalizing effects of the First World War, the economic hardships leading up to the Second World War, the subsequent rise in emigration from Latin America and Asia, or, finally, the Civil Rights movement of the 1960s and its backlash. Not knowing any of this, Webster could not have seen how race and religion came to propel nativism in times of economic difficulty and how in this context language legislation has developed as a way to control immigration. Nor could Webster have seen himself (or his views) as an agent propelling the United States to a moment when the 1981 Select Committee on Immigration and Refugee Policy would quote his comments on a national language within its proposal to retain command of English as a requirement for naturalization.[4] Webster's specifically eighteenth-century views on the role of language in a new republic had become evidence for historical continuity and modern immigration policy.

---

[3] See further Machan, 'Politics and the Middle English Language', *Studies in the Age of Chaucer*, 24 (2002), 317–24.

[4] Webster, *Dissertations on the English Language* (1789; rpt. Menston: Scolar Press, 1967), 397; James Crawford (ed.), *Language Loyalties: A Source Book on the Official English Controversy* (Chicago, IL: University of Chicago Press, 1992), 101. On language legislation and early American immigration, see John Higham, *Strangers in the Land: Patterns of American Nativism, 1860–1925*, 2nd edn. (New Brunswick, NJ: Rutgers University Press, 1988).

Relying on the retrospection of linguistic history, speakers not only construct the linguistic past but also, like Cameron's verbal hygienists, sometimes believe that they can know the linguistic future and can take action to achieve or prevent that future. But while speakers certainly can foster the development of a future they already see as given, evidence against their ability to make accurate linguistic predictions, particularly in sociolinguistic areas, is considerable. In 1600, prior to the British settlement at Jamestown, Virginia, no speaker would have had any reason to imagine the growth of the United States—which wouldn't even exist for over another century and a half—much less the impact its use of English would have on the structure and global dissemination of the language. At that same movement, well before the Highland Clearances and the mining of coal to sustain the Industrial Revolution, neither would any speaker have reason to imagine the overwhelming shift of monoglot Gaelic and Welsh speakers to English in the centuries to come.

From the opposite perspective, wildly errant predictions also demonstrate the limitations on foresight into the linguistic future. In his *Dissertations*, for example, Webster confidently supposed that the birth of the United States, coupled with the new associations of peoples and ideas that it entailed, would 'produce, in a course of time, a language in North America, as different from the future language of England, as the modern Dutch, Danish and Swedish are from the German, or from one another'.[5] Even allowing for the vagueness of 'in a course of time', and Oscar Wilde notwithstanding, this has not happened. Similarly erroneous and even more specific was Henry Sweet's 1877 assertion that within a century 'England, America, and Australia will be speaking mutually unintelligible languages, owing to their independent changes of pronunciation'.[6]

The limitations of linguistic foresight and its implications for agency appear in still smaller time frames. According to the 1940 United States census, from a white population of 118,214,870, some 1,858,024 individuals (1.6%) spoke Spanish as a mother tongue. By contrast, the 2000 census records 254,762,734 United States residents over the age of five, 26,771,035 (or 10.5%) of whom speak Spanish to some degree.[7] To foresee this increase in the number of Spanish speakers and their percentage among the general American

---

[5] Webster, *Dissertations on the English Language*, 22–3.

[6] Sweet, *A Handbook of Phonetics* (Oxford: Clarendon Press, 1877), 196.

[7] Campbell Gibson and Kay Jung, 'Historical Census Statistics on Population Totals by Race, 1790 to 1990, and by Hispanic Origin, 1970 to 1990, for the United States, Regions, Divisions, and States', Population Division, US Census Bureau, September 2002, Working Paper Series No. 56, Table E-6; United States Census 2000, Summary Tables on Language Use and English Ability. Information can be accessed at http://www.censu.gov/index.html. Comparisons between censuses are made difficult by the fact that over time the categorization of factors like age and race have changed.

population, an analyst of 1940 would have needed to know, presciently, many developments of the following decades. Foremost of these are the Civil Rights movement, the elimination of immigration quotas in 1965, and rising emigration from Latin America since the 1960s. No analyst of 1940 could have used only contemporary data like birth rates, housing patterns, or educational backgrounds to predict a fivefold increase in the percentage of Spanish speakers by the end of the millennium. So, too, is it impossible today to predict either the emergence of Spanish as co-equal to English in the United States (as many do). Sociolinguistic patterns like those that contributed to the rise of Spanish—and similarly not now operative—could well lead to that language's contraction or the expansion of another language, such as Chinese, which in the 2000 census had 2,022,143 speakers over the age of five.

It is in these senses, then, that speakers serve as victims to the structural and sociolinguistic changes they further. They articulate particular vowels, syntactic structures, or, simply, their native language, but they do so for immediate reasons: to buy lunch, express opinions, and explain procedures. Only in very limited ways might speakers be seen—and see themselves—as agents who speak, in the first instance, to effect diachronic change and not to accomplish limited pragmatic goals. Such agency seems restricted to lexicon, and then to the stigmatization or amelioration of individual words, such as *Miss* and *gay*. At the levels of syntax and phonology, targeted change has not been a significant historical factor for English. And larger sociolinguistic changes of the kind I described for the global expansion of English and the American expansion of Spanish necessarily transcend the efforts and control of any one individual.

Yet if speakers are victims of changes in the language they speak, the language itself, both in structure and pragmatics, is certainly changed by them. Structurally, it is of course speakers' use of particular forms that maintains the forms' currency and renders them as historical substitutes for competing forms. While no fifteenth-century speakers may have viewed their selection of the verbal inflection [s] rather than [εθ] as part of a diachronic process that would culminate in replacement of the latter by the former, the fact that they, their children, and their children's children did use the [s] inflection constituted that replacement. Their usage is why most Anglophones now say *walks* rather than *walketh*. In general, pragmatic terms, these speakers' simple use of English, whether by conscious decision or not, sustained the language's viability, as even more so did other individuals' use of written English to conduct law courts, teach school, and transact all government and financial business. To be sure, while such usage enhances the long-term status of a language in terms of its numbers of speakers and domains of usage, other kinds can produce long-term constriction. An old schoolchild rhyme begins 'Latin is a language, as dead as it can be', and the reasons it is so (to the extent that it is so) are that its speakers shifted to other languages (including developments of Latin) and that its domains have become increasingly limited, now primarily to the classroom. One can continue to tinker with grammatical and discursive niceties for a language which is dead in this sense, though such tinkering is remote from the processes of language change that I described in the second chapter. Without speakers, there can be no changes of this kind.

So speakers are changed by language, but it, too, is changed by them, and this complexity in the agency of linguistic change appears with particular force in religious as well as civic programs. Policies and legislation on doctrine, education, immigration, voting, and legal process can all shape the opportunities to use one language or another and thus not only that language's viability but also, at least indirectly, its grammatical structures. At the same time, grammatical and sociolinguistic issues often nominally motivate such policies in the first place. Factors like the number of speakers of a minority language, their rate of immigration, the structural impact of their native language on English, and their presence in schools and the workforce can all lead to government action that can enhance or curtail these same factors. Language change is thus an ambivalent phenomenon, in the sense that even as a language changes, so, too, can speakers unintentionally or indirectly change the language.

There is another kind of ambivalence operative here, however. That is, if religious and civic policies guide the language use of individuals, the policies themselves are ultimately the creation of individuals. To be sure, any one speaker (or voter) may have little genuine influence on or sympathy with specific acts of public policy, whether they are the declaration of an official language, the proscription of immigrant languages, or the mandate of court interpreters. But short of a totalitarian state, and no Anglophone country merits this label, policy officials do necessarily emerge from the groups they govern and they do necessarily respond to the concerns of at least some individuals from those groups. Stated more forcefully, all speakers are invested in linguistic policy decisions, and all speakers have responsibility for them. The alternative approach, advocated by many critics of global English in particular, conceives a kind of agentless linguistic policy—or at least a policy that is the agent of a limited, malfeasant group—that overrides the wishes of both Anglophones and the non-Anglophones they encounter. Robert Phillipson thus imagines English 'as a kind of linguistic cuckoo, taking over where other breeds of language have historically nested and acquired territorial rights, and obliging non-native speakers of English to acquire the behavioural habits and linguistic forms of English'. And Alastair Pennycook has seen such predatory processes as inherent in the post-colonial expansion of English, though again in ways that represent language as somehow a wilful agent acting irrespectively of at least some of its speakers' desires: 'If one of the central aspects of colonial discourse has been to construct the native Other as backward, dirty, primitive, depraved, childlike, feminine, and so forth, the other side of this discourse has been the construction of the colonizers, their language, culture and political structures as advanced, superior, modern, civilized, masculine, mature and so on.'[8] Much like the embrace of global English that it opposes, this approach contributes to the very anxiety that this book discusses, for it renders speakers the victims of policy as well as sound change.

In this chapter I look selectively at how particular public policies have affected English change and variation, and, in turn, at how the use of English and other languages has driven these same policies. Adhering to the approach I have followed so far, my methods are neither exhaustive nor reductive. In its 1500-year history that now includes the entire globe, the English language and any number of regional or national policies have mutually shaped one another in significant ways. By the same token, a good deal of public policy has not affected language change, even indirectly, and some kinds of linguistic policy have produced or been associated with only minimal anxiety about language change. As Braj Kachru suggests, it may be the case that once Lord Macaulay's educational minute of 2 February 1835 was passed, 'the subcontinent was not the same, linguistically and educationally'. But the same cataclysmic significance cannot be attributed to the imposition of an English-only educational policy in Puerto Rico following the Spanish-American War; Spanish was reinstated in classrooms in 1952, and to this day over 95% of the population over the age of five speak Spanish as their dominant language.[9] Along with the mutual effects language change and policy have on each other, such varying contextual dimensions contribute to the difficulty of identifying clear cause-and-effects relationships between language change and various kinds of religious, social, and political change. By Kachru's analysis, for example, Macaulay's minute might indeed be argued to have produced social change. But it also could merely have portended subsequent administrative

---

[8] Phillipson, *English-Only Europe? Challenging Language Policy* (London: Routledge, 2003), 4; Pennycook, *English and the Discourses of Colonialism* (London: Routledge, 1998), 129.

[9] Kachru, 'English in South Asia' and John A. Holm, 'English in the Caribbean', in *The Cambridge History of the English Language*, v, Robert Burchfield (ed.), *English in Britain and Overseas: Origins and Development* (Cambridge: Cambridge University Press, 1994), 501 and 354; Selected Social Characteristics in Puerto Rico (http://www.censu.gov/index.html).

activities of greater sociolinguistic consequence (such as the founding of universities in Bombay, Calcutta, and Madras), or itself been the inevitable consequence of the revitalization of missionary activities, including the instruction of English, that followed William Wilberforce's 1813 declaration to Parliament that it should exchange India's 'dark and bloody superstition for the genial influence of Christian light and truth'.[10] These kinds of causal ambiguities contribute their own complications to discussions of language, and it is in this context that I want to explore how religious and governmental policies have fostered, channeled, and even created anxiety about language change and variation in particular.

Language planning and the word of God

Like nearly every one of the roughly 500 Amerindian languages spoken in North America before the arrival of European colonists, Passamaquoddy suffered badly from contact with French, Dutch, Spanish, German, and English. Today, it has only about 600 speakers in Maine and nearby parts of Canada, and most of these, as is commonly the case with dying languages, are elderly; they are all bilingual with English. In response to such situations, tribes have adopted differing policies to increase a language's number of speakers and domains. One group inventively pursued the strategy of having the Disney cartoon *Bambi* dubbed in Arapaho, so that pre-school children could be exposed to the language in an entertaining and playful context.[11] Allen Sockabasin, of the Passamaquoddy tribe, has explored an equally inventive policy. Drawing on connections between language, community, and religion, he has translated English songs, poems, and prayers, including the rosary, into Passamaquoddy. Sockabasin has also had his translations professionally recorded and issued on CDs, which he distributes for free. Whether such recordings are sufficient to revitalize the language may be doubtful, but they do forcefully point to how language planning can make use of the emotional ties speakers have for particular domains of language use. 'I know when I say "my creator" in my language', Sockabasin observes, 'there is no other definition. It's who made me.'[12]

---

[10] Quoted in Kachru, 'English in South Asia', 504.

[11] Stephen Greymorning, 'Reflections on the Arapaho Language Project, or When Bambi Spoke Arapaho and Other Tales of Arapaho Language Revitalization Efforts', in Leanne Hinton and Ken Hale (eds.), *The Green Book of Language Revitalization in Practice* (San Diego, CA: Academic Press, 2001), 287–97.

[12] Quoted in Katie Zezima, 'One Man's Goal: For a Tribe to Pray in Its Own Language', *New York Times*, 15 November 2003, A11.

Language planning has two general impulses: corpus planning, which addresses specifics of usage and grammar and therefore typically takes the form of grammar books, dictionaries, and rhetorics; and status planning, which attempts to adjust the relative social functions of a given variety in relation to other varieties and which subsumes Sockabasin's efforts on behalf of Passamaquoddy. In either case, language planning characteristically has objectives beyond simple communication or the refinement of a linguistic code. These objectives may be presumptively ethical ones, such as the protection of a minority group's linguistic rights, and such protection typically depends on state or institutional support of some kind. Besides having eleven official languages and translating its documents into several more, for example, the European Union actively fosters the status of minority languages by allocating funds towards the maintenance of linguistic and ethnic diversity.[13] But it can also be possible to realize such objectives without the assistance of a financial and bureaucratic infrastructure. Thus, the constriction of sexist usage in many Anglophone countries has occurred largely under a popular initiative, as has the ameliorization of much sexist and racist terminology.

The kinds of social objectives that language planning characteristically serves bespeak other initiatives than group or individual civil rights, however. As Robert Cooper describes these initiatives, 'Language planning is typically carried out for the attainment of nonlinguistic ends such as consumer protection, scientific exchange, national integration, political control, economic development, the creation of new elites or the maintenance of old ones, the pacification or cooption of minority groups, and mass mobilization of national or political movements'.[14] These are the initiatives of dominant, ruling groups, be they political, economic, or religious, that manage areas like 'consumer protection' and 'scientific exchange' and that are also the groups likely to have the financial and administrative means for enforcing language policy. In the modern world, the most typical kind of language planning, whether of corpus or status, involves government-funded initiatives

---

[13] Phillipson, *English-Only Europe?*, 10. This policy has not been without controversy, on which see John Tagliabue, 'Soon, Europe Will Speak in 23 Tongues', *New York Times*, 6 December 2006, A10. On language planning generally, see Robert L. Cooper (ed.), *Language Spread: Studies in Diffusion and Social Change* (Bloomington, IN: Indiana University Press, 1982); Joshua Fishman (ed.), *Advances in Language Planning* (The Hague: Mouton, 1974); James W. Tollefson, *Planning Language, Planning Inequality: Language Policy in the Community* (London: Longman, 1991); and Robert Hodge and Gunther Kress, *Language as Ideology*, 2nd edn. (London: Routledge, 1993). On the ethics of language planning, see Juan Cobarrubias, 'Ethical Issues in Status Planning', in Cobarrubias and Joshua A. Fishman (eds.), *Progress in Language Planning: International Perspectives* (The Hague: Mouton, 1983), 41–85.

[14] Robert L. Cooper, *Language Planning and Social Change* (Cambridge: Cambridge University Press, 1989), 35.

implemented through educational programs. As the prerogatives of an elite, then, the initiatives and programs of language planning can reproduce ideology as much as they realize putatively linguistic goals.

The teaching of English as a second language is a case in point. This is currently an extremely lucrative, global activity for both the United States and Great Britain that has a presumptively linguistic objective and that achieves varying success in varying environments. To the extent that they render language a purchasable commodity and testify for the socioeconomic superiority and desirability of their teachers' homelands, however, ESL and TOEFL initiatives are also sometimes understood to inculcate Western economic values along with phonology, morphology, and syntax.[15] Pointing to issues such as the limited availability and success of ESL initiatives, some critics even argue that inadequate command of English as a second language reflects neither speakers' abilities nor their motivations. Rather, these critics trace inadequate language learning to policies that simultaneously cultivate a need and a desire to learn English but also limit speakers' opportunities to learn effectively. By manipulating the availability of English on the world linguistic market, such cultivation is thought to sustain a sociopolitical hierarchy with Anglophone nations at the top. When ESL programs emphasize the acquisition of language meant to apologize for immigrant language difficulties—which in some instances are effectively dialect differences—even the details of the programs can appear as complicit in such sociolinguistic policy.[16]

Whether economic values in such programs are incidental or primary in relation to grammatical ones is of course an arguable point, and many individuals might well reject claims that second language acquisition by its very nature reproduces a hierarchy that disadvantages those in the learning groups. But it's not necessary to make claims as broad as these in order to recognize that language planning is implicated in social policy and, therefore, that language has the potential to be a socially meaningful symbol and force—like clothing or music or hairstyles—that can further the objectives of a ruling or aspiring elite. This is the case, indeed, with the many examples I consider in this chapter but also with a variety of non-Anglophone examples. Early in the seventeenth century, for example, Cardinal Richelieu engaged in language planning by establishing the Académie Française, whose efforts to stabilize grammar, rhetoric, and vocabulary would serve as the linguistic counterparts to more general governmental efforts to stabilize society.[17] Social policy of an

---

[15] Robert Phillipson, *Linguistic Imperialism* (Oxford: Oxford University Press, 1992); Alastair Pennycook, *The Cultural Politics of English as an International Language* (London: Longman, 1994).

[16] James W. Tollefson, *Planning Language, Planning Inequality*, 7, 104–35.

[17] Cooper, *Language Planning and Social Change*, 3–11.

aspirant group likewise underwrote Ivar Aasen's nineteenth-century efforts to define a new Norwegian, or Nynorsk, as in part a nationalistic testament to cultural independence from Sweden, as well as Elias Lönnrot's collection and composition of the *Kalevala* poems in expression of the integrity of Finnish culture even under Tsarist rule. In both of these examples, a linguistic code mediated not simply social policy but national identity too, and this may well be one of the pre-eminent characteristics of language planning in the modern era.[18] Still other examples show language furthering one social identity or repressing another: Stalin's imposition of the Cyrillic alphabet on the nascent Soviet republics; the role of Tagalog in various Philippine nationalistic efforts; semantic debates over the character and integrity of Serbian, Croatian, and Bosnian languages in the former Yugoslavia; and the status of English as a tool of Western capitalism for groups in Iran, the Philippines, and China who are seeking closer or looser affiliations with the West.[19]

As a response to change and variation, language planning for religion and theology, in the broader history of English, has both facilitated shift to English and forestalled it. For Passamaquoddy, religion actually motivated the language's contraction as well as its revival: it was the decision of Jesuit missionaries to use French and Latin that initiated shift in the Passama-quoddy community, just as it is Sockabasin's decision to translate prayers into Passamaquoddy that injects vitality into it. At essentially the same time as Christian missionary work contributed to the demise of Passamaquoddy, however, language planning in the service of religion helped to forestall shift to English in various Celtic regions. The early identification of Welsh and Scots Gaelic with, respectively, Methodism and Presbyterianism did much to sustain the languages for their speakers during early modern social and economic upheaval, while, more pragmatically, the 1588 publication of a vernacular Bible provided symbolic and material support for Welsh in par-ticular. But if in these instances, religious language planning helped forestall shift and its concomitant disruption of culture and tradition, when the shift did occur, mostly in the nineteenth century, economics proved to be the stronger determinant by producing among both Anglophones and non-Anglophones the sense that variation from English was debilitating for the latter. This conjunction between religion, language planning, and economic expansion proved even stronger in Australia, south Asia, the antipodes, and South America, where planning led to the abandonment of indigenous

---

[18] Cf. Cooper, *Language Planning and Social Change*, 69, and Einar Haugen, *Language Conflict and Language Planning: The Case of Modern Norwegian* (Cambridge, MA: Harvard University Press, 1966).

[19] See Tollefson, *Planning Language, Planning Inequality*, and Tove Skutnabb-Kangas and Robert Phillipson (eds.), *Linguistic Human Rights: Overcoming Linguistic Discrimination* (Berlin: Mouton de Gruyter, 1994).

languages by non-Anglophones and also Anglophones' encouragement of a shift to English. The same, basic language plan obtained in each case: to convert indigenes, theologically if not also economically, by means of a language shift accomplished through education and the translation of the Bible and prayers into native languages. The thinking went that without such a shift, divergence between Anglophones and indigenous cultures would persist, to the putative detriment of both in various ways: Anglophones would lose opportunities for the conversion of non-believers as well as economic growth, and non-Anglophones would lose the promise of participation in the culture shared by the world's dominant groups. Through shift, however, linguistic, economic, and cultural variation would all (hypothetically) diminish together. As at Babel, language diversity thereby generated anxiety, and this kind of anxiety, channeled through religious policy, has been present in some form since some of the earliest days of English.

During the late ninth-century reign of King Alfred the Great—to begin with an early example—England began to emerge from a half century of depredations and colonizing efforts by mostly Danish Vikings. Beyond whatever the weaknesses of defense and political organization may have done to invite and enable the raids, responsibility for them was popularly understood to lie in the moral failures of the Anglo-Saxons, just as Gildas had earlier attributed the Angles' and Saxons' invasion to the similar failures of the British and as later Norman historians would explain their own invasion as God's scourge on the laxity of Anglo-Saxon England. When Viking raids resumed with even greater ferocity a century later, Wulfstan, bishop of Worcester, voiced this characteristically Augustinian historiographic viewpoint as a context for his explanation of the state of Anglo-Saxon England: 'Beloved men, recognize what the truth is: this world is in haste and it is drawing near the end, and therefore the longer it is the worse it will get in the world. And it needs must thus become very much worse as a result of the people's sins prior to the advent of Antichrist; and then, indeed, it will be terrible and cruel throughout the world.'[20] It was Alfred's reign that was largely responsible for England's earlier civic and moral emergence, and it was he who had rallied the English forces in a bleak winter of 878–9 and gradually reasserted Anglo-Saxon control over lands that the Danes had occupied. By 886 he had achieved a kind of political balance through the Treaty of Wedmore, distinguishing the lands that he controlled from those in the Danelaw, which remained in Viking power. If England as a political entity still lay well in the future, Alfred's military and political efforts had

---

[20] Michael Swanton (ed. and trans.), *Anglo-Saxon Prose* (London: Dent, 1975), 116–17.

done much to foster a centralized government with its own courts, law codes, and text production.

In this dynamic context of social disorder and organization, the king shifted his focus from social to linguistic matters, specifically to the state of learning in England, the demise of language use, and the possibilities that translation afforded for a return to stability. Alfred himself began this return through his translation of Gregory the Great's pastoral handbook *Cura Pastoralis*, to which he prefaced a survey of English learning. There, thinking back to his youth in a time before Viking raids intensified in the 850s, Alfred remembers a world of secular and religious scholars, devout kings, righteous service, and a love of wisdom. He looks around and sees that this world has passed, replaced by one in which few people south of the Humber river and even fewer north of it can understand the divine service in English or translate a letter from Latin to English. He sees burnt and desolate churches—once filled with books and treasures—and an ignorant populace, unable to read the books that would aid them. In Alfred's voicing, this populace shares his trauma, his recognition that they have been severed from the past that would give their present meaning: 'Our forefathers who formerly held these places loved knowledge, and through it they acquired wealth and left if to us. One can see their footprints here still, but we cannot follow after them and therefore we have now lost both the wealth and the knowledge because we would not bend our mind to that course.' History is here a path, and success, intellectual as well as material, lies in retracing and continuing the steps of tradition. More specifically, history is a path of books, now lost because the books, written in Latin, are illegible. And as depraved as the English may have been to invite the Viking depredations, the lapse in linguistic memory that renders the past unreadable may be the greater failure. Having asked himself why his predecessors did not translate books from Latin into English, Alfred realizes just how far the present has fallen linguistically as well as morally: 'They did not imagine that men should ever become so careless and learning so decayed.' The king's remedy for this situation is predictably, even necessarily, linguistic. Describing the passage of Holy Writ and exegesis from the Hebrews to the Greeks and then to the Romans, he proposes that these same books now be translated into English. To provide an institutional context for the production and distribution of these translations, he further proposes that free-born youth be taught to read English: 'afterwards one may teach further in the Latin language those whom one wishes to teach further and wishes to promote to holy orders'.[21]

---

[21] Swanton (ed. and trans.), *Anglo-Saxon Prose*, 31–2.

There is far more than nostalgia here. Alfred's policy collapses morality, history, and language, with a failure in one mirroring lapses in the others. While cause and effect may be moot, since variations in all three necessarily co-occur, language (he claims) provides the means to restore stability everywhere. Just as the loss of treasure and wisdom follows upon shifts away from Latin and literacy, so Alfred's program of translation and education will serve as the means to and confirmation of England's political and moral pre-eminence. Through his rationalization of translation, moreover, the king situates England in the *translatio studii* and *imperii*—in a cultural tradition that renders Winchester the Rome or Athens of the early Middle Ages.

Alfred's is thus a nuanced approach to anxiety about language change and variation. Such change may indeed be the origin and symbol of social dissolution. But if the English people can reassert control over language, eliminating variation and restoring England's linguistic practice to an immutable moment from the past, the resulting stability will advance the country beyond where it had been. In this way, Alfred evokes not simply the Tower of Babel but the pre-lapsarian Garden of Eden—metaphors of a cultural achievement that, he implies, is achievable by means of language management. If Alfred's policies failed to reach this goal, they did much to suspend the variation and change that the king laments and further linguistic achievement in England, with the educational program he described apparently extended in several foundational Christian works that joined the *Pastoral Care* in English translation at about this time: Gregory's *Dialogues*, Orosius's *History of the World*, Bede's *Ecclesiastical History*, Boethius's *Consolation of Philosophy*, and St Augustine's *Soliloquies*. Although the resumption of Viking raids in the late tenth century negated many of Alfred's political and literary achievements, the corpus planning in which he engaged was thus clearly successful in the short term. Representing language change through a heuristic that was religious as well as political, Alfred's policy channeled together recognition of the devastation wrought by the Vikings—the hand of God in earthly affairs—and the power of language in order both to reflect these conditions and to provide a means of redress. The circumstances that led to Alfred's program may indeed have been desperate, but there is nothing urgent in his calm assertion about the long-term stabilizing potential of language, once it is removed from the diurnal world of change.

But the fact that King Alfred did not permanently restore English culture through language planning on variation and change bears further consideration. When Viking raids resumed, they did so after Alfred's program of translation and education, after the Benedictine Reform these helped underwrite, and after the emergence of Winchester as a seat of learning and center for the production of the West Saxon koine in which many Old English texts survive. All these achievements would seem to have accomplished much of the restoration that Alfred envisioned, and so the success of the raids undermines the very claim that language change can be either cause of or solution to larger social disturbance. Indeed, a century later the Normans and Angevins rehearsed this same thinking and achieved much the same result. Through the Conquest, they reconfigured England's linguistic repertoire by introducing French, cultivating diglossia, and at the very least neglecting (if not repressing) production of manuscripts in English. Whatever success the Normans had in stabilizing the country by stabilizing linguistic variation was as short-lived as Alfred's, for by the middle of the twelfth century England witnessed the anarchy of King Stephen's reign and by the thirteenth the barons' revolt. For Normans and Anglo-Saxons alike, it seems, the real, divisive issues were not linguistic.

This was the case, too, at the height of the Lollard controversy. Inspired by John Wyclif, a theologian and graduate of Balliol College, Lollardy flourished at the end of the fourteenth and beginning of the fifteenth centuries. It was less a movement, however, than an association of movements, some learned and some popular, some avowedly political and some not. Lollard beliefs, likewise, ran a spectrum from the mildly heterodox to the overtly heretical, such as Wyclif's own denial of the doctrine of transubstantiation. For such views, Wyclif was condemned, in succession, by Pope Gregory XI in 1377, the Blackfriars Council in 1382, and Archbishop Courtenay of Canterbury in 1382. One of the prominent issues in Lollard rhetoric, both for and against, was their language planning over the role of the vernacular in Church worship and practice.

Portions of the Gospel had been translated into Old English, which had also been used for numerous sermons and homilies, and a pre-Lollard Anglo-Norman Bible translation is also extant. But since the Norman Conquest and within the dynamics of diglossia, Latin dominated all written and spoken religious activity in late-medieval England. This domination proceeded not simply from St Jerome's Vulgate Bible as the standard text of God's word but also, with the twelfth-century rise of scholasticism, from theological discussion at Oxford and Cambridge. For their part, the Lollards tended to represent this dominance of Latin as part of a larger obfuscatory process that concealed from believers the specifics of Scripture and their faith, the gaps between Scripture and received opinion, and the moral failures of those who managed Church practice. Making theology available in the vernacular was thus viewed as part of a process of integrity and virtue that could contribute to the conviction of English faith. According to one commentator, the refusal to render God's word in English amounted to a wilful and cursed attempt to hinder the salvation of the populace: 'For, if a master of skole knoweþ a sotilte to make his children clerkis, and to spede hem in here lernynge, he, hidynge þis lore from hem þat ben able þerto, is cause of here vnkynnynge. So, if writynge of þe gospel in Englische and of good doctrine þerto be a sotiltee and a mene to þe comoun pepel to knowe þe ry3t and redi weye to þe blisse of heuene, who loueþ lasse Crist, who is more cursed of God þan he þat lettiþ þis oon knowynge?'[22] In the prologue to the second Wycliffite Bible translation, the righteousness of a demand for vernacular translation produces desperation among believers: 'For, þou3 couetouse clerkis ben wode bi symonie, eresie and manie oþere synnes, and dispisen and stoppen holi writ as myche as þei moun, 3it þe lewid puple crieþ aftir holi writ to kunne it and kepe it wiþ greet cost and peril of here lif.'[23] The Lollards' opponents recognized full well that translation was in effect a wedge issue that opened up social and ecclesiastical concerns far beyond simply the language in which one read the Bible. To the chronicler Henry Knighton, in translating the Bible 'from Latin into the language not of angels but of Englishmen', Wyclif 'made that common and open to the laity, and to women who were able to read, which used to be for literate and perceptive clerks, and spread the Evangelists' pearls to be trampeled by swine. And thus that which was dear to the clergy and the laity alike became as it were a jest common to both, and the clerks' jewels became the playthings of laymen, that the laity might enjoy now forever what had once been the clergy's talent from on high.'[24] Through translation some of the fundamental distinctions of late-medieval society—literate from illiterate, clergy from laity, men from women—were at risk, and with them the more encompassing distinction between metaphorical jewels and jests.[25]

Language change and variation figured provocatively and complexly in this late-medieval controversy. Given the prominence of these linguistic topics in their policies and their willingness to defend them literally to the death, the Lollards certainly embraced change. And yet their motivation, many of them argued, was not the declaration of some new truth but the recovery of

---

[22] Anne Hudson (ed.), *Selections from English Wycliffite Writings* (Cambridge: Cambridge University Press, 1978), 107.

[23] Hudson (ed.), *Selections from English Wycliffite Writings*, 67.

[24] Knighton, *Knighton's Chronicle, 1337–1396*, ed. and trans. G. H. Martin (Oxford: Clarendon Press, 1995), 243, 245.

[25] For an account of the Lollard movement, see Anne Hudson, *The Premature Reformation: Wycliffite Texts and Lollard History* (Oxford: Clarendon, 1988). For a concise account of the relations between Lollardy and English, which has lately been the focus of much critical commentary, see Margaret Aston, 'Wyclif and the Vernacular', in Anne Hudson and Michael Wilks (eds.), *From Ockham to Wyclif, Studies in Church History*, Subsidia 5 (Oxford: Blackwell, 1987), 281–330.

transcendent, immutable truths that had become obscure through Church policy over time. Regarding fundamental Christian law, one writer notes that 'Crist in þe houre of his assencioun comaundid to hise diciplis to preche it to alle pepelis—but, we be siker, neiþer only in Frensch ne in Latyn, but in þat langage þat þe pepel vsed to speke, for þus he tauȝt hymself'.[26] If made intelligible to all people, the Bible would appear with its original sense, stripped of excrescence and therefore less liable to misunderstanding.

This attention to translation as not disruption but a linguistic and moral stabilizing process appears in a variety of ways. The prologue to the Bible translation, for example, follows St Augustine's injunctions in *De Doctrina Christiana* and takes pains to advocate the collation of Latin texts in order to arrive at correct readings. It even describes a process that carefully distinguishes variants: 'And where þe Ebru bi witnesse of Ierom, of Lire and oþere expositouris discordiþ fro oure Latyn biblis, I haue set in þe margyn bi maner of a glose what þe Ebru haþ, and hou it is vndurstondun in sum place.' Having specified how to render in English syntactic structures like Latin ablative absolutes and words like *autem*, the writer even suggests the potential English has for being more accurate than the Latin of received tradition: 'I purpose wiþ Goddis helpe to make þe sentence as trewe and open in English as it is in Latyn, eiþer more trewe and more open þan it is in Latyn.'[27] In the same vein, the prologue to one of the Wycliffite Glossed Gospels offers a detailed account of how gloss and text are distinguished: 'þe text of þe gospel is set first bi itsilf, an hool sentence togider, and þanne sueþ [follows] þe exposicioun in þis maner: first a sentence of a doctour declaringe þe text is set aftir þe text, and in þe ende of þat sentence, þe name of þe doctour seiynge it is set, þat men wite certeynli hou feer [far] þat doctour goiþ.'[28] A similar use of translation to channel textual (and social) stability runs collectively through the texts of the various Wycliffite translations themselves. Although physically the two hundred or so extant copies of the Wycliffite Bible vary from New Testament extracts to simple quartos to lavishly illuminated folios, linguistically Wycliffite books in general display consistency that suggests not simply the coordinated reproduction of texts but the cultivation of a sociolect as well.[29]

---

[26] Hudson (ed.), *Selections from English Wycliffite Writings*, 108.

[27] Hudson (ed.), *Selections from English Wycliffite Writings*, 69, 68.

[28] This prologue occurs in Cambridge, Trinity College MS B.1.38 and is quoted in Kantik Ghosh, 'Manuscripts of Nicholas Love's *The Mirror of the Blessed Life of Jesus Christ* and Wycliffite Notions of "Authority"', in Felicity Riddy (ed.), *Prestige, Authority, and Power in Late Medieval Manuscripts and Texts* (Woodbridge: D. S. Brewer, 2000), 20.

[29] On the physical format of Wycliffite Bibles see Henry Hargreaves, 'The Wycliffite Versions', in G. W. H. Lampe (ed.), *The Cambridge History of the Bible*, ii, *The West from the Fathers to the*

In effect, while critics like Knighton saw translation into English within the context of Lollard social disruption, much Lollard practice conceived language change as a necessary disruption that would restore linguistic stability and reduce the possibility of further change. As with King Alfred's revival of learning, the linguistic goal was to transcend change and variation. It was Church orthodoxy, in fact, that could be charged with pernicious change, since, as Wyclif argued, theological terms like *transsubtanciacio* ('transubstantiation') were all recent inventions in the schools and not words—or concepts—with a historical or scriptural foundation.[30] Conversely, even if the Latin language of St Jerome's Vulgate may have remained constant, in this case linguistic constancy, due to variability in interpretation and lapses in human conduct, had helped obscure the original immutability of the word of God. Such language policies served a more general Lollard goal of not so much remaking or revolutionizing the Church as returning it to the condition from which it had deviated, and so again like Alfred's policies—and, indeed, like much of the language anxiety I examine in this book—they involved fundamental paradoxes. Such policies advocated language change in order to restore language immutability, just as they cultivated stabilizing linguistic practices in order to effect change. And critics of Lollardy had paradoxes of their own. The fifteenth-century prelate Reginald Pecock, for example, maintained that since much of Lollardy's popular, heretical success could be attributed to its use of English, English should also be used by those seeking to refute the heretical arguments.[31]

That language in itself represented a significant point of contention in the debates over Lollardy is beyond doubt. William Thorpe, in an account of his 1407 'testimony' before Thomas Arundel, archbishop of Canterbury, states a version of perhaps the broadest theoretical justification for translation into English. To Thorpe, the key points are that the essence of the Gospel does not rest in the words of any particular version and therefore that an English rendering can do as well as a Latin one: 'Ser, by autorite of seint Ierom, þe gospel is not þe gospel for redying of þe lettre, but for þe blieue þat men haue

---

Reformation (Cambridge: Cambridge University Press, 1969), 387–415. For the Lollards' linguistic habits see generally Hudson, *The Premature Reformation*, 174–227, and M. L. Samuels, 'Some Applications of Middle English Dialectology', in Margaret Laing (ed.), *Middle English Dialectology: Essays on Some Principles and Problems* (Aberdeen: Aberdeen University Press, 1989), 64–80.

[30] Aston, 'Wyclif and the Vernacular', 300.

[31] Pecock, *The Repressor of Over Much Blaming of the Clergy*, ed. Churchill Babington, Rolls Series 19, 2 vols. (London: Longman, 1860), i, 128; *The Reule of Crysten Religioun*, ed. William Cabell Greet, EETS os 171 (London: Oxford University Press, 1927), 17–22.

in þe word of Crist—þat is þe gospel þat we bileue, not þe lettre þat we reden. Forþi þe lettre þat is touchid wiþ mannes honde is not þe gospel, but þe sentence þat is verily bileued in mannes herte þat is þe gospel.'[32] The issue appears prominently in a number of treatises from various viewpoints, and Lollard books were eventually burnt in a very public fashion. The status of English also figured significantly in official responses to Lollardy. Archbishop Arundel's own 1409 *Constitutions* proscribed both translation of the Bible into English and the possession of Bibles in English that dated to Wyclif's lifetime, while Bishop William Alnwick's 1429 investigations of heresy in Norwich maintained that knowledge of the Creed, Pater Noster, or Ave Maria in English could be regarded as proof of heresy.

But from the broadest sociolinguistic perspective and not that of Lollardy alone, English and translation were not the sole or primary motivating factors here, since at this very moment other domains advanced the vernacular without comment or controversy. Indeed, as exemplified by Chaucer's *Boece*, a rendering of the *Consolation of Philosophy*, academic standards of defining and glossing meaning could be successfully used in the production of vernacular translations of school texts. In rendering this work in English, that is, Chaucer incorporated into his translation extensive expansions and explanations from scholastic commentary traditions on the Latin *Consolation*. Chaucer thereby not only clarified his own work's sense but acted himself as a commentator, and in the process he implicitly advanced the claim that English could be used in ways historically restricted to Latin. If the ten extant medieval manuscripts (or fragments) of the *Boece* do not indicate a ground swell of interest among readers, neither do they give any sign that the work was resisted or suppressed because of Chaucer's innovative use of English. Even more pointed and potentially far-reaching indications that the status of English could be advanced without controversy come from the reign of Henry V. During this comparatively brief period (1413–22), the king served as at least an inspiration for some early fifteenth-century English poetry, employed the language in his correspondence, and perhaps fostered the cultivation of an English sociolect in the Chancery and other offices of government text production.[33] And a still greater sign of the late-medieval acceptance (if not

---

[32] Anne Hudson (ed.), *Two Wycliffite Texts*, EETS 301 (Oxford: Oxford University Press, 1993), 78.

[33] On Chaucer's translation, see Machan (ed.), *Chaucer's Boece*, Middle English Texts 38 (Heidelberg: Carl Winter, 2008), xi–xx. Derek Pearsall has suggested that Henry's support of English may be in part a response to Lollardy's use of the vernacular. See Pearsall, 'Hoccleve's *Regement of Princes*: The Poetics of Royal Self-Representation', *Speculum*, 69 (1994), 386–410.

necessarily embrace) of English is the almost decade-by-decade increase in the rate of manuscripts produced in English during the fourteenth and fifteenth centuries.

It is yet another paradox of late-medieval English sociolinguistics, then, that its practices both suppressed and advanced the expanded use of the vernacular and thus channeled non-linguistic concerns through language in very much a situational fashion. As a rhetorical figure, paradox necessarily points to something behind itself—some higher truth or conflict or realization—that would in this case affirm that these linguistic policies are not simply whimsy or sleight of hand. The resolution of this linguistic paradox again lies in the fact that the issues underlying it are not essentially linguistic. The Lollard controversy foregrounded change and variation and thereby fostered concerns about them, but it used these concerns to channel anxiety over narrowly religious policy and what has been called vernacular theology. Lollardy's linguistic ambitions were actually rather limited. It did not assay status language planning that would have transformed the role of English within the linguistic repertoire of late-medieval England; it did not seek to insert English into the domains of law, court culture, and business; and it did not seek to institutionalize English grammars, rhetorics, and dictionaries. By the same token, neither did opponents like Knighton indicate that they hoped to suppress the use of written English in general, which, as I have said, was expanding significantly at this very moment. For all sides of the argument, the diachronic change and synchronic variation of language could be used to focus the truly consequential issues of theology and Church government, and they thereby offered reason to argue and believe that the contemporary alteration of language would produce transformation of these same issues. If language change mirrored moral and institutional failure, it could also putatively lead to their eventual correction, and in this vein religion and culture—not language—remained as much the primary issues for the Lollards as they had been for King Alfred and would be for American nativist movements or the revival of Passamaquoddy. The limited linguistic consequences of Lollardy can thus be seen to follow from the misdirection that defined its representations of change and variation. When the status of English within England's linguistic repertoire did finally change, accompanied by changes in the corpus and its management, it did so not because of religious policy but through the early modern institutionalization of English in government and legal proceedings, education, and business, made possible by growths in printing and literacy and enabling the nationalism and ideology of linguistic standardization that sustained this change.

The government of language

A distinction between secular and religious policies is not easily drawn in the examples of Alfred's translation program and the representation of language change in Lollard activities. Alfred was of course a king, but his policy focused on the translation of key ecclesiastical texts and the preparation of men for Holy Orders, while Lollard activities, though concentrated on theological matters, ultimately were associated with the social unrest of the 1381 Peasants' Revolt and other civil disturbances of the period. These kinds of overlap perhaps inevitably emerged from the investiture that the medieval English crown and Church had in one another. With the increasing separation of Church and state in predominantly Anglophone regions since the early modern period, however, the former's role in language planning has diminished. In England, perhaps the last and most significant acts of religious linguistic policy were self-erasing ones that indirectly helped to exclude the Church from language planning by furthering the use of vernaculars and thereby relaxing any centralized control over sacred language. I refer here to Reformation proclamations like the 1549 First Act of Uniformity, which required the English Book of Common Prayer in public religious observance and restricted other languages—Hebrew, Greek, Latin—to private worship.[34] But also, more generally, I have in mind the Roman Catholic Council of Vatican II (1962–5), which mandated a shift from Latin to local vernaculars for religious services, since this shift had the similar effect of further constraining Church opportunities for language planning.

Institutional as well as ideological reasons situate contemporary language planning of all kinds, primarily, within the provenance of government rather than the Church. Beyond whatever impact the rise of scientific methods and religious skepticism may have had on individual perceptions of language, it is government—local, regional, or national—that characteristically has the funding and infrastructure to manage language planning. Taxes provide the means to maintain institutions like schools and courts, which in turn serve as the avenues for the articulation and enforcement of policies about language use and change. Indeed, language planning as it exists today, ultimately impinging on all aspects of daily life, was in many ways made possible only by the development of political states, which have joined together institutional infrastructure, technological developments in printing, mandatory education, the discipline of modern linguistics, and notions of nationalism.

[34] G. R. Elton, *The Tudor Constitutions: Documents and Commentary*, 2nd edn. (Cambridge: Cambridge University Press, 1982), 402–5.

If individual schools provide instruction in English or other languages, for example, they do so using modern technology and according to modern understandings of language acquisition, within government-regulated educational policies that are maintained by schoolboards and courts, and against a background of nationalist discourse about the relations between language and society.

Educational policy reflects and channels social anxieties through language change and variation in several distinct ways. Perhaps most simply, policies can create shift and transform social identity by suppressing the use of non-English languages in classrooms, as has been the practice in nearly all contact situations until fairly recently. Irish, Welsh, and Scots Gaelic were thus actively discouraged and sometimes even proscribed in nineteenth-century Irish, Welsh, and Scottish classrooms, as were Aboriginal languages in Australia, Spanish in Puerto Rico, and Maori in New Zealand. In Wales, the 1861 educational code even tied government funding to elementary students' proficiency in English and arithmetic, leaving schools little reason to teach Welsh and every reason to suppress it. And whatever reasons there may have been to teach Welsh became moot by the British 1870 Education Act, which simply prohibited the use of the language in schools.[35] In all these regions save Puerto Rico, the schoolroom proscription of an indigenous language contributed to a significant shift to English both directly and indirectly. Recent studies have shown, that is, that the use of a dominant language like English in the classroom, irrespective of the educational impact of what happens in that classroom, furthers shift in other ways. When children return home from school, they introduce the dominant language into domestic domains, bringing with it not only bilingualism but also the social values associated with that dominant language. This same conclusion appeared as long ago as an 1839 report by the Edinburgh Gaelic School Society, which indicates that Scottish educational policies affected Gaelic-speaking parents as well as their children: 'it is difficult to convince [the parents] that it can be any benefit to their children to learn Gaelic, though they are all anxious, if they could, to have them taught English.'[36] And in this way, as in the United States, just three generations can lead from monoglot, non-Anglophone parents, to bilingual children, to monoglot, Anglophone grandchildren. By itself, this kind of shift

---

[35] Mari C. Jones, *Language Obsolescence and Revitalization: Linguistic Change in Two Contrasting Welsh Communities* (New York: Oxford University Press, 1998), 10; Stephen May, *Language and Minority Rights: Ethnicity, Nationalism and the Politics of Language* (London: Longman, 2001), 170.

[36] Quoted in Daniel Nettle and Suzanne Romaine, *Vanishing Voices: The Extinction of the World's Languages* (Oxford: Oxford University Press, 2000), 138.

can also lead to personal and familial trauma over a speaker's history, identity, and ethnicity, as famously described by Richard Rodriguez.[37]

In instances where such shift has been compelled, the brutality of its methods can channel additional trauma through language. Welsh children discovered speaking their native language at school had the 'Welsh knot' (or 'not'), a knotted rope, placed around their neck, and wore it until another child's linguistic transgression earned the knot. At day's end, the last child wearing the rope was punished, sometimes by being beaten with the rope. Tally sticks that recorded instances of using Irish or Gaelic served similar purposes in Irish and Scottish classrooms.[38] Even more brutally, speakers of Aboriginal or Amerindian languages suffered not only direct corporal punishment for speaking a language other than English but also forced removal to boarding schools. According to one historical account of the Navajo reservations,

> In the fall the government stockmen, farmers, and other employees go out into the back country with trucks and bring in the children to school. Many apparently came willingly and gladly; but the wild Navajos, far back in the mountains, hide their children at the sound of a truck. So stockmen, Indian police, and other mounted men are sent ahead to round them up. The children are caught, often roped like cattle, and taken away from their parents, many times never to return. They are transferred from school to school, given white people's names, forbidden to speak their own tongue, and when sent to distant schools are not taken home for three years.[39]

Once the Indians arrived at the boarding schools, additional efforts were made to manage their linguistic as well as social variance from the Anglo population at large. At the Carlisle Indian Industrial School in Pennsylvania, founded in 1879, new arrivals had their braids cut and clothes replaced. In what amounted to a re-enactment of Babel, not only were they forbidden to speak their own languages but also speakers of different languages were scattered among each other in the barracks, so as to minimize the possibilities of maintaining tribal groups or languages.[40] The United States Bureau of Indian Affairs abandoned all such policies by 1934, but the long-term failure and detrimental effects of a compelled shift to English have become ingrained in Native American culture.[41]

---

[37] Rodriguez, *Hunger of Memory: The Education of Richard Rodriguez: An Autobiography* (Boston, MA: D. R. Godine, 1982).

[38] Jones, *Language Obsolescence and Revitalization*, 10; Viv Edwards, *Multilingualism in the English-Speaking World: Pedigree of Nations* (Malden, MA: Blackwell, 2004), 97–9.

[39] Quoted in David H. DeJong, *Promises of the Past: A History of Indian Education in the United States* (Golden, CO: North American Press, 1993), 118.

[40] Sally Jenkins, *The Real All Americans: The Team that Changed a Game, a People, a Nation* (New York: Doubleday, 2007), 78.

[41] See DeJong, *Promises of the Past*, and Crawford (ed.), *Language Loyalties*, 41–51.

It is important to recognize, I think, that not all shift was accomplished in brutal ways for pusillanimous reasons. A kind of historically myopic self-righteousness makes it possible to dismiss as simply examples of the Western avowal of the 'white man's burden' sociolinguistic activity that was in some cases sincerely meant and sincerely appreciated. In 1663, for example, John Eliot issued a translation of the Bible into the Natick dialect of Massachusetts on the conviction that it would serve as a vehicle for the establishment of a nation founded on Christian principles—which was precisely what the Massachusetts Bay Colony had hoped to accomplish—and would thus allow Natick speakers to transcend European limitations as embodied in European languages. Less theologically but perhaps just as benevolently, other early European visitors to North America sought to record American Indian languages as an expression of a Romantic desire to improve the human condition and preserve cultural origins that were sometimes perceived to be as ancient as Greece's.[42] Even Carlisle was founded with the best of intentions by Captain Henry Pratt on the firm belief that assimilation to Anglo culture offered Native Americans the best chance for prosperity and success in an America largely predisposed to contain if not exterminate them. In an editorial in the first issue of the school newspaper, he defined Carlisle's purpose in this way: 'Instead of educating soldiers to go to the western plains to destroy with powder and ball, it is proposed ... now to train at this institution a corps of practical, educated, and Christian teachers, who will by precept and practice induce their tribes on the plains to adopt the peaceful pursuits of Christian people.'[43]

It is also important to acknowledge, though, that Eliot and Pratt were exceptions to the often unambiguously cynical manipulation of language change for non-linguistic reasons, of which the experience of the Hawaiian islands is paradigmatic. An indigenous population of approximately 800,000 at Captain James Cook's 1778 landing had declined by 1893 to perhaps 40,000 individuals with varying degrees of competence in the Hawaiian language. As in other Pacific regions (such as New Zealand), partly the decline of speakers owed to the introduction of diseases for which the indigenous people lacked immunities, and partly it owed to the paradoxical Western attitude that saw Hawaiians as having both the virtue of noble savages and the simplicity of children—and for both reasons as a people in need of and unable to prevent westernizing intervention. Laura Fish Judd, an early Anglo resident, thus observed in 1880, 'If the Italian is the language of the gods, the French of

---

[42] Edward G. Gray, *New World Babel: Languages and Nations in Early America* (Princeton, NJ: Princeton University Press, 1999), 56–84, 112–38.

[43] Quoted in Jenkins, *The Real All Americans*, 81.

diplomacy, and the English of business men, we may add that the Polynesian is the dialect of little children. It is easier to say "hele mai", than "come here", and "I wai", than "give me water".[44] While many early schools conducted education in Hawaiian, they also worked expressly to assimilate indigenes to Anglo culture by requiring students, as part of their oral exercises, to renounce wooden gods, identify Western countries, and recite passages from the Bible. Nonetheless, despite the decline in the population and the educational influence of the West, a nativist sentiment persisted and experienced a resurgence in the 1890s with the cultivation of the hula dance and the emergence of a class of *kahuna* ('priests') focused on traditional activities and beliefs.[45] Though Hawaiian was in probably irreversible decline by 1893, then, it still had some life. What changed matters was the resolve of Anglo businesses to bring closure to their expanding influence over the islands. Over the course of a century they had wrested control of plantation lands and workers from local chiefs, in order to guarantee the continued, duty-free export of sugar into the United States.[46] In 1893, accordingly, the Hawaiian monarchy was overthrown, making Hawaii an independent (though American controlled) republic. Another step in this quiet acquisition of the islands occurred in 1896, when Hawaiian was proscribed in schools and English required. And in 1900 the Organic Act extended the English-only policy to the conduct of government business.

For the purposes of this book, the crucial point here is that, unlike at Carlisle, this suppression of language variation furthered not the presumptive good of the Hawaiians but, quite nakedly, the monetary gain of financiers. The effectiveness of these policies has been nearly complete. In 1880, 150 schools used Hawaiian to teach 4,078 pupils; 60 used English for 3,086 students. In 1902, no Hawaiian schools remained, while 203 schools used English for 18,382 students.[47] By 1983, when not even 50 children could speak Hawaiian, a language revival program was established, reintroducing students to Hawaiian culture as well as language. As of 1978 Hawaiian has been the co-official language of what is now the state of Hawaii, though long-term prospects for the language's maintenance remain dim.[48]

[44] Quoted in Albert J. Schütz, *The Voices of Eden: A History of Hawaiian Language Studies* (Honolulu, HI: University of Hawaii Press, 1994), 26.

[45] Schütz, *The Voices of Eden*, 347–50.

[46] Nettle and Romaine, *Vanishing Voices*, 94–7, and Sam L. No'eau Warner, 'The Movement to Revitalize Hawaiian Language and Culture', in Hinton and Hale (eds.), *The Green Book of Language Revitalization in Practice*, 133–44.

[47] Schütz, *The Voices of Eden*, 352.

[48] 'Major Effort Is Under Way to Revive and Preserve Hawaii's Native Tongue', *New York Times*, 15 April 2007, A18.

The motivations behind the Bureau of American Indian Affairs' policy of removing Native American children from reservations to English-only boarding schools displaced not economics but essentially genocidal ambitions to language change and variation. Nominally, removals took place out of concern for the Native Americans. John H. Oberly, the superintendent for Indian education, thus observed in 1885, 'It is an understood fact that in making large appropriations for Indian school purposes, the aim of the Government is the ultimate complete civilization of the Indian. When this shall have been accomplished the Indian will have ceased to be a beneficiary of the Government, and will have attained the ability to take care of himself.' Without removal to boarding schools, Native Americans, it was alleged and feared, would become extinct. Yet 'civilization' is of course a loaded term in this context, and few bureaucrats shared the compassion of Captain Pratt, the founder of Carlisle. An 1868 commission composed of government officials and army generals offered one gloss of 'civilization' and its relevance to language variation: 'Through sameness of language is produced sameness of sentiment, and thought; customs and habits are moulded and assimilated in the same way, and thus in process of time the differences producing trouble would have been gradually obliterated. By civilizing one tribe others would have followed...Schools should be established, which children should be required to attend; their barbarous dialects should be blotted out and the English language substituted.' Twenty-one years later the federal commissioner of Indian affairs, J. D. C. Atkins, offered much the same gloss and relevance: 'The first step to be taken toward civilization, toward teaching the Indians the mischief and folly of continuing in their barbarous practices, is to teach them the English language. The impracticability, if not impossibility, of civilizing the Indians of this country in any other tongue than our own would seem to be obvious, especially in view of the fact the number of Indian vernaculars is even greater than the number of tribes.'[49]

In New Zealand (or Aotearoa), contact between English and varieties of the indigenous Maori language illustrates still other ways by which government policies have fostered, in sometimes brutal fashions, anxiety about language change and variation. A Polynesian people, the Maori first arrived at the uninhabited North and South Islands late in the first millennium, probably coming from Tahiti and before that the Marquesas Islands. An influx of additional Polynesian immigrants in the fourteenth century fortified the descendants of the original group, and by 1642, when Abel Tasman captained the first European ship to dock in New Zealand, Maori language and culture,

---

[49] Quoted in Crawford (ed.), *Language Loyalties*, 48, 51.

the latter known for its carving and weaving in particular, were well and diversely established. Barely a century later, however, the sociolinguistic character of the area began to change swiftly and radically with the 1769 arrival of Captain Cook. European seal hunters landed in 1792, and by 1807 so, too, had whalers from the United States, Norway, Spain, and the East India Company. At this time, perhaps nearly 200,000 predominantly monoglot Maoris resided in New Zealand. By 1840 this population had decreased by 40%, and by 1890 it totaled about 45,000 individuals, a decline of roughly 75% over the course of the nineteenth century.[50]

The reasons for this decline are of course varied. As in Hawaii, North America, Africa, and Asia, Europeans introduced potentially fatal illnesses and diseases like measles, for which the indigenous populations had no antibodies, and also venereal diseases, which resulted in sterility. The trading of weapons for goods and the cultivation of strategic alliances that pitted individual groups against one another further contributed to the eradication of the Maoris. For the study of the anxiety attendant on language change, however, the most significant factors are the sociolinguistic ones. In 1838, only about 2,000 Europeans resided in New Zealand, but within four years, due to the attraction of farming and whaling opportunities, that number reached 10,000. In the latter half of 1861, after the discovery of gold, the European population of the South Island's Otago alone leapt from 13,000 to more than 30,000.[51] In this way, already in 1858 the population of pakehas (basically, 'Europeans') reached 59,000, thereby outnumbering that of Maoris less than a century after the appearance of the first English ship.[52] In addition to the advantages attendant on their control of technology and institutions such as the court system, Anglophones thus soon had simple numbers on their side. Even more sociolinguistically significant than this, the school system, as in India, contributed to a dramatic shift in the area's linguistic repertoire.

The earliest mission schools used Maori as a medium of education, with a Maori translation of the Bible appearing in 1827.[53] As I noted in Chapter 1, recent critics have emphasized the fact that language instruction is never value-free, since it always carries with it some of the ideals and principles of the culture it sustains, and in this light it can be argued that, ironically, this early instruction in Maori became a policy that may ultimately have helped to

---

[50] Ranginui Walker, *Ka Whawhai Tonu Matou: Struggle without End* (Auckland: Penguin Books, 1990), 80–1.

[51] Laurie Bauer, 'English in New Zealand', in Burchfield (ed.), *English in Britain and Overseas: Origins and Development*, 383.

[52] Walker, *Ka Whawhai Tonu Matou*, 113.

[53] Walker, *Ka Whawhai Tonu Matou*, 85.

undermine the language. By fostering the Western technology of literacy in a fundamentally oral society, missionaries implanted Western culture and created a means for the acquisition of land in accordance with Western conceptions of property. Further, by privileging some dialects as languages to be used for instruction in schools, missionary policy helped to simplify Maori linguistic diversity and establish belief in a monoglot culture analogous to the model of England and other dominant European powers.[54] The initiative to flatten out variation within Maori or between it and English appears with particular force in the first significant grammar and dictionary of Maori, published by Thomas Kendall and Samuel Lee in 1820. In order to teach the language to Europeans, who were likely educated in the highly synthetic languages of Latin and Greek, the authors willfully misrepresented Maori so as to make its grammar seem familiar. According to their preface, a 'particular object of the work, is the instruction of the European Missionary in the Language of New Zealand ... and for this end it was that Examples in declension and conjugation have been given, after the manner of European Grammars; when, in fact, there exists no such thing in the language in question'.[55]

Supplemented by the continued denigration of Maori as the inferior, debased language of an inferior, debased people, Maori literacy in effect worked to accelerate a linguistic shift to English that English literacy only furthered. The Native Schools Act of 1867, thus, directed that village schools be conducted in English, while the Native School Code of 1880 mandated that teachers have some familiarity with Maori, not to maintain the language but to ease the transition of students in the earliest grades and to facilitate the teaching of English. By 1905 the Inspector of Native Schools had promoted the proscription of Maori on playgrounds, which, as with Native American languages in the United States, Aboriginal languages in Australia, and Celtic languages in Ireland, Wales, and Scotland, came to mean the sometimes violent proscription of Maori in general.

The statistical concomitants of such policies are again striking: in 1900, over 90% of Maori primary students spoke Maori as their first language; by 1960, only 26% did; and by 1979 there was genuine concern that soon Maori would follow the pattern of Cornish and Manx and have all its speakers shift to English. The 1982 establishment of early-childhood Maori immersion programs through Te Kōhanga Rao, the 1986 creation of the Waitangi Tribunal to hear Maori grievances—an implicit recognition of a desire to protect the

---

[54] Peter Mühlhäusler, *Linguistic Ecology: Language Change and Linguistic Imperialism in the Pacific Region* (London: Routledge, 1996), 104–240. This book contains a wealth of historical quotations about the alleged barbarism of the Maori language and people.

[55] Quoted in Schütz, *The Voices of Eden*, 252.

language—and the 1987 Maori Language Act, which made Maori and English co-official languages that could both be used in courts of law, have led to some resurgence in the numbers of speakers and domains of usage. But even so, with Maori speakers overrepresented in low-paying jobs, unemployment, and low levels of education, the vitality of the language remains tenuous.[56] According to the 2006 National Census of New Zealand, 565,329 individuals were ethnically Maori; this represents about 14% of a national population currently estimated to be over four million. While Maori does hold co-official status with English, perhaps only 157,000 people are fluent with the language, most of whom are in fact Maori by descent.[57] The Maori population may have rebounded tenfold in one hundred years, then, but like the Celtic-speaking populations of Ireland, Wales, Cornwall, and Scotland it has shifted over-whelmingly to English.

Emblematic of the sociolinguistic issues implicit in the fairly dramatic shift of Maori speakers to English is the Treaty of Waitangi, signed on 6 February 1840, at a time when Maori speakers still outnumbered Anglophones. The first occasion on which the word *Maori* was used as a collective proper noun for all the indigenous peoples of New Zealand—who discriminated among themselves by tribal names—the treaty was written in both English and Maori, which had been a written language for about twenty years and which therefore sustained an oral, not a textual, culture. Most of the roughly five hundred Maori who 'signed' the treaty, indeed, did so only by making some kind of a mark. In English, the first article of the treaty gave 'sovereignty' to the Queen and her representatives over the whole of the region, but in the Maori version the word that corresponds to 'sovereignty' is 'kāwanatanga', a word that better translates as 'governorship'. The Maoris thus likely believed that they were ceding not their autonomy but rather the governance of imported British institutions. And this misunderstanding was reinforced by the second article, which in the Maori version used 'rangatiratanga', which does mean something like 'absolute chieftainship', to describe the Maoris' relationship to their lands, homes, and possessions. Here, interlanguage variation helped to erase itself by fostering a situation that accelerated the Maoris' shift to English; if Anglo-phones had sovereignty, that is, Maori held no interest for them or advantage

    [56] Walker, *Ka Whawhai Tonu Matou*, 146–8, 238–40; Mühlhausler, *Linguistic Ecology*, 246–7; Edwards, *Multilingualism in the English-Speaking World* 59, 106, 117; May, *Language and Minority Rights*, 285–308; Richard A. Benton, 'Language Policy in New Zealand: Defining the Ineffable', in Michael Herriman and Barbara Burnaby (ed.), *Language Policies in English-Dominant Countries: Six Case Studies* (Clevedon: Multilingual Matters, 1996), 62–98; Jeanette King, 'Te Kōhanga Reo: Māori Language Revitalization', in Hinton and Hale (eds.), *The Green Book of Language Revitalization in Practice*, 119–28.
    [57] http://www.stats.govt.nz/census/default.htm.

for the Maoris themselves. And from this linguistic confusion (if not misdirection) also followed many of the political, social, and economic difficulties of the next century and a half.[58]

For indigenous Hawaiians, Native Americans, Maoris, and, indeed, most of the linguistic minority groups that English contacted inside and outside of the British Isles, the intensity of policies designed to affect shift and eliminate variation seems surprising. Economically, technologically, and educationally disadvantaged to begin with, such groups would seem to have posed little threat to the institutional and commercial advantages of Anglophones, who in most of these regions (as in New Zealand) attained significant numerical superiority as well in a fairly short time. Even less clear is how a minority language not viable in business or government—and often lacking a written form—could in and of itself pose a threat to English and its speakers. What makes these policies clear (and familiar) is recognition of how they channel non-linguistic concerns into variation and change—into variation from English and the change of non-Anglophones to its use.

Maori itself was never a threat to English; its speakers were, potentially, to the farming, whaling, and mining industries. And if the variation of their language was erased—if they substantially shifted to English—at least some cultural traditions would be suppressed if not erased as well. In their place would be a sociolinguistic world that would disproportionately advance the non-linguistic concerns of some speakers (Anglophones) over others (Maoris). Whether in such situations non-native speakers—or, for that matter, speakers of a non-standard variety—can ever acquire precisely the same opportunities and advantages as native speakers of Standard English merely by changing their language seems doubtful. Even as the Maori overwhelmingly shifted to English, indeed, a kind of stage Maori was cultivated in early twentieth-century Anglophone writing as the representation of an English dialect putatively spoken by Maoris alone. This wasn't the case. The variety, in some ways like Dickens's cockney, reflected stereotypes as much as reality, and what was linguistically real was shared with lower-class pakehas in what amounted to a class, not an ethnic, sociolect: 'I been come all te way from Noo Zeelan to fight te Sherman soldier in Parani and make him clear outer t'this country. When I come here some feller been tell me all about t'that dirty trick all te Sherman been up tin Parani an Peljimi. No good you say t'that all gammon, it te true talk all right.'[59] If language had been the only issue,

58 Walker, *Ka Whawhai Tonu Matou*, 90–7; Bauer, 'English in New Zealand', 383; May, *Language and Minority Rights*, 286–7; and Donald McKenzie, *Oral Culture, Literacy and Print in Early New Zealand: The Treaty of Waitangi* (Wellington: Victoria University Press, 1985).

59 Quoted in Shaun F. D. Hughes, 'Was There Ever a "Māori English"?', *World Englishes*, 23 (2004), 576.

then once the Maoris shifted languages, there would have been no reason to fashion Maori English. In terms of the *conceptualization* of the Maoris, the dialect served to reinforce their isolation as an ethnic group, even though they now spoke English. And in this way, as a Labovian stereotype Maori English points even more strongly to the way language variation can stand in euphemistically for non-linguistic issues. To me, however, the most striking issue here is that such use of variation is by no means unique to New Zealand or, indeed, to the modern post-colonial world: it is characteristic of English in its recorded history. This same kind of supererogatory anxiety animates the Norman mythologizing of language contact between English and French, which I considered in the previous chapter, and it also runs through responses to the continued use of non-Anglophone languages in multilingual settings.

Bilingual education, whether its goal is maintenance of more than one language or transition to English alone, has been a particularly vitriolic issue in the United States. The Bilingual Education Act of 1968—officially, Title VII of the Elementary and Secondary Education Act—established federal guide-lines, and subsequent revisions of the act and Supreme Court decisions have kept the issue a prominent and controversial part of federal policy. In the 1974 case Lau v. Nichols, for example, the United States Supreme Court ruled on behalf of a group of Chinese-American parents whose non-Anglophone children had received no special aid for their language skills and who were consequently (the parents argued) performing poorly in school. While the Court of Appeals had ruled in favor of the school district, observing that 'every student brings to the starting line of his education career different advantages and disadvantages caused in part by social, economic, and cultural background', the Supreme Court maintained that 'there is no equality of treatment merely by providing students with the same facilities, text-books, teachers, and curriculum; for students who do not understand English are effectively foreclosed from any meaningful education'.[60] Some of the controversy about bilingual education arises from the fact that unimpeach-able conclusions about long-term efficacy are difficult to draw in light of the variation among programs, their assessment methods, the sociocultural con-texts of individual schools, and the pressures of political groups. As with diachronic structural change, it's impossible either to control for all variables but one or to test conclusions by reproducing a given set of conditions. Perhaps not surprisingly, then, competing studies have produced data both supporting and challenging the notion that bilingual education provides the

---

[60] Quoted in Crawford (ed.), *Language Loyalties*, 252, 253.

most effective transition to English competence for students who do not speak the language at home.[61]

Yet the intensity of current American responses to linguistic variation as filtered through bilingual education can also be tied chronologically to rising rates of immigration, increasing tax burdens, and backlash to civil rights legislation in general. From the 1980s onward these have produced an increasingly politicized environment for bilingual education, rendering it an outlet for anxiety about patriotism and employability. President Ronald Reagan once commented that it 'is absolutely wrong and against American concepts to have a bilingual education program that is now openly, admittedly dedicated to preserving their [i.e., non-Anglophone students'] native language and never getting them adequate in English so they can go out into the job market and participate'. Reagan's Secretary of Education, Terrel Bell, justified the diversion of funds from bilingual education by noting, 'We will protect the rights of children who do not speak English well, but we will do so by permitting school districts to use any way that has proven to be successful'.[62] Funding, indeed, has proved one of the most divisive issues. Since ultimately the same tax base that underwrites education also underwrites social services, the military, and everything from federal parks to border control, a decision to support bilingual education has many implications for government activity and national identity. Such a decision generates controversy not only over taxes in general but in its prioritizing of one cause over another through the allocation of funds. A clear indication of this aspect of the controversy is the fact that, even as critics have lambasted the expense, government funding has *never* provided bilingual education for more than a fraction of the Limited English Proficiency students who express an interest in transitional programs to English.[63] When the Bilingual Education Act was allowed to lapse in 2002, then, it did so in response to anxieties not simply or primarily about language or education but also about taxes, government regulation, immigration, race, and national priorities. And by doing so, it fueled anxieties in all these same areas.

---

[61] James Crawford, *Bilingual Education: History, Politics, Theory, and Practice*, 4th edn. (Los Angeles, CA: Bilingual Educational Services, 1999), 102–56.

[62] Quoted in Crawford, *Bilingual Education*, 53.

[63] Ronald Schmidt, Sr., *Language Policy and Identity Politics in the United States* (Philadelphia, PA: Temple University Press, 2000), 17. Also see Crawford, *At War with Diversity: US Language Policy in an Age of Anxiety* (Clevedon: Multilingual Matters, 2000), 84–103; Sandra del Valle, *Language Rights and the Law in the United States: Finding Our Voices* (Clevedon: Multilingual Matters, 2003), 217–74; and Roseann Dueñas González and Ildikó Melis (eds.), *Language Ideologies: Critical Perspectives on the Official English Movement*, i, *Education and the Social Implications of Official Language* (Urbana, IL: NCTE, 2000).

Like education, immigration alone has a significant impact on every government's spending, whether directed at customs agents, border guards, social services for immigrants, court translators, workplace guidelines, or voting rights. Also like education, immigration shapes individuals' views of their country: its values, economic stature, race, ethnicity, and level of civic responsibility. And in any of these areas language planning can facilitate government policy by fostering and channeling anxiety about language change and variation. Australia, New Zealand, Canada, and the United Kingdom have all regulated immigration in part through evaluations based on an individual's command of English, for instance. The relatively small regional variation in Canadian English, further, is partly a response to political anxieties, following the 1867 Confederation, over the possibility of American expansion into western territories. The government at that time facilitated Canada's own westward expansion of the railroads, which brought with them a great many teachers, bankers, and government officials from Ontario. In this way, political anxiety likewise served to expand Anglophone regions and contain the Francophone population largely in Quebec. Given the relative uniformity of Canadian English, variation and change retained—and continue to retain— the power to channel non-linguistic anxieties. While Anglophones may have come to dominate western territories, new immigrants continued to arrive in the nineteenth century, leading the *Calgary Herald*, in 1899, to call for restrictions and quotas by evoking the familiar narrative of language change: 'This policy of building a nation on the lines of the Tower of Babel, where the Lord confounded the language so that the people might not understand one another's speech, is hardly applicable to the present century.'[64]

In the United States, which experienced its own increase in immigration from southern and eastern Europe at this same time, an inability to read or speak English fluently could factor into judgements of immigrants as mentally deficient and thus lead to the disqualification of many individuals from these regions. In 1912, Henry Goddard found this to be the case with 83% of the immigrant Jews he studied, 80% of the Hungarians, 79% of the Italians, and 87% of the Russians. Language shift, race, and social engineering likewise coalesced in the Australian policy of the 1920s and 1930s that directed the forced seizure of mixed Aborigine-European children, who were to be raised among Anglophones and married to others with increasingly less Aboriginal

---

[64] Quoted in Edwards, *Multilingualism in the English-Speaking World*, 28. See further R. K. Chambers, '"Lawless and Vulgar Innovations": Victorian Views of Canadian English', in Sandra Clarke (ed.), *Focus on Canada* (Amsterdam: John Benjamins, 1993), 1–26; and Laurel Brinton and Margery Fee, 'Canadian English', in *The Cambridge History of the English Language*, vi, John Algeo (ed.), *English in North America* (Cambridge: Cambridge University Press, 2001), 422–40.

blood until the entire group would genetically and linguistically merge with the full-blooded Europeans.[65]

The channeling of extra-linguistic concerns through this kind of language planning becomes particularly salient in moments of non-linguistic social crisis. While the United States had never had any formal federal language policy, for example, the events of the First World War produced state and local restrictions on language as well as immigration. When the country entered the war, concerns about treason and national loyalty led a number of states to enact laws that restricted the use of non-English languages (particularly German) in public, at schools, and even on the telephone. Perhaps most famously, the 1919 Siman Act in Nebraska proscribed the teaching of any foreign language until students were in the eighth grade, leading to the arrest of Robert Meyer for teaching a Bible story in German to a group of younger children. In upholding Meyer's conviction for wrongfully teaching a foreign language, the Nebraska Supreme Court emphasized not language but safety and citizenship:

The salutary purpose of the statute is clear. The Legislature had seen the baneful effects of permitting foreigners, who had taken residence in this county, to rear and educate their children in the language of their native land. The result of that condition was found to be inimical to our own safety. To allow the children of foreigners, who had emigrated here, to be taught from early childhood the language of the country of their parents was . . . to educate them so that they must always think in that language, and, as a consequence, naturally inculcate in them the ideas and sentiments foreign to the best interests of this country.

For its part, in overturning the state court's ruling in Meyer v. Nebraska, the United States Supreme Court depended just as heavily on the non-linguistic effects and implications of language planning, specifically on the rights of Meyer to pursue his profession and of parents to educate their children in ways they see fit. 'Practically,' the Court reasoned, 'education of the young is only possible in schools conducted by especially qualified persons who devote themselves thereto . . . Mere knowledge of the German language cannot reasonably be regarded as harmful . . . Plaintiff in error taught this language in school as part of his occupation. His right thus to teach and the right of parents to engage him so to instruct their children, we think, are within the liberty of the amendment.'[66] In terms of how language can stand in for

---

[65] Edwards, *Multilingualism in the English-Speaking World*, 27–31.

[66] Crawford (ed.), *Language Loyalties*, 235–6. See also del Valle, *Language Rights and The Law in the United States*, 30–9; and Dennis Baron, *The English-Only Question: An Official Language for Americans?* (New Haven, CT: Yale University Press, 1990), 144–50.

non-linguistic issues, the similarity of the courts' arguments, despite the fact that they use them to reach opposite conclusions, is here striking. Like the lower court whose ruling it overturned, that is, the Supreme Court invests language change and variation—neutral linguistic phenomena—with the power to mediate individual freedom and national identity.

Immigration and social diversity intersect most generally with language planning and change in laws regarding the official status of English and other languages. In the late twentieth century these connections were especially prominent in the United States, which witnessed movements to make English the official language of not simply the country but also individual states, counties, and even municipalities.[67] One indication of the non-linguistic motivation of these movements is the history of US English, one of the pre-eminent organizations. Founded by John Tanton and S. I. Hayakawa in 1983, US English began as an offshoot of another organization that Tanton had founded in the previous decade: Federation for American Immigration Reform. Serving as they do to channel extra-linguistic social concerns about immigration, economic recession, increased taxation, and the formation of national culture, these movements sometimes strain to maintain even a nominal focus on language policy.[68] In April of 2005, for instance, Joe Manchin, the governor of West Virginia, vetoed a bill that would have made English the state's official language, not because he did not support the idea, and not because non-Anglophones present particular problems—or, for that matter, even make up a constituency—in a state wherein only 2.7% of the population does not speak English at home. He did so, rather, for the legalistic reason that the legislation had violated the state's constitution by being tacked onto other legislation, specifically onto the funding of municipal recreation boards.[69] The putative need for such legislation thereby remained unchallenged.

Such strains and concerns are neither uniquely American nor uniquely modern, however. The 1536 Act of Union of England and Wales offers the earliest expression of a broad government policy for containing social and linguistic change and variation through the declaration of languages' relative status. After stating that English should be the language used in all Welsh courts, the Act adds 'from hensforth no personne or personnes that use the

---

[67] See Baron, *The English-Only Question*; Larry Rohter, 'Repeal Is Likely for "English Only" Policy in Miami', *New York Times*, 14 May 1993, A7; Jodi Wilgoren, 'Divided by a Call for a Common Language: As Immigration Rises, a Wisconsin County Makes English Official', *New York Times*, 19 July 2002, A8.

[68] Carol L. Schmid, *The Politics of Language: Conflict, Identity and Cultural Pluralism in Comparative Perspective* (Oxford: Oxford University Press, 2001), 44–5, 32–56.

[69] 'English-Only Bill Is Vetoed', *New York Times*, 18 April 2005, A17.

Welsshe speche or langage shall have or enjoy any maner office or fees within the Realme of Englonde Wales or other the Kinges dominions upon peyn of forfaiting the same office or fees onles he or they use and exercise the speche or langage of Englisshe'.[70] The 1537 Irish 'Act for the English Order, Habite, and Language' similarly mandated English for all those who wished to be recognized as 'his Highness true and faithfull subjects'. And in the 1616 Act for the Settling of Parochial Schools, James I mandated the same situation for Scottish schools. Now that 'the vulgar English tongue be universally planted', the Act observes, 'the Irish language, which is one of the chief and principal causes of the continuance of barbarity and incivility amongst the inhabitants of the Isles and Highlands, may be abolished and removed'.[71] The striking thing about such language legislation in the history of English is that while it might lead to policies on education and business, by itself it has in fact had little impact on language use and shift. The shift of Welsh speakers to English, for example, depended more on the economic opportunities associated with the incursion of Anglophones into Wales than it did on the legal restrictions on the status of Welsh. Indeed, the limitation of such laws is clear from the fact that to this day, even though English is the official language—a language so declared by law—in neither the United Kingdom nor the United States, Anglophones of both countries enjoy numerical superiority as well as control over powerful domains of economics, education, and government. For all these reasons, they also have the prerogative of channeling non-linguistic issues through linguistic ones.

In predominantly Anglophone countries attempts to legislate the status of non-English languages have also been more common of late and have betrayed anxieties of their own about change and variation. If the English Only movement's efforts to pass a Constitutional amendment declaring English the official language of the United States point to anxiety over immigration and taxation, thus, the 1921 declaration of Irish as co-official with English in the Irish Free State uses language to signal a desire to effect political and cultural independence from England. This use of language planning to channel concerns over national identity appears likewise in Canada's 1988 Official Languages Act, which helped to protect the official rights of Francophones and Francophone communities; the 1993 Welsh Language Act, which did much the same for the status of Welsh in Wales; the 1992

---

[70] Quoted in Glanville Price, *The Languages of Britain* (London: Edward Arnold, 1984), 106–7.

[71] The Irish Act is quoted from Patricia Palmer, *Language and Conquest in Early Modern Ireland: English Renaissance Literature and Elizabethan Imperial Expansion* (Cambridge: Cambridge University Press, 2001), 137; and the Scots Act quoted is from Nettle and Romaine, *Vanishing Voices*, 140.

Native American Languages Act, which sought to promote and revitalize Amerindian languages; and the 1996 South African Constitution, which declared English one of that country's eleven official languages.

In such circumstances, English can be assigned so much symbolic, cultural weight that it can serve as a reason for a non-native group to maintain its linguistic variation from the Anglophones around them, even though the primary point of contention remains non-linguistic. From the middle of the nineteenth century, for instance, Chinese speakers raised concerns that education in English, particularly through missionary schools, would be a vehicle for introducing Western culture and values to China; and despite other profound ideological differences, their communist successors raised these very same concerns to support their own efforts to retard the spread of English. Contemporary speakers of indigenous African languages have expressed similar anxieties, singling out the World Bank and the International Monetary Fund as institutions that advocate language policies to further their own non-linguistic economic agenda. 'The hidden push for English, in particular,' Alamin Mazrui claims, 'can be seen as part of a right wing agenda intended to bring the world nearer to the "end of history" and to ensure the final victory of capitalism on a global scale.'[72] In every one of these cases, the official sanctioning or proscription of variation between English and other languages has served socially symbolic as well as—perhaps more than—communicative ends, with language becoming salient confirmation of an ethnic (or national) group's independent identity. While Anglophones have agitated about the persistence of indigenous languages and indigenous speakers about the introduction of English, for both groups language variation produces an anxiety that centers, ultimately, on social issues.

Policies like these recall the religious policies I discussed above: they seek to use change as a way of fostering linguistic and cultural stability that is resistant to further change, and they invest language with the power not simply to reflect culture but to transform it. In this way, such policies also project just how much language can be made to mediate non-linguistic issues. Whether or not one personally accepts the argument that the spread of English is part of a vast, global, capitalist conspiracy, the very belief that it is again testifies for the anxiety associated with language change and variation. Status planning on behalf of minority languages attests to this same anxiety. By themselves, legislation and business activity can do little to accomplish

---

[72] Mazrui, *English in Africa after the Cold War* (Clevedon: Multilingual Matters, 2004), 54. See also Kingsley Bolton, *Chinese Englishes: A Sociolinguistic History* (Cambridge: Cambridge University Press, 2003), 226–58.

or retard the revival of a dying language. Language revival must also be backed by government or private funding for educational and economic programs, and it must speak to ideas that are already broadly shared rather than attempt to initiate them. In Cooper's analysis of language planning and national languages, 'Symbols are created not by legislation but by history. Irish and Kiswahili are not national symbols because the Irish and Tanzanian constitutions proclaim them as national languages. They are national symbols because of their association and identification with their national liberation movements and with their citizens' shared memory.'[73] While such association and identification can not be compelled by fiat on speakers, they recall arguments about a global Anglophone conspiracy, in that they reflect a strong belief in the power of change and variation to shape non-linguistic concerns.

Shared memory, of course, is an elusive quality, often situationally defined and contested. Sociolinguistic developments in Australia offer a final case in point. As immigration patterns changed following the Second World War, showing less dependence on Great Britain, so, too, did internal conceptions of the nation, which came to accept and advance an Australian variety of English as well as a broader, multicultural identity. In advocating the maintenance of Aboriginal and Torres Strait languages as well as the acquisition of a non-English language by all Anglophones, the 1987 National Policy on Languages formalized a memory of Australia as a multilingual place in which change and variation were natural occurrences. This same memory was itself contested four years later, in the 1991 Australian Language and Literacy White Paper, which focused less on languages as cultural resources and more on English literacy and other educational concerns. As Michael Clyne summarizes this dynamic reformation of Australian national and linguistic identity, 'Throughout the history of Australia and the six British colonies that preceded the federated nation, there has been an open-ended tension between English monolingualism as a symbol of a British tradition, English monolingualism as a marker of Australia's independent national identity, and multilingualism as a reflection of a social and demographic reality and of an ideology of an independent multicultural and outreaching Australian nation.'[74]

---

[73] Cooper, *Language Planning and Social Change*, 103.

[74] Clyne, *Dynamics of Language Contact: English and Immigrant Languages* (Cambridge: Cambridge University Press, 2003), 9. See also Uldis Ozolins, *The Politics of Language in Australia* (Cambridge: Cambridge University Press, 1993); Michael Herriman, 'Language Policy in Australia', in Herriman and Burnaby (eds.), *Language Policies in English-Dominant Countries*, 35–61; and Edwards, *Multilingualism in the English-Speaking World*, 116–17.

Language, nation, identity

In modern Anglophonic states, government funded and regulated language planning is predominant (if not pervasive), whether its focus is the language used in classrooms, business, or courtrooms; the rights of immigrants and the non-Anglophone languages they might speak; or the status of non-Anglophone languages in states dominated by English, as is the case in most (but not all) countries in which English is an indigenous language. I have suggested ways in which this planning, while directed at variation and change, has an ultimate goal both more general and non-linguistic, and in this way channels anxiety about race, taxation, and other social issues towards and through anxiety about language. To this end, American legislatures and law courts have consistently avoided pronouncing the existence of something like linguistic rights, such as the United Nations' Universal Declaration of Linguistic Rights and the European Charter for Regional or Minority Languages. They have relied instead on the United States Constitution's fourteenth amendment—specifically, its guarantees of legal due process and the right to pursue life and liberty—as the justifications for bilingual education and the like. In this way, what are popularly envisioned to be linguistic issues are redressed more generally as issues of civil rights. To understand these better, I want now to place them within the context of how language figures in the construction of nation and national identity. It is within this context as well that I will return to the notion of individuals' responsibility for their government's language planning on their behalf.

The role of language in national identity depends significantly, of course, on the conception of nationhood at a given time, and for England, glimmers of both nationalism and linguistic nationalism appear throughout the pre-modern period. In the prologue to his fifteenth-century *Troy Book*, for instance, John Lydgate claims that his patron Henry V wanted the Troy story told in English so that all inhabitants of England might read it:

> By-cause he wolde that to hyge and lowe
> The noble story openly wer knowe
> In oure tonge, aboute in every age,
> And y-writen as wel in oure langage
> As in latyn or in frensche it is;
> That of the story the trouthe we nat mys
> No more than doth eche other nacioun:
> This was the fyn of his entencioun.[75]

[75] Lydgate, *Troy Book*, ed. Henry Bergen, 4 vols., EETS es 97, 103, 106, 126 (London: Kegan Paul, 1906–35), Prologue, lines 111–18.

There is a suggestion, here, of the importance of language in the construction of a nation, but it is only that: a suggestion. Lacking the social structures and ideology that make possible modern nationalism and a standard language, neither Henry nor any of his immediate successors could do much to cultivate a sense of linguistic nationalism: the population was predominantly illiterate, the culture would continue for over a century to conduct much of its education and official business in Latin and French, and English itself, while increasingly consistent in orthography, lacked codification and the formal support of education or standardization. All these characteristics began to change in the seventeenth and eighteenth centuries, and the advent of industrialization and its impact on social organization (e.g., increased urbanization and bureaucratic infrastructure) accelerated the change still more. It is in this period that, in Benedict Anderson's famous analysis, England, other European countries, and the Thirteen Colonies acquired the intellectual and institutional means to imagine themselves as a community— to conceive a group with shared interests and culture from among a collection of individuals largely unknown to one another.[76]

Philosophically, the clearest early statements on the relation between language and national identity are those of the eighteenth- and nineteenth-century German Romantics Johann Herder, Wilhelm von Humboldt, and Johann Gottlieb Fichte, who in various ways articulated connections between blood, soil, and language. In Herder's prize-winning essay 'On the Origin of Speech', presented to the Berlin Academy of Sciences in 1770, he asked: 'Has a nationality anything dearer than the speech of its fathers? In its speech resides its whole thought domain, its tradition, history, religion and basis of life, all its heart and soul. To deprive a people of its speech is to deprive it of its one eternal good . . . With language is created the heart of a people.'[77] And in his posthumously published but widely influential *On Language*, von Humboldt provided a detailed argument of how language constitutes the definitive trait of a nation and its people: 'The *mental individuality* of a people and the *shape of its language* are so intimately fused with one another, that if one were given, the other would have to be completely derivable from it . . . Language is, as it were, the outer appearance of the spirit of a people; the language is their

---

[76] Anderson, *Imagined Communities: Reflections on the Origin and Spread of Nationalism*, rev. edn. (London: Verso, 1991). For further consideration of the limitations of English linguistic nationalism before the modern period, see Machan, *English in the Middle Ages* (Oxford: Oxford University Press, 2003), 161–78.

[77] Quoted in Ronald Wardhaugh, *Languages in Competition: Dominance, Diversity, and Decline* (Oxford: Blackwell, 1987), 54. On the role of language in nationalism, both historically and today, see further May, *Language and Minority Rights*, 52–90.

spirit and the spirit their language; we can never think of them sufficiently as identical.'[78] By these analyses, whether language causes nationhood or reflects it may be moot, but without a common language there can be no nation of shared culture and tradition, and without a nation, there can be no formal, political state.

This view of the linguistic integrity of the nation-state has had considerable impact on the anxiety associated with language change and variation. Indeed, the legacy of the imagined communities that Anderson sees uniting modern nations—a legacy reinforced by the Babel model of change and variation—is that to be imagined, nations require a single dominant language and that, therefore, any true nation perforce has such a language. The modern Western conception of nationhood is often so dependent on the predominance of one language, that by a kind of syllogism, multilingualism can be seen to under-mine nationhood: if nations by definition are monoglot, then a multilingual society cannot become a nation.[79] And unless they somehow occurred for entirely internal reasons, even language shift or radical structural change can easily be seen to challenge the cultural and political integrity of a people and their view of themselves. Given this line of reasoning, indeed, Grimm's explanation of the First Consonant Shift as an expression of Germanic pride and impetuosity makes perfect sense: it could have occurred without violating the social and linguistic integrity of the Germanic people only if its occurrence was a *sign* of that integrity. And to Grimm it was.

Since Herder's formulation of language as 'the heart of the people', of course, notions of nationhood and statehood—and of ethnicity within them—have become increasingly less stable and more controversial. One common argument contends that it is ethnicity that is pre-modern, even primordial, and that national or state groupings are imposed upon it, while another essentially reverses these positions, maintaining that the existence of modern nations leads to the situational fabrication of ethnicity. In suppress-ing the separatist inclinations of minority language groups in the various republics, for instance, the Soviet Union (it could be argued) did much to

[78] Von Humboldt, *On Language: the Diversity of Human Language-Structure and Its Influence on the Mental Development of Mankind*, trans. Peter Heath (Cambridge: Cambridge University Press, 1988), 46.

[79] See further Robert McColl Millar, *Language, Nation and Power: An Introduction* (New York: Palgrave, 2005). As Sue Wright concisely puts the issue, 'recognition of pluralism was at odds with nationalist claims to be language communities with the distinctive and unique ways of thinking that Herder had suggested. An early objective in the nationalist project was thus to achieve linguistic convergence within the group and to differentiate the national language from all allied dialects on the continuum' (*Language Policy and Language Planning: From Nationalism to Globalisation* [Basingstoke: Palgrave Macmillan, 2004], 35).

foster those same inclinations, just as, more generally, ethnicity arises and persists in modern, industrial society through what has been called an internal colonial model and its division of labor along cultural rather than strictly class lines.[80] And yet another common argument describes ethnicity as neither primordially nor politically determined, but instead as a process. In this view, rather than some kind of Platonic category, ethnicity is a construction—and not necessarily an intentional one—that over time interprets and associates cultural activity in ways that allow ethnic identities to take shape in relation to one another.[81]

All these arguments need to accommodate the complications posed by linguistic change and variation. If nationality or ethnicity are in some sense essentialist, for instance, there must be a way to account for the preservation of identity despite alterations across time and space in a language's grammatical structure as well as in speakers' mental conceptualizations of it. And if they are not, if they are situationally defined, we need a way to identify when sociolinguistic phenomena achieve a kind of integrity that includes some practices or individuals as variants and excludes others as categorically different. Recent attempts to get around these analytical complexities through a category of hybridity, which focuses on overlaps and liminal areas in social categories, solve some difficulties but create others, for the very category of hybridity is itself open to the accusation that it simply offers another version of the ethnicity it attempts to evade.[82]

These are not airy, academic debates. Romantic notions of the immanence of language in statehood remain influential to this day; a common motto of Welsh language movements, for example, has been 'cenedl heb iaith, cenedl heb galon'—'a nation without a language is a nation without a heart'.[83] And the foundational premise of the United States English Only movement is that the ability to speak English is part of the definition of the country. Such debates also have real financial and social consequences for the conceptualization of language change and variation and, in turn, for how this conceptualization relates to more general social concerns. Indeed, however ethnicity has been formed in the modern era, minority languages have consistently

---

[80] Andrew Dalby, *Language in Danger: The Loss of Linguistic Diversity and the Threat to our Future* (New York: Columbia University Press, 2003), 124, and Michael Hechter, *Internal Colonialism: The Celtic Fringe in British National Development* (New Brunswick, NJ: Transaction Publishers, 1999).

[81] A good discussion of post-Conquest England from this perspective is Hugh M. Thomas, *The English and the Normans: Ethnic Hostility, Assimilation, and Identity 1066-c1220* (Oxford: Oxford University Press, 2003).

[82] See further May, *Language and Minority Rights*, 19–51, and Wardhaugh, *Languages in Competition*, 39–63.

[83] Wardhaugh, *Languages in Competition*, 85.

helped to define and enforce the notion of a nation-state. If ethnicity has been one way to maintain identity and social leverage in conglomerate, immigrant societies, for instance, it has also been part of the cultural residue that a nation, depending on circumstances, sees itself as repressing, transcending, or assimilating. In this way, a dominant group can style itself as the nation partly through its use of minority groups and languages. According to Tom Nauerby, then, 'The national languages were actually the exact opposites of what nationalist mythology supposed them to be... they were not the primordial foundation of nations, but the more or less artificial products of the nation-building process itself'.[84]

By this kind of analysis, one ethnic group in effect appropriates the concept of nation, using its language as a way to define it. At one end of a spectrum for implementing such a policy, one could place the Soviet Union or revolutionary France, both of which fairly aggressively, even brutally, advanced the cause of the nation by suppressing minority languages and utilizing Russian and French, respectively, as ways to stabilize political action. At the other end, Norway and its treatment of Nynorsk has been offered as a more benign example of nation-building through language. Fashioned by Aasen in the nineteenth century out of the Norwegian rural dialects that showed the least linguistic influence of the Dano-Norwegian elite that had governed Norway since the late fourteenth century, Nynorsk has been cultivated since then as a *landsmål*, a speech deeply rooted in the land. Yet if in this way Nynorsk can be said to have underwritten a concept of nation, even it has also served, according to some critics, to maintain the privilege of upper-rank Norwegian groups; in this scenario, an elite that does not speak Nynorsk justifies its status, in part, though a subordinated, imagined joint class of rural farmers and urban laborers.[85] Somewhere in between these extremes are most Anglophone countries. In all of them, any group's appropriation of statehood has been and will remain aggressively contested, precisely because none of them has one ethnic group so predominant that the country might be judged monoethnic (like Iceland), wherein language, nation, ethnicity, and state truly do coalesce. For both the United Kingdom and the United States, this situation certainly hasn't stopped individual groups from claiming cultural primacy, but the mere fact that such claims have been so aggressively contested of late undermines any individual claim.

---

[84] Nauerby, *No Nation Is an Island: Language, Culture, and National Identity in the Faroe Islands* (Aarhus: Aarhus University Press, 1996), 8.

[85] See Gregg Bucken-Knapp, *Elites, Language, and the Politics of Identity: The Norwegian Case in Comparative Perspective* (Albany, NY: State University of New York Press, 2003). On Nynorsk more generally, see Haugen, *Language Conflict and Language Planning*.

In such political models language variation and change are of great consequence as correlates of ethnicity and nationhood. Since the latter are typically identified in the ways they manifest themselves, as in clothing or ritual or, indeed, language, arguments about these correlates often stand in for arguments about social and cultural identity. Managing change and variation becomes a way of managing social identity, then, whatever relation these phenomena actually bear to it and however complexly that identity is fashioned. In nineteenth-century Wales, for instance, contact between Welsh speakers and Anglophones played out in a nexus of social issues of which language was only one part. In the slate industry widespread in southern Wales, those who spoke Welsh also tended to be renters who were politically liberal and religiously non-conformist. By contrast, H. Paul Manning points out,

Lord Penchyn, the most influential of the owners, was combination *rentier* and capitalist, owning the largest slate quarry (with a 40 percent market share) as well as having an enormous landed estate of some 50,000 acres, which meant that he stood as both employer and landlord to many of the workers, and was a Tory MP and an Anglican to boot, at a time when Welsh Nonconformist Liberalism stood not only for home rule for Ireland and possibly Wales, but also for Disestablishment of the church and for the tenant-farmer (*gwerin*) against the passive landed wealth of the squirearchy.[86]

Talking about and controlling Welsh thus served indirectly to talk about and control—mediate—a host of non-linguistic concerns.

Similar issues have appeared in contact between English and the roughly 250 indigenous languages in the Philippines, though there with a result quite different from that in Wales. In 1901, following the Spanish-American War, 1,000 Anglophone teachers came to the region as part of a concerted policy to counter and constrain linguistic variation. By 1925 this policy did limit variation by producing some shift to English, but it did little to improve the educational achievement of native Filipinos, for a study at that time showed that they lagged behind their American counterparts in reading and writing. It was partly in response to this situation that when the Commonwealth of the Philippines was established in 1935, English and Spanish were made co-official. Following the Second World War and Philippine independence in 1946, reaction against English as a colonial legacy increased and came to focus on one indigenous language—Tagalog—as a symbol and vehicle of national unity. Today, English is still widely spoken but mostly in a native variety

---

[86] Manning, 'The Rock Does not Understand English: Welsh and the Division of Labor in Nineteenth-Century Gwynedd Slate Quarries', in Brian D. Joseph *et al.* (eds.), *When Languages Collide: Perspectives on Language Conflict, Language Competition, and Language Coexistence* (Columbus, OH: Ohio State University Press, 2003), 48.

(Taglish).[87] If the example of Wales presents a fairly consistent dichotomy between powerful interests mediated by English and less powerful ones mediated by Welsh, the example of the Philippines illustrates a continually shifting sense of national identity reflected in the shifting relations of Spanish, English, and Tagalog.

South Africa offers a still more complex example of how managing change and variation can stand in (often ineffectively) for managing issues of economics, politics, and race. The first white settlers appeared on the Cape in 1652, and by 1795 British Anglophones had taken control of the region. By the early part of the nineteenth century, even though speakers of Dutch outnumbered Anglophones by a ratio of five to one, attempts were made to define the area through English. In 1811, for instance, knowledge of English was specified as a pre-requisite for civil service. Dutch was declared co-official with English in 1882, but twenty years later this designation was restricted to English alone. The dynamic between these languages—and Afrikaans, which joined English and Dutch as co-official in 1925—bespeaks an attempt to foster national culture through language and, more significantly, stands startlingly out of synch with the linguistic and social realities of a region in which the vast majority of the population spoke and speaks only one or more indigenous African languages like Zulu. While these realities do figure largely in the 1996 constitution of the new South Africa, which declared eleven official languages and thus gestured strongly towards a multilingual, multiethnic conception of nationhood, language management remains a limited means for generating social identity. According to the 1996 census, English was only the fifth most commonly used language, with about 3.4 million speakers; Zulu was first, with 9.2 million, and Afrikaans third, with 5.8 million. When use of a second language was calculated, the statistics changed in a reflection of perceived social utility. Zulu remained first, with 25 million speakers, but English moved up to third, with 17.6 million speakers, and Afrikaans dropped to fourth, with 16 million speakers. Within the additional contexts of strong ethnic divisiveness and the institutionalization of a continuum of varieties of English, the South African linguistic repertoire provides little support for an argument that managing change and variation can be at all effective as a way of creating social identity as well: if given the opportunity, its speakers choose languages not as national political statements but for the immediate social utility they are understood to provide.[88]

[87] See further Roger M. Thompson, *Filipino English and Taglish: Language Switching from Multiple Perspectives* (Amsterdam: John Benjamins, 2003).

[88] On the history of language policy in South Africa, see Nkhelebeni Phaswana, 'Contradiction or Assimilation? The South African Language Policy, and the South African National Government', in

For Wales, the Philippines, and South Africa, it might be said that language planning has been relatively modest and that whatever failures it experienced could thus be attributed to its own ineffectuality. The Soviet Union provides a non-English illustration that is anything but tepid but in the end just as inconclusive. By imposing a shift to Russian, Stalin could in many ways accurately claim that he controlled the identity of the individual and collective Soviet Socialist Republics. Yet the break-up of the Soviet Union and the subsequent rejection by many former republics of Russian and the Cyrillic alphabet provides a useful corrective to such claims. In its entirety the Soviet example suggests that connections between language and social identity can be as much by fiat as through Herder's 'heart of the people', that language policies meant to manage language change succeed or fail in sometimes unpredictable ways, and that speakers always, figuratively as well as literally, have something to say about the language they use. They also suggest that for all this, there is something deadly serious about individual and state investment in the significance of change and variation.

For the Soviet Union, deadly serious meant the deaths of millions of innocent people. For the United States, it has meant a struggle since the founding of the republic over the relations between English and nationhood and all the ideas and practices that depend on these relations. Within this context, anxieties about language change and variation have contributed significantly to the formation of national and ethnic identity. Originating as it did in the eighteenth century, the United States emerged against a distinctive linguistic background: the nationalism of Herder and the German Romantics, the virtual completion of the codification of written English, the increased expansion of print, and a concomitant rise in literacy. Coupled with the period's proverbial emphasis on human thought and reasoning, such characteristics lead John Howe to follow others in describing the founding of America as 'in a fundamental sense, a linguistic act...Embarked on an unprecedented experiment in republican independence, members of the revolutionary generation employed written language as an essential instrument of political action through which they articulated political ideologies, negotiated political conflict, recorded political accomplishments, and charted

Sinfree Makoni *et al.* (eds.), *Black Linguistics: Language, Society, and Politics in Africa and the Americas* (London: Routledge, 2003), 117–31. On South African varieties of English, see Daniel Gough, 'Black English in South Africa', in Vivian de Klerk (ed.), *Focus on South Africa* (Amsterdam: John Benjamins, 1996), 53–77; Susan Watermeyer, 'Afrikaans English', in de Klerk (ed.), *Focus on South Africa*, 99–124; and Roger Lass, 'South African English', in Rajend Mesthrie (ed.), *Language in South Africa* (Cambridge: Cambridge University Press, 2002), 104–26. More generally see Vic Webb, *Language in South Africa: The Role of Language in National Transformation, Reconstruction, and Development* (Amsterdam: John Benjamins, 2002); 68–88 offer statistics on language use.

the political future.'[89] Indeed, the formative years of the republic, between the Revolution and the Civil War, witnessed an overriding concern with language and what it meant to speak and write *as* an American. And this concern was expressed not just by imaginative writers (e.g., Cooper and Whitman) but also in educational and political circles, making it one of the new country's defining discursive traditions.[90] Howe characterizes opposing poles of thought about language and politics in the period that once more recall the Bible's competing explanations of change and variation. More significantly—and familiarly—for the concerns of this chapter, both views invest change and variation with terrific non-linguistic significance and thereby transfer to language what are properly the issues of nationhood and government organization.

At one extreme were writers who 'utilized language as if it constituted a fixed and unvarying medium of expression existing apart from the changing contexts of history, a medium stable in its grammar and vocabulary, certain in its meanings, and unambiguous in its capacity to express universal truth'. In a pre-Babel mode, such language would be resistant to change precisely because of its powers of transparent expression; and by extension, linguistic change and variation would imply the failure of human behavior as well as, more simply, the instability of a political process. At another extreme, embracing thinking more akin to the account of language change in Genesis 10, 'other political writers understood that language, far from constituting an autonomous realm of universal meaning separated from the flux of history, was inextricably embedded in human experience'. Language here serves as 'an instrument of political exploration and creativity to be deployed in the construction of a continuously unfolding political future'.[91] More than just the inevitable byproducts of natural language, change and variation from this perspective play crucial roles in the continual, situational adjustment of both language and politics. Their absence would indicate, indeed, the unnatural failure of political thought and action to keep pace with social development.

In the colonial period and early days of the republic, up through the Constitutional Convention of 1787, belief in the constancy of language (specifically political language) prevailed. In 1776, the year of the Declaration of

---

[89] Howe, *Language and Political Meaning in Revolutionary America* (Amherst, MA: University of Massachusetts Press, 2004), 2.

[90] See further Michael P. Kramer, *Imagining Language in America: From the Revolution to the Civil War* (Princeton, NJ: Princeton University Press, 1992). On the role that a feeling of discontinuity from the past played in this discourse, see John Algeo, 'External History', in Algeo (ed.), *English in North America*, 1–58.

[91] Howe, *Language and Political Meaning in Revolutionary America*, 5.

Independence, John Jay even described a homology between political unity, the new country, Providential design, and English: 'Providence has been pleased to give this one connected country, to one united people; a people descended from the same ancestors, speaking the same language, professing the same religion.'[92] It is this belief that underwrote John Adams's advocacy of an American language academy. Comparing the United States to Athens and Rome and positing as necessary a connection between democracy and language, he once located motivation for such an academy in English's role as the world's pre-eminent tongue: 'As eloquence is cultivated with more care in free republics than in other governments, it has been found by constant experience that such republics have produced the greatest purity, copiousness, and perfection of language. It is not to be disputed that the form of government has an influence upon language, and language in its turn influences not only the form of government, but the temper, the sentiments, and manners of the people.'[93] Neither the conviction in the fixedness of language nor the commitment to an American academy died with Adams. In 1889, indeed, an essay in the *North American Review* still called for the creation of the latter: 'No other means will so effectively secure unity, prevent sectionalism, and abolish dialects.'[94]

When colonial writers like Charles Brockden Brown advocated only the gradual change of language, and not its revolution and reconstruction, disapproval and avoidance of neologisms, semantic extension, metaphor, and the like acted not merely as idle stylistic gestures. They expressed, rather, a sense that the social and political processes to which these tropes pointed should themselves be slowed.[95] This approach to language, politics, and change explains why an 1857 newspaper editorial would see the primary contribution of Noah Webster, the founding father in any history of American English, to have been the preservation of putatively absolute constancy and regularity in American speech: 'Here, five thousand miles change not the sound of a word. Around every fireside, and from every tribune, in every field of labor, and every factory of toil, is heard the same tongue. We owe it to Webster.'[96] Precisely this same point about the immanence of linguistic

---

[92] Quoted in May, *Language and Minority Rights*, 209.

[93] 'A Letter to the President of the Congress' (5 September 1780), quoted in Crawford (ed.), *Language Loyalties*, 31. On the early emphasis on the constancy of language, see Howe, *Language and Political Meaning in Revolutionary America*, 38–62.

[94] Quoted in David Simpson, *The Politics of American English, 1776–1850* (Oxford: Oxford University Press, 1986), 13.

[95] Simpson, *The Politics of American English, 1776–1850*, 46–7.

[96] Quoted in Harlow Giles Unger, *Noah Webster: The Life and Times of an American Patriot* (New York: John Wiley and Sons, 1998), xii.

constancy in political stability—and, more importantly, about how instability in one produces instability in the other—was made when the regularity attributed to Webster's influence was denied to American English, and with it its implications for any American social achievement. In 1864, for example, the dean of Canterbury collapsed linguistic and moral failure in his assessment of the American Civil War: 'Look at the process of deterioration which our Queen's English has undergone at the hands of Americans...and then compare the character and history of the nation—its blunted sense of moral obligation and duty to man...and its reckless and fruitless maintenance of the most cruel and unprincipled war in the history of the world.'[97] In a more benign version, the use of change and variation to reflect marginal, inconstant behavior—and thus by implication to associate linguistic and political regularity with each other—emerges from the tendency of the early novelists like James Fenimore Cooper, very much unlike contemporary writers like Kelman and Welsh, to use non-standard and dialect forms primarily with minor characters and never with his narrators.[98]

Already during the War of Independence this belief in the constancy of political language was challenged. If such language were stable, fixed, and transparent, after all, it becomes difficult to account for the breach of trust and confidence that led the colonists to distrust the king and to foment what they viewed as justified revolution. For colonial America, stable language had resulted in political failure, which in turn implied the importance of adaptable, flexible language that was suited to specific situations. Buoyed by the emergence of federalism and its emphasis on a new, centralized government, Howe's other extreme of linguistic thinking gradually asserted itself. 'Federalists employed language in ways that were politically inventive', he notes, 'as a creative instrument essential to the ongoing task of exploring America's evolving republican experiment. The triumph of Federalism in 1787–88 brought the legitimation, not just of a "new science of politics", but of a new political language as well.'[99] If Adams and his advocacy of an American

---

[97] Quoted in Geoffrey Nunberg, *Going Nucular: Language, Politics, and Culture in Confrontational Times* (New York: PublicAffairs, 2004), 150.

[98] Simpson, *The Politics of American English, 1776–1850*, 149–201. Simpson points out, however, that Natty Bumpo, Cooper's protagonist in the 'Leatherstocking' series, is a special case as a 'dialect speaker who is not simply subordinated to the polite usages and values of the socially superior characters, and who seems to bear about him a definite degree of authorial approval and conviction' (168). On the role of English in the literary formation of early American identity, also see Christopher Looby, *Voicing America: Language, Literary Form, and the Origins of the United States* (Chicago, IL: University of Chicago Press, 1996).

[99] Howe, *Language and Political Meaning in Revolutionary America*, 224–5. On the early view that standard languages were a way for European elites to maintain social privilege and hierarchy, see Gray, *New World Babel*, 159–63.

language academy epitomize arguments for linguistic stability, Thomas Jefferson was one of the most prominent of the early voices for a new approach to language change and variation. A polymath who studied American Indian languages and advocated the study of Old English as a requirement at the newly founded University of Virginia, Jefferson championed what he called 'neology', which encompassed semantic expansions as well as neologisms. In a letter to Adams, indeed, he maintained that without neology 'we should still be held to the vocabulary of Alfred or Ulphilas; and held to their state of science also'. In an 1813 letter to John Waldo, Jefferson laid open the political implications of this view of change and variation. Language in England might remain as constant and immutable as the country and political process it supported, but as for Americans, 'we shall ... enlarge our employment of it, until its new character may separate it in name as well as in power, from the mother-tongue'.[100] For the American experience to have been reasonable and politically meaningful, language had to adapt. Yet if language change thereby produced anxiety in its absence rather than its presence, the anxiety itself remained just as palpable in the implication of linguistic change and variation in what are essentially non-linguistic issues of nation formation.

As Alexis de Tocqueville would later champion it, by this view America would be a place where language, like society, would be given free rein, develop communally, and show a consistency devoid of sociolinguistic hierarchies. In his widely read and influential *Democracy in America* (1835), de Tocqueville, very much under the influence of Herder and the German Romantics, not only posited 'democracy' and 'language' as essentialist categories but also presumed an essentialist connection between them. In aristocracies, such as those that still prevailed in Europe, 'language must naturally partake of that state of repose in which everything remains. Few new words are coined because few new things are made.' But in democracies like the United States, there is a 'competition of minds' and 'many new ideas are formed'. Change, linguistic as well as political, is what defines democracies and advances them beyond aristocracies: 'democratic nations love change for its own sake, and this is seen in their language as much as in their politics. Even when they have no need to change words, they sometimes have the desire.' And given de Tocqueville's sense that democracies are fundamentally populist political systems, it follows that their many new words—and the ideas they express—will not be intellectual or philosophical (as in aristocracies) but mostly words taken 'to express the wants of business, the passions of party, or the details of the public administration'. The language of a

---

100 Quoted in Howe, *Language and Political Meaning in Revolutionary America*, 80, 82.

democracy will thus continually grow in these areas, 'while it will gradually lose ground in metaphysics and theology'. By extension, if democracies characteristically lack the social divisions of aristocracies, because in democracies individuals of all social ranks intermingle, so, too, must the language of democracies like America lack the social and regional variation found in Europe. De Tocqueville's argument is thus almost hermetically sealed, expressing the same anxiety over change and variation that Jefferson had: whatever changes de Tocqueville did observe in American English—and English was not a language he himself spoke—had to reflect only the simple fact that the United States was a democracy.[101]

The most articulate and frequent advocate of this position, of course, was Webster. Unlike Jefferson, Webster was a federalist, but the two shared a commitment to the controlled change of language as a necessary aspect of the new country's political identity. In fact, for Webster the transition from federalism to linguistics was slight. He believed strongly, for example, in a standard, written language that was in many ways the grammatical equivalent of federalism's centralized government, and it is from this political perspective that he wanted English to change so as to reflect America. And even though the advent of historical linguistics and the work of comparativists like Sir William Jones had generally displaced belief in Babel and its account of a single language scattered by divine judgement, Webster held tightly to the monogenesis of language. Indeed, he espoused beliefs in the evolution of all modern languages from the Chaldean spoken by Noah and in the descent of European languages from Japheth's lineage in particular.[102]

As has been characteristic of the language anxiety that I have explored in this book, contradictions run through Webster's positions on language, language change, and the relation of the two to American character. On one hand, he saw written and spoken English as the expression of the people in general, which in the United States still meant a primarily agricultural population. Just as in de Tocqueville's analysis, this agricultural base would work against divisions of labor and the creation of a social elite, whose language use a dictionary like Johnson's could be seen to support.[103] The practical means

---

[101] De Tocqueville, *Democracy in America*, ed. Phillips Bradley, 2 vols. (New York: Vintage, 1945), ii, 68–74. De Tocqueville's notion that as a putatively classless society, the United States necessarily lacked regional and social variation was earlier expressed by the American Timothy Dwight. See Frederic G. Cassidy, 'Geographical Variations of English in the United States', in Richard W. Bailey and Manfred Görlach (eds.), *English as a World Language* (Ann Arbor, MI: University of Michigan Press, 1982), 187.

[102] Unger, *Noah Webster*, 286.

[103] Simpson, *The Politics of American English, 1776–1850*, 59, 70–1.

for expressing this egalitarian sociolinguistic identity of American English took shape in his grammar, spelling-book, and dictionary. For Webster these linguistic aids, appearing at a time when literacy was increasing and public education becoming more generally available, if still rather limited, not only differentiated and regulated American English but also served cultural, political, and moral purposes:

We have therefore the fairest opportunity of establishing a national language, and of giving it uniformity and perspicuity, in North America, that ever presented itself to mankind. Now is the time to begin the plan. The minds of the Americans are roused by the events of a revolution; the necessity of organizing the political body and of forming constitutions of government that shall secure freedom and property, has called all the faculties of the mind into exertion; and the danger of losing the benefits of independence, has disposed every man to embrace any scheme that shall tend, in its future operation, to reconcile the people of America to each other, and weaken the prejudices which oppose a cordial union.[104]

But on the other, as much as Webster affirmed the importance of language change to the identity of the American republic, he regarded this change as best restricted in scope and directed towards the end not of a continually evolving language but of one evolved to the point that, like British English in Jefferson's view, it might remain a fixed reflection of a fixed country. In this he recalls not only Jefferson but also the Lollards, King Alfred, and modern language legislation. As early as 1785, while stressing the importance of creating a national language that would demand respect at home and abroad, Webster observed: 'Nothing but the establishment of schools and some uniformity in the use of books can annihilate differences of speaking and preserve the purity of the American tongue.'[105] He likewise felt that just as the egalitarian, agricultural basis of American society worked against social and regional variation in language, so, too, this basis would lead to the atrophy and elimination of dialects.[106] In his *Dissertations*, while identifying and excoriating various regional pronunciations and linguistic habits, Webster indicates that such differences ultimately owe to carelessness and are thus correctable: 'Great efforts should be made by teachers of schools, to make their pupils open the teeth, and give a full clear sound to every syllable. The beauty of speaking consists in giving each letter and syllable its due proportion of sound, with a prompt articulation.'[107] It is for such reasons,

---

[104] Webster, *Dissertation on the English Language*, 36.
[105] Quoted in Unger, *Noah Webster*, 96.
[106] Simpson, *The Politics of American English, 1776–1850*, 77.
[107] Webster, *Dissertation on the English Language*, 109.

too, that he omitted dialect words—crucial and salient markers of variation—from his dictionary.

The popular traces of Webster's commitment to linguistic change are largely limited to orthographic variants like *theater, honor,* and *jail* in the United States as opposed to *theatre, honour,* and *gaol* in the United Kingdom and much of the former Empire. Far more significant has been Webster's resistance to change and variation. In this vein, it's worth recalling that his grammar and spelling-book were often packaged and sold with a copy of the Bible, thereby linking together physically as well as conceptually regularity in language and morality. Moreover, like early modern *vulgaria,* which inculcated Latin in schoolboys through sentences about the privileges and intelligence of the wealthy, Webster's speller, used in virtually every nineteenth-century American school, drove home its orthography alongside adages on nation, virtue, and the common good. As an illustration of *love,* Webster offered 'The *love* of God is the first duty of man', and as an illustration of *patriotism,* '*Patriotism* is the characteristic of a good citizen, the noblest passion that animates a man in the character of a citizen'.[108] As the 1981 Select Committee on Immigration citation of him suggests, Webster the social conservative has remained most memorable among thinkers who have invoked language as a necessary medium of forming the republic and maintaining its unity amidst the social, religious, and ethnic diversity of the United States. It is an irony of many kinds that in 1859, on the eve of the war that would fracture the country, Jefferson Davis, the future president of the Confederacy, should likewise have seen Webster and his linguistic ministrations as symbols of the states' unity: 'Above all other people, we are one, and above all books which have united us in the bond of common language, I place the good old Spelling-Book of Noah Webster. We have a unity of language no other people possesses, and we owe this unity, above all else, to Noah Webster's Yankee Spelling-Book.'[109]

Webster can serve as such an ambivalent symbol of linguistic constancy and change, and of the dangers and benefits commonly attributed to the latter, precisely because the issues for which he has been appropriated are linguistically unresolvable. They are not, in fact, primarily linguistic at all but rather social concerns filtered through language change and variation. In United States language planning at least, they dynamically and necessarily supplement each other as modern-day evocations of the conflicting accounts of change and variation in Genesis 10 and 11. What drives this dynamic in the

---

[108] Quoted in Unger, *Noah Webster,* 306; also see 344.
[109] Quoted in Unger, *Noah Webster,* 343.

United States and elsewhere are the connections between language policy and ethnic—and then national—identity. Language planning, and policies on change and variation in particular, serves as a heuristic for explaining history and social interaction. To a modern pluralist, Ronald Schmidt points out, the dominance of English is 'the unjust result of a very unequal competition between different language groups'.[110] To assimilationists, this same dominance is not only natural and appropriate but besieged by non-Anglophone individuals and the policies that allow and encourage them to remain so. Like Norman chroniclers, assimilationists can fabricate a monolingual American past, just as they attribute variation and change to external, disruptive forces. For pluralists and assimilationists alike, the euphemistic role of language in such discussions becomes especially prominent at moments of social crisis. A few months after the United States entered World War I, for instance, then-former president Theodore Roosevelt authored a jingoistic document entitled 'The Children of the Crucible' that emotively collapsed patriotism, history, and national identity into the English language: 'We must also have but one language. That must be the language of the Declaration of Independence, of Washington's Farewell address, of Lincoln's Gettysburg speech and second inaugural. We cannot tolerate any attempt to oppose or supplant the language and culture that has come down to us from the builders of the Republic with the language and culture of any European country.'[111] Thirty-nine distinguished citizens (including Roosevelt) signed 'The Crucible'.

While there may be much to choose from here in terms of the sentiments of such arguments, there is in fact little difference between their strategies and consequences. The English Only movement's push for a constitutional amendment designating English the official language of the United States may well be demagogic and even hysterical. But so, too, are arguments that make blithe, unsupportable generalizations about historical shift and that describe a vast Anglophone conspiracy insidiously spreading capitalism and genocidally erasing indigenous cultures by means of the Internet, instruction in English as a foreign language, and global economics.[112] Such extremes depend on a disregard for linguistic history, imagine language change as a problem that government language policy creates and can correct, credit

---

[110] Schmidt, *Language Policy and Identity Politics in the United States*, 77.

[111] Quoted in Crawford (ed.), *Language Loyalties*, 85.

[112] See, for example, Thomas Ricento (ed.), *Ideology, Politics and Language Policies: Focus on English* (Amsterdam: John Benjamins, 2000); Phillipson, *Linguistic Imperialism*; Skutnabb-Kangas and Phillipson (eds.), *Linguistic Human Rights*; Norman Fairclough, *Language and Power* (London: Longman, 1989); Robert Hodge and Gunther Kress, *Language as Ideology*, 2nd edn. (London: Routledge, 1993); Tollefson, *Planning Language*; and Pennycook, *The Cultural Politics of English as an International Language*.

language planning with far more initiative and influence than has historically been the case—how much real impact has the Académie Française, for example, had on the direction of spoken French?—and, ultimately, transfer responsibility for how change and variation are conceived from individuals to institutions.

Throughout this book I have suggested that as linguistic phenomena, change and variation have no intrinsic meaning. They are, in an absolute sense, as value-free as a phoneme, a piece of inflectional morphology, or even a word as the construction of phonology and morphology. By the same token, like all these phenomena change and variation can be invested with great meaning that in turn has great social consequence. If words like *gay* or *nigger* become socially charged or taboo, they do so not because of anything inherent in their phonological or morphological shape. Even their semantic reference alone fails to account for their effect, since meaning changes diachronically as well as varies synchronically and since there are other socially acceptable words (such as *homosexual*) that have the same general referents. It is their pragmatics—the ways in which speakers use them—that renders words powerful, sacred, benign, obscene, racist, and so forth. Should a word like *nigger* suddenly disappear, racism would not perforce disappear with it, any more than sexism disappeared with the spread of *Ms* at the expense of *Mrs* and *Miss*. Natural language is an inherently creative system, and humans are inherently creative beings; they always have found and always will find ways to express their thoughts. So long as speakers have a social or intellectual need for them, new words can always be found to bear the pragmatic weight speakers desire. Arguments over whether change is natural or unnatural, whether political language is stable or adaptive, and whether Webster was a linguistic innovator or preservationist remain unresolvable because they fail to account for the fact that in these cases language points to something else. And the something else, ultimately, is where opinions truly divide.

Language policies, like literary effects, are ways to generate pragmatic weight and invest social meaning. Specifically, in their treatment of language change and variation they have been ways for speakers to construct ethnicity, nationality, and statehood. As all the examples of this chapter suggest, they have played extremely important roles in this regard, underwriting both the intellectual achievement of King Alfred's revival of learning and the moral degradation of the forced removal and language shift of non-Anglophone children in Australia and the United States. When speakers argue about the significance of change and variation, as in the early days of the United States, they argue about fundamental issues of history, identity, and the future. At the same time, since the meaning of change and variation is what speakers invest in it, such arguments never address what generates this meaning. Almost perversely, the mere fact that language can be judged to have so much non-linguistic significance proves not this significance but that the issues are not linguistic. And just as the elimination of racist words would not eliminate racism, so the elimination of language change and variation would not eliminate the disputes over identity that they channel. It is again worth recalling that God visited His punishment upon Nimrod at a time when there was *no* change and variation, when communication was so complete as to allow for the building of the Tower.

Neither the hysteria of the English Only movement nor that of the augurs of linguistic imperialism does much to alleviate the anxiety associated with change and variation. It does much, in fact, to augment it. It obscures the fact that pragmatics is an individual as well as social way to generate meaning and that from this perspective individuals are as much the producers of language as its victims. In every aspect of language use—phonemic split, syntactic expansion, lexical diffusion—individual speakers provide the usage that constitutes the data of a language, whether one's interests are the data themselves or the data as means towards an abstraction like the *langue* or an ideal speaker-listener. In the case of language planning, the influence of religious and government policies on how individuals might view change and variation is considerable. And popular entertainment as well as court decisions and school policies can lead speakers to become complicit in the subordination of their own variety, eager to shift from Maori, Welsh, or Spanish, for example, to English as a language whose communicative, economic, and even ethical superiority they readily accept.[113]

But an important distinction is to be drawn here. In effect, a minority speaker's shift to English may well be coerced by circumstances and economic necessity; this was certainly the case with speakers of Hindi and Native American languages. Decisions to invest meaning in change and variation, to adhere to language planning as a way of redirecting other concerns about ethnic and national identity, and to claim prescience about the sociolinguistic future are not coerced in this fashion. They are matters of choice for individuals as well as policy-makers. And prior to seeing change and variation as confirmations of a preconceived national character or as symptoms of decline and dissolution, speakers have yet another choice. And that is the choice not to channel non-linguistic anxieties through language and thereby displace the genuine issues of concern.

---

[113] For an analysis of how linguistic subordination can work, see Rosina Lippi-Green, *English with an Accent: Language, Ideology, and Discrimination in the United States* (London: Routledge, 1997).

5

Say the Right Thing

When a dictionary's not enough

'The rock-bottom practical truth', Wilson Follett once wrote, 'is that the lexicographer cannot abrogate his authority if he wants to. He may think of himself as a detached scientist reporting the facts of language, declining to recommend use of anything or abstention from anything; but the myriad consultants of his work are not going to see him so...the work itself by virtue of its inclusions and exclusions, its mere existence, is a whole universe of judgments, received by millions as the Word from on high.'[1] By this reasoning, in orthography, sense, and usage, English is what the dictionaries say it is, and while thus general and theoretical in scope, Follett's observation actually responded to a very specific event: the September 1961 publication of *Webster's Third New International Dictionary*. Deriving ultimately from Noah Webster's 1828 *American Dictionary of the English Language*, which in turn derived from his 1806 *Compendious Dictionary of the English Language*, *Webster's Third* (as it was and is called) represented a tradition of financial, linguistic, and even cultural achievement. For many Americans—and, for that matter, readers worldwide—the Merriam-Webster company stands next only to Oxford University Press as the pre-eminent maker of dictionaries, and the cry 'Look it up in *Webster's*' serves as an emblem of the authority invested in it and in dictionaries in general.

Webster's Third was a long time in the making. A second edition had appeared in 1934, and work on the third was well under way when Philip Gove assumed editorial responsibility in 1951. A scholar of eighteenth-century literature by training, Gove was very much a traditionalist, committed to

---

[1] Quoted in Herbert C. Morton, *The Story of 'Webster's Third': Philip Gove's Controversial Dictionary and Its Critics* (Cambridge: Cambridge University Press, 1994), 189–90. The following account draws on Morton's splendid book, as well as on James Sledd and Wilma R. Ebbitt (eds.), *Dictionaries and THAT Dictionary: A Casebook on the Aims of Lexicographers and the Targets of Reviewers* (Chicago, IL: Scott, Foresman, 1962).

preserving qualities that had made Merriam-Webster a household name, but also to altering the form and content of the dictionary in ways that reflected how English had changed in the quarter century since the previous edition. He thus modified the phonetic transcriptions and the procedures for cross-referencing and the like, eliminated proper nouns, and added 100,000 new words (as well as many new senses) to what had appeared in 1934. He likewise worked to eliminate impressionistic racial or ethnic judgements from the definitions (*Webster's Second* had defined the Maori, in part, as 'vigorous and athletic, tall in stature, and pleasing in features, and brave and warlike') and, in general, to substitute concise and logical phrasal definitions for the some-times loosely structured and expansive definitions of the previous edition. By these means, *Webster's Third* appeared as a formidable symbol of its own authority: 450,000 entries contained in 2,662 pages (not including a 72-page preface outlining the book's methods and conventions) that weighed 13½ lbs and was listed at $47.50. Even for a book issued today, such statistics would be impressive; for one issued nearly a half-century ago, they are extraordinary.

For all this, much of the volume's early reception bordered on the hostile, attributing to Gove (and *Webster's Third*) not merely inaccuracy but malfea-sance and outright, willful ineptitude. Elsewhere in his review, indeed, Follett charged the dictionary with jettisoning 'a century and a third of illustrious history' and claimed that 'it plumes itself on its faults and parades assiduously cultivated sins as virtues without precedent'. *Webster's Third*, he asserted, 'is out to destroy...every obstinate vestige of linguistic punctilio, every surviv-ing influence that makes for the upholding of standards, every criterion for distinguishing between better usages and worse'. Even more sardonically and personally, David Glixon charged, 'It would seem that permissiveness, now on the wane in child-rearing, has caught up with the dictionary makers. Having descended from God's throne of supreme authority, the Merriam folks are now seated around the city desk, recording like mad.'[2] According to an editorial in the *New York Times*, 'Webster's has, it is apparent, surrendered to the permissive school that has been busily extending its beachhead on English instruction in the schools. This development is disastrous because, intentionally or unintentionally, it serves to reinforce the notion that good English is whatever is popular.'[3] Not all reviews were so critical or vitupera-tive. Many academic journals, particularly those in Britain, praised the book for its scholarly care, imagination, and erudition. But the negative reviews, often in prominent forums like the *New York Times* or *Life* magazine, reached

---

[2] Quoted in Morton, *The Story of 'Webster's Third',* 187–8, 172.
[3] Quoted in Sledd and Ebbitt (eds.), *Dictionaries and THAT Dictionary,* 78.

the widest audience and largely set the agenda for any subsequent, positive reviews, by placing them in the position of first having to defend the dictionary from the accusations made against it.

There are several oddities here. For one thing, the most critical and widely read reviews were often the most factually inaccurate. For example, Dwight Macdonald in the *New Yorker* blistered the dictionary as failing to follow the model of its predecessors, slavish to fashionable linguistics, and biased against historical sources in its citations. Yet as often cited as this witty review was, it was also profoundly ignorant about lexicography, the methods and contents of *Webster's Second*, and even the design and contents of *Webster's Third* itself. Macdonald simply misunderstood the book's citation and cross-referencing procedures, and he failed to appreciate that a very traditional source like Shakespeare was the most commonly cited authority—cited three times more frequently than the next most common authority, which happened to be the even more traditional Bible. For another thing, at issue were not simply *Webster's Dictionary* but also the Merriam-Webster company, both of them venerable in American letters and therefore, one would think, unlikely institutions to elicit the lexicographical equivalent of road rage. And for a third, the cause of the *New York Times*'s indignation and its readers' *schadenfreude* was neither social policy nor legislation but, ultimately, just a book— a dictionary—which reviews credited with the ability to cause not only a language but a society to rise and fall.

Macdonald, Follett, and others clearly touched a nerve in their assertion that readers saw dictionaries as unimpeachable and absolute authorities on language—in Follett's phrase, as 'a whole universe of judgments, received by millions as the Word from on high'. Whether dictionaries ever have had or even claimed this authority is perhaps immaterial, for it is readers who have invested them with it. And this disconnect between lexicographers' and readers' expectations surely produced at least some of the latter's frustration and outrage. *Webster's Third* did indeed decline to make some of the judgements of which Follett speaks; the label 'colloquial' was omitted, for instance, while 'slang' was greatly restricted on the theory that the distinction it implies—between slang and non-slang—isn't as fixed or universal as one might imagine. The dictionary's definition of *ain't* is a case in point. In the sense 'am not', the definition stated, *ain't* was 'disapproved by many and more common in less educated speech, used orally in most parts of the U. S. by many cultivated speakers esp. in the phrase *ain't I*'. The dictionary labeled the sense 'have not' as substandard. This could well be regarded as a model of restrained, non-judgmental description of linguistic reality—many people really do say *ain't*—and yet many reviewers interpreted the definition as a prescriptive grammar claim that *ain't*, a slang word, was now perfectly acceptable, non-stigmatized language. They saw the dictionary as in effect *advocating* the word. And in this curious way, the definition became a symbol of everything that was putatively wrong with *Webster's Third* as a book that refused to make any value judgements, that never distinguished prestige from non-prestige forms, and that in general furthered permissiveness in society as well as language. Merriam-Webster itself may also have been responsible for some of these misreadings and reactions. Its publicity program for *Webster's Third* presented the book, inaccurately, as not simply revolutionary in methods but also directed to families as an arbiter of language—the sort of book to be kept beside the dining-room table for reference and word games. The company thereby encouraged fundamental confusion already present among readers (and Merriam-Webster) who failed to distinguish prescriptive grammar, which was what Follett and others sought, from descriptive grammar, which is what Merriam-Webster and Gove sought and in fact gave.

But even this confusion would seem to fail to account for the controversy and moral indignation that *Webster's Third* incited. The battle metaphor of a 'beachhead' in the *New York Times*, read by a generation who remembered and may well have participated in the landings at Normandy and in the Pacific, seems designed to foster just this response. Glixon's rhetoric perhaps goes even further, emotively conflating the dictionary with bad parents and fallen angels. In reference to such responses, Herbert Morton points out that 'the central issue was not merely the dictionary itself, though it was that primarily; it was also what the critics thought the dictionary symbolized. At stake, so it was made to appear, was the preservation of the English language and the survival of deeply rooted cultural traditions.'[4]

Dictionaries have perhaps always had unusual authority and consequence in the United States, where they might be seen as substitutes for the language academy for which John Adams argued unsuccessfully.[5] Yet dictionaries in general necessarily play prominent roles in shaping attitudes towards language not only by specifying words' meanings but also, more generally, by including or excluding particular words and by specifying status and usage conventions for those that are included. Drawing on Foucault's notions of discursive conventions and how they construct the identity of the objects they

---

[4] Morton, *The Story of 'Webster's Third'*, 2.

[5] Allen Walker Read, 'The Allegiance to Dictionaries in American Linguistic Attitudes', in *Milestones in the History of English in America*, ed. Richard W. Bailey (Durham, NC: Duke University Press, 2002), 110–20. There was some hope, too, that the *Oxford English Dictionary* would serve in place of a language academy in the United Kingdom. See Lynda Mugglestone, *Lost for Words: The Hidden History of the Oxford English Dictionary* (New Haven, CT: Yale University Press, 2005), 143.

describe, John Willinsky thus observes, 'At heart, the dictionary is a school-book; it contributes to the disciplining of language, as easily as to its study'.[6] It is language's ability to discipline social experience, in turn, that constitutes its social power and seems to underlie the anxieties generated by *Webster's Third*. By effectively defining language—disciplining it to exist in a certain way, and thereby turning it into a discipline—dictionaries can serve as tools for discriminating among educated and non-educated speakers and, by extension, social classes and concomitant economic and political influence. Put another way, practical decisions about contents, the rhetoric of definitions, labeling, and even pronunciation guides have implications for conceptions of morality, propriety, and social class.[7] By extension, to know what is in an English dictionary—better still, to control what is in a dictionary—is to know what English is, which increasingly since the early modern period has itself been knowledge of terrific social consequence. In this vein, the dispute over the alleged permissiveness of *Webster's Third* seems very much an expression of post-war America's anxiety over 'the survival of deeply rooted cultural traditions', whether they be traditional gender roles, child-rearing, the value of education, high culture, or capitalism. At the very moment when the Soviet Union seemed to be winning the space race—Yuri Gagarin had become the first man in space in April 1961, four months before the dictionary was published—the *New York Times* in fact mockingly described *Webster's Third* as 'Bolshevik'.[8]

The largest issue here is metalinguistics, or linguistics that concerns itself with linguistics. Like any discipline, linguistics, alongside pursuing its inquiry of language phenomena, is in part focused on defining its methods of inquiry as well as those phenomena, and such definitions have consequences for how we understand the achievements of language. How we define language, for instance, will affect how we understand interlanguages like pidgins and creoles. And whether we accept language as a fixed, determinable code will shape attitudes toward social and regional variations. It is this nexus of academic debate and social consequence that this chapter explores. In particular, I want to consider how, through definitions of natural language in general as well as English in particular, the discipline of linguistics has helped cultivate anxiety about the natural attributes of language, including change and variation. As with literary narratives and legislative policy, I will

---

[6] Willinsky, *Empire of Words: The Reign of the OED* (Princeton, NJ: Princeton University Press, 1994), 44.

[7] For consideration of the ideological dimension of some of these practical decisions, see Henri Béjoint, *Tradition and Innovation in Modern English Dictionaries* (Oxford: Clarendon Press, 1994), 107–39.

[8] Quoted in Morton, *The Story of 'Webster's Third'*, 182.

suggest, linguistics has itself served as a way to channel extra-linguistic concerns through language.

Language standards

The variation and change that natural languages experience always leave them susceptible to transformations that hinder communication. Dante acknowledged as much in his *De Vulgari Eloquentia*, perhaps the medieval period's most detailed and sophisticated account of language and grammar, when he traced the development of vernacular languages across Europe and noted in general that 'no human language can be lasting and continuous, but must needs vary like other properties of ours, as for instance our manners and our dress, according to distance of time and place'. For Dante, grammar was invented precisely as a way of resisting the changeability that lies at the heart of natural language and that leads to failures in communication:

Hence were set in motion the inventors of the art of grammar, which is nothing else but a kind of unchangeable identity of speech in different times and places. This, having been settled by the common consent of many peoples, seems exposed to the arbitrary will of none in particular, and consequently cannot be variable. They therefore invented grammar in order that we might not, on account of the variation of speech fluctuating at the will of individuals, either fail altogether in attaining, or at least attain but a partial knowledge of the opinions and exploits of the ancients, or of those whom difference of places causes to differ from us.[9]

Grammar thereby enables humans to transcend the limitations of language and connect themselves not only to their peers but also to the ancients from whom, in evolving humanist thought, they had declined in so many ways. It is this stabilizing quality that characterizes and distinguishes written, prestigious languages from non-regularized spoken vernaculars and that therefore holds out to the latter a means to achieve the status of the former.

In 1490 William Caxton, who must have been around seventy at the time, expressed a similar sentiment, perhaps less grandly, by commenting on how much English had changed in his own lifetime: 'our langage now vsed varyeth ferre from that. which was vsed and spoken whan I was borne'.[10] Inasmuch as Caxton refers to what was 'spoken' when he was young, he evokes, from a diachronic perspective, the very qualities of variation—specifically, its

---

[9] Dante, *De vulgari eloquentia*, in Alex Preminger *et al.* (ed. and trans.), *Classical and Medieval Literary Criticism: Translations and Interpretations* (New York: Frederick Ungar, 1974), 420–1.

[10] Caxton, *The Prologues and Epilogues of William Caxton*, ed. W. J. B. Crotch, EETS os 176 (1928; rpt. New York: Burt Franklin, 1971), 108.

tendency to obscure communication—that Dante sees grammar as resisting. And, synchronically, this same sense of unintelligibility, of not using the same language, can confront contemporary tourists speaking structurally distinct varieties, such as New Zealand and African American Vernacular English, or Geordie and South African English. It is, however, the written channel, the focus of Dante's concerns, that presents perhaps the clearest examples of how time and space work against constancy in language and communication. To compare passages of English from different moments in the language's history, as I did in Chapter 2, is to confront the fact that, diachronically, English has indeed changed in ways that render varieties from different epochs mutually unintelligible.

To counteract this potential for mutual intelligibility and thereby increase the communicative and social influence of a language, users of every major Western European language (including English) since the early modern period have followed Dante's lead, with varying degrees of success, and worked to cultivate spoken and written varieties with two primary qualities. First, these cultivated varieties display minimum variation in form. In spoken language, this means consistency in pronunciation or stress patterns, while in written language it means consistency in orthography, punctuation, and discursive practices. Second, these varieties manifest maximum variation in function, which means that whether spoken or written they can be used in a number of domains for a number of purposes. Together, these qualities foster a standard as a variety with wide intelligibility among speakers separated by geography or time, and they also encourage and even require its use in influential circumstances. In effect, they allow languages to transcend variation and change as a way of improving (if not guaranteeing) communication.[11]

Standardization is thus at once a historical and a contemporary process. Historically, it involves the selection and codification of a particular variety in grammar books, rhetoric handbooks, and, of course, dictionaries, all of which distinguish right forms from wrong ones. The contemporary element of standardization derives from the fact that to be a standard a variety cannot simply be defined as such. It must be maintained and cultivated in sequential synchronic moments across time, through its acceptance as a standard by the language's users and through an elaboration of its functions, largely by means of its explicit instruction in schools. Its significance thus continuously evolves, building on its historical inception, subsequent interpretations of this inception, and subsequent interpretations of its current use.

[11] This key formulation of a standard as a variety displaying minimal variation in form and maximum variation in function originates with Einar Haugen, 'Language, Dialect, Nation', in *The Ecology of Language*, ed. Anwar S. Dil (Stanford, CA: Stanford University Press, 1972), 237–54.

For Western European vernaculars (again as Dante suggested), Latin, with its long history of codification and institutional prominence in schools and law courts, provided much of the model and inspiration for the immobilization of language that underlies standardization. To be sure, in his 1528 *De Recta Latini Graecique Sermonis Pronuntiatione* Erasmus lamented the variable and sometimes mutually unintelligible pronunciations of this language, then utilized by none as a first language, learned primarily through rigorous classroom instruction, and written and spoken in only select domains. And in England, John Hart's 1569 *Orthographie* likewise documents that English pronunciations of Latin differ from those used by speakers of other vernaculars.[12] But throughout much of its written history, and even taking into consideration the significant syntactic and lexical differences between the classical and medieval versions, Latin for the most part did remain considerably more fixed than any vernacular, particular in scholarly conceptions. The most ancient, most influential works, of Cicero or Virgil, had long since been completed by the early modern period, and textual criticism, the critical tool that made Humanism possible, promised to determine and deliver their correct texts once and for all.

Medieval Christian exegesis had infused this demonstrable grammatical regularity with moral and even eschatological qualities. It was St Augustine, for example, who drew a distinction between *vox* as external sound and *verbum* as internal concept in a way that paralleled a distinction between the fallen world and the eternal *logos* of Christ. Within this framework, the emphasis of linguistic study needed to be the cultivation of semantics and regular grammatical construction, since a simple description of ordinary change and variation could only confirm the fallen nature of the world— both materially and linguistically.[13] The contemporary fluctuations that disturbed Erasmus did so not simply because of grammatical solecism, then, but because of their ethical implications. And it is for reasons like these that schoolmasters throughout early modern Europe strove toward consistency and regularity in the instruction and uses of Latin, employing a pedagogy that depended on rote memorization of morphology and vocabulary and also, as importantly, on the translation into and out of the vernacular sentences that modeled acceptable grammar and sentiments (*vulgaria*). Joined to print technology, which provided wide access to (in many cases) virtually identical

---

[12] Hart, *An Orthographie* (1569; rpt. Menston: Scolar Press, 1969), Bii[r].

[13] See further Vivien Law, *The History of Linguistics in Europe from Plato to 1600* (Cambridge: Cambridge University Press, 2003), 94–111; and John Fyler, *Language and the Declining world in Chaucer, Dante, and Jean de Meun* (Cambridge: Cambridge University Press, 2007), 1–59.

texts, Latin demonstrated that prestigious, eloquent, moral, and learned language was that which eluded change and variation.

Early codifiers of English focused on the absence of just this constancy in describing their own language. So long as the language deviated from Latin and Greek in its regularity, its potential to displace their cultural authority could remain only that. Hart, indeed, saw his composition of the *Orthographie* as a selfless gesture for the benefit of the language and his countrymen, all diminished by this deviation: 'no man ought to trauell in this life onely or chiefly for himselfe and his next bloud, to the hindrance of others, but for the common welth of his country, though with daunger of life, or the price thereof in deede. Whoso may profite his country in any condicion, and especiallye wyth small cost and no daunger, he were vnnaturall to be a niggarde thereof.' And English, it seems, sorely needs Hart's ministrations:

But in the modern & present manner of writing (as well of certaine other languages as of our English) there is such confusion and disorder, as it may be accounted rather a kind of ciphring, or such a darcke kind of writing, as the best and readiest wit that euer hath bene, could, or that is or shalbe, can or may, by the only gift of reason, attaine to the ready and perfite reading thereof, without a long and tedious labour, for that it is vnfit and wrong shapen for the proportion of the voice.[14]

Accordingly, he addressed his work to reforming English spelling, including the identification of permissible sound-values for graphs, the invention of necessary new graphs, and the determination of spellings that correctly reflect speech.

About a decade later, Richard Mulcaster's *Elementarie* was even more specific than the *Orthographie* about the communicative discord produced by variation in English. To Mulcaster, this instability extended particularly to the relations between graphs and sounds: 'euerie letter almost being deputed to manie, and seuerall, naie to manie and well nigh contrarie sounds and vses, euerie word almost either wanting letters, for his necessarie sound, or hauing some more than necessitie requireth, [I] began to despare in the midst of such a confusio [sic], euer to find out anie sure direction, whereon to ground Art, and to set it certain'.[15] And for William Bullokar, a few more years later in his *Amendment of Orthographie*, the need to identify variation as a problem was a strong enough given in metalinguistic discourse that he could articulate it even as he also affirmed the greatness of the current form of English: 'So that for lacke of true ortography our writing in Inglish hath altered in euery age,

---

[14] Hart, *An Orthographie*, Aiiii^{r-v}, Aiii^r.
[15] Mulcaster, *The First Part of the Elementarie*, (1582; rpt. Menston: Scolar Press, 1970), 77.

yea since printing began...and if now be a time of the most perfect vse of the same, which must be confessed for the great learning dispensed in this land at this day...thinke it the great gift of God, if a perfectnesse be now surely planted, not to be rooted out as long as letters endure.'[16] English is at once perfect and degenerate—one of the many contradictions animating metalinguistic discussion then and still today.

While Hart, Mulcaster, and Bullokar saw orthographic instability as the source of English's most pressing problems, Richard Verstegan, in his 1605 *A Restitution of Decayed Intelligence*, foregrounded controversy over English's unstable vocabulary and its propensity to borrow words from other languages. Some critics 'think our toung thereby much bettred' through such borrowing, according to Verstegan, but others say 'that it is of it self no language at all, but the scum of many languages' and still others 'that it is most barren, and that we are dayly faine to borrow woords for it...out of other languages to patche it vp withall'.[17] With a thirty-three-page alphabetized list of 'our moste ancient English woords' and their modern synonyms and orthographic equivalents, Verstegan's *Restitution* sided with those who thought lexical stability should come internally, from English's native word stock. But other critics, such as Richard Carew in his 'Excellency of the English Tongue', advocated that an infusion of learned borrowings—derisively labeled 'inkhorn terms' by their opponents—was the best way for English to achieve lexical balance. And still other critics, like Thomas Wilson, saw inkhorn terms as a problem precisely because they represented variance from whatever constancy English already had. In his 1553 *Arte of Rhetorique*, he couches this argument in the kind of emotive associations that critics of *Webster's Third* would use four centuries later:

Among al other lessons, this should first be learned, that we neuer affect any straunge ynkehorne termes, but so speake as is commonly received: neither sekyng to be ouer fine, nor yet liuyng ouer carelesse, vsyng our speache as most men do, & ordryng our wittes, as the fewest haue doen. Some seke so farre for outlandishe Englishe, that thei forget altogether their mothers language. And I dare swere this, if some of their mothers were aliue, thei were not able to tell, what thei say, & yet these fine Englishe clerkes, wil saie thei speake in their mother tounge, if a man should charge them for counterfeityng the kynges English.[18]

---

[16] Bullokar, *The Amendment of Orthographie for English Speech* (1580; rpt. Amsterdam: Theatrum Orbis Terrarum, 1968), 2.

[17] Verstegan, *A Restitution of Decayed Intelligence*, (1605; rpt. Ilkley: Scolar Press, 1976), 204.

[18] Wilson, *The Arte of Rhetorique* (1553; rpt. Gainesville, FL: Scholars' Facsimiles and Reprints, 1962), 86[r].

It certainly wasn't the case, then, that all early grammarians agreed on what should be stabilized or how this should take place. What they did share was a sense that if English was to attain the expressibility and status of Latin and Greek, its variation needed to be controlled and channeled. At the same time, by designating vocabulary as acceptable or unacceptable and making these designations accessible only to readers who had access to handbooks like the *Orthographie*, the *Elementarie*, and the *Arte of Rhetorique*, these early metalinguistic discussions helped to fashion language into a marker of social rank. Only the kind of noble who once could use Latin as a concomitant of education and status—someone like Kynaston—would be able to learn which English words to use for the same purpose.[19] In another few generations Daniel Defoe, drawing on the inspiration of the Académie Française and its dictionary, infused this grammatical and social discussion with political overtones by making grammar a point of national pride and suggesting that 'the *English* Tongue is a Subject not at all less worthy the Labour of such a Society than the *French*, and capable of much greater Perfection. The Learned among the *French* will own, That the Comprehensiveness of Expression is a Glory in which the *English* Tongue not only Equals but excels it Neighbors.'[20] English, to Defoe, needed to be purged of irregularities and purified in style, and these perceived needs led him, and later Jonathan Swift, to call for the creation of England's own language academy, a call that is still sometimes repeated today.[21]

The burst of codification in the seventeenth and primarily eighteenth centuries indicates just how strong a hold this valuation of linguistic stability took on the minds of Anglophones. The first extant English grammar of English was Bullokar's 1586 *Pamphlet for Grammar*, and by 1600 only one other such grammar had appeared. By 1700 there were just an additional thirty. During the course of the eighteenth century, however, 236 more English grammars were published.[22] Dictionaries proliferated in this period in a similar fashion. The earliest English dictionary is Robert Cawdrey's 1604 *A Table Alphabeticall*, but between it and Johnson's 1755 *Dictionary* there

---

[19] See further Paula Blank, 'The Babel of Renaissance English', in Lynda Mugglestone (ed.), *The Oxford History of English* (Oxford: Oxford University Press, 2006), 212–39.

[20] Defoe, *Essays upon Several Projects* (London: Thomas Ballard, 1702), 229–30.

[21] John Honey, *Language Is Power: The Story of Standard English and its Enemies* (London: Faber and Faber, 1997), 164.

[22] See Ian Michael, *English Grammatical Categories and the Tradition to 1800* (Cambridge: Cambridge University Press, 1970); 549–87 enumerate the English grammars, and 588–94 order them chronologically. Another five English grammars appeared only in manuscript during this period. More generally, see G. A. Padley, *Grammatical Theory in Western Europe, 1500–1700: Trends in Vernacular Grammar*, 2 vols. (Cambridge: Cambridge University Press, 1985 and 1988).

appeared at least another twenty dictionaries, some of them, such as Nathan Bailey's 1721 *An Universal Etymological English Dictionary*, appearing in over twenty editions.[23] Grammars and dictionaries alike drew heavily upon one another, so that the amount of original work this codification represents is considerably less than these publication figures suggest. Nonetheless, codification thereby emerges as one of the pre-eminent linguistic concerns of the early modern period, cultivating stability in orthography, punctuation, rhetoric, and vocabulary and defining principles of language change built on analogy, etymology, history, logic, and usage. The standardization of spoken language has lagged behind that of written, beginning in earnest only with Walker's 1791 *Critical Pronouncing Dictionary*, though this delay was quickly remedied. In England the following century witnessed, for example, both the expansion of public schools as boarding institutions that cultivated (among other things) constancy in language, and also the distribution, to an increasingly literate society, of handbooks designed to help speakers eliminate stigmatized forms like 'dropped h'. Daniel Jones's 1917 *An English Pronouncing Dictionary* proved particularly influential in inculcating the ideology of a spoken standard language as well as the specific form of what was regarded as correct English pronunciation. Its value judgements of good and bad pronunciation have framed discussion of varieties of English literally far afield—in New Zealand, for example—from what Jones himself spoke and described.[24]

It is the breadth of such cultivation—its geographic, chronological, and social range—that has had the greatest consequence in the creation of a standard and its implications for linguistic change and variation. By itself, minimalization of forms—regularity in orthography and so forth—carries little significance. It may be the one structural characteristic of standards that differentiates them from other varieties, but it alone cannot transform a variety into a standard, and the forms this minimalization defines as standard—a pronunciation of *have* with an initial [h] ([hæv]) rather than one

---

[23] DeWitt T. Starnes and Gertrude E. Noyes, *The English Dictionary from Cawdrey to Johnson, 1604–1755* (Chapel Hill, NC: University of North Carolina Press, 1946).

[24] For a survey of standardizing works in the early period, see Manfred Görlach, *Explorations in English Historical Linguistics* (Heidelberg: C. Winter, 2002), 137–212. For general discussion of the kinds of issues such works examined, see Sterling Andrus Leonard, *The Doctrine of Correctness in English Usage, 1700–1800* (1929; rpt. New York: Russell and Russell, 1962); Richard W. Bailey, *Images of English: A Cultural History of the Language* (Ann Arbor, MI: University of Michigan Press, 1991), 179–213; and Linda C. Mitchell, *Grammar Wars: Language as Cultural Battlefield in 17th and 18th Century England* (Aldershot: Ashgate, 2001). On the details of spoken standardization, see Lynda Mugglestone, '*Talking Proper': The Rise of Accent as Social Symbol*, 2nd edn. (Oxford: Oxford University Press, 2003). On the use of Jones's standard in discussion of New Zealand English, see Elizabeth Gordon *et al.*, *New Zealand English: Its Origins and Evolution* (Cambridge: Cambridge University Press, 2004), 12.

without it ($[\wedge v]$) or a spelling like *which* rather than *hwich*—have no intrinsic quality that makes them standard. Already in the fifteenth century, in fact, printed English in general displayed considerably less variation than did written English of the previous century, and one variety in particular, Chancery English, had consistency even in the shapes of graphs, to go along with its orthographic, morphological, and lexical consistency. Developed within the government office of the Chancery and influential on other government writing and on English writing and printing in general, Chancery experienced, at least implicitly, some of the codification associated with standards.[25] And a century later, as in Hart's *Orthographie*, written English can already sometimes appear virtually identical to what lexicographers like Johnson or grammarians like Bishop Lowth would come much later to advocate: 'As of this part of difference, I shall write more at large after I haue briefly shewed you the two other vices of vsurpation of powers and misplacing of letters.'[26] Here, inasmuch as 'shewed' remains a recognized if obsolete variant of 'showed', the only formal differences with modern Standard English involve the distribution of *u* and *v*. Such similarities have increasingly led some critics to describe English as having been standardized already in the late-medieval period. John Fisher has argued, for instance, that Chancery English is the specific variety from which modern Standard English arose, while others have spoken more generally and casually of 'the standardization of much written English in the early fifteenth century'.[27] And still other critics have even identified a standard Old English in the tenth-century West Saxon koine in which most Old English writing survives.

But there is a fundamental and profound difference between a minimalization of forms of the sort encouraged by centralized copying houses or the development of print and standardization as an ideological and institutional gesture. The one might be called standardized language, the other standard language. If printed English of the sixteenth and even fifteenth centuries shared many of the formal characteristics of Modern English, it was framed by none of the social structures that render a variety a standard: selection,

---

[25] On the development and characteristics of Chancery English, see John H. Fisher, *The Emergence of Standard English* (Lexington, KY: University of Kentucky Press, 1996), 65–83; and also Fisher, Malcolm Richardson, and Jane L. Fisher (eds.), *An Anthology of Chancery English* (Knoxville, TN: University of Tennessee Press, 1984).

[26] Hart, *An Orthographie*, Eiiii^v.

[27] Fisher makes this argument in *The Emergence of Standard English*, as does Thomas Cable in 'The Rise of Written Standard and English', in Aldo Scaglione (ed.), *The Emergence of National Languages* (Ravenna: Longo Editore, 1984), 75–94. The quotation comes from Jocelyn Wogan-Browne et al. (eds.), *The Idea of the Vernacular: An Anthology of Middle English Literary Theory, 1280–1520* (University Park, PA: Pennsylvania State University Press, 1999), 340.

codification, and broad-based elaboration of function. All these are post-medieval, even post-early-modern, developments. Indeed, as I have noted, grammar books and dictionaries developed over the course of the seventeenth century and mostly in the eighteenth, and in at least the early part of this period Latin continued to be the language of instruction in grammar schools and at Oxford and Cambridge. It was in this period, too, that English came to be invested with political significance in the formation of England as a nation. These are the forces that produce what has been called the ideology of a standard—a way of thinking about language that invests cultural and linguistic prestige in one variety and that accordingly conceptualizes a hierarchy of other varieties and the sociolinguistic consequences of their use.[28]

It is this ideological component that ultimately creates a standard language from standardized language by transforming what might be simply a minimalization of variation into the practical and theoretical suppression of variation and change. Standard languages above all depend on the investing of meaning, on the ascription of social or cultural significance to linguistic forms that are otherwise simply tokens in a grammatical system. Indeed, a vowel, it might be said, is only a piece of acoustic phenomenon until speakers assign social value to it as a good or bad pronunciation. More concisely, attitude as much as form makes a standard what it is. Of even greater consequence as an ideological gesture, the very *concept* of standardization can make standards seem natural, inevitable varieties and in the process shape our perception of all linguistic activity. Indeed, to see a standard vernacular in pre-modern England, where it could not possibly occur, is to testify for the standard ideology's naturalization of linguistic regularity.

For all these reasons I would say that if 1066 and the Battle of Hastings serve as the convenient and conventional transition date from Old to Middle English, and 1476 and Caxton's establishment of the first English printing press as that from Middle to Early Modern English, then 1755 and the publication of Dr Johnson's *Dictionary* well symbolize the undisputed existence of Standard English. And by 'Standard English' I mean not a historical stage in the language's development but a specific, cultivated variety of the language: primarily, a written variety constant in orthography, punctuation,

28 For a critique of attempts to identify a standard English in the Middle Ages, see Jeremy J. Smith, 'Standard Language in Early Middle English?', in Irma Taavitsainen *et al.* (eds.), *Placing Middle English in Context* (Berlin: Mouton, 2000), 125–39. On the ideology of a standard more generally, see James Milroy and Lesley Milroy, *Authority in Standard Language: Investigating Standard English*, 3rd edn. (London: Routledge, 1999). They define standard ideology as 'a public *consciousness* of the standard. People *believe* that there is a "right" way of using English, although they do not necessarily use the "correct" form in their own speech' (25). They attribute the decisive establishment of this ideology to the eighteenth century (29).

morphology, syntax, and usage, which, while it may have some regional variation (e.g., Standard British English as opposed to Standard United States English) is everywhere also the language and object of classroom instruction, can be referenced through several forms of codification, and is recognized as the standard language in powerful domains of business, education, and government. And the timing of just when Standard English can be said to come into existence is significant, because as a response to variation and change, a standard language is also a response to the cultural context of its creation.

When grammatical discussions progressed in the seventeenth and eighteenth centuries, Standard English emerged not simply in codification but through ways of conceptualizing language. As a medium of ideas that also stood metaphorically for cultural and national stability, a relatively invariable form of English—and as importantly the very *notion* of such a form—came to stand for the language as well. In this way change and variation could be both linguistically and socially deviant and as such open to further qualifications of their deviance. By that I mean that once change and variation have been generally marked as channels for extra-linguistic anxieties—once it has been demonstrated that they can assume extra-linguistic signification—additional non-linguistic concerns can easily be mediated through them. Indeed, in the past few centuries, as formal features of both spoken and written language have become increasingly codified, the attribution of social meanings to variation and change has been an increasingly prominent part of the standardization process.

In the case of Standard English, as Defoe's interest in the Académie Française demonstrates, early grammatical discussions drew much of this meaning from presumptive associations between language and national identity. The opening sentence of Alexander Gill's 1621 *Logonomia Anglica* is thus 'The English nation and language have one origin: they go back to the Saxon and Angle peoples of Germany'.[29] Perhaps inevitably, associations like these evoke comparisons between English and prestigious antique or modern languages. In his 1605 *Remains concerning Britain* William Camden thus notes, 'I think that our English tongue is, I will not say, as sacred as the Hebrew or as learned as the Greek; but as fluent as the Latin, as courteous as the Spanish, as Court-like as the French, and as amourous as the Italian, as some Italianated amorous have confessed'.[30] More simply and eloquently, in his *Elementarie* Mulcaster, having described the English of his day as the best

---

[29] Gill, *Logonomia Anglica* (1621; rpt. Menston: Scolar Press, 1968), no sig.
[30] Camden, *Remains Concerning Britain* (1605; rpt. Yorkshire: EP Publishing Limited, 1974), 33.

there ever was or would be, waxed rhapsodic on the intrinsic value of his language and on the intrinsic connections between it and its speakers: 'I loue Rome, but London better, I fauor Italie, but England more, I honor the Latin, but I worship the English.'[31]

By aligning the character of the English language with the character of England itself, early grammarians like Camden and Mulcaster fostered a sense of language that marked change and variation as politically as well as socially significant. Through a kind of syllogistic logic that recalls the equation of nationhood with monolingualism, if the achievements of English stood as testaments to the emerging greatness of the country, then linguistic deviance could likewise reflect and even contribute to political dissolution. And by extension, variation already present in the form of regional orthography or morphology needed to be suppressed in the advance of Standard English. The written record of this period documents just this homogenization of writing, as in Early Modern Scots, where documents show the gradual insertion and dominance of southern English forms for the weak preterite, relative pronoun, and so forth.[32] Stability in the realms of language and social interaction were therefore connected even before Standard English can be said to exist, although by the same token this connection is one of the elements that made Standard English possible. For critics as enthusiastic as Camden, who praised the achievement of contemporary English, whatever faults there were in the language were there precisely because the present age was too given to fashion and novelty. 'Hitherto will our sparkful youth laugh at their great-grandfathers English,' he intones, 'who had more care to do well than to speak minion-like, and left more glory to us by their exploiting of great Acts, than we shall do by our forging of new words and uncouth phrases.'[33] In a similar vein, Verstegan points out that 'people in former ages were nothing so curious or delighted with varying their speech, as of late ages they are grown to bee, but kept their old language as they did their old fassion of apparel; in both which the world hath of later ages more then in former bin delighted; and in this age of ours much more than euer'.[34] When Mulcaster grants, therefore, that the English of his day must continue to change, he phrases his praise of his own English in a way that implicates the uncertain future of England in the certain variation and decline of its

---

[31] Mulcaster, *The First Part of the Elementarie*, 254.
[32] See Amy J. Devitt, *Standardizing Written English: Diffusion in the Case of Scotland 1520–1659* (Cambridge: Cambridge University Press, 1989).
[33] Camden, *Remains Concerning Britain*, 29.
[34] Verstegan, *A Restitution of Decayed Intelligence*, 197.

language: 'whatsoeuer shall becom of the English state, the English tung cannot proue fairer'.

As codification developed, so, too, did this connection between order in language and order in society. Through the efforts of writers as diverse as Thomas Hobbes, John Locke, Edmund Burke, and Dr Johnson, it, too, might in fact be regarded as having become naturalized—that is, become an unexamined assumption about language in many Anglophone communities.[35] In a private letter of 1638, even before these other writers had publicly defined the issue, Milton observed: 'For when speech is partly awkward and pedantic, partly inaccurate and badly pronounced, what does it say but that the souls of the people are slothful and gaping and already prepared for any servility? On the other hand, not once have we heard of an empire or state not flourishing at least moderately as long as it continued to have pride in its Language, and to cultivate it.'[36] It is just this kind of a presumed and unquestioned connection between social and linguistic order that underlies the policy issues I considered in the previous chapter.

In channeling political concerns through language, early modern metalinguistic discussion helped fashion change and variation as detrimental, if still natural, features of human language. Early critics reinforced this connection when, from a narrower perspective on communication, they described the purpose and achievement of language to be the transference of pure, unadulterated ideas from speaker to listener or from writer to reader. For Carew, 'the first and principal point sought in every language is that we may express the meaning of our minds aptly to each other'.[37] Subsequent linguistic discussion, even when not overtly political, has often reinforced this pre-Babel notion that human language should serve as the means for relaying ideas in their totality and that variation and change are therefore counterproductive processes. In his *Essay on Human Understanding*, for example, Locke characterized language as arbitrary and conventional and words as signs of ideas. Connections between physical words and invisible ideas cannot be natural, Locke reasoned, or there would be only one language. Because language proceeds from sense perception, moreover, 'those of one Country, by their customs and manner of Life, have found occasion to make several complex *Ideas*, and give names to them, which others never collected into

---

[35] For an overview of these connections, see David Simpson, *The Politics of American English, 1776–1850* (New York: Oxford University Press, 1986), 32–51.

[36] Milton, *Complete Prose Works*, 8 vols., gen. ed. Don M. Wolfe (New Haven, CT: Yale University Press, 1953–82), i, 330. The letter, written in Latin and translated in this volume, is to Benedetto Buonmattei.

[37] Carew, 'The Excellency of the English Tongue', in Camden, *Remains Concerning Britain*, 42.

specifick *Ideas*. This could not have happened, if these Species were the steady Workmanship of Nature; and not Collections made and abstracted by the Mind, in order to naming, and for the convenience of Communication.' Very much in line with St Augustine, however, Locke also contends that arbitrary language can be shaped and managed so as to avoid some kind of moral relativism and instead recover, so far as is possible, the stability of God's truths. Whether through imprecise expression or shifting pronunciation and usage, failures in communication occur when the words speakers use neither '*stand . . . for the reality of Things*' nor invoke the intended 'Ideas *in the minds also of other Men, with whom they communicate*'. Indeed, Locke understands the purpose of any language to be to enable the exchange of ideas, involving external signs that make one's invisible ideas known to others: 'To make Words serviceable to the end of Communication, it is necessary . . . that they excite, in the Hearer, exactly the same *Idea*, they stand for in the Mind of the Speaker. Without this, Men fill one another's Heads with noise and sounds; but convey not thereby their Thoughts, and lay not before one another their *Ideas*, which is the end of Discourse and Language.'[38]

Rather than naturalize variation and change, an argument like this (later advanced by David Hume and others) points to the importance of maintaining linguistic regularity, for the consequences of imprecision or the misuse of language are misused and imprecise ideas and hence communication. It is for reasons like this that Descartes had already provided an argument against accepting animal communication as language: inasmuch as human language consists of the exchange of ideas, communication among animals cannot be linguistic, since, lacking human minds, animals have no ideas to communicate.[39] And these same reasons underwrote the period's notion of universal grammar, which understood thought as subject to rational principles and language as the image of thought, so that language perforce had to—or perhaps *should*—reflect the laws of reason.[40] Even the prevailing alternative argument about the character of language agreed with philosophers like Locke on at least this one point. In the eighteenth century, through such efforts as Horne Tooke's *Diversions of Purley*, this argument took the form of advocacy for the 'genius' of each language, that is for the intrinsic character

---

[38] Locke, *An Essay Concerning Human Understanding*, ed. Peter H. Nidditch (Oxford: Clarendon Press, 1975), 432–3, 407, 406, 478.

[39] See Roy Harris, *The Language Machine* (Ithaca, NY: Cornell University Press, 1987), 30. A dated but still valuable overview of eighteenth-century positions on language can be found in Leonard, *The Doctrine of Correctness in English Usage*, 19–44.

[40] See further Hans Aarsleff, *The Study of Language in England, 1780–1860*, 2nd edn. (Minneapolis, MN: University of Minnesota Press, 1983), 13–43.

of a language's form and semantics. For the present discussion, the important point is that any variation from this character would necessarily be, again, deviation. Locke, Tooke, and even Whorf thus share at least this: the same essentialist connection between language and culture, as well as the sense that variation is semantically obfuscatory and socially debilitating.

The ways in which a standard ideology has come to channel social concerns through change and variation have proliferated in the modern world, affecting ethnic and social groups as well as individuals and, in turn, national varieties, sociolects like African American Vernacular English, the argot of young speakers, and so forth. In fact, the mediation of social concerns through language, including change and variation, has become so prolific that Deborah Cameron has invented the term verbal hygiene to describe 'the urge to meddle in matters of language'.[41] This meddling can take many forms, appearing in certain kinds of classroom instruction and linguistic analysis, as well as in commentary by popular essayists like William Safire and John Honey. The focus of discussion may be nominally linguistic—correct pronunciations, usages, and punctuation—and its implication is always that perfect communication, as before Babel, is possible and attainable, if only prescriptive grammatical rules were obeyed. But the discussion more generally serves as 'the arena where certain social conflicts find symbolic expression'. Above all, as with the uproar over *Webster's Third*, these conflicts engage issues like moral relativism, authority, and permissiveness in society. 'In the case of language,' Cameron suggests, 'it might be argued that investment in traditional authority manifests not just a general preference for continuity over change, but also an attachment to values and practices that were impressed on people in the formative stages of their personal linguistic histories.' In its most direct and brutal form, such investment disallows any speech judged non-standard, and, more importantly, those who speak it as well. In most Anglophone areas it may be impossible (or at least difficult) to refuse to hire individuals on the basis of their race or sex, but it is certainly legal in many cases to refuse to do so because of the putatively incomprehensible variety they speak: 'linguistic bigotry is among the last publicly expressible prejudices left to members of the western intelligentsia'. More subtly, in Cameron's analysis, in both the United States and the United Kingdom recent efforts to revive traditional grammar instruction and affirm the importance of Standard English have been the means to advance a politically orthodox agenda:

---

[41] Cameron, *Verbal Hygiene* (London: Routledge, 1995), vii.

conservatives use 'grammar' as the metaphorical correlate for a cluster of related political and moral terms: *order, tradition, authority, hierarchy* and *rules.* In the ideological world that conservatives inhabit, these terms are not only positive, they define the conditions for any civil society, while their opposites—*disorder, change, fragmentation, anarchy* and *lawlessness*—signify the breakdown of social relations. A panic about grammar is therefore interpretable as the metaphorical expression of persistent conservative fears the we are losing the values that underpin civilization and sliding into chaos.[42]

The very notion of traditional grammar instruction informing these connections presents its own difficulties, for the halcyon days it recalls never were. For one thing, since the modern profession of English instruction came into existence in the late nineteenth century English teachers have been describing each generation of student-writers as worse than the previous one. And for another, even those individuals whose long-ago grammar instruction may well have been superior to anything available today are also often remembering and glorifying an era that restricted that kind of education by sex, class, and race.

From the perspective of formal linguistics, Germanic philology, which emerged in the nineteenth century as the dominant approach to change and variation, developed linguistic genealogy with much the same nostalgia and socializing effects. As conceptual tools, tree diagrams, showing the progression of (say) Indo-European to Centum to Germanic, implied the discrete character of languages and described change as an exceptionless and regular process. The extension of this analysis into English necessarily promoted similar notions of linguistic stasis and change. In many ways, indeed, the history of English as an academic discipline also typically has been the history of standardization, a history that moves from the dialects of the Old and Middle English periods, through the codification of the early modern one, to the emergence of a global modern Standard English in the eighteenth century, to, at least in some accounts, an implicit culmination in modern American English.[43]

Given the historical contexts of standardization and modern linguistics, this implication of Standard English in what is widely understood to be the language's history was perhaps inevitable. From a literal if limited perspective, it can be said that early critics recognized and defined—'invented' would be

---

[42] Cameron, *Verbal Hygiene,* 13, 14, 12, 95. On the complaint tradition, also see Bailey, *Images of English,* 237–66, and Milroy and Milroy, *Authority in Standard Language,* 24–46.

[43] See, for example, Albert C. Baugh and Thomas Cable, *A History of the English Language,* 5th edn. (Upper Saddle River, NJ: Prentice Hall, 2002); and Seth Lerer, *Inventing English: A Portable History of the Language* (New York: Columbia University Press, 2007).

the early modern word—diachronic change and synchronic structure at the same time. Even as seventeenth-century grammarians like Verstegan or Cawdrey were codifying contemporary English, that is, bibliophiles like Francis Junius were inaugurating Anglo-Saxon studies. In this way, the history of English as a discipline not only emerges from a standard ideology but also, emphasizing continuity above all, legitimizes the standard variety of English as the pre-eminent one and non-standard ones as merely deviations. While critics like H. C. Wyld could thus imagine a history for Standard English and might even accept the legitimacy of rural dialects, they saw urban varieties as simply vulgar. 'It is as though uneducated speakers are not allowed to be involved in language history,' comments James Milroy.[44] And this use of historical continuity and stability as qualities that legitimate linguistic forms and varieties continues today with standard ones but also, in a gesture that again points to the naturalization of a standard ideology, with non-standard ones.

Creoles offer a case in point. Seeing them as defined not historically but structurally, Salikoko S. Mufwene rejects prevalent conceptions of African American Vernacular English as a stable variety that developed linearly from the days of slavery. He argues, indeed, that attempts to trace African American Vernacular English to a pervasive Plantation Creole and then to something like the Gullah variety still used on the seacoast islands of South Carolina reflect the kind of historical imperative and monogenesis that a standard ideology fosters with regard to variation and change. 'There is no historical justification', he suggests, 'for assuming that there was ever a time in the seventeenth or eighteenth century when every African-American spoke the basilect of a Gullah-like variety. Nor is there any particular justification for assuming that AAVE must have developed from a Gullah-like variety and that its speakers must have aimed at speaking like whites.'[45] African American Vernacular English, for Mufwene, should be only an umbrella term, not the label of a fixed or even semi-regular variety that the ideology of standardization encourages critics to find.

In this way, history itself acquires ideological force, providing affirmation of a linguistic structure's naturalness and continuity in the language. The mere existence and development of particular usages over centuries—including

---

[44] Milroy, 'The Legitimate Language: Giving A History to English', in Richard Watts and Peter Trudgill (eds.), *Alternative Histories of English* (London: Routledge, 2002), 11. See also Shana Poplack, Gerard van Herk, and Dawn Harvie, ' "Deformed in the Dialects": An Alternative History of Non-Standard English', in Watts and Trudgill (eds.), *Alternative Histories of English*, 87–110; and Milroy, 'The Consequences of Standardization in Descriptive Linguistics', in Tony Bex and Richard J. Watts (eds.), *Standard English: The Widening Debate* (London: Routledge, 1999), 16–39.

[45] Mufwene, 'African-American English', in *The Cambridge History of the English Language*, vi, John Algeo (ed.), *English in North America* (Cambridge: Cambridge University Press, 2001), 321.

Standard English as a variety—become confirmations of their claim to be transcendent, essential forms of English. ' "Antiquity" as a virtue of the English language', notes Richard Bailey, 'thus emerges as a significant part of the image of the language. But the fact of antiquity is one thing; its uses are another, and "educated" people have been expected to employ antiquity to their own advantage in presenting themselves as "discriminating" users of English. Highly refined national and class distinctions have been built around etymological nuance.'[46] In effect, antiquity thereby works against variation and change, so that even with over two-thirds of the current global Anglophone population now living outside of the United Kingdom and the United States, the antiquity of British English still serves as one of the strongest arguments for its primacy among the increasingly diverse varieties of Modern English. It was the putative failure of British English to live up to the responsibility of antiquity that so delighted my radio interviewer in July of 2000.

With the exception of sociolinguistics, even much modern formal linguistic theory has furthered the attitudes toward variation and change that are foundational to the standard ideology and that were developed in eighteenth- and nineteenth-century metalinguistic discussion. Ferdinand de Saussure's landmark *Cours de linguistique générale*, thus, propelled twentieth-century criticism in this direction when it emphasized the synchronic state of a language over its diachronic change. And this is the direction taken by subsequent structuralist linguists, such as Charles Fries in his 1952 *The Structure of English*, and in turn by the transformational approaches that replaced structuralism. 'Linguistic theory is concerned primarily with an ideal speaker-listener', Noam Chomsky famously declared, 'in a completely homogeneous speech-community, who knows its language perfectly and is unaffected by such grammatically irrelevant conditions as memory limitations, distractions, shifts of attention and interest, and errors (random or characteristic) in applying his knowledge of the language in actual performance.'[47] Less theoretically, it is the same direction taken by Basic English, Charles K. Ogden's effort to reduce and stabilize English as a secondary language for technical discourse through the reduction of its vocabulary to just 850 words. Beginning with the suppositions that a global language was a political necessity (particularly between the two world wars), that an artificial language like Esperanto was not viable, and that of the natural languages English was the most logical choice, Ogden set about simplifying English, not producing an interlanguage version. In the words of his colleague and

---

[46] Bailey, *Images of English*, 274.
[47] Chomsky, *Aspects of the Theory of Syntax* (Cambridge, MA: MIT Press, 1965), 3.

champion, I. A. Richards, 'If a language is to be easy to learn we must not only cut its words down to a minimum and regularize its grammar; we must also study very carefully the meanings of every one of its words and decide upon the central, pivotal or key meaning of each one of them. Parallel to the reduction and ordering of its vocabulary, there must be a reduction and ordering of the meanings of the words it recommends.'[48] Perhaps the most famous version of this kind of thinking, however, is fictional as well as satiric: Newspeak as Oceania's medium of consistent if rigidly controlled communication in the novel *Nineteen Eighty-four* by George Orwell, himself a sometime supporter of Basic English.

Not only have such theories shaped the status of variation and change through their overt emphasis on synchronic structure, however. By cultivating abstract systems like Saussure's *la langue* or Chomsky's 'competence', they have also furthered the notion articulated by both Locke and the Genesis account of the Tower of Babel that complete communication is the possible and reachable goal of human speech. In these systems, when speakers fail to understand one another, they do so not because such failure is an inalienable part of the human condition but because they do not speak the same *langue* or because their linguistic competence has been obscured by the vicissitudes of daily performance.[49] In all these ways, metalinguistic discussions have made a twofold contribution to the anxiety surrounding change and variation. First, of course, they have framed language discussions in such a way as to emphasize a view of language as static. And second, by agreeing on this one point, even as they disagree on many others, they have rendered it as part of what might be called a metalinguistic horizon—a set of ideas whose validity is demonstrated by the fact that they serve as presumptions in discussions of other issues, even when these discussions are carried out by critics whose other views differ as much as do those of Locke, Tooke, Sir William Jones, Whorf, and Chomsky.[50] Like the connection between social and linguistic order, that between variation and deviation has become naturalized.

Dialects, dictionaries, and pidgins

Metalinguistic discussions that limit or challenge variation have a peculiar, counter-intuitive characteristic: in order to identify and advocate a standard, they need also to identify the non-standard forms and varieties that the

---

[48] Richards, *Basic English and Its Uses* (London: Kegan Paul, 1943), 22.

[49] Harris, *The Language Machine*, 44–5.

[50] Aarsleff explains that part of what motivated Jones were his objections to the work of Tooke and others as impressionistic and even whimsical (*The Study of Language in England*, 127–32).

standard will avoid. While a standard may have one acceptable spelling, meaning, or pronunciation for a word, there may be many non-standard ones, and the act of specifying the standard will likely entail specifying, at least implicitly, all the likely unacceptable alternatives as well. When used as an adverb, for example, *there* is the only correct spelling, not *their*, *they're*, or *thar*, and the correct pronunciation of this word is [ðɛr] or [ðejər], maybe even [ðɑr], but not [bɛr], [ðɛn], [ðæt], and so forth. At a theoretical level the number of possible non-standard variations of any given standard form is virtually infinite, although because utterly random variation allows for no language at all, actual non-standard variation is rather more limited for spoken and written language. In any case, all such non-standard forms serve a crucial role in standardization: their existence constitutes the variation from among which standard forms can be isolated. In a grandly metaphorical way, they might even be said to represent the competing narrative of variation in Genesis 10 to that of stasis in Genesis 11. Standards need not simply to acknowledge non-standard forms, then, but even in a sense to maintain them. A language that somehow truly lacked variation, with uniform pronunciation and syntax by all users in all circumstances, could not itself be regarded as a standard, for if there is only one form for any given linguistic item, there cannot be a selection of that form. By the same token, if there somehow were only one variety of a given language, already necessarily used in all domains, there could be no elaboration of that language's function. Even codification would seem to be impossible, since all it could do would be to identify invariable usage: prescriptive and descriptive grammar would be the same.

In the early modern period, commentary on non-standard varieties in fact proliferated alongside grammars and dictionaries. One strain of thought at this time flirted with contradicting the entire ideology of standardization by accepting change and variation as inevitable. As the preface to his *Logonomia Anglica*, for example, Gill's description of the history of English and its many changes ('quam tandem mutacionem') serves as the work's premise, and he later identifies six regional varieties of English, offering the most detailed comparative account of their structure up to that time. To illustrate the 'Borealium' (northern) variety, he points to a distinctive centralized variant of the diphthong that had developed from Middle English /u/: 'au *for* ou, *as* gaun, *or also* geaun, *for* goun *toga*'.[51] Likewise evidently embracing Genesis 10, Carew went so far as to regard such regional varieties as one of English's strengths: 'Moreover the copiousness of our Language appeareth in the

---

[51] See Gill, *Logonomia Anglica*, 16.

diversity of our Dialects, for we have Court and we have Country English, we have Northern and Southern, gross and ordinary, which differ each from other, not only in the terminations, but also in many words, terms, and phrases, and express the same thing in diverse sorts, yet all write English alike.'[52] More moderately, Verstegan compares English in particular to the dispersion of the Germanic languages in general, and notes that change is entirely natural. In this regard, he cites the differences between the speech of Londoners and that of 'the countrey people that neuer borrow any words out of Latin or French'. For Verstegan, it is the relation between plain geographic distance and variation that most clearly reveals the latter's naturalness: 'wee may note our Cornishmen, who beeing sequestred from the Welshmen, but by a little arme of the sea do also varie from them in their language, though not so much as the Britons in *France*, who are yet more seperated: and yet was the language of these three originally one, which their speeches albeit somewhat differing, do yet sufficiently witnes'.[53]

Verstegan here sounds very much like a nineteenth-century comparativist, pointing to parallels in other language families and thus to higher-order linguistic principles as an explanation for English in particular. Yet his largely descriptive view of English's social and regional varieties is joined by other far more judgmental strains of criticism that invested the varieties with social significance, much as the standardizing tradition did for individual forms. Over forty years earlier Hart, too, had noted that 'Tongues haue often chaunged'. But he went on to suggest that the naturalness of change did not prevent change from being abused. If 'the fancies of men' have produced linguistic change and variation, they ought also be able to 'correct the vicious writing of the speach'.[54] For all of his own descriptivism, Gill passes even stronger judgement, suggesting that use and pronunciation in fact lead to linguistic corruption and identifying the Western variety of English as so corrupt as to be scarcely recognizable as English. The 'Occidentalium', he observes, is the 'greatest barbarity. And in fact if you should hear a farmer in Somerset, you would easily wonder whether English or some foreign tongue was being spoken.'[55] This view of dialects assumed a kind of formal status in John Bullokar's 1616 *English Expositor*. The first English dictionary to define the word *dialect*, the *Expositor* did so in a way that represented dialects as divergences from some putatively accentless variety—a view that persists, of course, into the present: '*Dialect*. A difference of some words, or

---

[52] Carew, 'The Excellency of the English Tongue', 49.
[53] Verstegan, *Restitution*, 195, 198.
[54] Hart, *An Orthographie*, Dii[r].
[55] Gill, *Logonomia Anglica*, 18.

pronunciation in any language: as in England, the Dialect or manner of speech in the North, is different from that in the South, and the Western Dialect differing from them both... So euery countrey hath commonly in diuers parts thereof some difference of language, which is called the Dialect of that place.'[56] But it was Sir Isaac Newton, of all people, who articulated this judgemental view of regional variation in the broadest critical perspective: 'The dialects of each language [are] soe divers and arbitrary [that] a generall language cannot bee so fitly deduced from them as from ye natures of things themselves wch is ye same in all nations and by which all language was at ye first composed.'[57] From the primacy of nature descends language, and from language evolve dialects, which are to that extent farther removed from and less expressive of nature.

As I noted in Chapter 3, at least a superficial awareness of England's dialect diversity, both social and regional, can be traced to the Middle Ages. In the thirteenth century, Roger Bacon commented in this way on the general regional differences of English: 'We see also that within the same language there are various idioms [diversa idiomata], that is manners and peculiarities of speech, as there are in English among northerners, southerners, easterners, and westerners.'[58] And a century earlier, in his *Gesta Pontificum*, William of Malmesbury not only acknowledged regional variation but also complained that some varieties were not mutually intelligible with others and hinted at the emergence of sociolects as well: 'Indeed, the entire language of the Northumbrians, especially in York, grates so stridently that none of us southerners is able to understand it. This situation came about because the north is in the proximity of the barbarians, with the result that it was distant from the former English kings and the current Norman ones, who are known to be situated more in the south than the north.'[59] While Malmesbury ties speech patterns to social position, and offers more than a hint of regional pride and even disdain, he does not explicitly situate regional varieties within an interpretive hierarchy that connects social features like rank, occupation, and sex to linguistic features like vocabulary and pronunciation. Both Bacon and Malmesbury, indeed, offer remarks more suggestive of idle curiosity than evocative of the systematic identification of discrete varieties whose

[56] Bullokar, *An English Expositor: Teaching the Interpretation of the Hardest Words Used in Our Language* (London: John Legatt, 1616), s. v. Blank identifies this as the earliest such definition in 'The Babel of Renaissance English', 214.

[57] Quoted in Edward G. Gray, *New World Babel: Languages and Nations in Early America* (Princeton, NJ: Princeton University Press, 1999), 67.

[58] Bacon, *Opera Quædam Hactenus Inedita*, ed. J. S. Brewer (London: Longman, 1859), 467.

[59] William of Malmesbury, *De Gestis Pontificum Anglorum*, ed. N. E. S. A. Hamilton, Rolls Series 52 (London: Longman, 1870), 209.

social meanings creative writers could exploit in the way I earlier described as narratives of language change. And this remains the case through the Middle Ages, with Chaucer, John Trevisa, Caxton, and others all testifying to an awareness of regional variation but not to a modern sociolinguistic stratification of dialects. Within late-medieval England's linguistic repertoire, indeed, the pre-eminent distinction remained not that among varieties of English but between English and non-English languages.[60]

What changed in the early modern period, as part of the linguistic attitudes that a standard ideology fosters, was the emergence of a metalinguistic discussion to frame the status of regional variation and change. When measured against a standard, such variation became—had to become—inaccuracies and errors that need to be corrected. Beyond this, non-standard varieties' essential roles in the enforcement of a standard increased, since the errors they demonstrated acquired social as well as linguistic significance. Put another way, when vested with social implications, variation and change became more potent, enforcing social and linguistic norms in mutually supportive ways. And this connection between linguistic and social structure has become so strong in the history of English since the early modern period as to constitute, I would argue, a kind of symbiosis. Without the embedding of social and linguistic practices in one another—specifically, the channeling of social issues through variation and change—Standard English would itself not have been possible.

While Carew may have thought that 'all write English alike', despite the regional variations in their language, Gill describes a linguistically and socially variegated speech community. But the linguistic variation he sees in this community is itself socially charged. He sees the speech of the cultured class as inherently stable, and variation and change as natural only among what he describes as 'rustics': 'And what I say about these dialects, I would wish you to understand relates only to rustics; for among gentler temperaments, there is everywhere only one speech, pronunciation, and meaning—more cultivated by upbringing.'[61] In his 1589 *The Arte of English Poesie*, George Puttenham imbeds variation even more deeply in the geographic and social landscape. For Puttenham, in a passage I cited in full in Chapter 2, the varieties spoken in the country and by cliques of academics or lower-rank, uneducated individuals are linguistically inferior—odd, misshapen, and false—compared to that spoken by the cultured and educated. Anyone looking for the best language, according to Puttenham, should not look in 'marches and frontiers' or even

---

[60] See Machan, *English in the Middle Ages* (Oxford: Oxford University Press, 2003), 71–110.
[61] Gill, *Logonomia Anglica*, 19.

universities or 'in any vplandish village or corner of a Realme', but rather should follow 'generally the better brought vp sort...men ciuill and graciously behauoured and bred'.[62] The role of education in Puttenham's analysis points to a significant development in the use of linguistic performance to channel other kinds of anxiety. By his analysis, not simply did variation and change become identified with non-standard varieties but the speakers of those varieties became fated, at least for the foreseeable future, to perpetuate them. This is so because Standard English, spoken or written, was an art acquired at home and cultivated in schools and universities, already the special provenance of an intellectual, economic, and political elite. Not to attend a university or the right school is not to acquire the right variety of English and therefore not to belong with England's foremost sociolinguistic group.

Connections between non-standard varieties, social status, and variation and change developed at both the level of the varieties themselves and at that of the details of their individual grammars. Invested with social significance, specific linguistic forms like titles of address or the second person personal pronoun (whether *thou* or *ye*) served as tokens of social display that identified speakers' varieties and their concomitant social standing. *Master*, as a preface to a surname, thus marked a gentleman, just as surely as *thou* projected disdain onto one's interlocutor—a point wittily made in Shakespeare's *Twelfth Night*, when Sir Toby Belch, in his efforts to arouse Sir Andrew Aguecheek to compose a letter of challenge to what he imagines to be a rival suitor, observes: 'Taunt him the license of ink. If thou thou'st him some thrice, it shall not be amiss.'[63]

More generally, Puttenham's comments on class and culture portend what would harden into a discourse for talking about dialects, as in Thomas Sheridan's 1762 *Course of Lectures on Elocution*, where he identifies two general varieties in London: Cockney, which is current 'in the city', and the 'polite pronunciation', which is found 'at the court-end'. Of these two, the court dialect is far and away the most fashionable, and it can be learned only by speakers who have already been admitted to its speech community and whose speech, in circular fashion, confirms their social standing: 'by conversing with people in polite life, it is a sort of proof that a person has kept good company'. 'All other dialects', says Sheridan, 'are sure marks, either of a provincial, rustic, pedantic, or mechanic education; and therefore have some degree of

---

⁶² Puttenham, *The Arte of English Poesie* (1589; rpt. Menston: Scolar Press, 1968), 120.

⁶³ *Twelfth Night*, 3.2.39–40. See Joseph M. Williams, '"O! When Degree is Shak'd": Sixteenth-Century Anticipations of Some Modern Attitudes toward Usage', in T. W. Machan and Charles T. Scott (eds.), *English in Its Social Contexts* (New York: Oxford University Press, 1992), 69–101.

disgrace annexed to them.'[64] As disinterested as Old English and even most Middle English writers may have been in associating social standing and achievement with linguistic forms and varieties, this association between politeness, good company, and stable, standard language—and, conversely, between provincialism, variation, and non-standard language—had in fact become commonplace in Sheridan's day. In 1789, for example, Philip Withers matter-of-factly observed in a way that could well have inspired Shaw's Henry Higgins not only that language remained the best opportunity for the upper class to demonstrate its rank but also that the language of the lower classes was not even worthy of attention:

It is no Part of my Plan to notice all the Phrases current in Covent Garden and the *Purlieus* of St. Giles. They are below rational criticism. My Animadversions will extend to such Phrases only as People in decent Life inadvertently adopt.

In former Ages, a Gentleman was easily distinguished from the Multitude by his DRESS. In the present Period, all external Evidence of Rank among Men is destroyed. Every outward Distinction is also lost in the female World . . . It is utterly impossible, on a first View, to determine the Rank of *this Boarding-School Miss.* But the Moment the unhappy Girl attempts to speak, her Origin is disclosed, and her Finery and affected Airs excite sentiments of Pity and Contempt. Hence the Importance of early attention to Purity and Politeness of Expression: it is the only external Distinction which remains between a Gentleman and a Valet; a Lady and a Mantua-maker.[65]

Bad language has provided one particularly effective way by which variation might further these discriminations between gentlemen and their valets, both literal and metaphorical. It's reasonable to suppose that as long as humans could speak, they have sworn and blasphemed, and the Ten Commandments in fact expressly forbid taking God's name in vain. In the twelfth century Henry I attempted to control this type of variation by imposing a system of fines for swearing in royal residences that was proportionately linked to social standing—to whether the speaker was a lord, squire, yeoman or page.[66] But it is again the early modern period, especially the seventeenth and eighteenth centuries, that offered the first consistent distinctions between good language and various kinds of bad language, including swearing and blasphemy, and that systematically tied those distinctions to social standing. Just as an increased attention to the use of titles of address helped language to stabilize shifting social ranks in early modern England, so the identification and proscription of improper language allowed merchants, yeomen, and the

---

[64] Sheridan, *A Course of Lectures on Elocution* (1762; Menston: Scolar Press, 1968), 30.
[65] Withers, *Aristarchus, or the Principles of Composition*, 2nd edn. (London: J. Moore, 1789), 160–1.
[66] Ashley Montagu, *The Anatomy of Swearing*, 2nd edn. (London: Macmillan, 1973), 108.

like to distinguish themselves from a lower rank of rougher speaking, less educated but socially aspirant individuals. If in some situations swearing can be a form of dominance, that is, in others so, too, can its avoidance be.

What began as a sixteenth-century Puritan effort to censor bad language assumed increasing urgency and still greater moral overtones in the decades to come. Following the Restoration, thus, there emerged several societies devoted to cultivating religion and manners, and within this context language variation in the form of improper language served as a symptom of larger social ills. For this reason, groups like the Society for the Reformation of Manners and the Society for the Promotion of Christian Knowledge took action focused on the elimination of cursing, often through manuals of good behavior. One of these, Richard Allestree's 1731 *The Whole Duty of Man*, devoted twelve pages to swearing as both a religious and social transgression: a sin against God but also a mark of unreliability and dishonesty.[67] While the SPCK pursued its ends through charity schools using books like Allestree's, the SRM attempted to legislate against bad language in a formal way, and both groups generally channeled several social issues through the variation from good speech that bad language emblemized. Bad language, thus, became regarded as a characteristic of the lower ranks, even if, as with phonological features like 'dropped *hs*', it may be in reality no more common among them than among the educated middle and upper ranks. And what makes bad language bad are likewise the larger issues it channels: it points to social unrest, it produces social unrest, and it constitutes social unrest. To the extent that at least early metalinguisitic discussion stressed the importance for women in particular to use good language, this form of linguistic variation acquired gendered qualities as well, leading, ironically, to the sociolinguistic disparagement of feminized speech, whether by women or men. In other words, to vary from a putative norm and speak as a woman, even if this means avoiding a marked discursive habit like swearing, has often been the justification for social marginalization.[68]

While swearing and bad language may have become less provocative now than in the eighteenth century, they can still serve as vehicles for issues of class and social propriety. In the 1960s and 1970s, Mary Whitehouse, founder of the National Viewers' and Listeners' Association, was a particularly insistent British voice on the need to curtail all forms of bad language in books and

---

[67] Tony McEnery, *Swearing in English: Bad Language, Purity and Power from 1586 to the Present* (London: Routledge, 2006), 94–7.

[68] For a historical survey of this issue, see Bailey, *Images of English*, 246–66. For broader consideration of the sociolinguistic marginalization of women's speech, see Deborah Cameron, *Feminism and Linguistic Theory*, 2nd edn. (New York: St Martin's Press, 1992).

on television and radio. Warning often of obscenity, blasphemy, and drugs, and taking various kinds of legal action against particular works and productions, Whitehouse had larger objectives consistent with this history of managing social issues through language: '"Let's all be kids together", cry the adults as if only the fantasies of child's play help them to come to terms with what they have made of the world. And in so doing, they deny the young the basic security without which they cannot grow to a mature and responsible exercise of freedom.'[69] Like the critics of *Webster's Third*, writing at nearly the same time, Whitehouse was most troubled about features of language that were not linguistic at all.

In this context, I want to return to dictionaries and their own roles in specifying Standard English and fostering variation and change as conduits of extra-linguistic issues.[70] The earliest dictionaries in England are medieval wordlists like the *Medulla Grammatice* or the *Promptorium Parvulorum*, which tend to list Latin and English in one-word equivalents and which circulated in relatively few copies. While such works would seem to have little extra-linguistic impact, the social implications of dictionaries and their identifications of language, change, and variation do figure already in the early modern period. As I noted in Chapter 3, the earliest dictionaries to focus on slang, cant, and other linguistic variation did so in order to enlighten good citizens of the coded language that thieves and vagrants used to plot against them. Writing in 1610 about how one Cock Lorrell, in 1501, had organized a group of vagrants, Samuel Rid observes, 'first of all they thinke it fit to deuise a certaine kinde of language, to the end their cousenings, knaueries and villanies might not be so easily perceiued and knowne, in places where they come'.[71] This same association between dictionaries' potential to stabilize language and society as one maneuver in general is foundational in the development of English lexicography following Cawdrey's 1604 *A Table Alphabeticall*. As an aspect of codification, indeed, English dictionaries emerged against a background of religious and national self-definition, cultural aggrandizement, and global expansion. If France, Spain, and Holland offered competition for colonies and foreign markets, Latin and Greek (again) represented languages with expansive and nuanced lexicons, traditions of grammatical exegesis, and unimpeachable records of rhetorical achievement. In their constancy, regularity, and imperviousness to change, they were what speakers of every early modern vernacular hoped for in their own language.

---

[69] Quoted in McEnery, *Swearing in English*, 125.

[70] In fact, the earliest citation in the *OED* to 'Standard English' in its current sense is from the dictionary's own original 1859 proposal for publication (s. v., *standard*, n. (a.), B.I.3.e).

[71] Quoted in Blank, 'The Babel of Renaissance English', 226. See further Julie Coleman, *A History of Cant and Slang Dictionaries*, i, *1567–1784* (Oxford: Oxford University Press, 2004).

For English dictionaries, the challenge was to negotiate a compromise between the perceived need to supplement the native vocabulary with importations of Greek and Latin terms and thereby enhance the reputation as well as expressibility of English *vis-à-vis* the classical languages and other vernaculars; and a reluctance to transform the language into something so monstrous that it could no longer stand as a symbol of English achievement. In the same way that Webster would later frame discussion of English in America, change might have been accepted as necessary, but only up to some negotiable point, at which it would be replaced by stability. On one hand, then, Thomas Blount's *Glossographia* of 1656 accepted and recorded words like *advigilate* ('to watch diligently') and *adoxy* ('ignominy'). On the other, Edward Phillips's 1658 *The New World of English Words* dispensed such inkhorn terms, including *cinerulent* ('full of dust or ashes') and *cacologie* ('evil communication'), in a list of barbarous words and those 'illegally compounded' or derived from Latin and Greek.[72] At either extreme, early dictionaries in general volatilely reflected social change (whether for good or ill) in the words they recorded or excluded, and they thereby functioned as something of far greater consequence than did medieval wordlists.

Faced with the kinds of theoretical and practical difficulties occasioned by language change and variation, lexicographers have perhaps not surprisingly been more flexible and less authoritarian than many of their critics. What were certain and fixed for Defoe, Swift, Follett, or Macdonald—the character of English lexicon, morphology, and registers—were provisional and evolving for Gove and predecessors like James Murray and Dr Johnson. The latter began his lexicographical work exhibiting confidence and certitude in his linguistic judgements. His 1747 *Plan of an English Dictionary* meticulously examines the many practical difficulties involving borrowed words, pronunciation, orthography, etymology, inflections, and so forth. Summing up his objectives, Johnson announces to the Earl of Chesterfield, 'This, my Lord, is my idea of an English dictionary; a dictionary by which the pronunciation of our language may be fixed, and its attainment facilitated; by which its purity may be preserved, its use ascertained, and its duration lengthened'.[73] Elsewhere, in place of 'purity', Johnson and others focus in particular on 'propriety' as a distinctively eighteenth-century way once more to meld together grammatical correctness and social stability.[74] And in this regard, it's significant that while Dante's definition of grammar emphasized primarily a stabilizing quality, English definitions recalled Quintilian in also emphasizing the notion that grammar was the art of speaking and writing correctly.

---

[72] Starnes and Noyes, *The English Dictionary from Cawdrey to Johnson, 1604–1755*, 41–2, 55–6.
[73] Johnson, *The Plan of a Dictionary of the English Language* (London: J. and P. Knapton, 1747), 32.
[74] See Lerer, *Inventing English*, 179–80.

By the time he completed his 1755 *A Dictionary of the English Language*, however, Johnson had discovered that his earlier views about linguistic constancy and purity were theoretically and practically unsustainable. He still held strongly enough to a prescriptive view of grammar to describe *shabby*, for instance, as 'A word that has crept into conversation and low writing; but ought not to be admitted into the language'.[75] But in the preface Johnson described language change as being as natural as, and therefore no more preventable than, diurnal change in general. As all humans age, Johnson notes, so, too, do all languages continue to supplement, diminish, and change their lexicons:

When we see men grow old and die at a certain time one after another, from century to century, we laugh at the elixir that promises to prolong life to a thousand years; and with equal justice may the lexicographer be derided, who being able to produce no example of a nation that has preserved their words and phrases from mutability, shall imagine that his dictionary can embalm his language, and secure it from corruption and decay, that it is in his power to change sublunary nature, or clear the world at once from folly, vanity, and affectation.[76]

The comparison here to folly and vanity is striking, suggesting as it does that language change may well be sometimes regrettable, sometimes detrimental, and sometimes unnecessary. But it remains inevitable. And this inevitability leaves lexicographers struggling to decide not only what words to include but how to define their core senses, from which regional or other non-standard usages might be seen to deviate.

Given the social issues implicated in the definition of standard and non-standard language, a sociolinguistic gesture as powerful as this has predictably produced differences of opinion. To many of Gove's critics, for example, despite their belief that *Webster's Third* had shirked its historical responsibilities, that dictionary's presentation of the oldest definition as an entry's initial sense ran contrary to the best interests of users who wanted to know the most widespread current definition. For Johnson, writing against a backdrop of universal languages and the continuing influence of the Tower of Babel, this same conflict took shape as one between modern usage and etymological meaning, and Johnson's sentiments, unlike many of his contemporaries, rested with the former.[77] In this regard at least, Gove thus oddly appears the conservative and Johnson the modernist.

---

[75] Johnson, *Dictionary of the English Language* (1755; rpt. New York: AMS Press, 1967), s. v.

[76] Johnson, *Dictionary of the English Language*, i, Cii^r.

[77] See Allen Reddick, *The Making of Johnson's Dictionary, 1746–1773* (Cambridge: Cambridge University Press, 1990), 45–51.

In the *Oxford English Dictionary*, Murray confronted this same contradiction between the desire to delineate and define the vocabulary of English and the recognition that vocabulary and usage are fundamentally open. Following Johnson's lead, his preface also draws a comparison between lexicography and observations of the natural world, in both of which distinctions among individuals (objects, creatures, or words) become complicated by the changes of time and the variation of species. A naturalist may identify certain proto-typical objects or individuals that unmistakably form a core classification and use them to draw distinct species boundaries, even though the boundaries themselves must remain permeable to synchronic and diachronic variants. 'So the English Vocabulary', the preface continues,

contains a nucleus or central mass of many thousand words whose 'Anglicity' is unquestioned; some of them only literary, some of them only colloquial, the great majority at once literary and colloquial—they are the *Common Words* of the language. But they are linked on every side with other words which are less and less entitled to this appellation, and which pertain ever more and more distinctly to the domain of local dialect, of the slang and cant of 'sets' and classes, of the peculiar technicalities of trades and processes, of the scientific terminology common to all civilized nations, and of the actual languages of other lands and peoples. And there is absolutely no defining line in any direction: the circle of the English language has a well-defined centre but no discernible circumference.[78]

Murray spoke like a scientist and philologist (maybe even, with his echo of Alain de Lille's definition of God, as a theologian)—someone well versed in languages and linguistic theory. But if the *OED*, like many dictionaries, aspired to pure objectivity in its descriptions of words and their histories, culturally determined issues of propriety and prestige inevitably shaped its definitions and the limits of which linguistic changes (in vocabulary or word meaning) were acceptable as English. As a Victorian project, in fact, the *OED* excluded common vulgarity and labeled certain words and usages as archaic, colloquial, and dialectal.[79] The project was the 1857 brainchild of Richard Trench, the archbishop of Dublin, who conceived the dictionary to sustain ethics and faith and not merely lexicography. And it was a project that in documenting the history of English constituted a national achievement, perhaps mirroring the 1856 opening of the National Portrait Gallery and the 1882 publication of the *Dictionary of National Biography*. All of these contemporaneous projects, according to John Willinsky, were understood to give 'proof of an advanced and advancing civilization'.[80]

---

[78] Murray *et al.*, *A New English Dictionary on Historical Principles*, 10 vols. (Oxford: Clarendon Press, 1888–1928), i, xvii.

[79] See further Mugglestone, *Lost for Words*, 143–78.

[80] Willinsky, *Empire of Words*, 24.

The metalinguistic discussions of variation and change that I have been tracing here have several hallmarks. First, developing as they do from the standardization of English and the ideology of a standard, they involve very much a set of historical circumstances. And this means that as powerful and naturalized as the notion of variation as an aberration or deviation may be today, this notion has specific origins and does not reflect a transcendent or inevitable quality of language. Second, these origins establish Standard English and its putative absence of variation and change as, in effect, the birth language of a ruling elite who had the most to gain from this connection, who alone (at least early on) had the means to acquire and use one particular variety of the language, and who socially as well as linguistically had the most to gain by preventing change in general. And it should be added that while Standard English may have helped to sustain this elite's privileges, it did not create or define them; wealth, education, and social influence did that. Third, established in this way standard language and the variable non-standards it required served as general sociolinguistic principles and precedents that might be activated in response to any number of speech communities: they were templates that could be filled with various social meanings rather than simply isolated, unique, and fixed constructs. If linguistic variation could be used to demarcate the educated from the uneducated, for instance, or the provincial from the sophisticated, so, too, might it discriminate in sex, sexual orientation, ethnicity, national identity, character, personal outlook, and even patriotism. Variation and change could funnel, in fact, any social issue. And fourth, in its attention to grammar as well as the linguistic repertoire, the focus of this metalinguistic commentary has characteristically been arbitrary and opportunistic. Verbal inflections could have been invested as easily and logically with social meaning as personal pronouns, while the English of Kent or Wessex might have as easily been stigmatized as that of Somerset or, more frequently, northern England. And from a different perspective, the emergence of a London variety as the basis of Standard English depended on the proximity of printing presses and social and economic power rather than on any intrinsic virtues of that variety. When cultural and linguistic traditions reinforce one another, as in the stigmatization of northern British English or African American Vernacular English, they may mystify this opportunism, but they cannot validate it.

What all this means is that by the time dialectology began to develop as a subdiscipline of linguistics in the nineteenth century, metalinguistic commentary had already fashioned variation and change as degenerative processes and the regional and social varieties they produce as confirmations thereof. All such varieties, further, could carry implications for class, education, social prestige, and so forth. Given the ideology of a standard, and the imagined constancy and consistency of Standard English, dialects could appear, variously, as atavistic evocations of a simpler, antique historical moment, or as corruptions born of ignorance and dissipation. Foreshadowed in the confusion produced by the use of 'egges' for 'eiren' by Caxton's merchant, both views share the sense that dialects are aberrations that, in the presence of Standard English, should be or already are disappearing.

In his monumental 1905 *English Dialect Grammar*, even Joseph Wright invoked the expectations of standard ideology in both his notion of the 'purity' of dialects and in his sense of their evanescence in the evolution of a superior, stable variety. 'There can be no doubt that pure dialect speech is rapidly disappearing even in country districts', Wright observes, 'owing to the spread of education, and to modern facilities for intercommunication. The writing of this grammar was begun none too soon, for had it been delayed for another twenty years I believe it would by then be quite impossible to get together sufficient pure dialect material to enable any one to give even a mere outline of the phonology of our dialects as they existed at the close of the nineteenth century.' In many cases, for Wright, inculcation of the standard through education is evidently succeeding—or at least believed to be succeeding—in erasing variation. Put another way, the disappearance of pure dialects proves the success of English culture, just as does Wright's contention that in lower-class, uneducated, urban London 'the dialects are hopelessly mixed and now practically worthless for philological purposes'.[81] As Jonathan Marshall has pointed out, the presumption underlying such foundational dialectology—a presumption that embodied the expectations of a standard and that Mufwene identifies in analyses of African American Vernacular English—was that even regional dialects were (or should be) inherently stable: 'The methods used were not designed to deal with the fact that the same speaker may use a very wide variety of different pronunciations, and *explanations* for the variation were not normally to be found. Traditional dialectology focused on regions having "place", "difference", and "distinctiveness" as their most prominent features to be analyzed.'[82] What varieties of English could not do within the context of a standard ideology was function, simply, as testaments to natural processes of change and variation.

---

[81] Wright, *The English Dialect Grammar* (Oxford: Oxford University Press, 1905), vii, viii. For an account of the development of English dialectology in the nineteenth century, see Ossi Ihalainen, 'The Dialects of England Since 1776', in *The Cambridge History of the English Language*, v, Robert Burchfield (ed.), *English in Britain and Overseas: Origins and Development* (Cambridge: Cambridge University Press, 1994), 197–274.

[82] Marshall, *Language Change and Sociolinguistics: Rethinking Social Networks* (New York: Palgrave Macmillan, 2004), 2.

From this perspective, the historical reception of global varieties—whether colonial, commonwealth, or acquired as a second language—shows significant parallels with that of indigenous British varieties. In each case, it has been a dynamic of opposition—standard opposed to non-standard, or British (and sometimes American) English opposed to transplanted varieties—that has enabled conceptualization of all the varieties. It's worth remembering, indeed, that while 1776 might be advanced as the originary moment of American English, this same moment, in its creation of the first national variety outside the United Kingdom, also did much to foster a sense of British English as well, for British English can exist as a conceptual category only when it co-exists with other varieties from among which it can be selected.[83] And likewise in each case this linguistic dynamic has been invested with social meanings of the kind witnessed in metalinguistic discussions of British dialects. For speakers of these transplanted varieties, the sociolinguistic separation could be turned to purposes of positive self-identification, as was the case in the early American republic. A 1774 letter to the *Royal American Magazine* thus opined, 'The English Language has been greatly improved in Britain within a century, but its highest perfection, with every other branch of human knowledge, is perhaps reserved for this land of light and freedom'.[84] And since the early modern period the advancement of Scots as a distinct language and not a variety of English has been a prominent feature in discussions of language and nationhood in Scotland.[85]

But often the variation and change that have produced national varieties outside of the United Kingdom have been regarded with the same doubt and derision that have been directed at non-standard varieties. British (and American) global expansion has in fact exacerbated the complexities of variation and change in two significant ways in light of the ideology of a standard. First, in the very centuries when contact between English and other languages increased in number, kind, and linguistic complexity (i.e., with non-Indo-European languages), thereby producing probably more varieties than ever before, at the same moment traditions of codification worked the hardest to stabilize language and reduce and stigmatize variation. And second, even as the spread of English has confirmed the spread of Anglo-American culture in Africa, the antipodes, Latin America, and Asia, the inevitable

---

[83] John Algeo, 'What is a Briticism?', in A. N. Doane, Joan Hall, and Richard Ringler (eds.), *Old English and New: Essays in Language and Linguistics in Honor of Frederic G. Cassidy* (New York: Garland, 1992), 287–304.

[84] Quoted in Bailey, *Images of English*, 103.

[85] For a good survey of the historical issues, see J. Derrick McClure, 'Scotland', in Burchfield (ed.), *English in Britain and Overseas*, 23–93.

alterations of English in post-colonial situations have furthered anxiety about the state of the language and the significance of change and variation. To put the matter more pointedly: sociolinguistic impulses to stabilize language in fact have worked in a diametric contradiction with economic impulses to expand markets, which necessarily also created more contact situations and more second-language learners. This contradiction animates the poet Robert Bridges's summation of the motives of the Society for Pure English, founded in Oxford in 1913. Without irony or any recognition of inconsistency, he notes that two considerations called the society into existence: the 'English language is spreading all over the world', and

It would seem that no other language can ever have had its central force so dissipated—and even this does not exhaust the description of our specific peril, because there is furthermore this most obnoxious condition, namely, that wherever our countrymen are settled abroad there are alongside them communities of other-speaking races, who, maintaining among themselves their native speech, learn yet enough of ours to mutilate it, and establishing among themselves all kinds of blundering corruptions, through habitual intercourse infect therewith the neighbouring English.[86]

British disparagement of American English provided much of the counterpoint that drove Webster's arguments for a uniquely American language, but a strain of skepticism about the legitimacy of English in the United States has remained to the present. As recently as 1979, a peer in the House of Lords exclaimed, 'If there is a more hideous language on the face of the earth than the American form of English, I should like to know what it is!'[87] Similar skepticism over transplanted varieties of English has also figured in the larger metalinguistic discourses for talking about all such varieties, including those of Jamaica, Canada, Australia, South Africa, and New Zealand. As in the United states, in all these cases it was the divergence of the transplanted varieties that raised concerns. In 1857, for instance, the Revd A. Constable Geikie, addressing the Canadian Institute and providing the first recorded instance of the phrase 'Canadian English', described this variety as 'a corrupt dialect growing up amongst our population, and gradually finding access to our periodical literature, until it threatens to produce a language as unlike our noble mother tongue

---

[86] Bridges, 'The Society's Work' (Society for Pure English, tract XX, 1925), in W. F. Bolton and David Crystal (eds.), *The English Language*, 2 vols., ii, *Essays by Linguists and Men of Letters, 1858–1964* (Cambridge: Cambridge University Press, 1969), 87–8.

[87] Quoted in Richard W. Bailey, 'American English Abroad', in Algeo (ed.), *English in North America*, 495.

as the negro patua or the Chinese pidgeon English'.[88] An 1886 editorial in a Hawaiian paper saw the divergences of a developing indigenous variety—including the use of a pidgin—from United States English as a development requiring classroom attention: 'It is a sober duty for every instructor of Hawaiian youth to check the use of pigeon-English. Very much can be done by watchfulness in this particular. And as we look forward into the years, and think of the possibilities, there is every incentive to make teachers chary in their use of doubtful English, and alert to correct the language of playground and street.'[89] And in 1910, E. W. Andrews had characterized New Zealand English as arising from simple failure to duplicate correct British English: 'There is not enough difference between the environments of the Englishman and the New Zealander to produce the existing difference in pronunciation. It should evidently be the teacher's aim to stay the process, and if possible restore to the New Zealand speech the culture it has unfortunately lost. We must, therefore[,] examine the faults one by one, and enumerate the definite sounds of English that the colonial ear has failed to catch and reproduce.'[90]

India provides still another paradoxical illustration of how the divergence of a transplanted variety from particularly Standard English has marked out that variety and its speakers for calumny and derision. While Macaulay's 1835 minute encouraged the spread of English among indigenous people of India, for example, the inevitably distinctive form English in India took from natural processes of borrowing, nativization, and the like served as the object of ridicule. In his 1891 *Baboo English as 'tis Writ*, Arnold Wright described native Indian papers as 'badly printed, badly written', and saw their English, over a century after its introduction, as not a variety but a corruption born of ignorance and insensitivity to nuance. These papers, he continues, 'are for the most part edited by aspiring native students, whose imperfect knowledge of English leads them to perpetuate most ridiculous blunders. The injudicious use of metaphors and idioms is perhaps the greatest stumbling block of the native writers. He has learned a number of expressions by rote, and is not content unless he is always pressing them into his writings whether the occasion warrants or not.'[91] In effect, the English of such indigenous

---

[88] Quoted in J. K. Chambers, '"Lawless and Vulgar Innovations": Victorian Views of Canadian English', in Sandra Clarke (ed.), *Focus on Canada* (Amsterdam: John Benjamins, 1993), 6. See further, Richard W. Bailey, 'The English Language in Canada', in Bailey and Manfred Görlach (eds.), *English as a World Language* (Ann Arbor, MI: University of Michigan Press, 1982), 134–76.

[89] Quoted in Albert J. Schütz, *The Voices of Eden: A History of Hawaiian Language Studies* (Honolulu, HI: University of Hawaii Press, 1994), 301.

[90] Quoted in Gordon *et al.*, *New Zealand English*, 6.

[91] Wright, *Baboo English as 'tis Writ: Being Curiosities of Indian Journalism* (London: T. Fisher Unwin, 1891), 17.

populations serves as both confirmation and justification of Anglo-American political and economic influence: its existence confirms the existence of the latter, even as its quality also provides justification for the latter's introduction. Given the influence of the standard ideology in metalinguistic thinking, speakers of non-standard or national varieties can become complicit in their own subordination, furthering negative stereotypes of their own speech. This continues to be the case for some American speech communities and was so, at least until relatively recently, in Australia and other post-colonial countries.[92]

The interlanguages that have resulted from English's contact with indigenous languages through global expansion should also be considered in this light. Born of immediate social necessity, pidgins and creoles have terrific social utility, testifying for the vitality of languages and speech communities in contact with one another. And so it comes as no surprise that on occasion the speech communities that use them can rival those using natural languages in duration and number of speakers. Mobilian Jargon, composed from English and several indigenous languages, persisted across the southern United States from the early eighteenth century until the middle of the twentieth, for instance, and in Papua New Guinea Tok Pisin has become a national language, used alongside English in parliamentary debates, education, and various domestic settings. In the Philippines, Taglish is the most widely used variety of English.

What may be surprising is that for all this, Anglophones and metalinguistic theory have historically responded to these interlanguages and the variation and change they embody with the same double bind that I have described for transplanted varieties of English. As products of trade, missionary contact, and colonial expansion in general, pidgins and creoles are inevitable byproducts of history and might even be seen as affirmations of Anglophones' success. At the same time, they have been regarded as monstrous, the vulgar speech of vulgar people. Early North American colonists, thus, routinely commented on the stupidity of the American Indians and the pidgins used to communicate with them. This inability to empathize linguistically with other speech communities is at times striking, as in the Revd John Megapolensis's attempts, in the 1640s, to learn Mohawk by means of the structural categories of Latin. Whether his informants used Mohawk or a pidgin to provide equivalents for

---

92 On Australia see John Gunn, 'Social Contexts in the History of Australian English', in Machan and Scott (eds.), *English in Its Social Contexts*, 204–29. On the processes of linguistic subordination more generally, see Rosina Lippi-Green, *English with an Accent: Language, Ideology, and Discrimination in the United States* (London: Routledge, 1997). For additional examples of British disparagement of transplanted English, see Bailey, *Images of English*, 130–3.

English vocabulary is unknown, for Megapolensis could understand the speech only through its failure to adhere to recognizable (i.e., Latinate) linguistic structure: 'one tells me the word in the infinitive mood, another in the indicative; one in the first, another in the second person; one in the present, another in the preterit'.[93] Megapolensis's attitude is mostly of disbelief, but Anglophones in Hawaii took a more socially aggressive approach in the 1920s, by which time Hawaiian had all but disappeared, replaced by English, Hawaiian Pidgin English, and Hawaiian Creole English. The speech groups of the languages differed along class and ethnic lines, with the latter two being used nearly exclusively by indigenous people and immigrants. As a confirmation of this distinction, and as a mechanism to maintain it, a two-tier educational system developed that used proficiency in English as a placement criterion and that continued into the 1960s.[94]

For its part, metalinguistic discussion has often sustained such approaches to interlanguages. Finding no place for them in its stemmatic classification of language families, and no parallel for them in the linguistic habits and developing nationalism of Europe, nineteenth-century philologists used terms like 'baby talk' and 'mongrel dialect' to refer to pidgins and creoles as badly learned versions of presumptively stable European languages. Perhaps necessarily, such linguistic and cultural judgements were mutually reinforcing. In 1911, noting the omission of copulas in pidgins and creoles, William Churchill generally observed, 'The savage of our study, like many another primitive thinker, has no conception of being in the absolute; his speech has no true verb "to be"'. And a year later, Beatrice Grimshaw commented in this way on the indigenous variety of English of Rossel Island, southeast of Papua New Guinea: 'To be addressed in reasonably good English of the "pidgin" variety, by hideous savages who made murder a profession, and had never come into actual contact with civilisation, is an experience perplexing enough to make the observer wonder if he is awake.'[95] To a more recent critic pidgin English, generically conceived, remains a 'means of speaking which is not quite English, and yet is nearer to English than to anything else'.[96] For a time in the middle of the twentieth century, pidgin dialectalism even appeared as a learning disability alongside reading deficiencies and cleft palates. For its

---

[93] Quoted in Axtell, 'Babel of Tongues: Communicating with the Indians in Eastern North America', in Edward G. Gray and Norman Fiering (eds.), *The Language Encounter in the Americas, 1492–1800: A Collection of Essays* (New York: Berghahn Books, 2000), 36.

[94] Viv Edwards, *Multilingualism in the English-Speaking World: Pedigree of Nations* (Oxford: Blackwell, 2004), 128–9.

[95] Quoted in Peter Mühlhäusler, *Pidgin & Creole Linguistics* (Oxford: Blackwell, 1986), 26, 27.

[96] Charlton Laird, *The Miracle of Language* (New York: Fawcett, 1953), 238–9.

part, the very term 'creole' compels a distinct classification of language that, structurally, may be no different from a language like English, which has continuously borrowed forms and words throughout its history.[97]

While linguistics today generally takes a more sympathetic and expansive approach to interlanguages, vestiges remain of the anxiety associated with the change and variation they demonstrate. Such vestiges appear in arguments that the grammar of pidgins and the language of children reproduce the syntactic simplicity of a proto-language used prior to the cultural and linguistic expansions of humans somewhere around 100,000 BC.[98] They are even more apparent in the suspicion surrounding whether to label, say, Kriol, spoken in Belize, as an independent language or a variety of English. 'Simplicity is confused with inadequacy,' suggests Loreto Todd, 'and creole speakers are often judged to be speaking bad English rather than efficient creole.'[99]

The most general difficulty with the anxieties generated, one way or another, by the creation of new varieties and interlanguages is that the categories that give rise to them, like the categories of change and variation, can themselves be impressionistic value judgements. Interlanguages, new varieties, debased varieties, and varieties that aren't really varieties but rather collections of forms that reflect inadequate acquisition easily blend into one another, and this is so because any such distinctions rest as much (or more) on interpretive frameworks as on any structural phenomena. While nineteenth-century critics saw transplanted varieties of English as at best imperfect and at worst barbarous, more recent critics have exercised greater subtlety by working to define individual varieties' grammars, histories, and relation to their speakers' cultures. Of the South Asian English once ridiculed by Wright, for example, Braj Kachru observes that the variety can 'be characterized both in terms of its linguistic characteristics and in terms of its contextual and pragmatic functions'.[100]

Susan Butler provides one framework for categorical distinctions among new varieties and interlanguages by specifying five criteria that define a distinctive variety: a pronunciation standard, communal words and phrases to describe specific circumstances where the language is used, a self-conscious

---

[97] On the structural similarities between natural languages and creoles, as conventionally defined, see Sarah Grey Thomason and Terrence Kaufman, *Language Contact, Creolization, and Genetic Linguistics* (Berkeley, CA: University of California Press, 1988), and Mufwene, *The Ecology of Language Evolution* (Cambridge: Cambridge Univeristy Press, 2001).

[98] Derek Bickerton, *Language and Human Behavior* (Seattle, WA: University of Washington Press, 1995).

[99] Todd, *Modern Englishes: Pidgins and Creoles* (Oxford: Blackwell, 1984), 248.

[100] Kachru, *Asian Englishes: Beyond the Canon* (Hong Kong: Hong Kong University Press, 2005), 43.

awareness of the variety's history, a literature, and reference works.[101] By these criteria, Philippine English, African American Vernacular English, South Asian English, Chicano English, and so forth do indeed qualify as distinctive varieties of English. And in this vein it's worth noting that one of the most prominent features of recent debates over the validity of world English*es* has been the emergence of national dictionaries, which provide the codification that is necessary for any standard. A Jamaican English dictionary, thus, appeared in 1967, an Australian English dictionary in 1988, a South African one in 1996, and a New Zealand one in 1997.[102]

Randolph Quirk has provided a wholly different framework for interpreting the variation that informs the English used in many such communities. Challenging the judgement of what he regards as imperfectly learned English to be a variety tantamount to long-recognized regional and social varieties like Canadian English or United States English, he suggests that to use variation in this way, to legitimate social groups, is to practice what he archly labels 'liberation linguistics'.[103] Focusing on the social consequences of various linguistic forms and what he sees as linguists' ethical obligations, Quirk elsewhere suggests:

we need to ask ourselves who benefits if we encourage the institutionalizing as norms of certain types of language activity that could alternatively be seen as levels of achievement. It may temporarily comfort an individual to be told that his English is a communicatively adequate basilect . . . it may comfort a Ministry of Education in requiring less funding than a more ambitious language-teaching programme; it may, above all, seem comfortingly democratic. But will it serve the individual's own needs

---

[101] Butler, 'Corpus of English in Southeast Asia: Implications for a Regional Dictionary', in M. L. S. Bautista (ed.), *English Is an Asian Language: The Philippine Context: Proceedings of the Conference Held in Manila on August 2–3, 1996* (Sydney: Macquarie Library, 1997), 103–24.

[102] F. G. Cassidy and R. B. Le Page (eds.), *Dictionary of Jamaican English* (Cambridge: Cambridge University Press, 1967); W. S. Ramson (ed.), *The Australian National Dictionary: A Dictionary of Australianisms on Historical Principles* (Melbourne: Oxford University Press, 1988); Penny Silva (ed.), *A Dictionary of South African English on Historical Principles* (Oxford: Oxford University Press, 1996); H. W. Orsman (ed.), *The Dictionary of New Zealand English: A Dictionary of New Zealandisms on Historical Principles* (Auckland: Oxford University Press, 1997). Representative studies of newly recognized varieties are: Carmen Fought, *Chicano English in Context* (New York: Palgrave, 2003); Lisa Kim (ed.), *Singapore English: A Grammatical Description* (Amsterdam: John Benjamins, 2004); Braj B. Kachru, 'English as an Asian Language', in Bautista (ed.), *English Is an Asian Language*, 1–23; Andrew B. Gonzalez, 'When Does an Error Become a Distinctive Feature of Philippine English?', in R. B. Noss (ed.), *Varieties of English in Southeast Asia* (Singapore: Singapore University Press, 1983), 150–72; and Bolton, *Chinese Englishes*.

[103] Quirk, 'Language Varieties and Standard Language', *English Today*, 21 (1990), 3–10. Quirk's remark might be juxtaposed with David Crystal's lament: 'There has been little perception of the need for a "green linguistics"' (*Language Death* [Cambridge: Cambridge University Press, 2000], 32). A useful overview of the continuing argument about the status of putatively new varieties of English can be found in Bolton, *Chinese Englishes*, 1–49.

when he or she looks for a better job? Will it help the Ministers of Education when they look for a bigger supply of professionals? Will it serve democracy's goal of the individual's mobility within a coherent free society?[104]

As Quirk implies, it's certainly the case that recognition of indigenous varieties often has a political edge, as in the argument that Black South African English should become a kind of national language for the unity it would provide its speakers.[105] It's also of course the case, as my earlier discussion demonstrated, that Standard English has its own political edge.

The thing about competing frameworks for approaching transplanted varieties and interlanguages is that their differences are unresolvable. Philippine English qualifies as a variety of English only if one accepts Butler's interpretive categories, but the fact that it fits her categories cannot validate the conclusion that any collection of forms that does so qualifies as a variety, *unless* one has already accepted her overall model. Similarly, the history of a variety can be determinative only for someone to whom that category is already significant, and it isn't necessarily so to Quirk. Indeed, Quirk's analysis, rooted in an ethical framework rather than a structural or social one, would reject the concept of Philippine English, and however consistent this rejection is with his framework, it likewise cannot prove, any more than Butler's acceptance of Philippine English can prove, the transcendent accuracy of his interpretation.

The ethical orientation that motivates Quirk is itself fraught. For him, this orientation assigns linguists a moral responsibility to resist movements like 'liberation linguistics' when their ultimate impact will be the further social marginalization of particular speakers: 'And if the native varieties go their own way to a greater degree than seems at present likely, linguists may be called on to suggest some interference with nature as radical as crop biologists or livestock breeders have long taken for granted.'[106] But if in Quirk's view linguists' ethical obligation is to intervene in and manage the development of natural languages, Susan Dicker reflects the views of a good many other linguists when she adopts this same moral posture to argue that linguists need to labor to undermine any social attitudes or institutions that might sustain the very sociolinguistic positions that Quirk takes as givens. In response to the assertion that particular varieties or discourse practices can limit social and economic opportunities in the United States, she advocates

---

[104] Quirk, 'Language Variety: Nature and Art', in Noss (ed.), *Varieties of English in Southeast Asia*, 13.

[105] See Peter Titlestad, 'English, the Constitution and South Africa's Language Future', in Vivian de Klerk (ed.), *Focus on South Africa* (Amsterdam: John Benjamins, 1996), 163–73.

[106] Quirk, 'Language Variety: Nature and Art', 15.

neither more education in Standard English nor even broader sociolinguistic tolerance but rather an aggressive subversion of the cultural values and institutions that Standard United States English supports, with linguists, educators, and government officials actively promoting nationwide bilingualism. Rather than manage natural languages, linguists for Dicker must manage nature itself, enacting what Quirk might well have called 'guerrilla linguistics'.[107]

What Quirk and Dicker share—and share with Butler as well—is an anxiety and even alarm associated with the processes of language variation and change. For Quirk, it is tolerance of linguistic change that causes concern, while for Dicker and Butler change and variation serve as vehicles for socially disruptive transformation. All three critics seek to shape the meaning of change, and in so doing all three elide the very distinction between variation and its social significance that their analyses foreground so clearly.

I assemble these competing views not in order to suggest that the classification of a set of forms as corruptions, a social or regional variety, or an interlanguage is impossible to make or of no consequence. Quite the contrary. All speakers, and not just linguists, make such judgements all the time, and terrific consequences sometimes follow from them. In the United States perhaps one of the most prominent recent examples of this very point is the controversy surrounding a 1996 resolution by the Oakland, California, School Board. Confronting persistently low standardized test scores and graduation rates among primary and secondary students—who were and are predominantly low-income African Americans—and presuming to follow in the spirit of a 1979 Supreme Court decision that had rendered it incumbent on school districts to take into account differences between Standard United States English and African American Vernacular English as a home language, the Oakland School Board declared the latter (which it labeled Ebonics) a 'genetically distinct' language. The implications and objectives of this declaration were never entirely clear, but what is clear is that within a matter of days it became national news—the subject of critical commentary, vitriolic editorials, academic debate, and racist jokes.

And what drove the response was not the *fact* of a collection of linguistic forms and practices that the Board called Ebonics—everyone seemed to know what was being talked about—but rather the challenge of *categorizing* just what this fact was and is. Was Ebonics a language? Was it a sociolect? Was it, to use Quirk's terms, the institutionalization of an inadequate level of achievement? Was the declaration itself a serious linguistic judgement, a

---

[107] Dicker, *Languages in America: A Pluralist View* (Philadelphia, PA: Multilingual Matters, 1996).

largely empathetic response to a social situation, or a cynical attempt to manipulate public sentiment and attract federal funds? And above all, what would follow—pedagogically, linguistically, and socially—from the various answers to these questions? On the surface, this response, conducted mostly by individuals who lived far from Oakland and had no children attending school in the district, argued over a categorical judgement about what forms and varieties could be included in the history of English. But at its heart, reception of the Oakland decision, like responses to all of the transplanted varieties I have just considered, argued about issues of race, class, education, citizenship, taxation, and social and individual responsibility. Like questions over the status of Scots or Kriol—whether varieties of English or languages unto themselves—an example such as this points to the way large social issues of self-identification can be triggered by variation and change and played out through them. And this is why the classification of linguistic varieties is important.

The Oakland decision on Ebonics, later reissued in a slightly modified version, led to months of political commentary and caustic remarks in the popular as well as academic presses, the impact of which, a decade later, has been minimal on Oakland students and racial attitudes. Neither, I suspect, has the controversy had much impact on popular conceptions of change and variation. The very lack of a clear resolution suggests that in Oakland, as in other contexts, a great deal in fact depends on the interpretation speakers assign to change and variation in their language. It also suggests that unambiguous, non-controversial assignments are not easily made. At an abstract level, it may well be possible to draw neat distinctions between varieties, interlanguages, corruptions, and the social issues they mediate, but in the messy reality of language use, where most speakers live, this is not the case.[108]

Beyond language

Metalinguistic discussion of language has been nearly as changeable as English itself. And it has changed in ways that not only reflect social context but also configure language as supportive of that context. What St Augustine saw as a flawed but crucial means of communication, its vocabulary crafted by ancients so as to reveal the immanent, transcendent truths of the universe, Dante saw as an art, something these same ancients devised in order to transcend the immutable truth of change and preserve communication. To

---

[108] For a measured assessment of the decision and its aftermath, see Theresa Perry and Lisa Delpit (eds.), *The Real Ebonics Debate: Power, Language, and the Education of African-American Children* (Boston, MA: Beacon Press, 1998).

the early modern period in England in particular, grammar was the measure of English's inadequacies. Without a formal grammar—and, ultimately, a standard variety—English could not achieve stability and thereby attain the communicative achievements of Greek and Latin. Without these, neither could it confirm its (or England's) pre-eminence in the world. This same grammar, when invested in the seventeenth and eighteenth centuries with social meanings about class and status, has come to serve as a measure of the very social categories it also helped maintain in the cultivation of written and spoken standards.

Securely on this chronological side of this semantic development, George Sampson, in his widely read 1921 book *English for the English*, could see English and the study of its language and literature as moral forces that would give life, rather than merely a living, to working-class children and would preserve humanity and culture in the aftermath of nineteenth-century industrialization. Elementary education, he felt, was the most important level of education, and the cultivation of correct grammar and the study of English literature were its most important features: 'But, as we have said, English is really not a subject at all. It is a condition of existence rather than a subject of instruction. It is an inescapable circumstance of life, and concerns every English-speaking person from the cradle to the grave. The lesson in English is not merely one occasion for the inculcation of knowledge; it is part of the child's initiation into the life of man.'[109] This same period witnessed the foundation of the Society of Pure English, championed by Bridges and dedicated to preserving grammatical distinctions and protecting English from changes initiated by speakers both at home and abroad. By the 1975 Bullock report on the teaching of English in the United Kingdom, metalinguistic emphasis had shifted from the redemptive power of English to the importance of classroom methods and the encouragement of pedagogical and social acceptance of non-standard varieties. A decade later the Swann Report acknowledged the importance of ethnicity and the value of maintaining non-English languages at home, but opposed bilingual education on the grounds that instruction in languages other than English was not the business of schools. And this testament to the importance of preserving a particular variety of English appeared even as other metalinguistic discussion has championed the diversity of the language in the ways I have described in Chapter 4.[110]

---

[109] Sampson, *English for the English: A Chapter on National Education* (1921; rpt. with introduction by Deng Thompson, Cambridge: Cambridge University Press, 1970), 44.

[110] On recent educational policy in the United Kingdom, see Linda Thompson, Michael Fleming, and Michael Bryam, 'Languages and Language Policy in Britain', in Michael Herriman and Barbara Burnaby (eds.), *Language Policies in English-Dominant Countries: Six Case Studies* (Clevedon: Multilingual Matters, 1996), 99–121. On the contrary embrace of variation, see David Crystal, *The Stories of English* (Woodstock, NY: Overlook Press, 2004).

One constant in these discussions has been the channeling of non-linguistic issues through language, whether in St Augustine's approach to language as evidence of divine design or through contemporary pedagogical discussions of the role of Standard English in furthering or delaying social integration and advancement. Variation and change in particular have consistently figured in this regard. And they have done so by being both evidence for non-linguistic social arguments and the means to conduct the arguments themselves. If linguistic variability motivated the record that dictionaries like *Webster's Third* provide, serving in effect as their driving force, it has also provided the counterpoints that make a variety like Standard English possible—the competing narrative, to reprise Hayden White's terminology. Because of this, the metalinguistic framing of variation and change can be pre-determinative of sociolinguistic experience. I have already suggested how 'creole' as a label draws a structural distinction among what are often accidents of history. Within the ideology of standard language, similarly, certain linguistic data—forms, pronunciations, words, and usages—become non-standard before they can be mere variation, and they accordingly will carry with them whatever social meanings have already been invested in them. 'Linguistic stereotypes', Bailey remarks, 'eventually emerge with opprobius social evaluations attached to them; once a given feature is associated with that stereotype, it joins the value system already established for it ... the image, in short, anticipates the evidence.'[111] And so the evidence of sociolinguistic experience—the vulgarity of non-standard forms, varieties, and speakers—almost inevitably confirms the interpretations that speakers inherit.

In this chapter I have argued for ways in which metalinguistic commentary, like literary narratives and public policy, can be determinative in speakers' attitudes towards change and variation. The picture that emerges here is far from clear and offers no easy conclusions. As I noted in the opening chapter, I certainly do not claim that language change is the only phenomenon to mediate extra-linguistic anxiety or that mediating such anxieties is the only thing that language does. In fact, the metalinguistic discussions I have traced contain a good many contradictions. Standard language, as I've just observed, requires non-standard language to be defined and maintained as a distinct variety. British English requires American, Australian, and South African English to preserve its own identity. And colonialism and international activity produced transplanted varieties of English that have been at once confirmation of Anglo-American global achievement and examples of linguistic decline.

[111] Bailey, *Images of English*, 134.

Metalinguistic commentary on change and variation has produced its own contradictions, perhaps the most prominent of which has been the interpretation of print and standard language as both socially liberating and confining. Indeed, already in the eighteenth century Sheridan (the father of the playwright) envisioned print as a means for eliminating the linguistic and social stratification that Standard English fosters. By advancing literacy through a standard language, the press, for Sheridan, would be the means towards an egalitarian society.[112] Volumes like the 1880 *The Letter H Past, Present, and Future* offered a similar promise, that by eliminating stigmatized, variant pronunciations, speakers might exceed restrictions of class, employment, and education.[113] What a book like *The Letter H* also does, of course, is reinforce the social stigmatization of 'dropped h' not only among those speakers whose varieties don't drop it but also among those whose varieties do—and who thereby become complicit in the subordination of their own speech. And what it further does is hold out what I take to be a false promise: that by changing language alone, individuals can also change their social circumstances. Democracy's goal, as Quirk implies, may in fact be 'the individual's mobility within a coherent free society', but whether most adult individuals, with the aid of *The Letter H* or Jones's *Pronouncing Dictionary*, truly could or can change their accents is doubtful. And still more doubtful is whether such change, if it were possible, could also effect a change in an individual's social status and opportunity. For every Margaret Thatcher who is able to reinvent herself through dialect transformation, the examples of Dickens's fiction and fabricated Maori English suggest that there are many more individuals whose social standing will precede conceptions of whatever actually comes out of their mouths.

Emerging foremost from these contradictions is the fact that, whatever the nuances of any particular metalinguistic criticism, it tends to present variation and change as volatile issues whose most important implications are extra-linguistic. For Cameron, perhaps the crux of the verbal hygiene issue is a conflict over the possibility—or impossibility—of achieving perfect communication through value-free language and thereby preserving a stable representation of the world. 'The common language needed for public purposes', she observes, 'is portrayed above all as a *neutral* and *universal* language, one that is available to all parties equally and does not predetermine the outcome of their discussions.'[114] When speakers manipulate traditional,

---

[112] Sheridan, *A Course of Lectures on Elocution*, 256–62.

[113] Alfred Leach, *The Letter H Past, Present, and Future: A Treatise, with Rules for the Silent H Based on Modern Usage, and Notes on Wh* (London: Griffith and Farran, 1880).

[114] Cameron, *Verbal Hygiene*, 120.

standard language by avoiding the generic masculine pronoun, they certainly expose the partiality of their own language, but they also reveal the partiality of the putatively neutral standard. In these circumstances, speakers must make choices over which partiality they prefer, and such choices have potentially explosive powers of social reform and reaction.

The volatility of precisely this need to make a choice appears in more general metalinguistic debates over the meaning of variation and change. To critics like Tony Crowley and Robert Phillipson, linguistic variability has transformative power. It must be maintained, because if it is erased, through the spread of a standard or global English, then linguistic regularity becomes a means of repression and social domination.[115] John Honey shares Crowley's and Phillipson's sense of language's political consequences, though he sees this same variability as change that must be avoided, for it brings with it the repression of those denied access to Standard English. If Crowley and Phillipson champion non-standards as forms of self-expression and social validation, Honey judges that failing to instruct speakers in Standard English renders them, effectively, as wrong speakers subject to the attendant social consequences: 'causing children to learn standard English is an act of empowerment which will give them access to a whole world of knowledge and to an assurance of greater authority in their dealings with the world outside their own homes, in a way which is genuinely liberating'.[116] It is in this sense that Quirk has challenged the practice of what he sees as a kind of well-meaning but misguided 'liberation linguistics'. But there are two crucial points for me in all these views, whatever their individual differences: first, variation and change serve as flashpoints for extra-linguistic political concerns; and second, they do so in ways that the ideology of a standard renders natural and inherent in language—maybe even invisible—rather than constructed and situational.

Dr Johnson once observed, 'I am not answerable for all the words in my Dictionary'.[117] The *furor* over *Webster's Third* and the tensions fostered by metalinguistic discussions of English in general suggest something else. Not only have lexicographers like Johnson (and Gove) been answerable for their words, but their words have been answerable for cultural achievements far beyond language alone. While Dr Johnson's disavowal may be characteristically arch, it also points to a significant contradiction. It is true enough

---

[115] Crowley, *The Politics of Discourse: The Standard Language Question in British Cultural Debates* (London: Macmillan, 1989), and Robert Phillipson, *Linguistic Imperialism* (Oxford: Oxford University Press, 1992).

[116] Honey, *Language is Power*, 42.

[117] Quoted in Reddick, *The Making of Johnson's Dictionary*, 10–11.

that individuals are generally not the creators of the words and grammar they use or even the conceptions of language that frame them. We learn language through observation and use, and much of what we say and how we speak therefore goes unexamined. At the same time, there would seem to be limits to the responsibilities of linguistic systems in comparison to those of their speakers. If we suppose that *Webster's Third* somehow displays linguistic permissiveness—which is a supposition that depends on the prior supposition that such permissiveness exists—there remains another significant mental leap from this permissiveness to any consequences it might have for personal virtue and child-rearing. In precisely what way, one might ask, does the refusal to designate certain words as slang produce a permissive society? Given the fact that Anglophones typically consult English dictionaries for only meaning and orthography and not for moral or social purposes,[118] what evidence is there that such consultation will likewise influence personal much less cultural attitudes? And if the *OED* was meant as 'proof of an advanced and advancing civilization', is there reason to believe that the dictionary itself contributed to an advance of that civilization's inhabitants?

Any logic that regards answers to these questions as a self-evident 'plenty' is merely associational, I think. It is an assertion by fiat of cause-and-effect connections. Even for education and usage, areas most directly affected by what's in a dictionary, connections between the putative permissiveness of *Webster's Third* (or any other quality of any other dictionary) and extra-linguistic social activity are only and fundamentally intuitive. Or, perhaps, counter-intuitive, since for every pedant like Follett or Macdonald there must be thousands more Anglophones who merely speak, irrespective of what words a dictionary includes or how it labels and defines them. Most people, I suspect, rarely consult dictionaries at all.

Speakers have a good many choices in the language they use, including whether or not they wish to leave it unexamined. The ideology of a standard is itself the product of choice in historical circumstances and not an intrinsic quality of natural language, and the success of its contributions to the English language and Anglophone culture similarly reflects historically conditioned and therefore not inevitable choices. In other words, the effects of standard language depend on the ways in which speakers use the variety, for in itself a standard is neither inherently liberating nor inherently confining. Variation and change, however, are inherent in natural language, and they necessarily do occur in any speech community. By extension, the metalinguistic sense we make of them likewise reflects choices about society, its values, and the role of

---

[118] Béjoint, *Tradition and Innovation in Modern English Dictionaries*, 140–68.

language in it. And whether we follow Honey and decide standard language is liberating or follow Crowley and decide it is repressive, we will invest variation and change with the sociolinguistic significance that supports our decisions. But such decisions remain choices for which we as individual speakers are answerable. It is to this issue that I devote the concluding chapter.

6

Fixing English

When English is the definition

One of the courses I regularly teach is the History of the English Language.
This is a curricular staple in many universities that offer advanced degrees in
English language and literature, and for its historical breadth and the range of
language-related issues that it raises, it's also one of my favorites. Inevitably,
history of the language courses are structured chronologically, beginning
with the Indo-European language and people of around 5,000 BC, moving
through the Primitive Germanic grouping of about 2,000 BC to the Western
Germanic grouping of about 500 BC, and proceeding from there to the
beginning of Old English.

When exactly this beginning occurred presents one of the first challenges in
the course, perhaps because by this historical point an actual written record
(as opposed to hypothetical reconstructions) begins to appear, requiring
greater care with empirical argument, and because the history also becomes
sociolinguistically close enough to have consequences for modern speakers
and how they view themselves, their language, and their world. Does English
begin the moment speakers of varieties of West Germanic set foot in what
would become Great Britain—is its origin in fourth-, fifth-, and sixth-century
social and political action? Is its origin purely linguistic—does it begin later,
in perhaps the eighth century, when these transplanted British varieties of
West Germanic might well have become mutually unintelligible with the
Old Frisian and Old Saxon languages that remained on the Continent and
that otherwise are the Germanic varieties structurally most similar to Old
English? Does Old English begin in the seventh century, when the written
record begins, in which case its origins are material? Is the origin still later,
in the late ninth century, when an Anglo-Saxon nation-state begins to
emerge from the political and cultural achievements of Alfred the Great?
Or, in view of the fact that a Channel crossing alone would likely have little
impact on linguistic structure, does English really begin on the Continent?

And if so, at what point—when the West Germanic variety diverged sufficiently from the Germanic variety, when that variety diverged sufficiently from a larger grouping of generally Western Indo-European languages designated the Centum grouping, or when that grouping diverged sufficiently from Indo-European?

Textbooks for a course like this—and many are available—typically mimic this chronological progression, offering an introductory chapter or two on continental matters and then proceeding to English and its chronological development.[1] Such books perhaps inevitably present a teleological narrative line, for they cannot be histories if they do not identify beginnings, developments, and, perhaps most importantly, conclusions, and to do this means to identify what linguistic and social facts qualify for inclusion within the history and what merit exclusion. Relations between facts and their representation have loomed large in historical and literary discussions of the past quarter century, but as long ago as 1946 R. G. Collingwood defined the issues with a clarity that I think transcends anything written since. 'History is not a spectacle,' said Collingwood simply. 'The events of history do not "pass in review" before the historian. They have finished happening before he begins thinking about them. He has to re-create them inside his own mind, re-enacting for himself so much of the experience of the men who took part in them as he wishes to understand.'[2] In its selection of events and larger definition of its own concerns, historical writing is thus (as Hayden White later noted) an act of imagination and judgement—one that prefigures what's important and what's not—and as such it must conceptualize and validate, in addition to the past, some version of the present towards which the history inexorably advances.

What all this means for the history of English and its textbooks is that the decision about where to begin Old English is not peculiar or unique but emblematic of every decision about structure, variation, and change that a linguistic historian must make. In each case, in the identification of what constitutes the language, what constitutes its variants, and what constitutes plain error, English is not so much a simple event that passes in review before the historian but a prefiguration of the field, its relevance to the present, and the relevance of both to the future. As in David Lightfoot's inventive simile, 'a language, like Odysseus, turns out to be a mythical, imaginary creature. It may be a convenient and useful fiction, like Odysseus and the setting of the

---

[1] One exception is Barbara Strang's *A History of English* (London: Methuen, 1970), which begins with the present and regresses in time.

[2] Collingwood, *The Idea of History* (Oxford: Clarendon Press, 1946), 97.

sun, but in reality it is a derivative, the aggregate output of some set of grammars. We shall see that language is not a coherent, definable entity.'[3] While the history of English necessarily rests on empirical data, that history's claim that the language is defined by the acceptance of certain forms, variation, and change and the disavowal of others is only apparently or partially empirical. The history of English, I would suggest, is less a topic than an argument—or a value judgement, as I called it in Chapter 2—and part of what dictionaries do is provide confirmation for this argument. As an argument, moreover, this history is ultimately circular. It presumes some transhistorical identity for English, whatever alterations the language might experience, as a means for distinguishing English forms from non-English ones; and it then uses these same distinctions to define the language. Rather than a topic rooted in the empirical data of linguistic structure, indeed, the history of English is an argument serving shifting social expectations.

What all this means for linguistic change and variation is that they play crucial roles in the definition of English. As I also argued in Chapter 2, for the most part change and variation are regular and constant, if not always entirely rational—they proceed systematically in patterns that are sometimes predictable and often explicable retrospectively. Variation is so much a part of language, in fact, as almost to challenge the claim for any stable category like 'English', replacing it, *à la* Lightfoot, with an amorphous, continually shifting and reconfiguring structure. Or, as in Roger Lass's memorable phrase, a 'language is a population of variants moving through time, and subject to selection'.[4] It is for this very reason that emergent linguistics has increasingly come to see speakers' articulation of variation as the quality that produces and constitutes natural language: to vary is to speak. And this means that alongside the axiom of linguistic relativism—the notion that because all languages communicate what their speakers need them to communicate there can be no better or worse languages—stands another axiom that's been suggested by others and that I have teased out throughout this book: change and variation are structurally neutral. They simply and continuously happen. What I've also teased out, however, is the notion that if change occurs neutrally within often predictable patterns, its direction and, more importantly, its meanings are shaped by extra-linguistic factors. Here I offer a classroom metaphor.

---

[3] Lightfoot, *The Development of Language: Acquisition, Change, and Evolution* (Malden, MA: Blackwell, 1999), 77.

[4] Lass, *Historical Linguistics and Language Change* (Cambridge: Cambridge University Press, 1997), 377.

At any one synchronic moment, there is an aggregate of grammatical and lexical tokens uttered by those speakers who have some claim to be speaking English, whether that claim is historical (e.g., they live in primarily Anglophone countries like Canada or New Zealand), socioeconomic (e.g., they live in the United Kingdom or the United States), pedagogical (e.g., they are students of English as a second language), or even pragmatic (e.g., they are speaking to someone who also has a claim to be speaking English). And for many of these tokens there are alternatives—variants—whether among the speakers of one community or between those speakers and another community's. If one were to imagine a chalkboard or dry-erase board at the front of the ubiquitous history of the language class, one could represent all of the linguistically meaningful utterances produced by speakers with some claim to be speaking English as dots on that board. English would then be the subset of dots that are judged a part of and that constitute the language. By extension, diachronic representation—for which a much larger board would be necessary!—would begin with dots for all the utterances of anyone anywhere at any time who had some claim to be speaking English and would proceed to identification of that subset of utterances transhistorically acceptable as English. Given the ubiquity of change and variation, with possibly hundreds of millions of dots representing hundreds of millions of utterances on the board I've imagined, abstractions like the neogrammarians' claim that change admits no exceptions, or Saussure's *langue*, or Chomsky's ideal speaker-listener play vital roles in our understanding of language, its variation, and its change. Without them, we could not proceed, for we cannot examine every individual utterance by every individual English speaker of the past 1,500 years.

To return to Collingwood, however, diachronic and synchronic subsets of the utterances that qualify as English do not pass in review before the grammarian or historian who draws them. They are not simple facts but reflections, and justifications, of some pre-figuring of the field of synchronic and historical English linguistics that is itself, necessarily, based on some heuristic frame. Someone on some principle, that is, decides which dots to include and which to exclude, and in many ways decisions about such matters were much easier to make in the past than they are now. When Murray began editing the *OED* in 1879, cultural context allowed him to *know* what was and wasn't English, and even he, in the preface passage I quoted in Chapter 5, allowed for some imprecision. Since then, with increased recognition of global English dialects, the language's identity has lost much more precision, leaving lexicographers with far less certitude than Murray enjoyed. And when the cost of a dictionary's production is taken into account—as any modern publishing house must do—yet another principle factors into lexicographical selection. Such a nexus of linguistic, social, and economic principles has indeed shaped the various corrections and revisions of the *OED* since its initial completion in 1928.[5] There's nothing insidious about any of this—it's how human cognition makes sense of the world, by identifying and categorizing experience according to some principle. And to do this—to decide whether varieties and grammatical forms go away, and if they do, where they go—necessarily draws on perceptual as well as empirical data. Put very simply, an individual's sense of English rests as much on lived experience as on linguistic structure.

At the same time, it is precisely this process that makes the history of English an argument. To ask who makes this argument, or how it is made, is also to ask perhaps the largest question I have implicitly asked throughout this book: What is English? And this is not an idle question, since any claim to speak English carries with it significant cultural, socioeconomic, and political repercussions. Any answer to this question requires some sort of structural baseline: a grammar of the phonology, morphology, syntax, and lexis against which all possible English utterances can be evaluated. Do they conform to this baseline, do they vary from it but in ways that still qualify them as English, or is their variance so distinctive that they can no longer be considered part of the language? And these kinds of comparisons affect assessment not only of individual grammatical features, such as whether specific pronunciations, words, or inflectional morphology qualify as English, but also of the concentration of such features in what may or may not be considered a variety. Like grammatical features, regional dialects, sociolects, pidgins, and creoles all derive their identities through their distinctions from some putatively base form of English. Without this kind of baseline, indeed, no meaningful generalizations of any sort could be drawn about English: we would simply be unable to talk about synchronic variation and diachronic change unless we had some ideal against which to measure the variation and change.

But as conceptually necessary as such a baseline might be, it can also occasion, in two distinct ways, anxiety about language, its variation, and its change. First, whatever heuristic is used to identify the baseline, whatever frame historians and grammarian use to define the linguistic present in their own minds or re-enact linguistic history (to invoke Collingwood one final time), the end result necessarily advances a form of English used only by some speakers. Concomitantly, it advances the social and economic opportunities

---

[5] See Charlotte Brewer, *Treasure-House of the Language: The Living OED* (New Haven, CT: Yale University Press, 2007).

of those speakers over those of speakers who use another variety. Given my argument that no linguistic phenomena have meaning in and of themselves, it is always speakers who invest significance in them, deciding how to classify them, which are important, and what they express. And the truth of the matter is that in assigning such meaning, some speakers, to paraphrase George Orwell's *Animal Farm*, are more equal than others. If by birth I should happen to speak a variety that's particularly close to this baseline—and I do—I will have less occasion to worry over or attend to the grammatical forms I use than would someone whose variety qualifies as more peripheral English or even a creole. Change and variation might occasion anxiety for both of us but for different reasons: for me, over the investment I might have in maintaining the sociolinguistic distinction and priority of my own variety, which would in fact leave me in the more influential position to decide whether the other speaker's variety is English, a creole, or an undeveloped interlanguage; and for the other speaker, over the sociolinguistic differences implicated in the variation between our speech patterns. General issues like these undermine the specific assumption that somewhere there is a stable, 'real' English providing stable comparative detail for assessing other varieties. Where and how would the identity of this 'real' English be drawn today? And for that matter, since English has changed so much, where and how might it be drawn historically? Is 'real' English what was used prior to the loss of grammatical gender and the dual pronoun? Or after the Great Vowel Shift but before the influx of Latinate words? Or after the conclusion of the Second World War but before the appearance of transplanted varieties in Asia and the introduction of Spanish lexical items in the United States?

The previous chapter argued that as it has been written since the early modern period, the history of English as a conceptual category has been implicated in the development of standard English, and vice versa. Not only did the cultivation of both disciplines occur simultaneously in the sixteenth, seventeenth, and eighteenth centuries, but both also identified the same baseline in a learned variety of English concentrated in southeast England. It was this variety that formed the basis of standard spoken and written English, just as it was the development of Standard English that has served as a kind of master narrative in histories of English. English colonizing and merchandising efforts provided two bulwarks for this narrative: they depended heavily on literacy and Standard English in educational, missionary, and governmental activities, and they largely originated in the southeast of England, so that when English spread around the globe, a generally southeast variety became a literal model in the utterances of influential personages in the Raj, early America, and other colonial communities. To an extent,

indeed, all non-British varieties of English are ultimately dialectal developments of a southeast variety, since even when transplanted British dialects
co-existed (as in the United States) this one typically proved the most
influential.[6] If American English eventually became an alternate baseline, it
did so only after early British speakers repeatedly faulted it for failing to meet
expressed standards and only as a baseline whose claim to authenticity rested
on an entirely different claim: not historical, literary, or grammatical but
socioeconomic and political. In this way, of course, the anxiety occasioned
by divergence from some imagined baseline of English is neither countered
nor neutralized; it is instead accepted as the necessary byproduct of institutionalized variation, which now exists between two competing standards
as well among the varieties measured against those standards.

The other way by which a comparative grammatical baseline can cultivate
anxiety is the way this book has examined in detail: by the channeling of
educational, social, religious, and governmental issues through variation and

This institutionalized anxiety has appeared again more broadly in the
proliferation of English and its speakers over the past few centuries, which
replays the nervous tension expressed in eighteenth-century British responses
to the development of United States and New Zealand English. Whether
through calls to contain the diversification of English or through arguments
to acknowledge world Englishes, variation and change from a standard,
putatively fixed form of the language serve as flashpoints for linguistic and
political discussion. Histories of English have themselves contributed to the
anxiety I describe. Underwritten by a standard ideology, they still often
describe a process of decreasing synchronic variation since the Middle Ages,
leading to the early modern triumph of English, the emergence of standard
language, and culmination in some modern form like United States English.
And this historical spectacle is imagined despite a backdrop of a conservatively estimated one billion contemporary speakers of English as a first or
second language, in a plethora of indigenous, post-colonial, and what Braj
Kachru calls expanding-circle domains. All this means that contrary to the
narrative teleology of histories of the language and the structural inadequacies
that comparison with a standard can imply, contemporary English embodies
structured synchronic variation (i.e., sociolects and regional dialects) that
must well exceed that of any point in the language's history. English, I would
say, is more alive than it has ever been.

The other way by which a comparative grammatical baseline can cultivate
anxiety is the way this book has examined in detail: by the channeling of
educational, social, religious, and governmental issues through variation and

---

6 See Roger Lass, 'Where Do Extraterrestrial Englishes Come from? Dialect, Input, and Recodification in Transported Englishes', in Sylvia Adamson *et al.* (eds.), *Papers from the 5th International
Conference in English Historical Linguistics* (Amsterdam: John Benjamins, 1990), 245–80.

change. Alfred the Great's discussion of the decay of learning after ninth-century Viking raids, the late-medieval Lollard controversy, the cultivation and codification of standard written English, the suppression of indigenous languages in New Zealand and Hawaii, attempts to define a nation through English, arguments over whether the varieties spoken in post-colonial regions qualify as national varieties—all these sociolinguistic episodes displace anxiety over social concerns to linguistic change and variation. They channel concerns over economics, race, ethnicity, sex, and class into language issues that can then be managed through both corpus planning of English usage and status planning of the relative roles of varieties of English as well as of the role of English in relation to contact languages around the globe. Within a heuristic emblemized by the biblical account of Babel and articulated in narratives from the earliest days of English, Anglophone policies and institutions have designated the linguistically natural (change and variation) as unnatural and debilitating, and have therefore invested in it terrific social consequence. Whether from the reactionary perspective of St Augustine, John Hart, or the United States English Only movement, or from the skeptical and conspiratorial one of those who practice what Quirk labels liberation linguistics, change and variation serve, weirdly, as at once euphemisms and flashpoints. They stand in for social issues that are truly volatile and thereby neutralize them; but in so doing they themselves also occasion anxiety about the issues they represent. Blaming language and managing it through educational and governmental policy thus become almost instinctual responses to any social, racial, or economic conflict. 'The American people believe English should be the official language of the government,' former United States House Speaker Newt Gingrich accordingly once claimed, conflating language, class, and race. 'We should replace bilingual education with immersion in English so people learn the common language of the country and they learn the language of prosperity, not the language of living in a ghetto.'[7]

Given the disjunction between language variation and the meanings that accrue to it, these meanings and the social concerns that exercise linguistic liberationists as well as Gingrich can be effectively addressed only by separating them from these linguistic associations. In the first instance, what provides language with social meanings—and what allows it to serve euphemistically for a variety of non-linguistic concerns—is the individual and collective decision to identify some variation as natural and some as

---

[7] 'It's English or Tongues of "Ghetto" Life, Gingrich Says', *Milwaukee Journal-Sentinel*, 1 April 2007, 19A.

erroneous. In effect, it is a decision to construct the history of English through a non-linguistic argument by allowing the language's putative identity to underwrite political and social agenda. And so the way to change the situation, I would maintain, itself begins with a decision: a decision not to allow language to stand in for non-linguistic concerns but directly to address these concerns, whether as individual citizens or as members of political entities like cities, states, and countries.

To argue this much, and to act upon this argument, is not to embrace lax standards in education, social chaos, or the gradual, inexorable decline of both the art of using English well and the structural integrity of the language. For Deborah Cameron, in fact, 'The way to intervene in public debates like the one about English grammar is not to deny the importance of standards and values but to focus critically on the particular standards and values being invoked and to propose alternatives'.[8] However much synchronic variation English today displays, moreover, there remains some kind of shared cultural space embedded in and realized through English, and a profitable line of inquiry would examine this shared space and extrapolate from it both to revised views of grammar and to distinctions between language and social meaning.[9] To argue as I have, then, is to accept responsibility for what we as Anglophones do, and until now a significant part of our actions has been to respond to certain difficult non-linguistic issues as if they were linguistic and in the process avoid dealing with their full implications. The early modern codification of English shows that social stability cannot be maintained by means of descriptive grammar; fiction's use of non-standard varieties shows that racism and sexism cannot be transformed through rhetoric; the linguistic histories of New Zealand and the United States show that ethnic divisiveness cannot be eradicated, nor social equality achieved, through the elimination of indigenous and immigrant languages; and the persistence of a kind of transmuted ethnicity in former Celtic-speaking areas shows that global homogenization of culture through international business does not erase cultural identity, even as desultory attempts to revive Celtic languages suggest that the objectives of such business cannot be thwarted or advanced merely by the identification and protection of endangered languages. When change and variation do not constitute the problem, they also cannot offer the solution.

---

[8] Cameron, *Verbal Hygiene* (London: Routledge, 1995), 115.

[9] See, for example, Anna Wierzbicka, *English: Meaning and Culture* (Oxford: Oxford University Press, 2006).

The cost and value of variation

Without doubt, as natural and inevitable as variation and change may be, they impose a significant cost on speakers, their communities, and even, in a metaphorical sense, languages themselves. One way to measure this cost would be by imagining the kinds of sociolinguistic benefits that would be lost if standard language, in the way it counteracts variation and change, ceased to exist. In the absence of standard language, for example, print would also be difficult, for though in England it dates to the pre-standard fifteenth century, its emergence as the defining medium for written language—and all the social and institutional developments that emergence entailed—correlates with Standard English. Developing together as they did, print and standard language have provided a way to achieve a linguistic condition in which, even if speakers can still misunderstand one another, written language does not in fact change or at least changes relatively slowly. In turn, print and Standard English have enabled the growth of education, the proliferation of literacy, and the expansion of Anglophone politics and markets. They also make it possible for geographically and chronologically distant speakers to communicate with one another—for South Africans to write to Canadians, and for modern Australians to read what Jane Austen wrote. Print and standard language may get us as close as we can be to the pre-Babel condition of being 'of one language'.

A further measure of the cost of variation is that even with print and Standard English, confusion still arises, for Anglophones can use the same written and spoken language with such diversity as to thwart communication. Trivial communicative disconnects can occur whenever speakers of different sociolects or regional varieties encounter one another when shopping or, particularly, traveling. While these disconnects may be the source of literary achievement or innocent amusement—local pronunciation of place names seems a continual source of humor to all Anglophones—they can also produce frustration, confusion, and anger. And this can be the case both for an isolated traveler unable to understand directions or, like Caxton's merchant, to order a meal in a restaurant, as well as for social groups and nations attempting to achieve workable, legal relations with one another. The 1840 Treaty of Waitangi in New Zealand created the social confusion it did partly because of a disparity between the English and Maori versions, just as Macaulay's 1835 minute used the variation between the English of British colonials and that of the indigenous people of India to codify social and class distinctions, and just as Webster saw American dialect variation as the means to and confirmation of the claim of the United States to a cultural identity distinct from that of England. At issue here, too, is identity and its investment in the forms and varieties of language we use. To the extent that language does serve as a symbol of group, ethnic, or national identity, its variation and change necessarily can work against this identity by foregrounding and enabling the emergence of various subgroups within a language community. If difficult issues like these arise against a backdrop of Standard English, which to some extent limits linguistic diversification, one could reasonably expect that without a standard such difficulties would increase.

On a more literal level, the cost of variation and change can be seen in their impact on social services, voting, education, and so forth. Funded by taxes, such programs respond directly to the variation present in Anglophone populations by providing, or withholding, money tied specifically to an individual's command of English. For native speakers, the primary investment is a financial one in programs designed to bring a non-standard speaker or one who lacks command of standard written English to a given level of competency. However this level is identified, a proportionate relationship necessarily exists among a speaker's current competency, the level to which the speaker will be brought, and the financial commitment by a school or public office. Very simply, it costs money to erase social and regional variation, and the farther a speaker is from the standard, the more it will cost to erase that distance—which might not in fact be erasable. For non-native speakers, the question of investment may also be financial, involving the cost of ESL programs in relation to speakers' disposable incomes. But non-native speakers' investment can be more pointedly emotional and personal, turning on issues like speakers' initial command of English, the structural similarities between their native language and English, the favorability (or otherwise) of speakers' sociolinguistic context to the acquisition of English, and the extent to which their identity is interconnected with their native language.

If community financial decisions about sociolinguistic issues like these represent a choice about the relative use of tax dollars—what amount of money should go to national defense and what to immigrant education?—they also represent a choice about how a city or country wants to represent itself. Does it see itself as hostile, inviting, or indifferent to language variation among its own Anglophones or between them and the non-native speakers in their midst? And if it sees itself as inviting, as many cities and countries in fact do, does it see the most sincere, beneficial kind of invitation to non-native speakers to be a funded entitlement program or the mere assertion that they have the opportunity, like countless immigrants before them, to learn English, assimilate, and advance in society? How does a city or country see the relationship between what benefits the native Anglophones and what benefits the non-native immigrants? While it's easy to demonize answers to questions like these—and particularly those who give the answers—the questions themselves resist easy solutions, and therein lies part of their cost. In the summer of 2006 the mayor of the small town of Arcadia, Wisconsin (pop. 2,402), proposed making English the town's official language, requiring the presence of an American flag beside that of any other country, and mandating that federal officials be notified about any undocumented immigrant workers. Responding to a large influx of Spanish-speaking laborers from Mexico into the local dairy industry, he asserted, 'I do want to close the doors to those that would come there and drain our resources by living and working here illegally, while benefitting from our tax-supported services'.[10] If the mayor's solution seems excessive and even caustic—and it ultimately was rejected by the local city council—the financial and social costs and problems that he identified in connection with language variation are very real.

Education is the venue where this cost has been perhaps the most prominent. Part of this prominence emerges from the plain emotive fact that children provide the most visible face of education. Part emerges from the role classrooms play both as forums for non-native speakers' introduction to English and Anglophone communities and in this way as emblems of how a society sees itself or what it sees itself becoming. And part emerges from the breadth of those affected by educational programs for native and non-native speakers. Inasmuch as public education is a government-funded and regulated enterprise, that is, it affects *every* member of a community, even those who are not themselves students in schools or the parents or guardians of students. Every member of a community, consequently, is likely to have an opinion on education.

For all these reasons, the costs of language change and variation in education are wide as well as high; as steep as the monetary value of bilingual, transitional, and even monolingual programs may be, the price of these programs in a community's view of itself and its future is higher still. And the more non-native speakers move into Anglophone regions or seek to acquire English as a second language, the greater the cost of variation and change. In the United States, an influx of non-Anglophone workers from Asia and Latin America has occurred over the past few decades. Not primarily targeting large cities, as nineteenth-century European emigrants tended to do, many of these speakers have settled in rural areas in particular—like Arcadia, Wisconsin. Bringing their children with them, they have also dramatically

---

[10] Quoted in Brian Voerding, 'Aracadia Mayor: No Más', *La Crosse Tribune*, 19 August 2006, A2.

affected the direction and programs of many school districts. Since the federal Bilingual Education Act lapsed in 2002, local districts have borne responsibility not simply for educating these non-native speakers but for bringing them to federally mandated performance levels, and the cost of this education—in several senses—can be staggering. Between 1993 and 2002, the number of limited-English students in several states tripled; in North Carolina it quintupled. And if it can be financially onerous simply to accommodate such increases, it's also onerous to find qualified teachers, since comparatively few of those in teacher training specialize in English as a second language. Consequently, if school districts are to attract credentialed applicants, they need to supplement salaries with various kinds of bonuses.[11] And all this means that tax payers in the district, monolingual as well as multilingual, have a vested and vocal interest in how the school district responds to variation and change.

This leaves yet one more cost of variation and change, and that has been the level of anxiety it has produced, both among those who see these linguistic phenomena as problems and would return to a pre-Babel era and among those who would celebrate linguistic variation as a mark of human diversity. Dialogue, discussion, and dissent may be inevitable means towards progress and conflict resolution, but on this topic at least they have more typically produced discord than resolved it. For critics like Honey, Macdonald, and Quirk linguistic variation, while unavoidable, only serves to advance social disruption and inequity, while for critics like Phillipson and Crowley it reflects and furthers the identity of the individual groups who all speak what is only nominally the same language and who have the right to speak languages other than English. What both critical outlooks share is the conviction that in their response to variation, Anglophones respond also to each other's dignity, which they promote by either suppressing or fostering linguistic change. But despite this common goal, the dialogue between what Cameron calls verbal hygienists and what Quirk calls linguistic liber-ationists is unresolvable and finally, I believe, unconstructive. Indeed, it has become similar to discussions between political adversaries that begin with a question like, 'Do you want world peace?' And just as few politicians would answer 'no', so would few Anglophones, at least publicly, assert that they wanted actively to suppress the human rights and dignity of other speakers. Both sides of the linguistic debate thus claim a kind of moral high ground and thereby allow little possibility for a compromise meeting somewhere in

[11] See Yilu Zhao, 'Wave of Pupils Lacking English Strains Schools', *New York Times*, 5 August 2002, A1, 11.

the middle, at least so long as discussion foregrounds language as the problem and the solution in all manner of social issues. It is in this sense, then, that another cost of variation and change for Anglophones has been the increase in anxiety about them that extended discussion and consideration have produced. In doing little to ameliorate the channeling of social issues through linguistic ones, this discussion has in fact done much both to naturalize the connection and to amplify the concerns associated with it.

All that being said, linguistic variation and change also have clear value, and I do not here advance merely an intellectual interest in linguistic diversity or refer simply to some association between it and social diversity. Rather, as the inevitable byproducts of language contact and social achievement, variation and change testify to the vitality of an individual language and of the collectivity of languages in general. While linguistic change often may proceed mechanistically, with found facts like push chains accounting for a sequence of phonological alterations, social phenomena just as often prove to be the instigators of this change. When language changes in these instances, it does so because society has advanced in some way, and examples include everything from technological progress (which, as in the nineteenth century, might supplement lexicon), to cultural revolution (which, as in the early modern period, might lead to syntactic change in response to translation needs), to social movement (which, as at the time of the Great Vowel Shift, might utilize language as a means of group distinction).

Beyond serving as responses to expanding sociolinguistic experience, variation and change also constitute foundational aspects of English grammar and usage. At a synchronic level even more fundamental than borrowed lexicon or syntactic innovation, they enable features like strong verbs, variable morphological rules, and vowel alteration as a plural marker. They also produce variable stress patterns for related words (*photograph* as opposed to *photographer* and *photographic*); for the same word functioning as two different parts of speech (*present* the noun as opposed to *present* the verb); and for a word fulfilling two different discursive functions (pronunciation of a direct object when it's topicalized to appear as the first word in a sentence, as opposed to when it's not). This last issue points to the role variation more generally plays in communicative competence. If grammatically competent speakers are those who are able to produce well-formed sentences with a language's syntax, morphology, lexicon, and so forth, communicatively competent ones are those who know how to adapt this grammatical competence to the specific frames of particular domains. They know how to vary speech depending on their interlocutors, topic, and locale; they know that one uses different vocabulary with children and adults, that one doesn't bare one's soul to a stranger at a bus stop or tell raucous jokes at a funeral, and that accommodation to another's sociolect or regional dialect can be a means to show solidarity. All this is to say that such knowledge is knowledge about variable phenomena, and a speaker without it—a pre-Babel speaker who had no sense of the need to alter speech depending on circumstances—would qualify as what has memorably been labeled a 'faulty interactant'.[12] Whatever social meanings accrue to variation and change and however detrimental these meanings might be to certain speakers, the intrinsic value of variation to expression and speakers is thus no less essential.

This connection between variation and communicative competence deepens through consideration of the flip-side of my earlier comment about how linguistic variation can work against a large community identity. As a form of social display, language accomplishes more than the transference of ideas that Locke described so well. It foments revolution, expresses passion, and releases tension. And also, as I have noted before, like clothing, hairstyles, and musical taste, grammar and discursive habits can be ways of announcing— and interpreting—social identity. All these things can constitute individuals' self-representation and provide those around them with an impression of their age, background, education, ethnicity, and social outlook. In the terminology of M. A. K. Halliday, which I noted in the opening chapter, language functions as a social semiotic by encoding social distinctions in age, class, education, and so forth.[13] At the broadest level, going back to the ancient Greeks and their suspicion of foreigners, language has been a crucial means for establishing ethnic and national identity, and in its own history, English has indeed served and continues to serve distinct roles in the definition of group culture, whether the group is one defined by age-graded features, by lexicon that emerges from ethnic or non-native traditions, or by a conviction that language stands as a distinctive characteristic of national identity. Adolescents and speakers of national as well as non-standard varieties use language so effectively in representing themselves as members of a cohort that, Stephen May suggests, if language is not the pre-eminent determinant of a cultural group that Herder and other German Romanticists believed it to be, it is still a significant factor: 'language may not be intrinsically valuable in itself—it is not primordial—but it does have strong and felt associations with ethnic and national identity'.[14]

---

[12] See R. A. Hudson, *Sociolinguistics*, 2nd edn. (Cambridge: Cambridge University Press, 1996), 112–16.

[13] Halliday, *Language as Social Semiotic: The Social Interpretation of Language and Meaning* (London: Edward Arnold, 1978).

[14] May, *Language and Minority Rights: Ethnicity, Nationalism and the Politics of Language* (New York: Longman, 2001), 129.

By extension, both historically and today, as the geographical, ethnic, and social circumstances of Anglophones have changed, so, too, has English. The earliest Germanic groups, perhaps even before they left the Continent, encountered Roman paved roads for the first time and borrowed what became *street* for them. As Anglo-Norman barons occupied the Welsh marches later in the Middle Ages, they borrowed the Welsh word *crag* to describe the rocky outcrops they encountered. Later still, when English explorers returned from overseas, they brought with them not only goods from around the world but the words to describe them—like *ketchup* (Chinese), *bwana* (Swahili), and *chintz* (Hindi). More complexly, change and variation in the history of English testify for the development of sociolects derived from contact with non-native speakers or through native speakers' exploitation of what Halliday labels 'the sociolinguistic play potential of one's own variety of the language'.[15] Speakers of what may well be a non-standard variety, that is, foster its covert prestige and their own sociolinguistic identity by developing coded linguistic activity in syntax, lexicon, and discursive practices; in maintaining the integrity of their own variety, such speakers not only help to preserve their own social identity but also establish barriers of intelligibility between themselves and other, more powerful groups. And in this way, varieties as disparate as African American Vernacular English, Geordie, and Singapore English offer self-preserving group identification in much the same way as would have the divergence of the Ingvaeonic languages (Old Saxon, Old Frisian, and Old English) from Primitive Germanic or Webster's declared independence of United States from British English. The relatively recent presence of non-standard and even non-native speakers in publicly prominent positions like that of network news broadcaster points to this same value in variation as a reflection of changing group identities.[16] On a narrower but I tend to think no less significant scale, multilingual department store Santa Clauses, able to greet children as easily with 'Maligayang Pasko' and 'Feliz Navidad' as with 'Merry Christmas', likewise emblemize the flexibility of language in defining group identity.[17] Variation and change thus prove as consequential to representation as they do to grammatical structure and discourse conventions.

The advantages of variation can be pursued further, into a more abstractly linguistic realm. It's true enough that a concomitant of the twentieth and twenty-first century's global economy—and particularly of the role

---

[15] Halliday, *Language as Social Semiotic*, 160.

[16] Mireya Navarro, 'Breaking the Sound Barrier', *New York Times*, 23 July 2006, 9, 1 and 10.

[17] Patricia Leigh Brown, 'Santa Claus Packs a Bag of Languages at a California Mall', *New York Times*, 21 December 2003, A5.

of Anglophone countries in this economy—has been the curtailment of some languages and the contraction and even death of others. But as Mufwene has noted, another concomitant, typically overlooked in discussions that focus on language loss, has been something akin to the process of 'speciation in population genetics'.[18] From a grammatical point of view, change and variation point to the vitality of a language, since it is only living languages that can change, but also constitute the medium by which any language—to push Mufwene's biological metaphor—produces new varieties and languages. And in the area of speciation, English has of late been a particularly fertile language.

It remains unclear at least to me how statistically significant generalizations can be made about the degree of current global linguistic diversity in comparison to that in any pre-literate, statistically unanalyzable moment.[19] Nonetheless, I will grant that the approximately 6,000 natural languages used today may well represent a relative decrease from the number of languages spoken in some pre-modern epoch. At the same time, however, English itself—in its regional dialects, sociolects, and the various interlanguages (creoles and pidgins) to which it has contributed—embodies more structural and sociolinguistic diversity than it has at any moment in its recorded history. I wonder, then, if the situation of the modern industrialized world is not simply whether it does or does not display less linguistic diversity than did the pre-Columban world but whether its diversity skews differently. Today, that is, variation may predominate as a reflection and measure of what we now consider intra-linguistic variation in languages used by large groups of speakers (Spanish and Chinese, perhaps, alongside English) rather than of the divergence among structurally distant and distinct languages each of which has comparatively few speakers. And I would advance this line of reasoning still further. Placing the common claim that variation among languages has declined precipitously over time within a sociolinguistic context that nonetheless guarantees change, I wonder whether the implicit identification of linguistic variation with national languages isn't yet another naturalized

---

[18] Salikoko S. Mufwene, 'Language Endangerment: What Have Pride and Prestige Got to Do with It?', in Brian D. Joseph *et al.* (eds.), *When Languages Collide: Perspectives on Language Conflict, Language Competition, and Language Coexistence* (Columbus, OH: Ohio State University Press, 2003), 330.

[19] One study claims, for example, not only that language loss has accelerated in the modern period but that the perhaps 6,000 to 6,500 languages spoken today represent a significant drop from the 15,000 languages that the study somehow estimates were spoken between 100,000 and 10,000 BC. See Anna Ash, Jessie Little Doe Fermino, and Ken Hale, 'Diversity in Local Language Maintenance and Restoration: A Reason for Optimism', in Leanne Hinton and Ken Hale (eds.), *The Green Book of Language Revitalization in Practice* (San Diego, CA: Academic Press, 2001), 19–35.

legacy of Romantic thought. I wonder whether linguistic variation isn't really a kind of zero-sum game. I wonder whether variation might have remained constant between the Indo-European migrations and the present, though it is now more intra- than inter-linguistic, and only time can tell whether the pendulum of variation might some day swing back.

The title of this chapter turns on a pun, embracing *fix* both in the sense 'repair' and in the sense 'stabilize'. It's a pun, or at least a double meaning, present in metalinguistic discussions of English already in the early modern debates that helped fashion a grammar of Standard English. In his 1712 *Proposal for Correcting, Improving, and Ascertaining the English Tongue*, Jonathan Swift advocates that 'some Method should be thought on for ascertaining and fixing our Language for ever', a notion reprised forty years later by David Hume, who speaks of 'Eminent and refined geniuses . . . [who] . . . fix the tongue by their writings'.[20] It is Dr Johnson, however, who perhaps predictably makes the best use of this double meaning. In the preface to his *Dictionary*, he notes, 'Those who have been persuaded to think well of my design, require that it should fix our language, and put a stop to those alterations which time and chance have hitherto been suffered to make in it without opposition'.[21] These two senses are often in play, not only in metalinguistic discussions of English but also in the dynamics between language and culture. Much of what I have described in this book, indeed, could well be summarized by the seductive notion that if the language can be stabilized, the culture will be repaired, and vice versa.

But English isn't broken. It varies and changes because, despite the power of the myth of Babel, that's what natural languages do. While the written channel might well be regarded as relatively stable right now, the spoken channels—the many global sociolects and regional dialects—will never be. And whatever other connections English may have to the social institutions and actions of those who speak it, its own variability points to one thing above all: that linguistically, these social groups are vital and healthy.

Roses and any other names

While I was writing the first draft of this book, a controversy of the sort that could arise only in a university occurred in my home institution. It was the kind of controversy that I could imagine figuring in one of David Lodge's academic novels. It involved the nickname for the university's athletics teams.

---

[20] *OED*, s. v. *fix, v.*
[21] Johnson, *Dictionary of the English Language* (1755; rpt. New York: AMS Press, 1967), i, Cii^r.

In the early years of the university, several different names had been used, but beginning in the early 1950s the teams were known as the 'Warriors' and the image of the teams—on banners, uniforms, shirts, and so forth—was that of a non-descript American Indian. The selection of Warriors was not random, since the university was named for an Indian missionary, founded by an order of Catholic priests with a long history of working on missions and reservations, and located in an area that was once entirely inhabited by various Algonquian nations. Already in the 1960s some students, faculty, and local citizens began to express concern that the Warrior name and attendant imagery showed disrespect to Native Americans and ought therefore to be dropped. In the early 1970s the university did eliminate 'Willie Wampum', a student who dressed as a caricatured Native American and appeared at athletic events, especially basketball games, to cheer on the team and inspire the crowd's support. But the name Warriors remained into the 1990s, when, following a vote by students and faculty and against the wishes of a great many alumni, it was changed to Golden Eagles.

Largely because of disgruntled alumni, the nickname controversy never entirely died, and a decade later it again reached a moment of crisis when the university's board of trustees agreed to review the situation and make a definitive recommendation on whether the name should remain Golden Eagles, revert to Warriors, or become something entirely new. Leading up to the board's deliberations and vote, various university and civic groups expressed various opinions, which generally fell at one of two extremes: that Warriors was and always would be offensive to Native Americans, both as people and in the public conception of them, and that Warriors not only had a historical link to the university but need not be offensive, as witnessed by the many other universities that have retained the nickname, sometimes (but not always) tacitly morphing the warrior from a Native American to a medieval knight. For their part, Native Americans took positions on both ends of this spectrum. Campus rallies were held, interviews given to the local media, and opinion pieces published in magazines and newspapers. One of these, endorsed by several members of the faculty, appeared in the student-run campus newspaper.

The letter argued that faculty 'have a responsibility to comment on the issues of language and representation involved in the current debate' and, more generally, that words 'accrue meaning—both literal and connotative— only through historical usage and in real human communities'. Asserting that in the United States *warriors* 'connotes first and formatively American Indians', the letter maintains that whether 'this linkage ascribes to American Indians traits that seem negative or positive, it denies them the dignity and right of self-representation. In the case of sports, it appropriates and misuses American Indian experience.' For all these reasons, the letter concluded, 'Whatever the intentions of the Board of Trustees in considering reversing this name change, there can be no doubt that the wider community [of the university, city, and country] would perceive the return of the Warriors as a return to an era of racial insensitivity'. What direct impact this letter had on the board's decision, I don't know; it was only one of several expressions of this same basic sentiment during the months that the controversy dragged on. Eventually, the board did explicitly reject Warriors and, after briefly toying with the idea of yet another new name, agreed to retain Golden Eagles.

Though asked to sign this letter, I did not do so—not because I liked one name over the other in the abstract, nor because I felt it was appropriate to insult or limit the dignity of Native Americans or any other group. Partly I didn't sign because I didn't think it much mattered what the university called its teams; I thought that Warriors was a fine nickname for an athletic team, that it was odd to change it to Golden Eagles, that Golden Eagles was a fine nickname, and that amidst current curricular and institutional crises in higher education it was still odder to be debating the issue at all, much less contemplating a return to Warriors. Mostly I didn't sign, however, because I saw the argument as fundamentally flawed, as the sort of argument that anxiously muddies language change and social meanings in ways I have examined throughout this book.

Without in any way questioning the motives or integrity of the letter's signers, I am struck by the way it both faults speakers for the language they use and denies them responsibility for creating that language and, hence, the opportunity to change their language or, more importantly, their thinking and action. Responsibility rests instead with the language, in which meanings may accrue 'through historical usage and in real human communities' but which at some point—now, evidently—become impervious to these same usages and communities. While King Alfred, the Lollards, and Webster had all maintained that language should change only up to a point that they had determined and then become fixed there, this argument takes the mirror tactic that asserts change cannot take place after a point that the writers had determined. *Warriors* is judged necessarily to connote Native Americans, who, in turn, are judged necessarily delimited and demeaned by this same connotation. And this necessity is predicated on a pattern of usage throughout the history of the university and country. To use *warriors* again, then, is necessarily to invoke earlier usage patterns and therefore declare that the present university embodies the racial insensitivity, if not racism, present in these patterns.

To my mind, then and now, there are serious practical and theoretical problems with this line of reasoning that once more demonstrate how extra-linguistic social anxieties can be channeled through language change and variation. Derived from Old French *werreieor*, English *warrior*, in the sense 'One whose occupation is warfare; a fighting man, whether soldier, sailor, or (latterly) airman; in eulogistic sense, a valiant or an experienced man of war', occurs already in Robert of Gloucester's late thirteenth-century *Metrical Chronicle*, where the connotation is obviously of an armored soldier: 'Kniȝtes and oþer worrerours, þat to þis londe wende'. This same sense predominates in the fourteenth, fifteenth, sixteenth, and seventeenth centuries—alongside, I should note, an odd and expansive set of figurative usages involving women and animals—and the first recorded connotation of what we would today call indigenes does not occur until 1788: 'Many of their warriors, or distinguished men, we observed to be painted in stripes, across the breast and back.' Coming from John White's *Journal of a Voyage to New South Wales*, however, this passage refers not to Native Americans but to Aborigines. The first *OED* example with *warrior* as a reference to American Indians is from James Fenimore Cooper's 1826 *Last of the Mohicans*: 'A swarthy band of the native chiefs ... with the warriors of their several tribes'.[22]

The practical point here is not that *warriors* was never used to connote Native Americans until 1826; surely, there must have been significantly earlier (if unattested) usages in this sense. The practical point, as the faculty letter in fact notes, is rather that words do indeed have histories. But what the letter does not note as well is that these histories reflect the usage decisions of human speakers and not some kind of atavistic spirit—something akin to Milton's etymological fallacy—within the language itself. *Warrior* did not and does not always 'first and formatively' connote American Indians, even in the United States. A borrowing from French, it reflects the large-scale late-medieval English importation of French courtly practices (like chivalry) and the vocabulary associated with them; to be like the French would have required (or at least benefited from) words for specifically French institutions and practices, words such as *harness*, *majesty*, and *manor*, all of which are borrowed from French and first recorded in English at about the same time as *warrior* is.

Application of the word to indigenous peoples whom Anglophones encountered as they spread around the globe equally reflects decisions of individual and collective speakers. Given the European habit of framing perception and reception of New World phenomena within the context

---

[22] *OED*, s. v., *warrior*.

of historical experience, particularly that of the Antique as described and depicted in books, it was inevitable that Anglophones would think, probably early on, to designate as *warriors* the 'fighting men' they encountered in North America and elsewhere around the globe.[23] This was the label that would have best categorized and explained such people. Additionally, in view of the word's history, such extrapolated designations would seem at least initially to have been not merely descriptive but complimentary (or 'eulogistic' as the *OED* labels it), building on a lexical tradition that began with the appropriation of what was originally a term for a landed, noble fighting man. Two decades prior to Cooper's *The Last of the Mohicans*, for instance, Wordsworth wrote 'Character of the Happy Warrior', whose eponymous hero is not a mounted knight but someone who is diligent, moral, and compassionate, and who,

> . . . while the mortal mist is gathering, draws
> His breath in confidence of Heaven's applause:
> This is the happy Warrior; this is He
> That every Man in arms should wish to be.[24]

And two centuries prior to Wordsworth, in translating Giovanni Biondi's *History of the Civil Wars of England*, the Earl of Monmouth refers unambiguously to a seventeenth-century champion, again clearly not a mounted knight, who 'was rightly ranked in the number of the chiefe warriers of that age'. Within this lexical context alone, but also within the rhetorical context of representing indigenes as worthy opponents, there is by extension no denial of indigenous dignity in either White's or Cooper's use of *warrior* as cited above. And generalization from 'soldiers' to all Native Americans is a likewise logical choice and parallels the semantic extension of a word like *viking*, which in popular and academic usage has had its reference broaden from what might best be called a sea-going pirate of particularly the ninth and tenth centuries to all of the men, women, and children who lived in medieval Scandinavia.

Positive connotations for a *warrior* as a description of a Native American 'fighting man' continue throughout the nineteenth century. A *New York Times* headline of 23 April 1875, at the height of the so-called Plains Uprising, notes the 'Surrender of Hostile Comanche Chiefs and Thirty-Six Warriors', and a headline like this can be newsworthy only if the surrender itself is—which

---

[23] On the Antique as a frame for early modern perceptions of the New World, see Anthony Grafton, with April Shelford and Nancy Siraisi, *New Worlds, Ancient Texts: The Power of Tradition and the Shock of Discovery* (Cambridge, MA: Harvard University Press, 1992).

[24] Wordsworth, *The Complete Poetical Works*, ed. A. J. George (Cambridge, MA: Houghton Mifflin, 1932), 341.

would require that the 'Warriors' be formidable foes and not individuals lacking dignity. The article itself in fact goes on to distinguish the 'thirty-six braves' from '140 women and children', thereby drawing a clear distinction between indigenous 'fighting men' and indigenes in general.[25] And even on 15 July 1899, by which point any Native American aggressive resistance to Anglo expansion was long a thing of the past, the *Times* could still represent Native American fighting men as redoubtable with the headline 'Pursuit of Sioux Warriors' and the subheadline 'Three Parties of Indian Police are After Swift Bear and His Band—An Uprising Feared'.[26] The *Times* may well have exaggerated or even demonized the fleeing Sioux by describing them as *warriors*, of course, but such rhetoric would prove the point that in reference to Native Americans the word still had, at that time, neutral and even positive connotations in the way that it validates and perhaps glorifies pursuit by the United States army. Without the dignity of being 'fighting men', Swift Bear and his band could ill justify fears of an uprising. Just over a decade later, a positive, metaphoric use of *warrior* is traditionally ascribed to Glenn 'Pop' Warner in the pre-game pep talk that he gave to the football team of the Carlisle Indian School prior to its 1912 game against, of all places, the United States Military Academy at West Point, whose backfield featured, of all people, Dwight D. Eisenhower: 'These men playing against you today are soldiers. These are the Long Knives. You are Indians. Tonight we will know whether or not you are warriors.'[27]

Any caricaturing or denial of dignity in the connotations of *warrior* must have been one semantic step farther on. The experiences of Native Americans who fought in the First World War may have been a factor, since stereotypes of Indians as instinctive, natural fighters could have joined with

---

[25] *New York Times*, 23 April 1875, 1.

[26] *New York Times*, 15 July 1899, 1.

[27] Quoted in Alexander M. Weyand, *The Saga of American Football* (New York: Macmillan, 1955), 101. Although the *New York Times* report the day after the game does not list Weyand as having participated, he was the captain of the 1915 Army team and so it's reasonable to suppose he knew people who did. He claims to have gotten the quotation from Bill Stern, a popular sports broadcaster in the 1930s, 1940s, and 1950s. Pop Warner barely mentions the incident in his autobiography, but two Carlisle players (Gus Welch and Pete Calac) did attribute these sentiments to Warner in his pep talk, though they made no attempt to quote him verbatim. Evidently, Warner, who was a strong advocate of Carlisle and who was very loyal to his players, in general liked to use the fact that they were Indians playing white men as a motivational tool. See Robert M. Wheeler, *Jim Thorpe: World's Greatest Athlete* (Norman, OK: University of Oklahoma Press, 1975), 128; Bill Crawford, *All American: The Rise and Fall of Jim Thorpe* (Hoboken, NJ: John Wiley and Sons, 2005), 188; Lars Anderson, *Carlisle vs. Army: Jim Thorpe, Dwight Eisenhower, Pop Warner, and the Forgotten Story of Football's Greatest Battle* (New York: Random House, 2007), 278; Sally Jenkins, *The Real All Americans: The Team that Changed a Game, a People, a Nation* (New York: Doubleday, 2007), 7. Though Weyand's book is Jenkins's source, she offers a slightly different version of the quotation.

racial stereotypes to undermine the very success implicit in representations of Native American soldiers; their success, that is, confirmed that they were 'blood-thirsty warriors'.[28] But *warrior* clearly retained positive, self-representational qualities on the two-year anniversary of Armistice Day, when, at a memorial at the Tomb of the Unknown Soldier in Washington, D C, the Crow chief Plenty Coups concluded his speech by saying, 'I hope that the Great Spirit will grant that these noble warriors have not given up their lives in vain and that there will be peace to all men hereafter'.[29] And even today the word *warrior* can preserve not only its medieval associations with knight-hood, as at those American universities that use the name and a mounted knight as a mascot, but also its positive connotations for at least some Native Americans, as among the Portland, Oregon, group 'Warriors for Christ'. The goal of this group is 'to encourage and strengthen spiritual growth among Native Americans through evangelism and discipleship training, and to strengthen and plant Native churches on Indian reservations and urban areas throughout North America', and its web page emblazons its name over a picture of buffalo, a plains teepee, and a bonneted young man.[30] From a global perspective, the word likewise can retain laudatory, self-representa-tional connotations for other indigenous peoples, as in the 1994 novel *Once Were Warriors*, which holds out the word and its associations as symbols of the status lost to Maori culture in the brutal and economically debilitated urban housing projects of the New Zealand present.[31]

These practical problems in evaluating how meaning accrues to a word like *warrior* point to a larger theoretical problem. And that is what I've come to think of, in a metaphor that's perhaps grotesque but nonetheless apropos, as having your Sapir-Whorf hypothesis but eating it, too. The positions expressed in the faculty letter share many educational and governmental sentiments that I have traced throughout this book by attributing to language and language change an overarching and preemptive power to shape reality—to define experience in such a way, through grammar and discursive patterns, as (in this instance) to deny individuals 'dignity and [the] right of self-representation'. At the same time, like these other sentiments the letter's arguments are predicated on the notion that some individuals, at least, can transcend the determinative power of language, historically by creating and then limiting a word's connotations once and for all and currently by being able to evade the linguistic determination of experience in order to evaluate

---

28 Thomas A. Britten, *American Indians in World War I: At Home and at War* (Albuquerque, NM: University of New Mexico Press, 1997), 99–115.

29 Quoted in Britten, *American Indians in World War I*, 160.

30 http://www.warriorsforchristonline.org/index2.htm.

31 Alan Duff, *Once Were Warriors* (Honolulu, HI: University of Hawaii Press, 1994).

language itself and the process by which this same creation took place. By this line of reasoning, indeed, a word like *warrior* behaves in semantically peculiar, even unique ways. For unexplained reasons, the implicit claim seems to be that *warrior* may have been borrowed into English without Anglophones appropriating and misusing the experience of French chevaliers, and it may have had its meaning extended from 'mounted, armed fighting man' simply to 'fighting man' or even 'virtuous man' without similarly affecting the experience of early modern soldiers or morally upright individuals. But once applied to indigenous fighting men in the United States, the denotation and connotation of the word became permanently negative. It's as if the 'real human communities' that give the word its meaning exclude all those that existed before and after some historical moment at which the meaning of *warrior* is presumed to have become forever fixed.

Language thereby becomes both the manufacturing force that the strictest versions of Sapir-Whorf describe—the force that fashions reality and that renders individuals who speak different languages as the inhabitants of effectively different worlds—but also the literal subject of certain speakers, particularly malfeasant ones. In this way, language change once more channels social anxiety, for it is by linguistic change that the word *warrior* allegedly came first and foremost to mean 'Native American' in a way that denied indigenes 'the dignity and right of self-representation', and it is through resistance to linguistic change, the letter asserts, that the university could resist 'a return to an era of racial insensitivity'. Change and variation also become mystified yet again, since while speakers have the ability to invent words and change at least some of their meanings across time, after some point, for unexplained reasons, they lose this ability: they cannot now, evidently, recuperate *warrior*. And the ascription of all such developments to some vague historical agency like 'social power' as reflected in dominant institutions not only further mystifies change but also exonerates speakers from the responsibility for the language they use and their decisions to change it or leave it as is. It is just this kind of adaptation of the Sapir-Whorf hypothesis that I have opposed in this book, arguing instead that it is speakers who invest linguistic forms with meanings, which may in fact then shape their reality but for which they remain responsible. And I have argued that just as all interlocutors in a conversation are accountable for the direction and sense of their conversation, all Anglophones are accountable for English, for as James Milroy has observed, 'it is *speakers*, and not *languages*, that innovate'.[32]

---

[32] Milroy, *Linguistic Variation and Change: On the Historical Sociolinguistics of English* (Oxford: Blackwell, 1992), 169.

By extension when we respond to speakers *through* language alone, we depersonalize and obfuscate this accountability.

It may well be that there are some words that are so semantically contaminated that they cannot be rehabilitated in any way. It's difficult to imagine an athletic team called the *nazis* or the *niggers*, for example, because it's difficult to imagine that these words could ever become separated from their horrific—and not just demeaning—connotations. But even as I say this, I want to add that when it comes to language, human will can be a powerful mechanism for shaping pragmatics. Both *vandal* and *cossack*, for instance, would seem to have irrevocably negative connotations of brutality and destruction, and yet each is now used for United States university athletic teams. And these appear alongside various kinds of *devils, demons, buccaneers, vikings*, and, of course, *warriors*. There is even an institution that proudly and without any sense of irony or ethnic stereotyping designates its teams the 'Fighting Irish'.

From its historical associations with slavery and racism, *nigger* would seem particularly unlikely ever to be semantically ameliorated: it has become perhaps the most notorious word in English, so notorious, in fact, that its utterance in certain circumstances has been likened to a violent speech act akin to yelling 'fire' in a crowded theater.[33] With the widespread use of the form [nɪgə] in rap music, however, the word has lost these inflammatory associations in some domains, in the same way that *gay* and perhaps *queer* have themselves become ameliorated. In all cases, by casually using the words and not directing them as insults or simply avoiding them, as had been customary, speakers demystify them and denude them of at least some of their power to shock and offend. In some usages *nigger* has in fact come to serve almost as an endearment, particularly among young African Americans. But the limits of this usage—and the responsibility of speakers for fashioning not only what they say but what they do—appeared in an assault case in New York City in 2006. The fact that one young man beat another was not in dispute; what was in dispute was whether the attack qualified as a hate crime based on race, for which the penalty would be greater. And this qualification turned on the significance of the defendant's use of the 'n-word', as prosecutors and defense attorneys regularly referred to it throughout the trial, avoiding uttering the word *nigger* themselves. The defendant, having grown up in a racially mixed neighborhood, maintained that he used the word as part of his ordinary discourse and that it consequently did not have its overwhelmingly negative historical connotations. The prosecutors argued

---

[33] Randall Kennedy, *Nigger: The Strange Career of a Troublesome Word* (New York: Pantheon, 2002).

that it did, and in the end were able to secure conviction of first- and second-degree robbery as a hate crime.[34]

As the faculty letter's reference to historical usage indicates, the history of words matters: it offers a window on communities that used language and on how it and their world have shaped one another as well as the present. But it should be the whole history that matters, not just an expedient selection, and words that have the historical, visceral impact of *nazi* and *nigger* are few and far between in English. Even granting the historical associations of *warrior* with American Indians, one would be hard-pressed to locate usages and a social consensus that *warrior* was one of these contaminated words. Everything I have traced—from Robert of Gloucester to Pop Warner to modern New Zealand—suggests otherwise. And to my mind, further, to try to increase the corpus of damaged, unusable words only further serves to mystify language change, divert responsibility for usage from speakers, and (thereby) avoid the real social issues associated with the words. Prevention of a return to *warrior* offers a temporary satisfaction, but in doing so it also suppresses consideration of the very issues that seem to make the word into a problem. It is worth remembering, indeed, that words acquire negative and positive connotations in precisely the same way: speakers' usage. Just as speech communities have fashioned any word's history and negative connotations, so might they rehabilitate it. Just as they borrowed a word like *warrior* and changed its meaning in various ways, so might they continue to change it, its connotations, and, most importantly, the social issues it raises.

Words obviously do matter, and changing language can sometimes change the world in which we live. Words can affect how we see this world and can be at least a partial means for altering that world. Such was the case in the 1960s when, in the first wave of feminism, many speakers came to resist strongly the casual use of *girls* for women who worked in offices—a usage that required the untenable presumption that labeling these women as children or adolescents did not adversely affect others' perception of them. Forty years later, at least in the United States, this usage is almost literally unheard of and could well be, in any case, grounds for a sexual harassment law suit. And at the very least, this change in usage reflects some positive change in the status of female office-workers, though avoidance of *girl* has scarcely produced a society free of sexism.

---

[34] Corey Kilgannon, 'Tolerance for a Racial Slur Is a Test for Potential Jurors', *New York Times*, 18 May 2006, C17; and Kilgannon, 'Attacker Guilty of Hate Crimes in Howard Beach', *New York Times*, 10 June 2006, B1.

But it is my argument that throughout the history of English, and perhaps particularly in the wake of another of Orwell's works, 'Politics and the English Language',[35] change and variation—or their absence in an imagined pre-Babel world—have served far too easily as channels for non-linguistic issues and have thereby distorted discussion of vital social concerns. They have been used to imagine a world of perfect, unvarying communication, which in turn has been used to formulate all manner of institutional activity and to produce all manner of social anxiety. If the study of natural languages shows that such a world is impossible, the Tower of Babel—the myth that seems to explain so much—shows that even if perfect communication were possible, it would also be lethal, both offering an affront to God and leading to the scattering of humanity. As Orwell said so well, language can serve to mask otherwise unacceptable political and social activity, and it is easier to change human language than human actions and beliefs. In that sense, as with *girl*, manipulation of language can have positive benefits beside the negative ones Orwell describes—it can at least encourage social change by causing speakers to think about what they say.[36]

Ultimately, however, it is social activity, not the language, that is both the problem and its solution. Language is not responsible for sexism, racism, or various other kinds of social injustice. It may be a tool to such injustice, but it is a tool used by speakers, who have the power not merely to invent words and use them with negative connotations but also to reject these connotations. More importantly, speakers have the power to elect not to blame language change and variation for the social issues they encounter in the world—not to transfer non-linguistic anxieties onto linguistic topics—but directly to address these issues. Perhaps above all, my discussion of *warrior* illustrates just this point: that different speakers can invest different meanings into linguistic activity and that language does not determine social reality (as I understand the faculty letter to presume) but rather exists in a kind of symbiotic relationship with it. When we blame language and use it as a euphemism for something extra-linguistic, the something else always seems to find a way to persist and take on new forms. 'The euphemism treadmill', as Stephen Pinker calls it, 'shows that concepts, not words, are in charge: give

---

[35] Orwell's essay, which has been widely circulated, particularly in rhetoric handbooks, first appeared in *Horizon* in April of 1946.

[36] Cf. Ann Curzan's comment: 'Whether or not changing language eventually changes attitudes remains an open question; clearly, however, the simple fact that language reform requires speakers to think about a linguistic construction and its possible social implications—be they sexist, racist, or otherwise discriminatory—brings a level of awareness of these issues to a speech community that might not otherwise be achieved' (*Gender Shifts in the History of English* [Cambridge: Cambridge University Press, 2003], 180).

a concept a new name, and the name becomes colored by the concept; the concept does not become freshened by the name'. Having noted the replacement in common discourse of *Negro* by *black* and then by *African American*, he continues: 'We will know we have achieved equality and mutual respect when names for minorities stay put.'[37]

To assign blame to language, and to minister to it alone, provides short-term solutions to long-term social problems. It also creates still more problems, since to do so allows speakers to avoid the cause of a problem and examine only its symptom. The narrative, political, religious, educational, and linguistic issues I have examined here suggest just how debilitating such avoidance can be. Totalitarianism can exist with or without the word *nazi*, racism with or without *nigger* or *warrior*, and sexism with or without *girl*. Simply to change language, or to worry over what language change reveals about a changing society, allows speakers to evade responsibility for what they say. Of far greater consequence, it also allows them to deny responsibility for what they do.

---

[37] Pinker, 'The Game of the Name', *New York Times*, 5 April 1994, A21. A version of the issue Pinker describes affects even the naming of varieties of English predominantly used by minorities. What school teachers a half century ago might have called simply 'dialect' became, in the 1970s, Black English Vernacular, then African American English, then Ebonics, and then African American Language; and since the name for this variety has been so unstable and even contentious, there has never been at any one time consensus over just what label to use. Transformation of the name into an abbreviation—so African American Language becomes AAL, in opposition to the Language of Wider Communication, or LWC—reifies the name and further distances it not only from the variety to which it refers but also from whatever social issues are associated with that variety. See the usage in, for example, Geneva Smitherman, *Word from the Mother: Language and African Americans* (New York: Routledge, 2006).

Works Cited

Aarsleff, Hans, *The Study of Language in England, 1780–1860*, 2nd edn. (Minneapolis, MN: University of Minnesota Press, 1983).

Achebe, Chinua, *Anthills of the Savannah* (New York: Anchor, 1987).

Adams, J. N., *Bilingualism and the Latin Language* (New York: Cambridge University Press, 2003).

Aitchison, Jean, *Language Change: Progress or Decay?*, 3rd edn. (Cambridge: Cambridge University Press, 2001).

Algeo, John, 'What is a Briticism?', in A. N. Doane, Joan Hall, and Richard Ringler (eds.), *Old English and New: Studies in Language and Linguistics in Honor of Frederic G. Cassidy* (New York: Garland, 1992), 287–304.

—— (ed.), *The Cambridge History of the English Language*, vi, *English in North America* (Cambridge: Cambridge University Press, 2001).

—— 'External History', in Algeo (ed.), *English in North America*, 1–58.

Allen, Chadwick, *Blood Narrative: Indigenous Identity in American Indian and Maori Literary and Activist Texts* (Durham, NC: Duke University Press, 2002).

Alvarez, Lizette, 'It's the Talk of Nueva York: The Hybrid Called Spanglish', *New York Times*, 25 March 1997, A1, 14.

Anderson, Benedict, *Imagined Communities: Reflections on the Origin and Spread of Nationalism*, rev. edn. (London: Verso, 1991).

Anderson, Lars, *Carlisle vs. Army: Jim Thorpe, Dwight Eisenhower, Pop Warner, and the Forgotten Story of Football's Greatest Battle* (New York: Random House, 2007).

Arnold, Matthew, *On the Study of Celtic Literature and On Translating Homer* (New York: Macmillan Company, 1904).

Ash, Anna, Jessie Little Doe Fermino, and Ken Hale, 'Diversity in Local Language Maintenance and Restoration: A Reason for Optimism', in Hinton and Hale (eds.), *The Green Book of Language Revitalization in Practice*, 19–35.

Aston, Margaret, 'Wyclif and the Vernacular', in Anne Hudson and Michael Wilks (eds.), *From Ockham to Wyclif, Studies in Church History*, Subsidia 5 (Oxford: Blackwell, 1987), 281–330.

Axtell, James, 'Babel of Tongues: Communicating with the Indians in Eastern North America', in Gray and Fiering (eds.), *The Language Encounter in the Americas, 1492–1800*, 15–60.

Bacon, Roger, *Opera Quædam Hactenus Inedita*, ed. J. S. Brewer (London: Longman, 1859).

Bailey, Charles-James N., *Essays on Time-Based Linguistic Analysis* (Oxford: Clarendon Press, 1996).

Bailey, Richard W., 'The English Language in Canada', in Bailey and Manfred Görlach (eds.), *English as a World Language* (Ann Arbor, MI: University of Michigan Press, 1982), 134–76.

—— 'American English Abroad', in Algeo (ed.), *English in North America*, 456–96.

—— *Images of English: A Cultural History of the Language* (Ann Arbor, MI: University of Michigan Press, 1991).

Baron, Dennis, *The English-Only Question: An Official Language for Americans?* (New Haven, CT: Yale University Press, 1990).

Bauer, Laurie, 'English in New Zealand', in Burchfield (ed.), *English in Britain and Overseas: Origins and Development*, 382–429.

Baugh, Albert C. and Thomas Cable, *A History of the English Language*, 5th edn. (Upper Saddle River, NJ: Prentice Hall, 2002).

Bautista, M. L. S. (ed.), *English Is an Asian Language: The Philippine Context: Proceedings of the Conference Held in Manila on August 2–3, 1996* (Sydney: Macquarie Library, 1997).

Beadle, Richard, 'The Virtuoso's *Troilus*', in Ruth Morse and Barry Windeatt (eds.), *Chaucer Traditions: Studies in Honour of Derek Brewer* (Cambridge: Cambridge University Press, 1990), 213–33.

Beal, Joan C., *English Pronunciation in the Eighteenth Century: Thomas Spence's 'Grand Repository of the English Language'* (Oxford: Clarendon Press, 1999).

Bede, The Venerable, *Expositio Actuum Apostolorum et Retractatio*, ed. M. W. Laistner (Cambridge, MA: Medieval Academy of America, 1939).

—— *A History of the English Church and People*, trans. Leo Sherley-Price (Harmondsworth: Penguin, 1955).

Béjoint, Henri, *Tradition and Innovation in Modern English Dictionaries* (Oxford: Clarendon Press, 1994).

Ben-Rafael, Eliezer, *Language, Identity, and Social Division: The Case of Israel* (Oxford: Clarendon Press, 1994).

Benton, Richard A., 'Language Policy in New Zealand: Defining the Ineffable', in Herriman and Burnaby (eds.), *Language Policies in English-Dominant Countries*, 62–98.

Bernstein, Richard, 'A Snappy Slogan? In German? Don't Smile. Try English', *New York Times*, 21 December 2004, A4.

Berthelette, Thomas (ed.), *Jo. Gower de Confessione Amantis* (London: Berthelette, 1532).

Bex, Tony and Richard J. Watts (eds.), *Standard English: The Widening Debate* (London: Routledge, 1999).

Y Bibl Cyssegr-lan: Sef yr Hen Destament a'r Newydd (London: Robert Barker, 1630).

Bickerton, Derek, *Language and Human Behavior* (Seattle, WA: University of Washington Press, 1995).

Blake, N. F., *Non-Standard Language in English Literature* (London: Andre Deutsch, 1981).

—— (ed.), *The Cambridge History of the English Language*, ii, *1066–1476* (Cambridge: Cambridge University Press, 1992).

Blank, Paula, 'The Babel of Renaissance English', in Lynda Mugglestone (ed.), *The Oxford History of English* (Oxford: Oxford University Press, 2006), 212–39.

Bloomfield, Leonard, *Language* (New York: Holt, 1933).

Bodine, Ann, 'Androcentrism in Prescriptive Grammar: Singular "They", Sex-indefinite "He", and "He or She"', in Deborah Cameron (ed.), *The Feminist Critique of Language: A Reader* (London: Routledge, 1990), 166–86.

Bolton, Kingsley, *Chinese Englishes: A Sociolinguistic History* (Cambridge: Cambridge University Press, 2003).

Borst, Arno, *Der Turmbau von Babel: Geschichte der Meinungen über Ursprung und Vielfalt der Sprachen und Völker*, 4 vols. in 6 (Stuttgart: Anton Hiersemann, 1957–63).

Boulton, Marjorie, *Zamenhof: Creator of Esperanto* (London: Routledge, 1960).

Bradley, S. A. J., *Anglo-Saxon Poetry* (London: Dent, 1982).

Brewer, Charlotte, *Treasure-House of the Language: The Living OED* (New Haven, CT: Yale University Press, 2007).

Bridges, Robert, 'The Society's Work' (Society for Pure English, tract XX, 1925), excerpted in W. F. Bolton and David Crystal (eds.), *The English Language*, 2 vols., ii, *Essays by Linguists and Men of Letters, 1858–1964* (Cambridge: Cambridge University Press, 1969), 86–99.

Brinton, Laurel and Margery Fee, 'Canadian English', in Algeo (ed.), *English in North America*, 422–40.

Britten, Thomas A., *American Indians in World War I: At Home and at War* (Albuquerque, NM: University of New Mexico Press, 1997).

Brooke, James, 'For Mongolians, E is for English, F is for Future', *New York Times*, 15 February 2005, A1, 9.

Brown, Patricia Leigh, 'Santa Claus Packs a Bag of Languages at a California Mall', *New York Times*, 21 December 2003, A5.

Bryson, Bill, *The Mother Tongue: English & How It Got That Way* (New York: W. Morrow, 1990).

Bucken-Knapp, Gregg, *Elites, Language, and the Politics of Identity: The Norwegian Case in Comparative Perspective* (Albany, NY: State University of New York Press, 2003).

Bullokar, William, *The Amendment of Orthographie for English Speech* (1580; rpt. Amsterdam: Theatrum Orbis Terrarum, 1968).

—— *An English Expositor: Teaching the Interpretation of the Hardest Words Used in Our Language* (London: John Legatt, 1616).

Burchfield, Robert (ed.), *The Cambridge History of the English Language*, v, *English in Britain and Overseas: Origins and Development* (Cambridge: Cambridge University Press, 1994).

—— 'Introduction', in Burchfield (ed.), *English in Britain and Overseas: Origins and Development*, 1–19.

Burgess, Anthony, *A Clockwork Orange* (London: Penguin, 1972).

Burke, Peter, *Languages and Communities in Early Modern Europe* (Cambridge: Cambridge University Press, 2004).

Burling, Robbins, *The Talking Ape: How Language Evolved* (Oxford: Oxford University Press, 2005).

Burridge, Kate, *Blooming English: Observations on the Roots, Cultivation and Hybrids of the English Language* (Cambridge: Cambridge University Press, 2004).

Butler, Susan, 'Corpus of English in Southeast Asia: Implications for a Regional Dictionary', in Bautista (ed.), *English Is an Asian Language*, 103–24.

Bybee, Joan L., *Phonology and Language Use* (Cambridge: Cambridge University Press, 2001).

—— *Frequency of Use and the Organization of Language* (Oxford: Oxford University Press, 2007).

—— and Paul Hopper, 'Introduction', in Bybee and Hopper (eds.), *Frequency and the Emergence of Linguistic Structure*, 1–24.

—— and Paul Hopper (eds.), *Frequency and the Emergence of Linguistic Structure* (Amsterdam: John Benjamins, 2001).

Cable, Thomas, 'The Rise of Written Standard English', in Aldo Scaglione (ed.), *The Emergence of National Languages* (Ravenna: Longo Editore, 1984), 75–94.

Calvet, Louis-Jean, *Language Wars and Linguistic Politics*, trans. Michel Petheram (Oxford: Oxford University Press, 1998).

Camden, William, *Remains Concerning Britain* (1606; rpt. Yorkshire: EP Publishing Limited, 1974).

Cameron, Deborah, *Feminism and Linguistic Theory*, 2nd edn. (New York: St Martin's Press, 1992).

—— *Verbal Hygiene* (London: Routledge, 1995).

Campbell, Alistair, *Old English Grammar* (Oxford: Clarendon Press, 1959).

Carew, Richard, 'The Excellency of the English Tongue', in Camden, *Remains concerning Britain*, 42–51.

Cassidy, Frederic G. (chief editor), *Dictionary of American Regional English*, 4 vols. (Cambridge, MA: Belknap Press of Harvard University Press, 1985–).

—— 'Geographical Variation of English in the United States', in Richard Bailey and Manfred Görlach (eds.), *English as a World Language* (Ann Arbor, MI: University of Michigan Press, 1982), 177–209.

—— and R. B. Le Page (eds.), *Dictionary of Jamaican English* (Cambridge: Cambridge University Press, 1967).

Cawley, A. C. (ed.), *The Wakefield Pageants in the Towneley Cycle* (Manchester: Manchester University Press, 1958).

Caxton, William, *The Prologues and Epilogues of William Caxton*, ed. W. J. B. Crotch, EETS os 176 (1928; rpt. New York: Burt Franklin, 1971).

Chambers, J. K., '"Lawless and Vulgar Innovations": Victorian Views of Canadian English', in Sandra Clarke (ed.), *Focus on Canada* (Amsterdam: John Benjamins, 1993), 1–26.

—— *Sociolinguistic Theory: Linguistic Variation and Its Social Significance* (Oxford: Blackwell, 1995).

Chaucer, Geoffrey, *The Riverside Chaucer*, ed. Larry D. Benson, 3rd edn. (Boston, MA: Houghton Mifflin, 1987).

Ch'ien, Evelyn Nien-Ming, *Weird English* (Cambridge, MA: Harvard University Press, 2004).

Chomsky, Noam, *Aspects of the Theory of Syntax* (Cambridge, MA: MIT Press, 1965).

Clanchy, M. T., *From Memory to Written Record: England 1066–1307*, 2nd edn. (Oxford: Blackwell, 1993).

Clyne, Michael, *Dynamics of Language Contact: English and Immigrant Languages* (Cambridge: Cambridge University Press, 2003).

Cobarrubias, Juan, 'Ethical Issues in Status Planning', in Cobarrubias and Joshua A. Fishman (eds.), *Progress in Language Planning: International Perspectives* (Berlin: Mouton, 1983), 41–85.

Coleman, Julie, *A History of Cant and Slang Dictionaries*, i, *1567–1784* (Oxford: Oxford University Press, 2004).

Collingwood, R. G., *The Idea of History* (Oxford: Clarendon Press, 1946).

Connor, George Alan *et al.*, *Esperanto: The World Interlanguage* (London: A. S. Barnes, 1948).

Cooper, Robert L. (ed.), *Language Spread: Studies in Diffusion and Social Change* (Bloomington, IN: Indiana University Press, 1982).

—— *Language Planning and Social Change* (Cambridge: Cambridge University Press, 1989).

Crawford, Bill, *All American: The Rise and Fall of Jim Thorpe* (Hoboken, NJ: John Wiley and Sons, 2005).

Crawford, James (ed.), *Language Loyalties: A Source Book on the Official English Controversy* (Chicago, IL: University of Chicago Press, 1992).

—— *Bilingual Education: History, Politics, Theory, and Practice*, 4th edn. (Los Angeles, CA: Bilingual Educational Services, 1999).

—— *At War with Diversity: US Language Policy in an Age of Anxiety* (Clevedon: Multilingual Matters, 2000).

Crowley, Robert (ed.), *Piers Plowman* (London: Crowley, 1550).

Crowley, Tony, *The Politics of Discourse: The Standard Language Question in British Cultural Debates* (London: Macmillan, 1989).

—— 'Curiouser and Curiouser: Falling Standards in the Standard English Debate', in Bex and Watts (eds.), *Standard English: The Widening Debate*, 271–82.

Crystal, David, *The Cambridge Encyclopedia of the English Language* (Cambridge: Cambridge University Press, 1995).

—— *Language Death* (Cambridge: Cambridge University Press, 2000).

—— *Language and the Internet* (Cambridge: Cambridge University Press, 2001).

—— *English as a Global Language*, 2nd edn. (Cambridge: Cambridge University Press, 2003).

—— *The Stories of English* (Woodstock, NY: Overlook Press, 2004).

Crystal, David, *The Fight for English: How Language Pundits Ate, Shot, and Left* (Oxford: Oxford University Press, 2006).

Cursor Mundi, ed. Richard Morris, EETS os 57, 59, 62, 66, 68, 99, 101 (London: Trübner, 1874–93).

Curzan, Ann, *Gender Shifts in the History of English* (Cambridge: Cambridge University Press, 2003).

Dalby, Andrew, *Language in Danger: The Loss of Linguistic Diversity and the Threat to Our Future* (New York: Columbia University Press, 2003).

Daley, Suzanne, 'In Europe Some Fear National Languages are Endangered', *New York Times*, 16 April 2001, A1, 10.

Daniel, Samuel, *Musophilus: Containing a General Defense of Learning*, ed. Raymond Himelick (West Lafayette, IN: Purdue University Studies, 1965).

Dante, *De Vulgari Eloquentia*, in Alex Preminger *et al.* (ed. and trans.), *Classical and Medieval Literary Criticism: Translations and Interpretations* (New York: Frederick Ungar, 1974), 412–46.

—— *The Paradiso*, trans. John Ciardi (New York: Mentor, 1970).

Defoe, Daniel, *Essays upon Several Projects* (London: Thomas Ballard, 1702).

DeJong, David H., *Promises of the Past: A History of Indian Education in the United States* (Golden, CO: American Press, 1993).

De Klerk, Vivan (ed.), *Focus on South Africa* (Amsterdam: John Benjamins, 1996).

Del Valle, Sandra, *Language Rights and the Law in the United States: Finding Our Voices* (Clevedon: Multilingual Matters, 2003).

De Tocqueville, Alexis, *Democracy in America*, ed. Phillips Bradley, 2 vols. (New York: Vintage, 1945).

Deutscher, Guy, *The Unfolding of Language: An Evolutionary Tour of Mankind's Greatest Invention* (New York: Henry Holt, 2005).

Devitt, Amy J., *Standardizing Written English: Diffusion in the Case of Scotland 1520–1659* (Cambridge: Cambridge University Press, 1989).

Dickens, Charles, *Great Expectations*, ed. Angus Calder (London: Penguin, 1965).

—— *Nicholas Nickleby*, ed. Mark Ford (London: Penguin, 1999).

Dicker, Susan J., *Languages in America: A Pluralist View* (Philadelphia, PA: Multilingual Matters, 1996).

Dixon, R. M. W., *The Rise and Fall of Languages* (Cambridge: Cambridge University Press, 1997).

Dobson, E. J., *English Pronunciation 1500–1700*, 2nd edn., 2 vols (Oxford: Clarendon Press, 1968).

Dryden, John, *The Works of John Dryden*, ed. Edward Niles Hooker and H. T. Swedenberg, Jr., 7 vols. (Berkeley, CA: University of California Press, 1956–).

Duff, Alan, *Once Were Warriors* (Honolulu, HI: University of Hawaii Press, 1994).

Eakin, Emily, 'Going at the Changes in, Ya Know, English', *New York Times*, 15 November 2003, A15, 17.

Echevarría, Roberto González, 'Is "Spanglish" a Language?', *New York Times*, 28 March 1997, A29.

Eco, Umberto, *The Search for the Perfect Language* (Oxford: Blackwell, 1995).

Edwards, Viv, *Multilingualism in the English-Speaking World: Pedigree of Nations* (Malden, MA: Blackwell, 2004).

Elton, G. R., *The Tudor Constitutions: Documents and Commentary*, 2nd edn. (Cambridge: Cambridge University Press, 1982).

Elyot, Sir Thomas, *The Boke Named the Gouernour* (1531; rpt. Menston: Scolar Press, 1970).

'English-Only Bill Vetoed', *New York Times*, 18 April 2005, A15.

Fairclough, Norman, *Language and Power* (London: Longman, 1989).

Fisher, John H., 'British and American, Continuity and Divergence', in Algeo (ed.), *English in North America*, 59–85.

—— *The Emergence of Standard English* (Lexington, KY: University of Kentucky Press, 1996).

——, Malcolm Richardson, and Jane L. Fisher (eds.), *An Anthology of Chancery English* (Knoxville, TN: University of Tennessee Press, 1984).

Fishman, J. A. (ed.), *Advances in Language Planning* (The Hague: Mouton, 1974).

Forster, Peter G., *The Esperanto Movement* (The Hague: Mouton, 1982).

Fought, Carmen, *Chicano English in Context* (New York: Palgrave, 2003).

Fyler, John, *Language and the Declining world in Chaucer, Dante, and Jean de Meun* (Cambridge: Cambridge University Press, 2007).

Gazophylacium Anglicanum (1689; rpt. Menston: Scolar Press, 1969).

Gellrich, Jesse M., *The Idea of the Book in the Middle Ages: Language Theory, Mythology, and Fiction* (Ithaca, NY: Cornell University Press, 1985).

Gerald of Wales, *The Jewel of the Church*, ed. and trans. John J. Hagen (Leiden: E. J. Brill, 1979).

Ghosh, Kantik, 'Manuscripts of Nicholas Love's *The Mirror of the Blessed Life of Jesus Christ* and Wycliffite Notions of "Authority"', in Felicity Riddy (ed.), *Prestige, Authority, and Power in Late Medieval Manuscripts and Texts* (Woodbridge: D. S. Brewer, 2000), 17–34.

Gibson, Campbell and Kay Jung, 'Historical Census Statistics on Population Totals by Race, 1790 to 1990, and by Hispanic Origin, 1970 to 1990, for the United States, Regions, Divisions, and States', Population Division, US Census Bureau, September 2002, Working Paper Series No. 56.

Gill, Alexander, *Logonomia Anglica*, 2nd edn. (1621; Menston: Scolar Press, 1968).

Goddard, Ives, 'The Use of Pidgins and Jargons on the East Coast of North America', in Gray and Fiering (eds.), *The Language Encounter in the Americas, 1492–1800*, 61–78.

Gonzalez, Andrew B., 'When Does an Error Become a Distinctive Feature of Philippine English?', in Noss (ed.), *Varieties of English in Southeast Asia*, 150–72.

González, Roseann Dueñas and Ildikó Melis (eds.), *Language Ideologies: Critical Perspectives on the Official English Movement*, i, *Education and the Social Implications of Official Language* (Urbana, IL: NCTE, 2000).

Gordon, Elizabeth *et al.*, *New Zealand English: Its Origins and Evolution* (Cambridge: Cambridge University Press, 2004).

Görlach, Manfred, *Aspects of the History of English* (Heidelberg: Carl Winter, 1999).

—— *Explorations in English Historical Linguistics* (Heidelberg: Carl Winter, 2002).

Gough, Daniel, 'Black English in South Africa', in de Klerk (ed.), *Focus on South Africa*, 53–77.

Gower, John, *The English Works of John Gower*, ed. G. C. Macaulay, EETS es 81 (London: Oxford University Press, 1900).

Grace, Patricia, *Baby No-Eyes* (Honolulu, HI: University of Hawaii Press, 1998).

Graddol, David, *The Future of English?: A Guide to Forecasting the Popularity of the English Language in the 21st Century* (London: British Council, 1997).

Grafton, Anthony, with April Shelford and Nancy Siraisi, *New Worlds, Ancient Texts: The Power of Tradition and the Shock of Discovery* (Cambridge, MA: Harvard University Press, 1992).

Gray, Edward G., *New World Babel: Languages and Nations in Early America* (Princeton, NJ: Princeton University Press, 1999).

—— and Norman Fiering (eds.), *The Language Encounter in the Americas, 1492–1800: A Collection of Essays* (New York: Berghahn Books, 2000).

Greenberg, Joseph H., *Indo-European and Its Closest Relatives: The Eurasiatic Language Family* (Stanford, CA: Stanford University Press, 2000).

Greymorning, Stephen, 'Reflections on the Arapaho Language Project, or When Bambi Spoke Arapaho and Other Tales of Arapaho Language Revitalization Efforts', in Hinton and Hale (eds.), *The Green Book of Language Revitalization in Practice*, 287–97.

Grillo, R. D., *Dominant Languages: Language and Hierarchy in Britain and France* (Cambridge: Cambridge University Press, 1989).

Gumperz, John J. and Dell Hymes (eds.), *Directions in Sociolinguistics: The Ethnography of Communication* (New York: Holt, Rinehart and Winston, Inc., 1972).

Gunn, John, 'Social Contexts in the History of Australian English', Machan and Scott (eds.), *English in Its Social Contexts*, 204–29.

Halliday, M. A. K., *Language as Social Semiotic: The Social Interpretation of Language and Meaning* (London: Edward Arnold, 1978).

Hargreaves, Henry, 'The Wycliffite Versions', in G. W. H. Lampe (ed.), *The Cambridge History of the Bible*, ii, *The West from the Fathers to the Reformation* (Cambridge: Cambridge University Press, 1969), 387–415.

Harris, Roy, *The Language Machine* (Ithaca, NY: Cornell University Press, 1987).

Harrison, K. David, *When Languages Die: The Extinction of the World's Languages and the Erosion of Human Knowledge* (Oxford: Oxford University Press, 2007).

Hart, John, *An Orthographie* (1569; rpt. Menston: Scolar Press, 1969).

Haugen, Einar, *Language Conflict and Language Planning: The Case of Modern Norwegian* (Cambridge, MA: Harvard University Press, 1966).

—— 'Language, Dialect, Nation', in *The Ecology of Language*, ed. Anwar S. Dil (Stanford, CA: Stanford University Press, 1972), 237–54.

Hechter, Michael, *Internal Colonialism: The Celtic Fringe in British National Development* (New Brunswick, NJ: Transaction Publishers, 1999).

Herriman, Michael, 'Language Policy in Australia', in Herriman and Barbara Burnaby (eds.), *Language Policies in English-Dominant Countries*, 35–61.

—— and Barbara Burnaby (eds.), *Language Policies in English-Dominant Countries: Six Case Studies* (Clevedon: Multilingual Matters, 1996).

Higham, John, *Strangers in the Land: Patterns of American Nativism, 1860–1925*, 2nd edn. (New Brunswick, NJ: Rutgers University Press, 1988).

Hinton, Leanne and Ken Hale (eds.), *The Green Book of Language Revitalization in Practice* (San Diego, CA: Academic Press, 2001).

Hoban, Russell, *Riddley Walker: A Novel* (New York: Summit Books, 1980).

Hodge, Robert and Gunther Kress, *Language as Ideology*, 2nd edn. (London: Routledge, 1993).

Holm, John A., 'English in the Caribbean', in Burchfield (ed.), *English in Britain and Overseas: Origins and Development*, 328–81.

Homer, *The Odyssey*, trans. Richmond Lattimore (New York: HarperCollins, 1963).

Honey, John, *Does Accent Matter? The Pygmalion Factor* (London: Faber and Faber, 1989).

—— *Language Is Power: The Story of Standard English and Its Enemies* (London: Faber and Faber, 1997).

Howe, John R., *Language and Political Meaning in Revolutionary America* (Amherst, MA: University of Massachusetts Press, 2004).

Hudson, Anne (ed.), *Selections from English Wycliffite Writings* (Cambridge: Cambridge University Press, 1978).

—— *The Premature Reformation: Wycliffite Texts and Lollard History* (Oxford: Clarendon, 1988).

—— (ed.), *Two Wycliffite Texts*, EETS 301 (Oxford: Oxford University Press, 1993).

Hudson, R. A., *Sociolinguistics*, 2nd edn. (Cambridge: Cambridge University Press, 1996).

Hughes, Shaun F. D., 'Was There Ever a "Māori English"?', *World Englishes* 23 (2004), 565–84.

Hymes, Del, *Foundations in Sociolinguistics: An Ethnographic Approach* (Philadelphia, PA: University of Pennsylvania Press, 1974).

Ihalainen, Ossi, 'The Dialects of England Since 1776', in Burchfield (ed.), *English in Britain and Overseas: Origins and Development*, 197–274.

Isidore of Seville, *Etymologiarum sive Originum Libri XX*, ed. W. M. Lindsay, 2 vols., 2nd edn. (Oxford: Clarendon Press, 1962).

'It's English or Tongues of "Ghetto" Life, Gingrich Says', *Milwaukee Journal-Sentinel*, 1 April 2007, 19A.

Jager, Eric, *The Tempter's Voice: Language and the Fall in Medieval Literature* (Ithaca, NY: Cornell University Press, 1993).

Jenkins, Sally, *The Real All Americans: The Team that Changed a Game, a People, a Nation* (New York: Doubleday, 2007).

Jespersen, Otto, *Language: Its Nature, Development and Origin* (London: G. Allen and Unwin, 1922).

Johnson, Samuel, *The Plan of a Dictionary of the English Language* (London: J. and P. Knapton, 1747).

—— *A Dictionary of the English Language* (1755; rpt. New York: AMS Press, 1967).

Jones, Daniel, *An English Pronouncing Dictionary* (London: J. M. Dent and Sons, 1917).

Jones, Mari C., *Language Obsolescence and Revitalization: Linguistic Change in Two Contrasting Welsh Communities* (New York: Oxford University Press, 1998).

Joseph, Brian D. *et al.* (eds.), *When Languages Collide: Perspectives on Language Conflict, Language Competition, and Language Coexistence* (Columbus, OH: Ohio State University Press, 2003).

Kachru, Braj B., 'The Second Diaspora of English', in Machan and Scott (eds.), *English in Its Social Contexts*, 230–52.

—— 'English in South Asia', in Burchfield (ed.), *English in Britain and Overseas: Origins and Development*, 497–553.

—— 'English as an Asian Language', in Bautista (ed.), *English Is an Asian Language*, 1–23.

—— *Asian Englishes: Beyond the Canon* (Hong Kong: Hong Kong University Press, 2005).

Karttunen, Frances, 'Interpreters Snatched from the Shore: The Successful and the Others', in Gray and Fiering (eds.), *The Language Encounter in the Americas*, 215–29.

Keller, Rudi, *On Language Change: The Invisible Hand in Language*, trans. Brigitte Nerlich (London: Routledge, 1994).

Kelman, James, *How Late It Was, How Late* (London: Secker and Warburg, 1994).

Kennedy, Randall, *Nigger: The Strange Career of a Troublesome Word* (New York: Pantheon Books, 2002).

Kilgannon, Corey, 'Tolerance for a Racial Slur Is a Test for Potential Jurors', *New York Times*, 18 May 2006, C17.

—— 'Attacker Guilty of Hate Crimes in Howard Beach', *New York Times*, 10 June 2006, B1.

Kim, Lisa (ed.), *Singapore English: A Grammatical Description* (Amsterdam: John Benjamins, 2004).

King, Jeanette, 'Te Kōhanga Reo: Māori Language Revitalization', in Hinton and Hale (eds.), *The Green Book of Language Revitalization in Practice*, 119–28.

Knighton, Henry, *Knighton's Chronicle, 1337–1396*, ed. and trans. G. H. Martin (Oxford: Clarendon Press, 1995).

Kramer, Michael P., *Imagining Language in America: From the Revolution to the Civil War* (Princeton, NJ: Princeton University Press, 1992).

Krauss, Michael E., 'Keynote—Mass Language Extinction and Documentation: The Race Against Time', in Osahito Miyaoka *et al.* (eds.), *The Vanishing Languages of the Pacific Rim* (Oxford: Oxford University Press, 2007), 3–24.

Kynaston, Sir Francis (ed. and trans.), *Amorum Troili et Creseidae Libri duo priores Anglico-Latini* (London: John Lichfield, 1635).

Labov, William,'On the Mechanism of Linguistic Change', in Gumperz and Hymes (eds.), *Directions in Sociolinguistics: The Ethnography of Communication*, 512–38.

—— *Sociolinguistic Patterns* (Philadelphia, PA: University of Pennsylvania Press, 1972).

—— 'On the Use of the Present to Explain the Past', in Philip Baldi and Ronald N. Werth (eds.), *Readings in Historical Phonology: Chapters in the Theory of Sound Change* (University Park, PA: Pennsylvania State University Press, 1978), 275–312.

—— *Principles of Linguistic Change*, i, *Internal Factors* (Oxford: Blackwell, 1994).

—— *Principles of Linguistic Change*, ii, *Social Factors* (Oxford: Blackwell, 2001).

Laing, Margaret (ed.), *Middle English Dialectology: Essays on Some Principles and Problems* (Aberdeen: Aberdeen University Press, 1989).

Laird, Charlton, *The Miracle of Language* (New York: Fawcett, 1953).

Lalla, Barbara and Jean D'Costa, *Language in Exile: Three Hundred Years of Jamaican Creole* (Tuscaloosa, AL: University of Alabama Press, 1990).

Langland, William, *Piers Plowman: The B Version*, rev. edn., ed. George Kane and E. Talbot Donaldson (Berkeley and Los Angeles, CA: University of California Press, 1988).

Lass, Roger, *On Explaining Language Change* (Cambridge: Cambridge University Press, 1980).

—— 'Where Do Extraterrestrial Englishes Come from? Dialect, Input, and Recodification in Transported Englishes', in Sylvia Adamson *et al.* (eds.), *Papers from the 5th International Conference in English Historical Linguistics* (Amsterdam: John Benjamins, 1990), 245–80.

—— *Historical Linguistics and Language Change* (Cambridge: Cambridge University Press, 1997).

—— (ed.), *The Cambridge History of the English Language*, iii, *1476–1776* (Cambridge: Cambridge University Press, 1999).

—— 'Phonology and Morphology', in Lass (ed.), *1476–1776*, 56–186.

—— 'South African English', in Rajend Mesthrie (ed.), *Language in South Africa* (Cambridge: Cambridge University Press, 2002), 104–26.

Law, Vivien, *The History of Linguistics in Europe from Plato to 1600* (Cambridge: Cambridge University Press, 2003).

Leach, Alfred, *The Letter H Past, Present, and Future: A Treatise, with Rules for the Silent H Based on Modern Usage, and Notes on Wh* (London: Griffith and Farran, 1880).

Leland, Charles G., *Pidgin-English Sing-Song* (London: Trübner, 1876).

Leonard, Sterling Andrus, *The Doctrine of Correctness in English Usage, 1700–1800* (1929; rpt. New York: Russell and Russell, 1962).

Lerer, Seth, *Inventing English: A Portable History of the Language* (New York: Columbia University Press, 2007).

Lightfoot, David, *The Development of Language: Acquisition, Change, and Evolution* (Malden, MA: Blackwell, 1999).

Lippi-Green, Rosina, *English with an Accent: Language, Ideology, and Discrimination in the United States* (London: Routledge, 1997).

Locke, John, *An Essay Concerning Human Understanding*, ed. Peter H. Nidditch (Oxford: Clarendon Press, 1975).

Looby, Christopher, *Voicing America: Language, Literary Form, and the Origins of the United States* (Chicago, IL: University of Chicago Press, 1996).

Lusignan, Serge, *Parler vulgairement: les intellectuels et la langue française aux xiiie et xive siècles*, 2nd edn. (Paris: J. Vrin, 1987).

Lydgate, John, *Troy Book*, ed. Henry Bergen, EETS es 97, 103, 106, 126 (London: Kegan Paul, 1906–35).

Machan, Tim William, 'Kynaston's *Troilus*, Textual Criticism, and the Renaissance Reading of Chaucer', *Exemplaria* 5 (1993), 161–83.

—— 'Language Contact in *Piers Plowman*', *Speculum*, 69 (1994), 359–85.

—— 'Thomas Berthelette and Gower's *Confessio*', *Studies in the Age of Chaucer*, 18 (1996), 143–66.

—— 'Language and Society in Twelfth-Century England', in Taavitsainen *et al.* (eds.), *Placing Middle English in Context*, 43–66.

—— 'Politics and the Middle English Language', *Studies in the Age of Chaucer*, 24 (2002), 317–24.

—— *English in the Middle Ages* (Oxford: Oxford University Press, 2003).

—— 'Medieval Multilingualism and Gower's Literary Practice', *Studies in Philology*, 103 (2006), 1–25.

—— (ed.), *Chaucer's 'Boece'*, Middle English Texts 38 (Heidelberg: Carl Winter, 2008).

—— and Charles T. Scott (eds.), *English in Its Social Contexts: Essays in Historical Sociolinguistics* (New York: Oxford University Press, 1992).

MacMahon, Michael K. C., 'Phonology', in *The Cambridge History of the English Language*, iv, Suzanne Romaine (ed.), *1776–1997* (Cambridge: Cambridge University Press, 1998), 373–535.

MacWhinney, Brian, 'Emergent Approaches to Language', in Bybee and Hopper (eds.), *Frequency and the Emergence of Linguistic Structure*, 449–70.

'Major Effort Is Under Way to Revive and Preserve Hawaii's Native Tongue', *New York Times*, 15 April 2007, A18.

Manning, H. Paul, 'The Rock Does not Understand English: Welsh and the Division of Labor in Nineteenth-Century Gwynedd Slate Quarries', in Joseph *et al.* (eds.), *When Languages Collide*, 45–70.

Marshall, Jonathan, *Language Change and Sociolinguistics: Rethinking Social Networks* (New York: Palgrave Macmillan, 2004).

May, Stephen, *Language and Minority Rights: Ethnicity, Nationalism and the Politics of Language* (London: Longman, 2001).

Mazrui, Alamin M., *English in Africa: After the Cold War* (Clevedon: Multilingual Matters, 2004).

McArthur, Tom, *The English Languages* (Cambridge: Cambridge University Press, 1998).

McClure, J. Derrick, 'English in Scotland', in Burchfield (ed.), *English in Britain and Overseas: Origins and Development*, 23–93.

McEnery, Tony, *Swearing in English: Bad Language, Purity and Power from 1586 to the Present* (London: Routledge, 2006).

McKenzie, Donald, *Oral Culture, Literacy and Print in Early New Zealand: The Treaty of Waitangi* (Wellington: Victoria University Press, 1985).

McLarin, Kimberly J., 'To Preserve Afrikaners' Language, Mixed-Race South Africans Join Fray', *New York Times*, 28 June 1995, A4.

McWhorter, John H., *Doing Our Own Thing: The Degradation of Language and Music and Why We Should, Like, Care* (New York: Gotham, 2003).

Meyers, Walter E., *Aliens and Linguists: Language Study and Science Fiction* (Athens, GA: University of Georgia Press, 1980).

Michael, Ian, *English Grammatical Categories and the Tradition to 1800* (Cambridge: Cambridge University Press, 1970).

Michel, Dan, *Ayenbite of Inwyt*, ed. Richard Morris, EETS os 23 (London: Trübner, 1866).

Millar, Robert McColl, *Language, Nation and Power: An Introduction* (New York: Palgrave, 2005).

Milroy, James, 'Middle English Dialectology', in Blake (ed.), *1066–1476*, 156–206.

—— *Linguistic Variation and Change: On the Historical Sociolinguistics of English* (Oxford: Blackwell, 1992).

—— 'The Consequences of Standardization in Descriptive Linguistics', in Bex and Watts (eds.), *Standard English: The Widening Debate*, 16–39.

—— 'The Legitimate Language: Giving a History to English', in Watts and Trudgill (eds.), *Alternative Histories of English*, 7–25.

—— and Lesley Milroy, *Authority in Standard Language: Investigating Standard English*, 3rd edn. (London: Routledge, 1999).

Milroy, Lesley, *Language and Social Networks*, 2nd edn. (Oxford: Blackwell, 1987).

—— and Pieter Muysken (eds.), *One Speaker, Two Languages: Cross-disciplinary Perspectives on Code-Switching* (Cambridge: Cambridge University Press, 1995).

Milton, John, *Complete Prose Works*, 8 vols., gen. ed. Don M. Wolfe (New Haven, CT: Yale University Press, 1953–82).

—— *The Poems of John Milton*, ed. Roy Flannagan (Boston, MA: Houghton Mifflin, 1998).

Mitchell, Linda C., *Grammar Wars: Language as Cultural Battlefield in 17th and 18th Century England* (Aldershot: Ashgate, 2001).

Montagu, Ashley, *The Anatomy of Swearing*, 2nd edn. (London: Macmillan, 1973).

Morales, Ed, *Living in Spanglish: The Search for Latino Identity in America* (New York: St Martin's Press, 2002).

Morton, Herbert C., *The Story of 'Webster's Third': Philip Gove's Controversial Dictionary and Its Critics* (Cambridge: Cambridge University Press, 1994).

Mufwene, Salikoko S., *The Ecology of Language Evolution* (Cambridge: Cambridge University Press, 2001).

Mufwene, Salikoko S., "African-American English", in Algeo (ed.), *English in North America*, 291–324.

—— 'Language Endangerment: What Have Pride and Prestige Got to Do with It?', in Joseph *et al.* (eds.), *When Languages Collide*, 324–45.

Mugglestone, Lynda, *'Talking Proper': The Rise of Accent as Social Symbol*, 2nd edn. (Oxford: Oxford University Press, 2003).

—— *Lost for Words: The Hidden History of the Oxford English Dictionary* (New Haven, CT: Yale University Press, 2005).

Mühlhäusler, Peter, *Pidgin & Creole Linguistics* (Oxford: Blackwell, 1986).

—— *Linguistic Ecology: Language Change and Linguistic Imperialism in the Pacific Region* (London: Routledge, 1996).

Mulcaster, Richard, *The First Part of the Elementarie* (1582; rpt. Menston: Scolar Press, 1970).

Murray, Sir James A. H. *et al.*, *A New English Dictionary on Historical Principles*, 10 vols. (Oxford: Clarendon Press, 1888–1928).

Nauerby, Tom, *No Nation Is an Island: Language, Culture, and National Identity in the Faroe Islands* (Aarhus: Aarhus University Press, 1996).

Navarro, Mireya, 'Breaking the Sound Barrier', *New York Times*, 23 July 2006, 9, 1 and 10.

Nettle, Daniel, *Linguistic Diversity* (Oxford: Oxford University Press, 1999).

—— and Suzanne Romaine, *Vanishing Voices: The Extinction of the World's Languages* (Oxford: Oxford University Press, 2000).

Noss, R. B. (ed.), *Varieties of English in Southeast Asia* (Singapore: Singapore University Press, 1983).

Nunberg, Geoffrey, *Going Nucular: Language, Politics, and Culture in Confrontational Times* (New York: PublicAffairs, 2004).

Ohaeto, Ezenwa, *Chinua Achebe: A Biography* (Bloomington, IN: Indiana University Press, 1997).

Orsman, H. W. (ed.), *The Dictionary of New Zealand English: A Dictionary of New Zealandisms on Historical Principles* (Auckland: Oxford University Press, 1997).

Ozolins, Uldis, *The Politics of Language in Australia* (Cambridge: Cambridge University Press, 1993).

Padley, G. A., *Grammatical Theory in Western Europe, 1500–1700: Trends in Vernacular Grammar*, 2 vols. (Cambridge: Cambridge University Press, 1985 and 1988).

Page, R. I., 'How Long Did the Scandinavian Language Survive in England? The Epigraphical Evidence', in Peter Clemoes and Kathleen Hughes (eds.), *England Before the Conquest: Studies in Primary Sources Presented to Dorothy Whitelock* (Cambridge: Cambridge University Press, 1971), 165–81.

Palmer, Patricia, *Language and Conquest in Early Modern Ireland: English Renaissance Literature and Elizabethan Imperial Expansion* (Cambridge: Cambridge University Press, 2001).

Parkes, M. B. and Richard Beadle (eds.), *The Poetical Works of Geoffrey Chaucer: A Facsimile of Cambridge University Library MS Gg. 4.27*, 3 vols. (Norman, OK: Pilgrim Books, 1979–80).

Pearsall, Derek, 'Hoccleve's *Regement of Princes*: The Poetics of Royal Self-Representation', *Speculum*, 69 (1994), 386–410.

Pecock, Reginald, *The Repressor of Over Much Blaming of the Clergy*, ed. Churchill Babington, Rolls Series 19, 2 vols. (London: Longman, 1860).

—— *The Reule of Crysten Religioun*, ed. William Cabell Greet, EETS os 171 (London: Oxford University Press, 1927).

Pennycook, Alastair, *The Cultural Politics of English as an International Language* (London: Longman, 1994).

—— *English and the Discourses of Colonialism* (London: Routledge, 1998).

Perry, Theresa and Lisa Delpit (eds.), *The Real Ebonics Debate: Power, Language, and the Education of African-American Children* (Boston, MA: Beacon Press, 1998).

Phaswana, Nkhelebeni, 'Contradiction or Assimilation? The South African Language Policy, and the South African National Government', in Sinfree Makoni *et al.* (eds.), *Black Linguistics: Language, Society, and Politics in Africa and the Americas* (London: Routledge, 2003), 117–31.

Phillipson, Robert, *Linguistic Imperialism* (Oxford: Oxford University Press, 1992).

—— *English-Only Europe? Challenging Language Policy* (London: Routledge, 2003).

Pinker, Stephen, 'The Game of the Name', *New York Times*, 5 April 1994, A21.

Poole, Austin Lane, *From Domesday Book to Magna Carta 1087–1216*, 2nd edn. (Oxford: Clarendon Press, 1955).

Poplack, Shana, Gerard von Herk, and Down Harvie, ' "Deformed in the Dialects": An Alternative History of Non-Standard English', in Watts and Trudgill (eds.), *Alternative Histories of English*, 87–110.

Preston, Dennis R., *Perceptual Dialectology: Nonlinguists' Views of Areal Linguistics* (Dordrecht: Foris Publicatons, 1989).

—— 'The Story of Good and Bad English in the United States', in Watts and Trudgill (eds.), *Alternative Histories of English*, 134–51.

Price, Glanville, *The Languages of Britain* (London: Edward Arnold, 1984).

Prokosch, Eduard, *A Comparative Germanic Grammar* (Philadelphia, PA: Linguistics Society of America, 1939).

Pryce, Malcolm, *Last Tango in Aberystwyth* (London: Bloomsbury, 2003).

Puttenham, George, *The Arte of English Poesie* (1589; rpt. Menston: Scolar Press, 1968).

Quirk, Randolph, 'Language Variety: Nature and Art', in Noss (ed.), *Varieties of English in Southeast Asia*, 3–19.

—— 'Language Varieties and Standard Language', *English Today: The International Review of the English Language*, 21 (1990), 3–10.

Ramson, W. S. (ed.), *The Australian National Dictionary: A Dictionary of Australianisms on Historical Principles* (Melbourne: Oxford University Press, 1988).

Ray, John, *A Collection of English Words* (1691; rpt. Menston: Scolar Press, 1969).

Read, Allen Walker, *Milestones in the History of English in America*, ed. Richard W. Bailey (Durham, NC: Duke University Press, 2002).

—— 'The Allegiance to Dictionaries in American Linguistic Attitudes', in *Milestones in the History of English in America*, ed. Bailey, 110–20.

—— 'Amphi-Atlantic English', in *Milestones in the History of English in America*, ed. Bailey, 55–82.

—— 'British Recognition of American Speech in the Eighteenth Century', in *Milestones in the History of English in America*, ed. Bailey, 37–54.

—— 'Milestones in the Branching of British and American English', in *Milestones in the History of English in America*, ed. Bailey, 3–21.

Reddick, Allen, *The Making of Johnson's Dictionary, 1746–1773* (Cambridge: Cambridge University Press, 1990).

Ricento, Thomas (ed.), *Ideology, Politics and Language Policies: Focus on English* (Amsterdam: John Benjamins, 2000).

Richard of Devizes, *The Chronicle of Richard of Devizes of the Time of King Richard the First*, ed. and trans. John T. Appleby (London: Thomas Nelson and Sons, 1963).

Richards, I. A., *Basic English and Its Uses* (London: Kegan Paul, 1943).

Richler, Howard, *A Bawdy Language: How a Second-Rate Language Slept Its Way to the Top* (Toronto: Stoddart, 1999).

Rickford, John R., *Dimensions of a Creole Continuum: History, Texts & Linguistic Analysis of Guyanese Creole* (Stanford, CA: Stanford University Press, 1987).

Riddy, Felicity (ed.), *Regionalism in Late Medieval Manuscripts and Texts: Essays Celebrating the Publication of 'A Linguistic Atlas of Late Mediaeval England'* (Woodbridge: D. S. Brewer, 1991).

Ritt, Nikolaus, *Selfish Sounds and Linguistic Evolution: A Darwinian Approach to Language Change* (Cambridge: Cambridge University Press, 2004).

Rodriguez, Richard, *Hunger of Memory: The Education of Richard Rodriguez: An Autobiography* (Boston, MA: D. R. Godine, 1982).

Rohter, Larry, 'Repeal Is Likely for "English Only" Policy in Miami', *New York Times*, 14 May 1993, A7.

—— 'Learn English, Says Chile, Thinking Upwardly Global', *New York Times*, 29 December 2004, A4.

Romaine, Suzanne, *Socio-historical Linguistics: Its Status and Methodology* (Cambridge: Cambridge University Press, 1982).

—— 'Contact with Other Languages', in Algeo (ed.), *English in North America*, 154–83.

Sampson, George, *English for the English: A Chapter on National Education* (1921; rpt. with introduction by Denys Thompson, Cambridge: Cambridge University Press, 1970).

Samuels, M. L., *Linguistic Evolution, with Special Reference to English* (Cambridge: Cambridge University Press, 1972).

—— 'The Great Scandinavian Belt', in Laing (ed.), *Middle English Dialectology*, 106–15.

—— 'Some Applications of Middle English Dialectology', in Laing (ed.), *Middle English Dialectology*, 64–80.

Sapir, Edward, *Language: An Introduction to the Study of Speech* (New York: Harcourt-Brace, 1921).

Schlesinger, Jr., Arthur M., *The Disuniting of America: Reflections on a Multicultural Society*, rev. edn. (New York: W. W. Norton, 1998).

Schmid, Carol L., *The Politics of Language: Conflict, Identity and Cultural Pluralism in Comparative Perspective* (Oxford: Oxford University Press, 2001).

Schmidt, Sr., Ronald, *Language Policy and Identity Politics in the United States* (Philadelphia, PA: Temple University Press, 2000).

Schneider, Edgar W., *Postcolonial English: Varieties around the World* (Cambridge: Cambridge University Press, 2007).

Schütz, Albert J., *The Voices of Eden: A History of Hawaiian Language Studies* (Honolulu, HI: University of Hawaii Press, 1994).

Senior, Jennifer, 'Sign Language Reflects Changing Sensibilities', *New York Times*, 3 January 1994, A1, 8.

Shakespeare, William, *The Complete Works*, ed. Alfred Harbage (London: Penguin, 1969).

Sharp, Henry (ed.), *Selections from Education Records*, i, *1781–1839* (Calcutta: Superintendent Government Printing, 1920).

Shaw, George Bernard, *Complete Plays with Prefaces*, 6 vols. (New York: Dodd, Mead, 1962).

Sheridan, Thomas, *A Course of Lectures on Elocution* (1762; rpt. Menston: Scolar Press, 1968).

Silva, Penny (ed.), *A Dictionary of South African English on Historical Principles* (Oxford: Oxford University Press, 1996).

Simon, John, *Paradigms Lost* (New York: Potter, 1980).

Simpson, David, *The Politics of American English, 1776–1850* (New York: Oxford University Press, 1986).

Skutnabb-Kangas, Tove, 'Linguistic Diversity and Biodiversity: The Threat from Killer Languages', in Christian Mair (ed.), *The Politics of English as a World Language: New Horizons in Postcolonial Cultural Studies* (Amsterdam: Rodopi, 2003), 31–52.

—— and Robert Phillipson (eds.), *Linguistic Human Rights: Overcoming Linguistic Discrimination* (Berlin: Mouton de Gruyter, 1994).

Sledd, James and Wilma R. Ebbitt (eds.), *Dictionaries and THAT Dictionary: A Casebook on the Aims of Lexicographers and the Targets of Reviewers* (Chicago, IL: Scott, Foresman, 1962).

Smith, A. H. (ed.), *Three Northumbrian Poems* (London: Methuen, 1933).

Smith, Jeremy J., *An Historical Study of English: Function, Form and Change* (London: Routledge, 1996).

—— 'Standard Language in Early Middle English?', in Taavitsainen *et al.* (eds.), *Placing Middle English in Context*, 125–39.

Smith, Jeremy J., *Sound Change and the History of English* (Oxford: Oxford University Press, 2007).

Smitherman, Geneva, *Word from the Mother: Language and African Americans* (New York: Routledge, 2006).

Sontag, Deborah, 'Oy Gevalt! New Yawkese An Endangered Dialect?', *New York Times*, 14 February 1993, A1, 18.

St Augustine, *Confessions*, trans. R. S. Pine-Coffin (Harmondsworth: Penguin, 1961).

—— *Tractates on the Gospel of John 1–10*, trans. John W. Rettig, i of *The Fathers of the Church: A New Translation* (Washington, DC: The Catholic University of America Press, 1988).

—— *De Doctrina Christiana*, ed. and trans. R. P. H. Green (Oxford: Clarendon Press, 1995).

—— *The City of God against the Pagans*, ed. and trans. R. W. Dyson (Cambridge: Cambridge University Press, 1998).

Starnes, De Witt T. and Gertrude E. Noyes, *The English Dictionary from Cawdrey to Johnson, 1604–1755* (Chapel Hill, NC: University of North Carolina Press, 1946).

Stavans, Ilan, *Spanglish: The Making of a New American Language* (New York: Rayo, 2003).

Strang, Barbara, *A History of English* (London: Methuen, 1970).

'Surrender of Hostile Comanche Chiefs and Thirty-Six Warriors', *New York Times*, 23 April 1875, 1.

Swanton, Michael (ed. and trans.), *Anglo-Saxon Prose* (London: Dent, 1975).

Sweet, Henry, *A Handbook of Phonetics* (Oxford: Clarendon Press, 1877).

Taavitsainen, Irma *et al.* (eds.), *Placing Middle English in Context: Selected Papers from the Second Middle English Conference* (Berlin: Mouton de Gruyter, 2000).

Tagliabue, John, 'In Europe, Going Global Means, Alas, English', *New York Times*, 19 May 2002, A15.

—— 'Soon, Europe Will Speak in 23 Tongues', *New York Times*, 6 December 2006, A10.

Taylor, Dennis, *Hardy's Literary Language and Victorian Philology* (Oxford: Clarendon, 1993).

Thomas, Hugh M., *The English and the Normans: Ethnic Hostility, Assimilation, and Identity 1066–c1220* (Oxford: Oxford University Press, 2003).

Thomason, Sarah Grey and Terrence Kaufman, *Language Contact, Creolization, and Genetic Linguistics* (Berkeley, CA: University of California Press, 1988).

Thompson, Linda, Michael Fleming, and Michael Bryam, 'Languages and Language Policy in Britain', in Herriman and Burnaby (eds.), *Language Policies in English-Dominant Countries: Six Case Studies*, 99–121.

Thompson, Roger M., *Filipino English and Taglish: Language Switching from Multiple Perspectives* (Amsterdam: John Benjamins, 2003).

'Three Parties of Indian Police are After Swift Bear and His Band—An Uprising Feared', *New York Times*, 15 July 1899, 1.

Titlestad, Peter, 'English, the Constitution and South Africa's Language Future', in de Klerk (ed.), *Focus on South Africa*, 163–73.

Todd, Loreto, *Modern Englishes: Pidgins and Creoles* (Oxford: Blackwell, 1984).

Tollefson, James W., *Planning Language, Planning Inequality: Language Policy in the Community* (London: Longman, 1991).

Toon, Thomas E., 'The Social and Political Contexts of Language Change in Anglo-Saxon England', in Machan and Scott (eds.), *English in Its Social Contexts*, 28–46.

Trudgill, Peter, *The Social Differentiation of English in Norwich* (Cambridge: Cambridge University Press, 1974).

—— *Sociolinguistic Variation and Change* (Edinburgh: Edinburgh University Press, 2002).

Truss, Lynne, *Eats, Shoots & Leaves: The Zero Tolerance Approach to Punctuation* (New York: Gotham, 2004).

Turner, George W., 'English in Australia', in Burchfield (ed.), *English in Britain and Overseas*, 277–327.

Twain, Mark, *Adventures of Huckleberry Finn*, ed. Henry Nash Smith (Boston, MA: Houghton Mifflin, 1958).

Unger, Harlow Giles, *Noah Webster: The Life and Times of an American Patriot* (New York: John Wiley and Sons, 1998).

'Universal Declaration of Linguistic Rights' at http://www.linguistic-declaration.org/index-gb.htm.

Usk, Thomas, *Testament of Love*, in *Chaucerian and Other Pieces*, vii, *Complete Works of Geoffrey Chaucer*, ed. W. W. Skeat (Oxford: Oxford University Press, 1897).

Verstegan, Richard, *A Restitution of Decayed Intelligence* (1605; rpt. Ilkey: Scolar Press, 1976).

Vitalis, Orderic, *The Ecclesiastical History of Orderic Vitalis*, ed. and trans. Marjorie Chibnall, 6 vols. (Oxford: Clarendon, 1969–80).

Voerding, Brian, 'Aracadia Mayor: No Más', *La Crosse Tribune*, 19 August (2006), A1, 2.

Von Humboldt, Wilhelm, *On Language: The Diversity of Human Language-Structure and Its Influence on the Mental Development of Mankind*, trans. Peter Heath (Cambridge: Cambridge University Press, 1988).

Walker, John, *A Critical Pronouncing Dictionary and Expositor of the English Language* (London: Robinson and Cadell, 1791).

Walker, Ranginui, *Ka Whawhai Tonu Matou: Struggle without End* (Auckland: Penguin Books, 1990).

Waller, Edmund, *The Poems of Edmund Waller*, ed. G. Thorn Drury (London: Lawrence and Bullen, 1893).

Wardhaugh, Ronald, *Languages in Competition: Dominance, Diversity, and Decline* (Oxford: Blackwell, 1987).

Warner, Sam L. No'eau, 'The Movement to Revitalize Hawaiian Language and Culture', in Hinton and Hale (eds.), *The Green Book of Language Revitalization in Practice*, 133–44.

Watermeyer, Susan, 'Afrikaans English', in de Klerk (ed.), *Focus on South Africa*, 99–124.

Wa Thiongo, Ngũgĩ, *Decolonising the Mind: The Politics of Language in African Literature* (London: James Currey, 1986).

Watts, Richard and Peter Trudgill (eds.), *Alternative Histories of English* (London: Routledge, 2002).

Waugh, Evelyn, *The Complete Stories of Evelyn Waugh* (Boston, MA: Little, Brown, and Co., 1998).

Webb, Vic, *Language in South Africa: The Role of Language in National Transformation, Reconstruction, and Development* (Amsterdam: John Benjamins, 2002).

Webster, Noah, *Dissertations on the English Language* (1789; rpt. Menston: Scolar Press, 1967).

Weinreich, Uriel, William Labov, and Marvin I. Herzog, 'Empirical Foundations for a Theory of Language Change', in W. P. Lehmann and Yakov Malkiel (eds.), *Directions for Historical Linguistics: A Symposium* (Austin, TX: University of Texas Press), 95–188.

Wells, H. G., *The Shape of Things to Come* (New York: Macmillan, 1933).

Wenzel, Siegfried, *Macaronic Sermons: Bilingualism and Preaching in Late-Medieval England* (Ann Arbor, MI: University of Michigan Press, 1994).

Weyand, Alexander M., *The Saga of American Football* (New York: Macmillan, 1955).

Wheeler, Robert M., *Jim Thorpe: World's Greatest Athlete* (Norman, OK: University of Oklahoma Press, 1975).

White, Hayden, *The Content of the Form: Narrative Discourse and Historical Representation* (Baltimore, MD: The Johns Hopkins University Press, 1987).

Whorf, Benjamin Lee, *Language, Thought, and Reality: Selected Writings*, ed. John B. Carroll (Cambridge, MA: Technology Press of Massachusetts Institute of Technology, 1956).

Wierzbicka, Anna, *English: Meaning and Culture* (Oxford: Oxford University Press, 2006).

Wilgoren, Jodi, 'Divided by a Call for a Common Language: As Immigration Rises, a Wisconsin County Makes English Official', *New York Times*, 19 July 2002, A8.

Wilkins, John, *An Essay towards a Real Character, and a Philosophical Language* (1668; rpt. Menston: Scolar Press, 1968).

William of Malmesbury, *De Gestis Pontificum Anglorum*, ed. N. E. S. A. Hamilton, Rolls Series 52 (London: Longman, 1870).

Williams, Joseph M., ' "O! When Degree is Shak'd": Sixteenth-Century Anticipations of Some Modern Attitudes toward Usage', in Machan and Scott (eds.), *English in Its Social Contexts*, 69–101.

Willinsky, John, *Empire of Words: The Reign of the OED* (Princeton, NJ: Princeton University Press, 1994).

Wilson, Thomas, *The Arte of Rhetorique* (1553; rpt. Gainesville, FL: Scholars' Facsimiles and Reprints, 1962).

Withers, Phillip, *Aristarchus, or the Principles of Composition*, 2nd edn. (London: J. Moore, 1789).

Wogan-Browne, Jocelyn *et al.* (eds.), *The Idea of the Vernacular: An Anthology of Middle English Literary Theory, 1280–1520* (University Park, PA: Pennsylvania State University Press, 1999).

Wood, Nicholas, 'In the Old Dialect, a Balkan Region Regaining Identity', *New York Times*, 24 February 2005, A4.

Woolley, Lisa, *American Voices of the Chicago Renaissance* (Dekalb, IL: Northern Illinois University Press, 2000).

Wordsworth, William, *The Complete Poetical Works*, ed. A. J. George (Cambridge, MA: Houghton Mifflin, 1932).

Wright, Arnold, *Baboo English as 'tis Writ: Being Curiosities of Indian Journalism* (London: T. Fisher Unwin, 1891).

Wright, Joseph, *The English Dialect Grammar* (Oxford: H. Frowde, 1905).

Wright, Laura, 'Macaronic Writing in a London Archive, 1380–1480', in Matti Rissanan *et al.* (eds.), *History of Englishes: New Methods and Interpretations in Historical Linguistics* (Berlin: Mouton de Gruyter, 1992), 762–70.

—— *Sources of London English: Medieval Thames Vocabulary* (Oxford: Clarendon Press, 1996).

—— (ed.), *The Development of Standard English, 1300–1800* (Cambridge: Cambridge University Press, 2000).

Wright, Sue, *Language Policy and Language Planning: From Nationalism to Globalisation* (Basingstoke: Palgrave Macmillan, 2004).

Zezima, Katie, 'One Man's Goal: For a Tribe to Pray in Its Own Language', *New York Times*, 15 November 2003, A15.

Zhao, Yilu, 'Wave of Pupils Lacking English Strains Schools', *New York Times*, 5 August 2002, A1, 11.

Index